TERROR AT SEA

Also by Douglas Stewart:

FICTION

Cellars' Market
The Dallas Dilemma
Undercurrent
Late Bet
Hard Place
M.O – a collection of crime short stories (contribution)

Under the pen-name Cameron Ross:
Case for Compensation
Villa Plot, Counterplot
The Scaffold

NON-FICTION

A Family at Law (with Gavin Campbell)
Roulette-Playing to Win (under pen-name Brett Morton)
Shipping at Risk (Contributor)
Piraten (German Edition of *Terror at Sea*)
The Brutal Seas (Previous Edition)

TERROR AT SEA

Douglas Stewart

MP PUBLISHING

TERROR AT SEA

First revised edition published in 2015 by

MP Publishing
12 Strathallan Crescent, Douglas, Isle of Man IM2 4NR British Isles
mppublishingusa.com

Cover designed by Alison Graihagh Crellin

Publisher's Cataloging-in-Publication data

Stewart, Douglas Lindsay.
Terror at sea / Douglas Stewart.
p. cm.
ISBN 978-1-84982-331-9
1. Piracy. 2. Pirates. 3. Hijacking of ships. 4. Maritime terrorism. 5. Organized crime. 6. Outlaws. 7. Criminals. I. Title.

KZ7212 .S74 2015
364.16/4 --dc23

ISBN 978-1-84982-331-9
10 9 8 7 6 5 4 3 2 1

Also available in eBook

Revised and updated edition of *The Brutal Seas: Organised Crime at Work* (2006)

This book is dedicated to those who have suffered the terror of a piracy attack, and to the families of those who have been murdered or suffered at sea while politicians postured.

CONTENTS

INTRODUCTION

Even as you read these lines, somewhere on the high seas mariners are being attacked by armed pirates, their faces masked, their weapons deadly. Their victims may be murdered, tortured, seized as hostages, or simply dumped overboard. Today, piracy is a multibillion dollar business. A recent worrying trend, bringing the threat closer to home, is the use of such ill-gotten gains to fund international terrorism. International law enforcement, despite a welcome increased will to combat crime at sea, has struggled to be effective in prevention and punishment.

In the so-called *golden days* of piracy, Blackbeard, Anne Bonny, and Mary Read roved the main, robbing and pillaging. They, however, faced the risk of arrest or sinking by the mighty navies that patrolled the oceans. Today, the profits are greater, the weapons more sophisticated, and the crimes are planned in Asian boardrooms or terrorist hideaways in lawless parts of Somalia. The new maritime threat of international terrorism adds a further dimension to the original activities of organised criminals and opportunistic young men.

In some chapters, names of victims may have been changed, but in other respects dramatised versions of events have been based on known facts from reliable sources such as the International Maritime Bureau.

Recently, the attack on the large container ship *Maersk Atlanta* (the subject of the 2013 film *Captain Phillips*) has captured the public imagination and raised awareness of the terrors of attack by armed pirates. But the man who has done more than anyone to alert the public to the dangers of modern piracy, to demonstrate the social cost in terms of lives lost, and to take up the fight against the Mr Bigs of piracy and their gangs of thugs, is Eric Ellen.

This book is not a biography of Eric Ellen; nonetheless, Ellen "The Pirate-Buster" towers over these pages like a colossus. Without his courage and dedication many appalling crimes about which the general public was either uncaring or ill-informed would have remained unsolved.

Ellen's international reputation was summed up in the legend inscribed on the Huntingdon Fellow Medallion, presented to him from the Mariners' Museum in Norfolk, Virginia: "*In appreciation to the foremost authority in the field of modern piracy and his quest to educate others about issues affecting the maritime industries.*"

Following his retirement from the ICC-International Maritime Bureau [IMB], of which he was the founder-director, Ellen agreed to speak to me personally and candidly, on the record, about the challenges and dangers he and his team had faced. The ICC-International Maritime Bureau, founded by Ellen in 1981, is a lynchpin in the war against maritime crime.

As chief constable of the Port of London Police Authority, Ellen had grown frustrated by the lack of resources available to combat ruthless criminals committing lucrative crimes. He saw the need for an agency able to operate without frontiers, and so the Bureau was born, with Eric running the Bureau from his home. Today, this London-based organisation has grown from a tower block in Barking to a new base in Wapping, still close to the once-great London docklands.

Gradually, Ellen's endeavour achieved well-deserved recognition. The FBI, Scotland Yard, MI5, MI6, Interpol and police throughout the world now rely on the Bureau's unrivalled international databank, acquired through exhaustive review of informers and other sources, for intelligence about organised maritime crime.

I first met Ellen in 1980 while researching *Undercurrent*, my novel on shipping crime. 'In my police force,' Ellen explained, 'I had no budget or authority to investigate major swindles or cross-border shipping crimes unless there was a connection to the UK. I was inundated with evidence of fraud or murder at sea but there was and is no single body tackling the problem.'

While the creation of the Bureau has made a difference, it could not hope to solve a global problem of such magnitude single-handedly. Its operation, according to Ellen, was 95% routine, 4% frantic action and 1% fear.

One of its key investigators in the murky world of Far East shipping crime was S. Lin Kuo. A former Taiwanese police inspector, Shiao Lin was a black belt in judo, a kung fu expert, and a sharpshooter with a .38 revolver. In Taipei, she had operated undercover, infiltrating vice and gambling dens while posing as a prostitute—highly dangerous work, requiring a cool head and sharp brain. This proved excellent training for investigating the Triads and other major-league gangsters encountered by the IMB.

'Following the launch of the Bureau, I invited Lin to join us in London, as I needed someone resourceful with her specialised knowledge. Since then, she has played a unique role as an investigator, undertaking over 30 in-depth investigations and receiving a number of death threats along the way—especially when researching forged and fraudulent seamen's licences. These she shrugged off, even while exposing organised crime in the Far East.

'If you spend your time investigating and trying to prevent highly profitable crime, it is not surprising you get death threats.' Ellen shrugs. 'Why should a Bureau investigator command any more respect from big-time gangs than others? They kill when it suits them. Did I worry about it? No. Not because the danger is not real—it is. My lifelong philosophy has been that if there is going to be a murder attempt, it will come at a time and place that is unexpected. On that basis, you just carry on doing what is right, regardless.'

Through educating its members and the wider community about crime at sea, the Bureau has played an effective role in crime prevention. In the last 25 years, the Bureau has also played detective, notching up some notable triumphs. But with limited funds, the Bureau cannot achieve everything; Ellen's successor, Captain Pottengal Mukundan, the present director of the IMB, has continued the fight by encouraging national governments to act effectively against the criminal gangs, to ensure a deterrent effect.

Thanks to its first director, the Bureau is now an accepted authority, its opinions respected. Captain Mukundan sees the Bureau operating more discreetly now. 'These days, we are involved in every major case of piracy. The Bureau is at the top table discussing every major maritime *initiative* on piracy. One of Eric's great achievements was to ensure that we commanded respect. Now, we prefer to operate more behind the scenes, acting as a facilitator and supporting governments and law enforcement agencies with our information and expertise.'

CHAPTER ONE
Organised Crime, Corruption and Murder - Piracy

One December day, MV *Baltimar Zephyr*, a mixed cargo carrier weighing 2,854 GRT and some 91 metres in length, was en route from Freemantle, Australia, to Singapore before proceeding to Calcutta. Singapore was still about 30 hours away to the north. To the west, 60 miles distant, lay the coast of Indonesia. The cargo of containers on deck meant that the ship was riding low in the water. The distance between sea level and main deck was only about 6 feet—no problem for pirates, even for a vessel making 12 knots.

The ship's master was Captain John Bashforth, 45, a popular and well-respected Englishman from Derbyshire. The Chief Officer was Teodolfo Pereja, 41, a Filipino national. The ship's cargo, tractors and mining equipment, was unlikely to appeal to pirates, being too bulky to steal. However, Bashforth knew that sometimes, in these waters, pirates would try to steal *the entire ship*. Had they been closer to shore, the most likely attack would have come from armed locals on a speedboat—a kind of maritime smash-and-grab raid. But out here, the chief risk was a visit from Indonesian naval personnel, speeding across from their warship to steal anything to boost their meagre incomes. Their targets would be the safe and the crew's cash and valuables.

Contrary to some reports, *Baltimar Zephyr* was not in the notorious Strait of Malacca. That particular gauntlet would be run after Singapore. She was in the Java Sea, some 150 miles north of Jakarta, still in an area notoriously infested with pirates. The weather conditions were *Sea State 2*, implying a swell of only about 6 feet, with a stiff breeze. Not conditions to deter experienced attackers.

The crew had no reason to be unhappy with Captain Bashforth. He had announced that the owners were providing a new washing machine and that a pig would be provided for their Christmas feast. During the day, he had issued written instructions: *extra security precautions were to be taken while the vessel was sailing through these dangerous waters. Doors to the accommodation were to be kept locked. Lookout was to be rigorous. In the event of armed pirates boarding the vessel, there was to be no resistance.*

It was a fine, moonless night. Bashforth, Pereja, and Acting Quarter-master Able-Seaman Charlito de Vera, 30, were on the bridge. De Vera had only joined the ship that November, in Hong Kong. Bashforth worked on the bridge till mid-evening. Most of the time, he discussed company business with Pereja. De Vera later stated that he overheard Pereja tell the master that he had a well-hidden cash hoard which no pirate would find; he was planning to buy a $2,000 computer in Singapore.

The accommodation on the *Baltimar Zephyr* was close to the stern. Below the winged bridge lay, in descending order, C Deck, B Deck, and A Deck. Captain Bashforth and his Chief Officer had their quarters on C Deck, the other officers on B Deck, while A Deck was for the crew. The main deck was stacked with containers.

An internal stairway linked the different decks to the bridge. Aft of the accommodation external metal stairs led up to the bridge, providing access to each deck but only through watertight steel doors. Inside each steel door was a further wooden door. By using the external stairway, either bridge door on the wings could be reached by way of the outside wraparound walkway. De Vera claims that at 2100, he had locked every door leading into the accommodation. No member of the crew admitted to opening any locked door.

With the two inner and outer doors locked, crew were able to exit without keys but the only way back in was to use a key or else force an entry. Sometimes, however, attackers possess a set of master keys. One lock was later found to have a piece of metal jammed in it. Was this the work of the pirates, or had the lock been sabotaged by a member of the crew? How did this tally with de Vera's assertion that everything was secure?

When Bashforth went below at 2245, somewhat later than usual, he left Pereja working by the dimmed lights of the Chart Room. The bridge was equipped with port and starboard radar screens. The Radio Room was also up there, but Bashforth always kept this locked to prevent its unauthorised use for personal calls home. Additional communications included telex, VHF Radio and Inmarsat Satellite Communication. There was also a mobile phone capable of making international calls. An internal telephone system linked the bridge to each cabin.

Pirates often attack a ship from astern; some ships post a permanent stern watch when sailing in dangerous waters. De Vera's duty involved checking astern every 20 minutes. This meant unlocking one of the bridge doors and patrolling the external walkway, looking especially for small craft approaching from the stern. Every exit presented an opportunity to forget to lock the door on return. De Vera claims he did not forget. However, just as a car's rear view mirror leaves a blind spot, the vessel's radar left a significant area in the wake where intruders could approach unseen. Nor did De Vera notice anything out of the ordinary. This check astern took only a couple of minutes. Thus, for about 18 minutes out of 20, the ship's stern was vulnerable and unobserved.

Except for the hiss of the air conditioning struggling to combat the steamy conditions, all was hushed in the half-light of the bridge. The crew were far below, relaxing in their cabins. Only Pereja and de Vera were on watch. The two men went about their tasks without speaking. Through the seven big windows they could see the ship's bows parting the swell in a surge of salty white froth. Closer to the accommodation the stacked containers blocked much of the view from the bridge.

It was nearly midnight. De Vera was looking forward to the end of his watch when he suddenly heard a sound behind him. Startled, he swung round and glanced into the Chart Room. He recoiled in terror, seeing an intruder, a shadowy figure in the gloom, a handkerchief obscuring his features. De Vera read the menacing hatred and determination in the eyes. The Chief Officer's hands were raised above his head in surrender. Horrified, de Vera noticed the gun pressed to his colleague's skull.

The pirates had probably used a rubber dinghy with a powerful motor. Dinghies can bounce along undetected in a ship's wake. In a swell, the easiest means of boarding is from the side. The containers stacked on deck meant the attackers were invisible from the bridge. Scaling a mere 6 feet with a grappling hook over the ship's rail is no obstacle for fit young pirates.

To attack a ship 60 miles out at sea would require extra fuel and sophisticated navigation equipment—impractical in a small craft. Locating a ship with a suitably low freeboard at night so far from land could hardly be achieved by chance. Eric Ellen is convinced that this points to an Indonesian naval mother-ship or some other vessel lying only a few miles distant.

The intruder was wearing Ray-Ban style sunglasses, a shirt, trousers and heavy work boots. Slung across his body was a rifle and in his hand was the gun, his finger poised on the trigger. De Vera could only describe the man as short, perhaps 5 foot 4 and of medium dark complexion. That description could fit thousands of Indonesians.

The gunman signalled to both men to lie on the floor. Shocked, they obeyed without question. *Baltimar Zephyr* continued to make 12 knots with nobody at the helm. Attacks like this often leave vessels unmanned, at risk of colliding with other ships or running aground. Tankers and LNG carriers pose a particularly deadly threat, but pirates do not concern themselves with such trifles.

The pirate wanted the Radio Room opened but the duo made clear they had no key. A shot then rang out, followed by the crash of breaking glass. The pirate had shot out the starboard radar screen. The *no-see zone* thus created implied a planned escape back to a mother-ship hovering nearby. He turned his attention to the locked Radio Room. When he failed to break in, he slashed the VHF radio cables and destroyed the bridge telephone system. Destruction of the communication systems also suggested that the aim was to ensure the attackers got away undetected, rather than planning to steal the ship, in which case they would have commandeered the bridge and overpowered the crew with a gang of 14 men or so.

The lone gunman on the bridge belonged to a gang, but precisely how many came aboard, or what they were up to, remains a mystery. No crew member was attacked or ordered to hand over valuables. It was unusual that only one pirate invaded the bridge. Attacks usually feature weight of numbers. Now the intruder put the gun to de Vera's head as he lay on the floor. 'Officer? Officer?' he hissed. De Vera murmured: 'No!' The pirate turned to Pereja, urging him to his feet. De Vera heard Pereja pleading: 'Please don't kill me. I have a family.' The gunman forced the terrified officer at gunpoint through the internal door toward the cabins with the obvious intention of finding valuables and the ship's safe.

De Vera lay petrified, alone and unguarded. He was unarmed. For all he knew, the ship might be swarming with a dozen armed pirates. About five minutes later, he heard a single shot from below. Too terrified even to stand up or attempt to hide, he never moved from the bridge and never saw another attacker. De Vera later told the authorities that the intruder must have climbed the internal staircase and entered the bridge that way, through another door on A, B or C Deck.

The piece of metal later found jammed in the lock thus acquired greater significance. After the attack was over, two of the crew confirmed they had found both the A Deck inner wooden door and external steel door open. It seems likely that this was the exit route used, if not also the point of entry. Of course, the intruder could have reached the bridge via the external staircase, but that had presumably been locked by De Vera. The Indonesian investigators, later, seizing on de Vera's evidence, accepted *as fact* that entry to the bridge could *only* have been through the internal door.

Precisely what happened after Pereja was forced from the bridge remains unclear. If he cooperated in the opening of the safe, surely his life should have been spared. At times, a ship's safe may contain some $30,000 for wages, but the Danish owners doubted there would have been a large sum of money in this safe. The safe was later found open and empty. However, the table in the Captain's Day Room was strewn with cash—US $153, Australian $150 and Hong Kong $240—probably personal money belonging to John Bashforth and certainly a worthwhile bonanza for poorly paid naval personnel or pirates.

Teodolfo Pereja was executed in cold blood in the Captain's Day Room. He had been forced to kneel and was then shot through the head from close range, despite having persuaded Bashforth to open the safe. In a desperate effort to save himself, the Chief Officer would surely have handed over his personal secret savings if his attacker knew about his money. Had someone on board tipped the pirates off that Pereja had a hoard of cash? Did they know he would be alone on the bridge with de Vera? Whether Pereja was murdered in Bashforth's presence before the safe was opened is unclear. It is unthinkable that a man like Bashforth would have got Pereja killed by refusing to open the safe—especially in light of his own written instructions issued earlier in the day: *no resistance*.

In Freemantle the previous week, Bashforth had broken a toe in an accident. This hampered his movements. Having failed to appease the gunman (or gunmen) by opening the safe and witnessing the fate of Pereja, he must have tried to escape, fleeing from his own cabin suite, down two flights of stairs to A Deck. Here, in a desperate attempt to save himself, he tried to barricade himself into the heads. Without his injured foot, he might have been quick enough to get inside and lock the door. As it was, the gunman caught him.

The body of the master, this popular, careful and well-respected Englishman, was discovered slumped in a corridor. He had been shot in the thigh and, fatally, in the chest. The ship's cook, Manuel Agravante, had been asleep on A Deck. He was woken by a gunshot, followed by a scream and then another shot. He gingerly peered out of his cabin door and saw the captain lying on the floor by the heads. Over him stood a hooded gunman wearing a ski mask. The gunman pointed the gun at Agravante but did not fire. Agravante hastily slammed and locked his cabin door. Someone briefly rattled the handle but gave up. This hooded figure does not match the man on the bridge, described by Charlito de Vera as wearing sunglasses and a cloth wound round the lower part of his face. If Agravante is to be believed, de Vera was *not* the only person to actually see an intruder, although the deeply flawed Indonesian investigation concluded otherwise.

Able-Seaman Igano was also asleep on A Deck. He heard footsteps and a scuffle, followed by two shots. Then there was silence. Igano huddled in his cabin, terrified. But nobody approached. After a few minutes, he peered out and saw the body of his captain, the feet still quivering. Shocked, he locked himself in his cabin. After about 40 minutes, he managed a furtive conversation with Able-Seaman Rosell in the next cabin. Were the pirates still aboard? Was anybody on the bridge? Who else was dead? Were the pirates running the ship? If not, who was? Neither knew. All seemed quiet. Giving each other courage, they escaped through the cabin portholes and hid in a nearby crane, peering about in dread of being seen or of what they might see. But of the pirates, there was no sign.

There is further evidence that more than one attacker was involved. The Chief Engineer, sadly now too traumatised ever to return to sea, heard the gunshots from his cabin on B Deck. He then heard voices talking in an unfamiliar tongue, as did the Second Engineer. The ship's Second Officer, Gueverra, was also on C when he heard shots. From the lower decks came the sound of running and of a door being slammed. He checked the time. It was precisely 2354. He too remained locked in his cabin. Much later, he activated the ship's fire alarm by heating the sensor in his cabin with a cigarette lighter. He, like others, had no idea what was happening, whether the ship was being controlled by the pirates or whether they had fled. Small wonder that the crew did nothing, simply waiting and hoping to survive before investigating.

Though nobody knew it, the attack was over; the pirates had departed. After killing the two senior officers, they had either fled in panic or left, satisfied with their booty. The Second Officer's sounding of the fire alarm heralded that the attack was over. For 90 minutes, the ship had sailed on autopilot with nobody in control. Crewmen gradually emerged from cabins and hiding places. Gueverra, now in command, used a mobile phone to contact the Danish owners. Distress calls were broadcast by radio transmitter and Inmarsat.

A lookout spotted a speedboat that must have come from a mother-ship. Gueverra ordered that petrol bombs be prepared to repel any further attack, but none came. Two vessels were spotted—one on the bow about seven miles distant, and another about 5 miles away to starboard. In the darkness, it was impossible to tell whether the ship to starboard was a naval or cargo vessel used by pirates as a mother-ship. Neither vessel answered the distress calls. Were both ships from the Indonesian Navy? Or were they just too frightened to get involved? Would-be rescuers had been attacked in similar circumstances.

Pereja's cash was never found. Either Pereja had concealed it too well or he had handed it over. Possibly, if other crew members knew about his cash, they might have disguised themselves as pirates and stolen it; but if so, they too must have hidden their loot well enough to prevent the Indonesian investigators from finding it. If, during the robbery, the thieves were recognised by either of the dead men, that would explain the cold-blooded executions. However, the sighting of the speedboat (if true) makes it highly unlikely that members of the crew were responsible for this crime.

Moreover, De Vera never informed the Indonesian investigators that he knew about Pereja's cached money. He revealed this only in the course of further interrogation. If he himself were guilty, De Vera would surely never have volunteered this information.

Another definite possibility is that somebody aboard was working as a mole for pirates. Planting a mole aboard a vessel was a common enough strategy employed by some gangs but usually in more sophisticated attacks than this one, often with the aim of stealing the entire ship. By mobile phone, a mole would report the ship's position, the location of the safe and any other information about cash or valuables. A mole could also open doors to the accommodation. Although the Indonesian authorities concluded there was just one attacker, there were probably many more. Normally, a gang uses surprise, speed, firepower and weight of numbers—an armed team charging along the quiet gangways, yelling, firing, terrifying the crew into handing over anything of value.

If there were only two attackers, this suggests the presence of a fifth-columnist. It is certainly odd that the rest of the crew were not threatened, nor was any serious attempt made to break into their cabins, although a couple of doors were rattled. This implies that the intruders had been briefed that the other crewmen had nothing worth stealing. It is also consistent with the notion that two of the crew were masquerading as pirates.

At dawn, following calm instructions from the experienced Danish ship managers, the ship continued heading for Singapore. Nobody wanted the vessel to be taken to an Indonesian port for investigation. For a further 24 hours, the ship sailed without incident. Stig Jensen, Managing Director of Baltimar ApS Ltd in Denmark, arranged a rendezvous for the ship on 13 December at 0700 with *Sea Dragon*, a vessel organised by the Singapore agents. Captain Suresh Prabhakar was ready to be transferred to take command. The meeting point was by the famous Horsburgh Light at the eastern end of the Singapore approach.

Baltimar Zephyr did rendezvous with Sea Dragon a few miles from Bintan Island. However, ill-advisedly, she was still in Indonesian waters. With impeccable timing, an Indonesian Naval Patrol Boat appeared. Despite protestations that the owners wanted her to enter Singapore, the warship ordered *Baltimar Zephyr* to proceed to an Indonesian port. There was no choice. Such is the law of the sea.

In Singapore, which prides itself on representing the best traditions of marine etiquette, a thorough and fair investigation of the double murders would have been undertaken. To have the enquiry conducted in Indonesia with major input from the Indonesian Navy was unacceptable. Justice in Indonesia was a marketable commodity. Official corruption was endemic. The IMB were convinced that many attacks on shipping had been approved or ordered by officers of the Indonesian Navy—probably up to flag officer rank. The levels of naval pay were so pitiful that the temptation to boost earnings by plundering ships must have been irresistible.

Baltimar Zephyr was forced into the port of Tanjung Uban on Bintan Island, only about an hour across the strait from Singapore. Prabhakar and a doctor from *Sea Dragon* went aboard. The Indonesian *investigation* involved a mixed group comprising naval officers, police, immigration, customs and a doctor. Behind the scenes, Rear Admiral Yusuf Effendi ruthlessly pulled the strings.

Ellen was approached almost immediately by the agents in Denmark. He reported the incident to the IMO, but just when an orderly investigation in Singapore had seemed assured, the Indonesian Navy had intervened. It was four days before the bodies of the victims were removed from the ship. What followed bore no resemblance to a double murder investigation.

From the outset, the Indonesians decided that the crew had mutinied under the leadership of the Chief Engineer. What evidence they had for this claim has never been revealed. Having decided that mutiny was the motive, the *investigation* set about finding evidence to prove their case, dismissing facts that did not fit.

In their search of the vessel, no murder weapon was found, although three bullets had been fired. If a crewman had used a weapon, it had either been lobbed overboard or well hidden. The gun had been a .45, similar to the FN.45s used by the Indonesian Navy. What *was* found beside the cash abandoned on the captain's table was a note, apparently uncrumpled. The Indonesian investigation claimed that this was consistent with murder by the crew. Their opinion was that the English was *too good* for Indonesian pirates, even though they knew that an Indonesian pirate involved in an earlier attack on the *Australia Star* spoke excellent English. The message in the note, scrawled in black marker pen, was starkly clear:

I NEED YOUR ALL
MONEY IF YOU
DO NOT LIKE
HURT NO SPEAK
FOLLOW ORDER
ALSO YOU TAKE
CREW MONEY

On the reverse side was written:
NO FOLLOW
YOU DIE

No fingerprint evidence was obtained from the note. The Indonesian investigation found no marker-type pen or paper aboard that could have been used. Had it been written by one of the crew as a bluff to conceal an onboard crime, the pen must have been thrown overboard along with any paper and any weapon used. That said, the wording is interesting. The note could have been *specifically targeted at Pereja*, the man with the secret hoard. It was handed to Pereja and contained two different orders: firstly, to hand over all *his* money (*I need your all money*), and, secondly, to empty the safe (*take crew money*). Implicitly, the crew's wages would be in the safe. The wording does suggest inside information that (1) Pereja had money and (2) that he would be on duty. All that was then needed was to establish which of the two on the bridge was the officer (*Officer? Officer*?).

Maybe the Chief Officer did not hand over his secret hoard, banking on the erroneous assumption that the pirate would not know about it. Instead, he led the gunman (gunmen?) to the Captain's Day Room, a tiny narrow office with room for a desk, chair and safe and not much more. Did Pereja's failure to hand over his own money so anger them that they killed him in revenge? This conjecture fits *if* they had an accomplice aboard who had briefed them about Pereja's hoard.

In a bizarre attempt by the Indonesians to identify the crew member who had allegedly carried out the attack, de Vera was blindfolded and made to lie on the bridge floor while the crew filed past. Each had to whisper "*Officer? Officer*?" De Vera recognised no voice. Handwriting tests were also conducted but none of the crew's writing matched the message. None of this discouraged the investigators from allocating blame to the crew. The words used in the writing test were the old English typing adage: "The Quick Brown Fox Jumps Over The Lazy Dog!"—farcical tests, quite meaningless to a group of Filipinos with a poor command of English.

The Indonesian investigation concluded that in a *Sea State 2* the ocean swell was too severe for an external attack; mutiny was the only possibility. Prabhakar told them that *Sea State 2* meant the sea was calm. The sighting of a speed boat 60 miles from land and evidence of what Indonesian pirates had *already* achieved in rougher conditions were both ignored. The previous April, nine pirates had succeeded in clambering aboard MV *Australia Star*, six times larger than *Baltimar Zephyr* and presenting a much higher freeboard; that ship had been making 17 knots at the time.

Six days later, the investigation concluded that, as the accommodation and bridge doors had been locked, and *Sea State 2* had prevailed, there must have been a mutiny. If the Indonesians had any special information to support this strange conclusion, it was never made public. At the insistence of the Indonesians, Prabhakar, as the new master, had to sign three extraordinary declarations to secure release of vessel and crew. He had no option: *no sign, no leave here.*

The first document authorised the investigation to cease and acknowledged that the external doors to the accommodation had been locked to the best of Prabhakar's knowledge. Prabhakar pointed out in writing that, as he had not been aboard the vessel, he had no personal knowledge! In the second declaration, he was made to admit that there was insufficient evidence of piracy and also to *apologise* to the Indonesian Government for inconvenience and for the barrage of hostile media comment about the incident—as if he had any control of the media, in which strong suspicions about the role of the Indonesian Navy had been expressed. The final declaration confirmed the *good treatment* from the investigators, acknowledging that they had 'behaved like perfect gentlemen throughout and tried their very best.' This formal note bizarrely ended: 'Wishing you all a Merry Christmas!' Whether Prabhakar had added these final words in a gesture of defiance, only he himself could say.

Prabhakar's sole aim was to get the ship and crew to the safety of Singapore. The owners had a business to run; cargo bound for Calcutta had been delayed. The investigation had been a farcical whitewash with no real attempt to establish the truth. One lighter moment occurred when an officer from Indonesian Intelligence triumphantly produced a piece of *blood-stained string* found in de Vera's cabin. To general merriment, it proved to be no more than a piece of *greasy* string!

Ellen, much travelled in the region, was not surprised by the outcome. Stig Jensen contacted him again after the vessel was released. He was disturbed about the way the investigation had been handled, especially by the allegations of mutiny. There was no evidence, and certainly none which implicated the Chief Engineer as its instigator.

Among the many reports on the case, Ellen found a death threat. 'There had been two deaths, both needless but there might easily have been a third. Someone involved in the investigation was warned that if he ever breathed a word of what he knew, he would be killed.' Ellen knew the identity of the person threatened; he took the threat most seriously. That showed how anxious certain people were to suppress the truth. The news of the murders caused international outrage. A British captain and a Filipino officer murdered, yet the only voices crying *mutiny* were Indonesian. The rest of the maritime world scoffed at the notion.

Back in England, Captain Bashforth's brother, Bob, a solicitor in Derbyshire, was most unhappy with the investigation. 'John was a meticulous person, careful and rather shy. He wanted all doors kept locked for good reason in these waters. He was late on the bridge because of his concern. He had written out special orders to keep the ship safe. I think one of the doors may have been faulty, enabling the pirates to enter the accommodation. I never heard any suggestion back then that sometimes Indonesian attackers had planted a gang member onboard. Hearing that years later may help to explain things that were unclear. Perhaps the door had been tampered with by a planted gang member.

'From everything I heard at the time, I was convinced the Indonesian Navy had been involved in piracy and I think they knew more about this than has ever been proved. The naval officers were so underpaid that I suppose robbing from passing cargo ships was a useful something on the side. As for their investigation, I thought it useless.'

As a lawyer, this is informed criticism from someone well able to recognise a whitewash.

Bob Bashforth's concerns resonated with the National Union of Marine, Aviation and Shipping Transport (NUMAST). In accordance with English practice following a violent death, an inquest was held in Derbyshire. This ancient fact-finding process involves a coroner who is usually an experienced lawyer. Evidence is routinely gathered and collated by the English police. Key witnesses are called and a verdict is given as to the manner in which the deceased met his death. For deaths abroad, however, the coroner has to rely on the cooperation of foreign authorities.

Her Majesty's Coroner called for the core evidence from Indonesia.

It was never provided. Despite this disgraceful lack of cooperation, the Coroner still possessed sufficient factual evidence to conclude that John Bashforth had been *unlawfully killed.* He added that 'the weight of the evidence indicated that the assailant was a member of a group of armed raiders who had boarded the vessel and escaped while it was underway.'

Between the attack and the inquest, the British Government was severely criticised. Following the Coroner's comments, pressure increased on the Government to instigate a proper investigation to catch the murderers. Questions were asked in the House of Commons. NUMAST was particularly effective in keeping the murders in the public consciousness and in lobbying MPs.

Between the Conservative Government and the Indonesian President Suharto there existed a strong commercial bond. Suharto had come to power with American support. Foreign governments, Britain, the USA and Germany in particular, curried favour with him, despite the abuse of human rights under his corrupt regime and the bloody conflict in Timor. Suharto rewarded Britain with huge orders for armaments, orders which would be compromised by allegations of corruption or aspersions cast on the integrity of the Indonesian Navy. The murders of Bashforth and Pereja were an embarrassment to the British Government, for whom the arms contracts equation was simple: *healthy exports plus improved unemployment figures equal electoral popularity*. The greater the tyrant, the more obsequious and grovelling foreign governments had to be to ingratiate themselves.

The UK's balance of payments has always relied heavily on the arms trade. Britain has supplied regimes where ultimately the arms deal has come back to haunt Ministers. In the fragile economic climate of the time, the Chancellor of the Exchequer urgently needed arms sales to Indonesia. The Foreign Office was well aware of Indonesian sensitivities.

But NUMAST was persistent, nor did the Union stand alone. Britain had a proud tradition of standing up for truth and protecting its citizens. In bygone days, a couple of gunboats would have been despatched to give *Johnny foreigner a damned good pasting*, delivering a clear message: Britain protected her own. Britain was one of the pioneers of international maritime trade; London was still a hub. The Government's feeble stance was viewed as shoddy. Left-wingers protested against the Government caving in to a regime like Suharto's. Conservative elements in the City, the big shipping companies, insurers, brokers, and bankers were uneasy at their failure to protect shipping. Pressure was coming from all sides.

Two years after the murders, the Indonesian Government announced that their file was closed. It was a further two years before a diplomatic breakthrough occurred. On a visit to London, the Indonesian Foreign Minister agreed to arrange to make the original files available for a British enquiry. This was a triumph for NUMAST and an endorsement of the British Government's persistent, quiet but effective diplomacy. Officers from the Organised Crime Group at New Scotland Yard were appointed to review the Indonesian investigation and to present a report.

Raking over cold ashes is never easy. Terms of reference were agreed with much difficulty and rules laid down on what could be made available to Detective Superintendent Jeffrey Rees (later a key figure in the aftermath of the death of Diana, Princess of Wales, in Paris) and Detective Inspector Suzanne Williams, who later represented Interpol in the Joint International Working Group of the Comité Maritime International, which led to the Model Laws approved in 2002. Her other experience included being a member of the Royal Protection Squad.

The documentation made available to Scotland Yard proved to be far from complete. The promised assistance was not what Scotland Yard were entitled to expect. Vital documents were withheld, although the detectives *were* shown a set of photos mounted in an album entitled "*Our Wedding*!" Nevertheless, working with the Danish management, with assistance from Singapore, and using photos of the renamed vessel itself, they were able to reach a number of conclusions:

- Enquiries revealed no crew tension justifying allegations of mutiny.
- The ship's log was not made available for the days leading up to the 11 December.
- The Indonesians cut off satellite communication from the ship after it was taken into port. Fortunately, unknown to them, the Chief Engineer had a mobile phone!
- The owner company had never had any complaints about Captain Bashforth or Chief Officer Pereja, both of whom they held in high regard.
- The clothing worn by Captain Bashforth was never subjected to forensic examination. Allegedly, it was sent to his brother. He never received it.
- No access was provided to the original Demand Note left by the pirates.
- Manner of access to the bridge by the intruder remained an uncertainty. Of various possibilities, they regarded forced entry through the door on A Deck as perhaps the most likely.

- Though aware that there had been unsubstantiated allegations that serving or former Indonesian servicemen had been engaged in piracy, they obtained no such evidence. The .45 gun used, however, was consistent with FN.45s used by the Indonesian Navy.
- One of the most sinister aspects of the affair lay in a message allegedly from the *Baltimar Zephyr* at the time that the transfer of Captain Prabhakar was to take place from *Sea Dragon*. The Indonesians claim that the Radio Officer of an Indonesian Naval vessel at the scene, the *Kri Mandau*, picked up a message, allegedly from *Baltimar Zephyr*, stating 'mutiny on board.' Not one listening station nor one other single vessel anywhere in the world heard any such message. Furthermore, the crew denied saying anything like that, nor had any previous distress calls suggested that.
- The fact that nothing was *apparently* stolen was used by the Indonesian investigators to support their view of a mutiny. However, they accepted the possibility that Pereja's cash might have been taken or that the pirates viewed the cash available as insufficient.
- The original investigation ignored the clear sighting of the *hooded man* by the ship's cook Agravante. This was not the man seen by de Vera on the bridge.
- The Indonesian authorities had failed to investigate the limited extent of visibility from the bridge to where the boarding may have taken place. The detectives believed but cannot be sure that the containers could have been a factor.
- The attack on the vessel's communications is inconsistent with a mutiny. The crew would have been endangering themselves.
- Despite official denials of any piracy problem, the report concludes that there *was* a problem in the region and that the statistics available provided good circumstantial evidence that should have been taken into account. The waters were, in their view, statistically the most dangerous in the world.
- The crew, who had been interrogated over five days, sometimes after being woken at night, remained consistent in their accounts of the night's events.
- The barrister appointed to represent the company's insurers had been refused access to the ship.
- The piece of metal found in the A Deck door lock was dismissed as not relevant by the Indonesian investigation.
- Three ski masks were found in de Vera's cabin. The original investigation concluded that these were a material fact but the young

seaman contended that he had bought them in different ports for use in cold weather. (It *is*, however, odd that he had three such potential disguises, especially given the hot places the vessel was visiting—*the author's view, not a comment from the detectives.*)

- The Indonesians stated that another crew had previously mutinied on a Malaysian ship, the *Mekong Express*. They also told the Scotland Yard officers that a Filipino crew had mutinied within 6 months of the *Baltimar Zephyr* incident. They explained that they had sent out helicopters and naval vessels. That incident was, they said, reported to the Singapore authorities. The Indonesian Navy had then sent the vessel back to Singapore. The Scotland Yard team wrote to the Singapore authorities and received a reply from Assistant Superintendent Yeoh Bak Sek. He confirmed by letter that *there was no record of any such mutiny having taken place*. 'Indeed, they were not aware of any mutinies in modern times.' A request by the detectives for the Indonesians to provide the name of this vessel for further investigation went unanswered.

The British investigation concluded that '*whilst we could never rule out crew involvement totally, our considered judgement is that it must be beyond any reasonable doubt that Captain Bashforth and Chief Officer Pereja were murdered by pirates intent on robbery, who boarded the Baltimar Zephyr from another vessel.*'

Under English law, that would be sufficient to convict any accused person before a criminal court. However, the officers were unable to establish who was involved in the attack. It is reasonable to assume that documents not produced probably pointed away from mutiny toward areas whose scrutiny would have been unwelcome to the Navy-led investigation.

Interestingly, what had been published at the time by the Indonesian team as a *definitive* decision of mutiny was, during the UK investigation, diluted to being a *"tentative"* conclusion only. But the perpetrators of these callous crimes can rest easy now. The files are truly closed.

Detective Superintendent Williams found interesting the possibility of a gang member working as a mole on the ship. When interviewed for this book, she said: 'We were unaware during the investigation that one technique used in piracy was to plant a gang member on target ships. We in the Metropolitan Police had no in-depth experience of piracy at that time. Piracy attacks have increased but are grossly under-reported for a variety of reasons. These include delays, lack of confidence in local investigators, insurance issues, the loss of face and the pride of the master. Now we at

Scotland Yard are much more conversant with armed attacks on ships. Limited budgets, however, remain a central problem.'

At the IMB, Eric Ellen was dissatisfied with the Indonesian investigation. 'What message did this shambles give to others who might have reported an attack? They think better of it. The Bureau needs the most accurate figures to show the extent of the problem to give us leverage. I felt sorry for the Scotland Yard team, but at least they had enough evidence to destroy any credibility in the Indonesian views.

'Our confidential sources in the region confirmed that the Indonesian Navy had been involved in piracy attacks. Reports of the craft used by pirates and their style of dress supported this. One Rear Admiral's name kept cropping up but there was no *smoking gun* that proved naval involvement with *Baltimar Zephyr*, and anyway other organised crime gangs were plundering around Indonesia too. Whilst it is encouraging that their Navy has been responding to international complaints and putting out more patrols, that is not nearly enough. The continuing attack figures prove that.

'There might have been the occasional rogue crew who attacked ships unknown to the Admirals, but for these attacks to occur so often for so long is proof enough that piracy was part of the unwritten policy of the Indonesian Navy. But capturing pirates is only a start. The top criminals have little to fear from the judicial system. The Government must clean up the police and the judiciary too.'

Gang leaders know they can usually bribe their way out of trouble. Besides the Navy, the powerful people behind the most lucrative attacks can influence politicians and are above the law. The armed masked men are mere foot soldiers, controlled by the real bosses who never see a ship. Theirs is a luxurious lifestyle, a world of boardrooms, fine wines and pampered mistresses. These powerbrokers operate international syndicates, some of them belonging to the much-feared Triad societies.

PART TWO
The Triads and the Far East

The ways of the Chinese Triads, their identity, the structure and scope of their operations are shrouded in mystery. Collaborating with his close contacts in the Hong Kong Organised Crime and Triad Bureau and elsewhere throughout the Far East, Eric Ellen has acquired unique insights into the way these powerful secret societies operate.

Maritime fraud in Southeast Asia bears the indelible imprint of organised crime. One Bureau staff member working on problems in the region was Shiao Lin Kuo, a former Taiwanese Police Inspector. Her experience made her keenly aware of the dangers of challenging the brutal grip of the bosses. Ellen acknowledges her input and the usefulness of informants, who are rewarded for their information but who also risk their lives.

Informants have helped trace ships and given tip-offs about planned crimes. They might have heard that a pirate crew was being put together or a ship set up as a *mother-ship*. A ship's master might suddenly go off sick and be replaced with a criminal. Such valuable confidential information has allowed the Bureau to save insurers and others fortunes over the past 30 years. On one occasion, an informant planted as a gang member was arrested. Ellen saw him manacled, arms and legs. 'It was pitiful. I intervened to try to get him released into my custody. After much acrimonious haggling with the police, the Commissioner eventually agreed. But there was a condition. At a karaoke night I had to sing the well-known pop song *The Streets of London*! There was precious little pleasure in that for me or my audience, but my man was released! Of course, he could never be used again.'

Rooted in tradition, some Triad societies still use old titles like *Dragon Head* for the kingpin. Key players are known by a number. But most use the terms *Cho Kun* (Chairman), *Cha So* (Treasurer) and *Heung Chu* (Incense Master) for the top triumvirate. As in a legitimate business, the Chairman is elected regularly! These all-male gangs exude an aura of power and menace, an invincible image constantly being burnished.

When Ellen was running the Bureau, he estimates that there were some fifty societies operating in Hong Kong, all independently of one other, each with its triumvirate and the foot soldiers who did the actual dirty work. The Triad society might hijack a ship itself or hire another gang to carry out the raid.

Though the waters of the Far East are much less dangerous today than even just a few years ago, thanks in part to patrolling naval vessels, Captain Mukundan's in-tray, like Ellen's before him, bulges with Far East problems, many with Triad involvement. Chinese justice and other security measures stifled the plague of ship-stealing for a number of years, but since 2006, Indonesian pirates have moved their attention from the former hotbed, the Malacca Strait, into the South China Seas. In 2006, there was just one reported attack, but in 2010 the figure had risen to over 30, according to IMB statistics. The area around the Natuna Islands has proved especially dangerous.

Ellen explained that ships are targeted well in advance, both for the value of the cargo and the vessel itself. A gang is then hired and the price is agreed. The criminal bosses formerly promised to spare no expense to ensure the legal representation and release of the pirates if they were caught. But many gangs have been abandoned by their bosses when captured, perhaps because so many hijackers have been caught that it is no longer financially viable to support them.

New recruits may receive small payments, but for many the privilege of an invitation to join a Triad society is incentive enough. They quickly participate in gang activities—street crime, drugs, fake Rolex watches, smuggling, prostitution, maritime crime. The cream of the new intake may eventually be permitted to recruit their own gang to operate under them. This process continues, the most successful gaining in power and responsibility, fitting their own gang into the overall structure.

The perception in the West is that the Triads employ violent tactics to enforce secrecy and obedience. This is true. To be successful, members need *clout*. Clout comes from respect achieved through violence and threats. Deaths in turf wars are frequent. Having achieved respect through brutality, the successful member seeks to create a respectable image, often using his ill-gotten gains to set up a legitimate business as a front. But to get elected as one of the triumvirate involves a lengthy process, developing a criminal empire and subcontracting parts of the action to other members of the same society.

When we speak of a violent attack on a ship's crew followed by hijacking as being the work of *Triads*, we're not talking of one organisation. It maybe just one society, acting alone, or a joint venture, perhaps directed by well-educated white-collar leaders. If it suits their commercial interests, Triad gangs will cooperate, a feature seen in international piracy or people-smuggling. An operation which involves stealing a ship in Indonesia but selling the cargo in China may be a joint venture between contacts in each country. Many years ago, there *was* an attempt to create a true Triad empire, calling itself *The United World Chinese Association*. The venture did not succeed, but had it done so, it would have been a force to reckon with.

Ellen believes the Triad leaders know they are impregnable; even though their identity is known, they are confident that it cannot be proved in court. They may officially be engaged in in-shipping, import-export, banking, insurance or commerce, maintaining a respectable front and enjoying a luxurious lifestyle.

If their underlings are caught, there is no chance that they will reveal names of the bosses. Retribution would be swift and merciless. *Omerta*, the code of silence, as in the Mafia, is fundamental. But whereas John Gotti and other mob leaders in the USA became widely recognised as iconic Godfathers of various crime families, the Triad structure is far more secretive; its leaders are more likely to have got themselves into key respectable positions in the community.

Shiao Lin and Ellen have confronted Triad leaders, Chairmen of Triad societies, who would pass for chief executives of multinational corporations. They have the brains, the social contacts, and the thugs. With their power and reputation, they can intimidate or bribe police, the judiciary, politicians. They appear civilised and respectable with no hint of the violence that brought them to the top, nor of their links to the violence still carried out at their command.

Shiao Lin (*Little Bamboo* in Chinese) is deceptively neat, svelte and dainty; her slender frame conceals her immense inner strength and courage. She first volunteered to work undercover against organised crime when still a police officer, living life on the edge working against Triad interests in Taiwan. Her smiling demeanour is beguiling. It is hard to believe that she infiltrated the toughest gangs before exchanging Taiwan for the IMB headquarters in London.

Shiao Lin would unearth every fact she could to prove a link with a crime, and then confront the suspect. She was undeterred, even when confronting top gangster figures. She was often sure she was being followed and watched. She found the experience uncomfortable but she was never afraid, even when she was up against local corruption as well as gangs. 'I think that being a woman is a help,' she says. 'It's good to be underestimated! If after confrontation I got no admission, then I would usually turn to the police. Often, I found the local police knew the Triad bosses but lacked evidence to warrant a prosecution.'

Not all these bosses are fabulously wealthy, even though they make huge profits from crime. A phantom ship operation can net them millions and yet they can still be hard up! They live so extravagantly; they are usually heavy gamblers and womanisers. A failed piracy attack can be costly, too.

One problem the Triads don't have is the current higher cost of money laundering. Tighter banking laws mean the cost of laundering money to beat the system has risen from 5% to 25%. The Triads operate their own money transfer system in which cash does not cross borders, so the authorities cannot monitor the transfer. If, as a part of a ship-stealing scam, money has to go from Shanghai to Singapore, a kind of IOU voucher is created; this is then redeemed privately in Singapore. The books balance because someone in Singapore will want to shift money to Shanghai and the position is reversed.

This resembles the Indian and Middle Eastern *Hawala* system. A network of contacts operate cashless transfers. A code may be used—perhaps the serial number on a banknote—to ensure that the right person collects at the other end. Money might move from Dubai to New York in a few hours by a few phone calls. Both money-transfer systems move millions of dollars, operating on trust. The penalties for double-cross would be severe. Al-Qaeda were suspected of using *Hawala* to fund the hijackers of the planes that struck on 11 September 2001. Secretive systems of transferring money without banks or apparent records are ideal both for fraud and for terrorists.

Opinions vary as to the number of pirate gangs operating around Indonesia. The situation constantly changes, dependent on potential financial gain versus the risks or alternative ways of making a fast buck. If the chances of big profits are reduced because of better policing, piracy declines and criminals concentrate on more lucrative alternatives.

International initiatives, like the creation of the Bureau or the work of the International Maritime Organisation, have only scratched the surface of piracy and shipping fraud in the Far East. The Philippines, a complex archipelago of some 700 small and large islands, presents a special challenge, being almost impossible to police, with many small harbours where ships with false papers may offload cargo so long as a sufficient number of palms are greased.

Captain Emilio Changco was a bespoke pirate with an indomitable belief in his own invincibility. His gang operated from Manila Bay, an ideal area for piracy. Changco needed no *mother-ship* operating at sea. His speciality was stealing ships around the huge port of Manila, usually vessels laden with cargo. In his heyday, Changco boasted that he could steal any ship selected from his *'display cabinet'*—a panoramic view of the bay from his seafront hotel room. Scattered across the bay lay vessels of every kind, awaiting loading or discharge of cargo. For those with $300,000 available in cash, his motto was: *You choose, I steal.* Nothing and nobody stood between Changco's band of thugs and success. Anyone foolish enough to resist would be tossed overboard. Only the fit, the lucky, and those who could swim survived.

There was nothing clandestine about Changco and his cutthroats. He was notorious among shipowners and police around the globe. Some owners even paid Changco to steal back their own pirated vessels! Others called on Changco's special skills for shipping fraud involving *singletons*. A company would own a single ship, a *singleton*, which would then be over-insured. The ship was often reaching its sell-by date and requiring an expensive refit. What better solution than to pay Emilio Changco to steal it and force underwriters to pay an inflated sum for its loss? Profitable for all concerned except for the 'names' at Lloyd's of London Insurers. At the time, Changco could sell the vessel with another hastily registered name under a different flag of convenience. Alternatively, the vessel could be profitably used as a phantom.

Typical of many thefts in Manila Bay was that of the *Silver Med*, a dry cargo vessel of 5,300 tons, Liberian-registered and operated by Middle East agents of Piraeus. When she was hijacked, she was carrying rattan bound for Taiwan. The incident bore all the hallmarks of Changco's style and panache. Shiao Lin, investigating organised maritime crime in Manila, discovered that one member of the syndicate behind this hijacking belonged to the medical profession! A gang of eight men disguised as police boarded the *Silver Med*. Captain William Chadwick, then the Chief of the Investigation Division in the Liberian Marine Safety Department, recalls: 'We received a message that, unexpectedly and without authority, she had just sailed while awaiting orders in Manila Bay.' A series of five incidents three months previous immediately aroused suspicion that this was a hijacking. The ship's crew—14 Indian officers, at least five Filipino ratings, and the Chief Officer's wife, were forced overboard. They were fortunate to survive.

Chadwick was able to trace the vessel to Kota-Kinabalu, North Borneo, in Indonesia. There the Port Authorities were asked to intervene, but when the police launch arrived, the ship had sailed. She changed names regularly. Under another name, *Sea Rex*, she was eventually seized at Luzon, back in the Philippines. There were four Filipinos and three Singaporeans aboard. Some suggested the ship might have been going on to China to be sold for scrap. It is more probable that she would have been used as a *phantom ship*, far more lucrative to the gangs. The rattan had of course disappeared—presumably sold off in some quiet, unquestioning port.

Changco's hubris was unimaginable. He was a brazen criminal and a callous murderer. Not only did his activities rob insurers of many millions, they also cost many people their lives. Vessels that vanished included the *Comicon*, with 25 crew missing, the *Antoinette*, *Cresat 1* and *Mayon*, the last three all from Manila Bay. When the bulk carrier *Negotiator* disappeared from anchorage at Subic Bay, Manila, her crew were never seen again. Captain Chadwick is convinced these ships would not have been sold for scrap—certainly not immediately. They would have been used as *phantom ships*, trading and stealing cargo in the region under other names—or perhaps used for people-smuggling by the Chinese snakeheads.

Changco had cocked a snook at the law for years when he made the mistake of stealing the oil tanker *Tabango*, owned by the Philippine National Oil Corporation. That crime was too much for the Government to swallow—action was taken at last. Now a sick man, unable to walk without a stick, Changco was arrested and jailed by the Filipino authorities. While *apparently* attempting a jailbreak by, improbably, scaling a high fence, he was shot dead. The likelihood is that he was silenced.

Changco earned himself a fortune against a background of poverty. He offered teenagers from the back-street slums of Manila a chance to be in a gang and steal ships. Illegal it might be, but it was a job and it beat abject poverty. Besides, there was the powerful thrill of boarding vessels in the bay and stealing them by force.

Changco is gone, but the Philippines still present dangers to shipping. Religious and political extremism have exacerbated the situation, while poverty and political and religious uncertainties erupt in bloodshed on a regular basis, draining resources and sapping community spirit. The risk of 'traditional' violent piracy is now augmented by the threat presented by local terrorists who have been lured into extremist factions by despair over a bleak and uncertain future.

The USA is supporting the Government against Al-Qaeda recruitment, but more conflict is inevitable. Poverty, the ready availability of weapons, and the presence of gangs ready to absorb disaffected youth mean that violent attacks against defenceless seamen will continue—whether motivated by fundamentalism or the more practical aim of putting food on the table.

Organised crime syndicates are a global problem. To illustrate the mysterious interplay between organised crime, corruption and the Indonesian Navy, let us go back to the murky world of Chew Cheng Kiat—alias *Mr Wong*. Mr Wong was another gang leader operating within an impoverished society. The task of combating crime anywhere is tough, but in a country like Indonesia, where corruption, nepotism and intimidation of police and judges is endemic, even containment, let alone eradication, is almost a lost cause. For too long, Indonesian waters were the most lawless seas on the planet. Maritime crime is and was only one facet of a much larger problem.

- Between 1999 and 2000, the sum of $22 billion provided by the International Monetary Fund was stolen from the national coffers. Terms and conditions for granting the loan were blatantly ignored.
- A son of ex-President Suharto was jailed for 18 months for his part in a crooked land deal worth multimillions. The Supreme

Court Judge in Jakarta who sentenced him was later gunned down by five assassins.

- In October 2001, the Speaker of the Indonesian Parliament was allegedly involved in embezzlement involving millions of US dollars.
- A Minister for Mines and Energy fell from power for alleged involvement in a scam involving the oil industry to the tune of $25 million.
- No official within the system will keep his job unless he joins the *simony* system. Customs officials, port authorities, court staff, immigration officers and traffic police are all part of this culture. They have to bid high to obtain their appointment and then continue paying. Eliminating the simony system presents a daunting challenge. A London lawyer visited Jakarta to investigate a shipping problem met some top officials, to whom he complained that his clients' rights had been abused. He then returned to his hotel. Later that evening, he was confronted by two armed thugs, who frogmarched him at gunpoint and put him on the next flight to Singapore. He was lucky to survive.

Mr Wong was engaged in piracy on a grand scale. Not for him the swift raid to grab a spot of cash and a few televisions. He preferred to steal entire ships, preferably with high-value cargo. He used the name Chew Cheng Kiat on occasion and claimed to be Singaporean, a graduate of Nayang University. He admitted to having a wife in Singapore and children in Australia, but he led at least a double life with several false trails and aliases. He also had a mistress on Batam Island.

His origins are shrouded in mystery. Eventually, the Singapore Government would issue a statement declaring that, despite his reputation, Mr Wong was not Chew Cheng Kiat. That name belonged to a Singaporean who had lost his passport some years earlier, the suggestion being that Wong had stolen his identity. The Government would not even confirm that Wong was Singaporean. Andreas Harsono, a journalist who met him, placed him by accent as Singaporean Chinese or Malaysian Chinese, as he spoke Malay with a Chinese accent.

In a James Bond movie, the bad guy is a larger-than-life figure—bullet-headed, sinister, or hulking and physically impressive. But Mr Wong's appearance was so ordinary that he blended into the background. Slim, with a round, cheerful face and rapidly thinning brown hair, his strong dark features suggesting Malay and Chinese ancestry—he laughed readily and handled media attention with easy good humour, although his eyes were wary. Yet this unassuming man was a ship-stealer of legendary proportions; he set his seal on many a phantom ship operation. Indonesian authorities contended that Wong was the Indonesian end of an organised crime group—possibly Triad-directed—involving China, Hong Kong, South Korea, Singapore and elsewhere.

As the small island Republic of Singapore grew ever more successful and prosperous, the population soared and it ran out of land. The solution adopted was to create allegiances with neighbours. To the north lies Malaysia, with which Singapore has not always enjoyed the best of relations. Johor Bahru, the closest point, is just a crowded bridge away from Singapore. Broadly to the south across the Strait lies the small island of Batam, an Indonesian possession and part of the Riau Archipelago, a mere 40-minute ferry crossing from Singapore. Thirty years ago, it was poor, undeveloped and in need of investment, while Singapore was hungry for growth: and thus the Golden Triangle of Singapore, Johor and Batam was born. Singapore could bring infrastructure, new business and prosperity to these poorer areas.

What started then as an investment in Batam has now exploded into the mainland province of Riau and the islands. The simple fishing communities on these islands, so attractive to tourists, harboured numerous pirates.

Singapore, the busiest port in the world, is a useful neighbour for a pirate. Moreover, Singapore has had difficulty protecting its waters. After vessels heading east pass the Horsburgh Light, open season begins for piracy. If Singapore had enjoyed better legal rights in the Phillip Channel and the Malacca Strait, Mr Wong's pickings would not have been so rich. The Golden Triangle was his stomping ground. 'There were three bilateral agreements made between Indonesia, Malaysia and Singapore,' confirms Captain Mukundan. 'Attacks had become so frequent that even Japan had volunteered to join in a taskforce to help keep this sea-lane safe—in the interests of its own shipping fleet.'

It never happened. As the crisis of local piracy boomed in the 1980s and 1990s, none of the three countries agreed. There was no *hot pursuit* agreement that would enable a Malay warship to enter Indonesian water without permission. However, the sharing of operational information between the littoral states and coordinating action against pirates has been impressive—an indication of what could have been achieved through cooperation and adequate funding.

Piracy is a reflection of the state of the economy. Until the crash of the rupiah in 1997, piracy attacks were falling in the Malacca Strait. These crimes had generally been opportunistic raids by locals rather than complex attacks involving ship-stealing. When poverty gripped the nation, crime levels rose.

Besides its own lively import-export scene, Singapore is an important port for bunkering, repairs and other business. Since the 1979 FERIT Report, the extent of shipping crime in the region has been well known in marine circles. Many of these sometimes vicious attacks were just fleeting forays by local thugs who would board a ship, rob her crew, empty the safe and then flee back to a tiny port on the Indonesian side. Here, the spoils would be divided—police and port officials taking their cut for turning a blind eye. The robbers generally came from Indonesia, in particular from harbours along the eastern seaboard of Sumatra. Using Singapore as a base to launch pirate attacks was not an option, though meetings of the kingpin Triad figures have regularly been held therein five-star hotels.

Mr Wong's role, like Changco's, was stealing ships to order. All that differed was the *modus operandi*. Changco operated from his waterfront hotel. Wong, however, spent much time on his mother-ship *Pulau Mas*, a small tanker of around 400 tons often seen around Batam. His gang stole to *his* orders, cherry-picking the ships that created the best profits, possibly acting under instructions from a Triad powerbroker. As a local gang leader, he and other bosses from China and Malaysia would select the vessels to be attacked and stolen. For years, this syndicate ran an impressive operation that earned multimillions.

The sudden new prosperity on Batam brought corruption and crime in its wake. Across the Strait, the great naval fleets of the world had always used Singapore as a safe haven. Vessels, especially those of the Royal Navy, were constantly present to protect British interests. American sailors, too, were often in town. In the '60s, for sex-starved crews, the highlight of a visit at Singapore was to experience the night life on Bugis Street; here, slender doe-eyed girls and beautiful transvestites were ready to cater for every taste. The modern Government of Singapore was none too enthusiastic about Bugis Street's colourful reputation. As the economy boomed, so did the demand for space. New tower blocks were needed. Bugis Street, the tiny red-light district near the Arab and Indian quarters, was ruthlessly sanitised and is now unrecognisable as the mariners' paradise of yore.

But Batam and Johor were different. They were beyond the iron grip of the Singapore Government. Singaporeans may accept a penal code where freedom of speech is restricted, chewing-gum is banned and jaywalking or failure to flush a lavatory are criminal offences. But they certainly revelled in the sordid aspects of the modern reincarnations of Bugis Street across the water in Johor and on Batam.

A lively nightlife developed. Karaoke bars, strip clubs, brothels and massage parlours sprang up. Money-changers (many of them *money launderers*) abounded. Life became fast-paced. Increasing numbers of hotels catered for businessmen and tourists. A sex industry flourished in the ferry-port town of Nagoya. Singaporeans, encouraged back home to live a disciplined life of austerity and moral rectitude, queue daily at the ferry terminal to enjoy the fleshpots of Batam. Wong was a regular, flitting across the Singapore Strait. At one time, his Indonesian girlfriend worked in a karaoke bar where seductive hostesses performed duets of various kinds.

Wong lived a double life. By reputation a shipowner or shipping agent, this status enabled him to discover details of vessels, crew, cargo, routes and times and to place his fifth columnist mole aboard, equipped with a mobile phone. Wong's role was intelligence, not the rough stuff. He was never the man with the machete or the Mk 47. In the fast-moving commercial bustle of Batam Island, Wong's activities attracted no more attention than those thousands of other Malay-speaking Singaporeans who came there to live, to work or to play. Singapore is a community characterised by harmonious racial relations, despite occasional tensions. Wong was not ostentatious: like most Singaporeans who live in a hot, humid climate, he generally wore casual white shirts and trousers and lived simply—just another face in the crowd.

Unlike Gotti, the Mafia don of New York's Gambino family, Wong did not act like a movie star, strolling the streets of Little Italy shaking hands. He could walk down Singapore's busy Orchard Road unobserved, stroll across the Padangun recognised, dine out unremarked. His face was never in the media. He more closely resembled the old style Mafiosi—secretive, keeping a low profile, shunning vulgar flaunting of power or wealth.

These Far East syndicates were well-informed. With members planted in reputable banks or shipping offices, they could access IMB Reports and Confidential Bulletins. A report might reach a syndicate leader within 24 hours, leaked by someone in a reputable bank. IMB's duty to alert members to scams and risks was complicated by the need to avoid evidence falling into the wrong hands. When investigating organised crime, Shiao Lin got so close to the gangs that she was able to identify the names of the bosses, but this information could not be published without revealing how much the Bureau knew. Somebody somewhere would leak the details, even though they were distributed to insurance members only.

Shiao Lin had been monitoring the region's rising crime figures, intending to prepare a report as a FERIT Mark 2. (FERIT reported on shipping crimes in the area back in 1979.) This benchmark investigation revealed the huge extent of shipping frauds. It should have sounded the death knell on complacency. But few prosecutions followed. The crime syndicates expanded their activities. From 1988, there was a marked increase in criminal activity: *phantom ships*, hijackings, deviations, cargo thefts, piracy attacks, documentary frauds and container theft proliferated.

In the '70s, rust buckets would be scuttled and insurance claims made. The new trend was to arrange the hijacking of an elderly ship and a claim was then made that way. The hapless crew were simply tossed overboard to make the attack look like piracy.

With regard to the phantom ship problem, one of the weaknesses in an already weak system concerned ship registration. A stolen ship needs a new identity; criminals managed to bribe officials in shipping registries to issue a *Certificate of Provisional Registry*. The normal fee was $5,000, but officials were bribed with ten times that amount to provide the certificate. The registry would be given false details about the ship's dimensions, weight and depth. Because no checks were carried out, one single ship could be registered with a string of bogus names and certificates. Wong used a string of false names for vessels hijacked.

Such crimes were highly profitable. The syndicates made hundreds of millions. Several gangs or syndicates were in operation in the Far East. Those run by Indian or Bangladeshi nationals were mainly interested in gold and cigarette smuggling or documentary frauds—selling non-existent cargoes based on false papers—whereas the phantom ship syndicates were mainly Chinese.

These criminals could usually speak English but between themselves they spoke Cantonese or Mandarin. Unsurprisingly, Shiao Lin's enquiries proved that some of the gang leaders like Wong were involved in legitimate shipping and international trade as a respectable front. Some possessed several passports and false identities, naturally obtained illegally. A Malaysian passport could be obtained for as little as $3,000.

Investigating such powerful figures is dangerous. 'Death threats?' Shiao Lin smiles cheerfully. 'You can't let that stand in the way of the job at hand. Particularly when I was exposing the false papers used by gangs for pirate crews, I was upsetting some influential people. But if you're a woman, people allow you to put your feet in deeper. They're not so defensive. You just have to go and deal with them and forget who you are…and who they are too. I don't give them a chance to look down on me because I'm a woman. I'm in a man's world.'

Beneath the veneer of respectability as a shipping executive from Singapore, Wong—having checked, through his contacts in shipping offices, which ships were sailing with what crew and, most importantly, with what cargo—would select a target with an attractive high-value cargo. He could then get one of his gang hired as a fifth columnist among the crew.

It was not known at the time of the attack on the *Baltimar Zephyr* that using moles planted aboard vessels was an established technique. It is most unlikely that Wong had any involvement in that attack. It did not bear his stamp: the cargo was not stolen, the ship was not hijacked, and he would not have been interested in petty cash. His gang would have overpowered the bridge and taken immediate control, assisted by their man on board. The crew would have been dumped on a liferaft and abandoned to their fate.

Just occasionally, the ship rather than the cargo was the big attraction, as in the case of the high-tech *Petro Ranger*. But generally the gangs go for the cargo—aluminium ingots or oil that they know they can sell in a port where no questions will be asked. One such deal can turn a profit of a couple of million.

Once Wong's target had been chosen and an advance deal to sell the stolen cargo arranged, action then moved to *Pulau Mas*, his mother-ship. A new name for the targeted vessel would be selected and registration papers prepared. He could save on registration fees (and bribes) because onboard he had the facilities to forge credible documents of ownership for future use, which he knew would pass muster for selling off cargo in a carefully selected port. The mother-ship also had ample paint for changing the name, repainting the funnel and effecting other changes to complete the disappearing trick.

The crewman planted on the target ship would keep Wong's team informed by mobile phone of the ship's position and the numbers on the bridge. When the decision was taken to attack, always at night, up to 30 masked and armed pirates would board the assault craft and speed the few miles from the mother-ship. Success was usually swift. Violent intimidation ensured minimal resistance. The crew would usually then be manacled and locked in a cabin while the pirates took command. The ship's name and identity would be changed by a lick of paint, the target ship metamorphosing into a phantom. There was no need for further bloodshed, but some piracy gangs, like the *Jump, Buddy Jump* mob, seemed to revel in killing. Lucky crews were abandoned in a boat, a liferaft, or on some remote island. The less fortunate were dumped overboard to die or simply murdered out of hand. The crews of the stolen tankers *Hualien* and *Tenyu* were never found.

Once the vessel has been stolen and a new crew put in place, she is ready to ply her trade as a phantom. Shipping agents find naïve or greedy traders, attracted by a bargain freight rate, ready to entrust their goods to a ship that does not legitimately exist. It's a trap and an obvious one.

'I'm sending timber from Manila to Phuket on the *Saucy Sue*, registered in Cyprus. OK?'A single phone call enquiry like that from a trader to the IMB asking this might prompt a response like *there's no such vessel of that type registered under that name.* An uninformed trader can kiss his timber goodbye. It would leave Manila but be sold in some obscure port. Result? More huge profit from this one phantom ship. This type of crime was repeated over and over.

Wong's gang was responsible for countless successful attacks, especially stealing tankers, with the trail leading to China. Significantly, one major attack went wrong back in 1998. Was this failure the start of his downfall? Or did *Petro Ranger* go wrong because he had *already* lost influence to another rival gang? Did this mistake and the financial losses that followed lead to his arrest? It seems possible, perhaps even likely.

Petro Ranger was attacked in April 1998 by Wong's gang shortly after leaving Singapore for Ho Chi Minh City. This was a sophisticated operation. The ship was new, large, and equipped with a state-of-the-art computerised bridge system. Moreover, her cargo of gas, oil and kerosene was itself of significant value—worth at least two to three million dollars on the black market in China. Wong's methodology was slick. His pirate teams had stolen a string of tankers, changed their identities and sailed them north to China. There, the oil would be secretly discharged into the Chinese black market.

On Wong's orders, 12 pirates took over *Petro Ranger*, which was manned by a crew of 21. Heavily armed with automatic rifles and machetes, the pirates had no problem in seizing the ship, but they needed the crew's help to understand the technology on the bridge. Though they suffered violent intimidation and minor injuries, the crew were not immediately murdered.

The blue funnel was painted red and the vessel renamed *Wilby*. Another phantom was being created. A tanker like this could earn the gang around $40 million after selling off the stolen cargo. Easy money. The Bureau had tried to combat this type of crime for years; they reckoned a phantom was being created every few weeks by attacks like this. Each phantom then traded repeatedly, using different names, stealing more cargoes.

Wong's operation involved discharging *Petro Ranger's* cargo in the South China Sea off Hainan Island. The procedures were tried and tested. The cargo would be offloaded into other vessels and smuggled into mainland China, where tax on fuel meant that it could be sold most profitably. Corrupt Chinese officials were in on the scam and normally made no waves. But this time the pirates were caught in the act of transfer and arrested—as were the original crew. There had been a glitch in the well-oiled machinery. Had the seeds of a crackdown or a turf war within China already been planted? Did someone want Wong's operation to fail, or was there a double-cross, perhaps involving bigger bribes?

Whatever the reason, what happened to the crew of *Petro Ranger* and to the pirates in China is extraordinary: the Indonesian pirate gang were released and allowed to go home to return to the job they knew best—stealing ships—while the genuine crew and their Australian captain were treated as criminals. Wong's friends in China may not have prevented the apprehension of the *Petro Ranger*, but at least they secured the release of the criminals. But the setback meant Wong's smooth operation was in disarray. The *Petro Ranger* fiasco damaged Wong's credibility.

It seems unlikely that Wong's gang was involved only in oil thefts, in view of the immense profits from other cargoes. The rash of attacks and hijackings within range of his *mother-ship* suggest he was involved in other crimes as well. Accounts as to how he came to be arrested vary. The fearless award-winning Indonesian journalist, Andreas Harsono, revealed two conflicting versions in *The Age*, a Thai newspaper.

According to one account, Rear Admiral Sumardi of the Indonesian Navy announced that Wong was arrested on 1 December 1998 in Hotel 88 on Batam Island. However, another version painted a picture of more sinister complexity. This suggested Wong had been arrested aboard *Pulau Mas* in the port of Johor *in Malaysian waters* a week previously. Associates of Wong, including his Batam girlfriend, claimed he was arrested in Johor. He had phoned from the Malaysian port claiming that Indonesians, including naval officers, had boarded his ship and demanded 50,000 Singapore dollars. The intruders had come from an Indonesian Naval Patrol Boat, the inference being that Wong was being targeted or blackmailed by people who believed they had information that could be used against him. According to Wong, *Pulau Mas* was commandeered and sailed back into Indonesian waters.

Captain Mukundan notes that *Pulau Mas* is officially listed in the Bureau's statistics as a victim of a piracy attack at Johor. Ironic fate decreed that the great ship-stealer should have his own vessel hijacked. Previous attempts around Batam or Bintan Islands to board his ship and catch Wong had always failed. Those efforts had been thwarted by the ship's sudden departure—probably through a warning to Wong from a corrupt official.

In Johor, the Indonesian Navy could not lawfully seize *Pulau Mas*. More probably, interested parties had used the navy to enforce payment of a claimed debt, forcibly returning Wong to be arrested on Indonesian soil. When the vessel was boarded in Johor, the ship proved to contain a prosecutor's dream: a comprehensive modern piracy kit, including 15 pairs of handcuffs, 14 face masks, knives, fake immigration stamps, date and time stamps, and 12 cartons of paint. There were also ship's stamps and sets of forged ship papers ready for use. A speedboat with a powerful 200-horsepower motor completed the naval team's haul.

After being forced to return to Indonesia, Wong was not immediately imprisoned or charged. In his bruised pride, Wong may well have regarded the episode as an arrest, but in reality the event suggests naval officers were abusing their power to help a crony recover a debt. In the week following his enforced return to Batam, Wong went about his business, rejoining his mistress on 29 November. Back ashore, among the gaudy sleaze of the island, he made no serious attempt to hide. He checked into the Hotel Kolekta, where he was always known as Mr Wong, using a passport in the name of Chong Kee Fong.

Indonesian Intelligence, *Guskamar Armabar*, were apparently behind his arrest, alleging Wong was the mastermind of a multi-nation syndicate. Rear Admiral Sumardi announced that Wong had admitted his syndicate was involved in five attacks on tankers, including that on the MT *Petro Ranger* (although Wong himself protested his innocence), the MT *Atlanta*, MT *Suci*, MV *Pendopo* and MT *Plaju*. There was no mention of any involvement in the attack on the MT *Tenyu*, another tanker, or indeed in *any* attack where the crew were murdered, although these deadly attacks were otherwise quite compatible with his style of operation.

Admiral Sumardi, like Ellen and Shiao Lin, believed the mastermind—probably a Triad, working through Wong—was China-based and that the tankers had all been stolen to order. These incidents alone would have produced a profit of $30 to $40 million, even allowing for bribes, backhanders and the crews' wages. The Admiral also gave the official explanation of events surrounding the arrest, where by a former member of the Wong gang tipped off the Intelligence Agency about the ship's precise location *in Indonesian waters*. In a top-secret lightning strike, Wong's lookouts and informers failed him and the ship was seized.

Despite the contradictions, evidence suggests that the ship *was* unlawfully seized in Johor, whether by authorised or dissident naval personnel or others disguised as naval personnel. Once *Pulau Mas* had been forcibly removed from Malaysian waters into the Indonesian jurisdiction, the arrest could officially be made. *Something* had changed: Wong's defence system had been destroyed, perhaps through a clean-up of corruption within the navy, or, more probably, through a clash with other gang leaders over the *Petro Ranger*—or with some influential person who had lost out in other deals with Wong.

Wong, along with seven others, was arrested in November 1998. He denied any wrongdoing but in late 1999 he was jailed and nobody shot the judge. Nobody intervened to save him through corruption—indications, perhaps, that his influence had waned. His initial sentence was seven years, later reduced to a derisory four. He is now free.

The Bureau urged the prosecution and conviction of 17 other pirates, but this never happened. One gang was caught after hijacking MT *Selayang*; others were apprehended by the Philippine Coast Guard on the MV *Inabukwa*. Thanks to excellent cooperation between the Philippine and Indonesian authorities, they were brought back to Indonesia and charged, tried and convicted, but the sentences were very lenient: the majority walked free due to time already served.

The climax of another attack in Indonesian waters occurred four years later, in a Bombay courtroom in February 2003 and under Indian law. The result was a triumph for justice, made possible only by intense international cooperation and the coordinating role of the Bureau.

Ports are hotbeds of gossip. Shipping agents like Wong can quickly discover which ships are valuable and vulnerable. The Japanese freighter MV *Alondra Rainbow* was handpicked by people in the know. She weighed 8,900 tons and carried 7,000 tons of cargo—aluminium ingots. Ship and cargo together were worth $20 million. In a violent attack by masked pirates off the Indonesian coast, the crew were transferred to a *mother-ship*. They were later cast adrift on a liferaft and not picked up for 11 days. The cargo was off loaded in a prearranged deal.

The Bureau traced the stolen vessel through its contacts and, after a dramatic shootout by the Indian Navy, she was seized in the Arabian Sea with the pirates still aboard, desperately trying to flood the engine room and set fire to the ship. One of the most expensive legal firms in Bombay was hired to defend, a clear indication that someone influential was behind this gang. At the time, India was not a signatory to the Rome Convention of 1988, which gives an arresting state jurisdiction over a piratical attack in waters outside its territory.

The legal question was the grounds on which India could exercise jurisdiction to prosecute. Indian law, originally based on English common law, has been codified. The issue was whether the old piracy laws had been carried forward. The 14 pirates were charged and convicted of the hijacking and sentenced to seven years hard labour—a good deterrent to other criminals. The tough stance taken by the Indian authorities and the courage with which they saw it through are praiseworthy, especially since the incident involved a foreign ship carrying a foreign cargo, hijacked by foreign nationals in the waters of another country.

In January 2005, the Malaysian authorities boarded an Indonesian tug and a barge, stolen in December 2004. The tug was towing the barge from the Philippines to Indonesia. Following a tip-off from the Bureau, three pirates and another person were taken into custody at Tawau in East Malaysia. Both vessels had been renamed and were flying under the Belize flag. But satisfaction at the recovery of the vessels was tempered by the disappearance of all nine crew members, presumed dead.

Without solid evidence, it would be incorrect to publish one Indonesian name that has appeared on the Bureau's files with great frequency. It might also prove dangerous. Soni Wee, an Indonesian pirate executed in China, reputedly worked for this man, a prominent member of Jakarta's business community. That connection would associate this public figure with the infamous savage attack on the *Cheung Son* as recounted in Chapter 7. This captain of industry, a friend of former President Suharto, is widely rumoured to have been involved, behind a front of reputable business interests, in activities including piracy, prostitution and people-smuggling. His influence, wealth and power present an insurmountable obstacle to investigation, let alone prosecution. Yet until such Titans of organised crime are brought down, there can be little realistic guarantee of safety for shipping in Indonesian waters. Before the recent emergence of the Somali pirates and the problems off Nigeria, there were no more dangerous waters in the world than the seas of Southeast Asia. The dry statistics gathered over the past 30 years cannot convey the horror of facing armed and masked pirates in the dead of night. Pirates in this region tend to attack by night, armed with guns, knives and machetes. However, the figures published in the ICC-International Maritime Bureau's regular reports are accurate only to the extent that crimes are reported. Most are not.

An ongoing initiative from 2004 saw Malaysia, Singapore, Indonesia and Thailand combine to safeguard shipping in the Malacca Strait and the Singapore Strait. The Indian Navy joined in 2006, and their involvement apparently coincided with a major decline in crime. Naval patrols and air reconnaissance have also proved effective. But the gangs moved on, seeking greener pastures. Their next focus of activity was the South China Seas, where incidents of attacks rose to 30 in 2010.

Poverty, opportunism, wealthy criminal financiers, and low risk of prosecution combine in an unholy alliance, creating a climate that encourages pirates to seek out lucrative and vulnerable prey. The Malacca Strait operations demonstrate what concerted efforts can do to reduce the levels of crime. But the relatively small size of the bottleneck here makes it easy to patrol by sea and air. The South China Seas and the waters off Somalia to the Indian Ocean present a challenge on a far different scale, as will be seen later.

CHAPTER TWO

Mass Murder? The MV *Estonia* Car Ferry Disaster

On the night of 27/28 September 1994, the MV *Estonia*, a Ro-Ro car ferry travelling from Tallinn, Estonia, to Stockholm, Sweden, sank in bad weather conditions—but not unusually so for the Baltic Sea. Of the 989 reported passengers and crew members, 852 drowned. There had been a bomb threat shortly before sailing.

What happened that night is explained in detail later in this chapter.

When given the chance to get to the truth, three Governments—Sweden, Finland and Estonia—united only to foster doubts and suspicion. What remains is a lingering suspicion that what happened was no tragic marine accident but more probably mass murder, and in any event a cover-up of unpalatable and secretive facts.

Killing 852 people out of 989 *officially* aboard, a death toll far worse than Pan-Am 103 over Lockerbie, warranted an unimpeachable and transparent investigation. It did not get one. The initial investigation by the Joint Accident Investigation Commission (JAIC) was carried out in private involving Governments with gross conflicts of interest, either on legal liability grounds or because of secrets that they preferred to conceal.

Poisoned Chalice

The JAIC concluded that the loss of the *Estonia* was a tragic accident at sea and finger-pointed to the strength of the ship as delivered by the German shipbuilders. Faith in the work of this tri-national Commission has continued to dwindle, and now, 20 years after that tragic night, voices still call for the full story to be revealed.

The evidence today points suspiciously toward the involvement of organised crime and the aftermath of the Cold War. Alternatively, secretive Government agencies may have pressured the Commission so that the JAIC members found themselves holding a poisoned chalice rather than the sword of justice. That could have suckered them into a less than frank appraisal of the sinking. Over the course of the three-year investigation, the Estonian chairman was forced to resign, the Swedish chairman had to resign after admitting to lies, and two other members of the Commission died. The pressures of seeking truth were indeed great.

Conspiracy theories abound after any curious major event, whether the death of Diana, Princess of Wales, the crash of TWA 800 or the assassination of JFK. Sifting truth from informed speculation and from the wilder extremes is difficult. Unfortunately, the JAIC shot itself in both feet:

- By its composition and chairmanship.
- By working in secret.
- By being driven to admit that lies were told about the investigation.
- By refusing to listen to or admit outside external evidence.
- By neglecting or refusing to undertake scientific tests that should have been done at the time with the available evidence.
- By concealment of evidence—and by being caught Watergate style.
- By declaring the wreck a *no-go zone* and attempting to bury the hull in concrete and gravel on the superficially laudable basis that the wreck was full of corpses.

Above and beyond calls for other apparent cover-ups and conspiracies to be exposed, the remarkable story of the loss of the *Estonia* is surely on the firmest ground. Only the most diehard disbeliever of conspiracy theories will not be persuaded that vested interests had a reason to conceal the true causes of the sinking. In this chapter, an attempt is made to catalogue the flaws in the official JAIC findings and to point to alternatives, one of which is a murderous set of explosions. But there are other possibilities. A fresh independent investigation has been needed ever since the final JAIC report, dated December 1997.

Since 2007, there has been a further attempt by the Swedish Government to dampen doubts, and in May 2008, further reports were published that—depending on your starting point—either put the issue to bed or simply raised more concerns. This latest investigation was a theoretical exercise only and is open to serious criticism for that reason. This too is discussed later.

Witness Evidence

Witness evidence after any disaster needs to be investigated properly and then tested in the fire of cross-examination. Even honest witnesses can be mistaken in the confusion of terrifying events. Conflicting testimony needs to be weighed. All material witnesses need to be interviewed. There have been suggestions that as many as 12 crew members disappeared and never gave evidence. One of them was a captain from the vessel, though he was off-duty and not in command that night.

Scientific evidence and expert testimony from a variety of quarters needs to be subjected to informed cross-examination. Expert evidence is notoriously unreliable. Ask any litigation lawyer! Two sides call expert evidence on an issue and despite both often having identical facts from which to work, the conclusions are often very different. Cynics contend that the opinion depends on who is the paymaster.

Experts must rely on *facts supplied*. If those facts are flawed because of inadequate investigation or from failure to supply all known facts, then the expert starts from a false premise and however distinguished, the outcome may be nonsense. By analogy, people rely on computers, but the expression *rubbish in, rubbish out* is pivotal in knowing whether the outcome is reliable. So it is with expert evidence.

In any far-reaching investigation, even fringe theories need to be considered, if only to be discarded when subjected to keen forensic legal analysis. The writer appeared as the solicitor representing an employee of a hospital where over 40 persons died in a fire. Finger-pointing and wild speculation as to the cause went in many directions, but at the Public Enquiry every aspect, however absurd, was explored so that the outcome was hard to challenge.

In contrast, the JAIC investigation was an insult to the families of the bereaved. Because it was so secretly and badly handled, it is scarcely surprising that cries of *cover-up* have lingered. Elusive truth may never be reached if secretive Governmental agencies want to prevent the public from knowing more, and it is tragic that because of the way this investigation was handled, the perception of cover-up remains. It may be that nothing sinister occurred that night, but turning deaf ears and blind eyes when so many had died was both callous and short sighted.

The author first wrote about this tragedy in November 2001. Everything that was written then still holds true, but subsequent events up to 2006 fortified the doubts about the investigation, and the more recent reports of 2008 have done nothing to douse the fires of concern. The bereaved families deserve nothing less than a proper investigation with witnesses and cross-examination. This will not happen unless litigation by the families ever moves forward. However, such litigation is often settled on confidential terms when inconvenient issues may be open to public scrutiny. This litigation has stumbled and stuttered and may now have fizzled out.

Roll-On, Roll-Off Ferries

Long before *Estonia* sank on 27/28 September 1994, many marine architects had regarded Roll-On, Roll-Off (Ro-Ro) ferries as unsafe. Ever since the *Titanic*, a principle of ship design has been to divide vessels into watertight compartments. This prevents the entire hull from flooding from one point of water ingress. It sounds like common sense. But Ro-Ro ferries defy this principle, as the car decks run from bow to stern like a giant cave. At the bow, as on *Estonia*, there is a visor. When at sea, this is locked down to keep the sea out. It pivots up and down on its hinges to form the upper part of the bow and during crossings should be clamped tightly down by what is known as the Atlantic Lock. The integrity of the hinges and locks operating the visor are essential to the safe operation of the vessel.

Behind the visor is a ramp used for vehicles going in and out. At sea, this becomes a giant door that also should be watertight once raised and tightly shut. Bearing in mind that these two vital parts guard access to the huge cavern of the car deck, it is essential that they are maintained in good repair and kept watertight. At the docks, the visor lifts up like those on knights' armoured helmets. The ramp is lowered. The economics of this design are impressive, as it reduces time in port by rapid loading and unloading.

However, in the ten-year period from 1978 to 1988, 5,300 passengers lost their lives due to this design. Before *Estonia*, there had been the sensational loss of the cross-channel ferry *Herald of Free Enterprise*. The vessel had sailed with its gaping bow doors open, a remarkable but not unique lapse in basic safety. When she was barely out of the Belgian port of Zeebrugge, heading for Dover on 6 March 1987, she started to fill with water and keeled over in 90 seconds in calm seas. One hundred and eighty-eight persons died, though many more were rescued as the disaster was so close to shore.

For the future of the Ro-Ro design, it might have been the end of the line. The speed with which the incoming water capsized the vessel was a stark warning. It was not entirely heeded, though modifications to the design of *new* vessels were made from 1990 to meet IMO requirements. Despite the dangers written large since 1912 of not having watertight compartments, commercial pressures prevailed. Seven years later, *Estonia* gave a more fearful example—save that it occurred, unseen and terrifyingly at night, in the middle of the wild blackness of the chill Baltic Sea.

MV Estonia's Final Days

The 21,000-ton Ro-Ro car ferry had been built in Germany in 1979/80. After various owners, by September 1994 she was owned by Estline Marine Co and operating under a bareboat charter. The corporate structure was complex, but underlying the name, the Estonian Government had an interest as co-owners. The Swedish company Nordstrom & Thulin were also co-owners and had responsibility for maintenance.

By chance on 27 September 1994 (the day the fateful voyage started), the Swedish Maritime Board inspected the vessel, as they were providing educational support to Estonians being trained to be safety inspectors. Swedish Chief Inspector Åke Sjöblom had apparently been so concerned about the condition of the visor and bow ramp, among a shopping list of issues, that he tried to prevent it from sailing. His other apparent concern was the incompetence of the crew.

A top-ranking Estonian who was being trained was notified of this view and sought instructions from his superiors, but they insisted the voyage should go ahead. There is some dispute about whether the Swedes tried to get the ship kept in port by appealing to their bosses back in Stockholm. In any event, the ship sailed. The evidence of Åke Sjöblom is so pivotal that it warranted full investigation under questioning, supported by contemporaneous documentary evidence of phone calls, notes and records. In their findings, the concerns noted that day were ignored by the JAIC, who concluded that the vessel was in tip-top condition and seaworthy except for some rubber repairs needed on the visor.

Perhaps it is not surprising that concern about seaworthiness of the bow area was ignored by the Estonian officials. In the previous January, the vessel, while under a previous name and ownership, had been in dry dock in Turku, Finland. Scheduled work included a major overhaul of the bow door area and strengthening the locking devices for the visor and bow ramp. The vessel was sold before the work was done, and Nordstrom & Thulin, presumably with support from the Estonian Government, determined the work not to be needed.

Bomb Threats

Not for the first time, that very day, there had been a phoned warning of explosives aboard the vessel. A conversation discussing the search between the ship and the Tallinn Harbour-Master's office on VHF was overheard by a witness on vessel *Linda* in the harbour. The speaker aboard *Estonia* said nothing had been found but the ship sailed about 30 minutes late.

The nation of Estonia was in its infant stages—emerging from Russian control following the collapse of the USSR and the end of the Cold War. Crime was rampant, involving turf wars between powerful gangs. There were rumours of troubles with the shipping company involving payment of protection money. The port of Tallinn had become favoured as a known route for drug and people-smuggling as well as high-level arms-running. The official figures for casualties make no allowance for a suggestion that there may have been some 150 Kurd refugees being secretly transported that night in a truck. These illicit trades invariably give rise to bribery in ports and to vendettas between rivals. With fortunes at stake, there are certainly gangsters who would put vengeance before the lives of the innocent.

Of these factors, by far the most interesting is the international arms-dealing for reasons that were hinted at in the earlier German edition of this book in 2002, but which have now accelerated toward pole position. In that version, the author concluded that the vessel did not sink from design defects coupled with the forces of nature, as the JAIC had decided, but rather had probably been severely damaged by explosives. Rumours then had been circulating that this route had been regularly used to transfer top-secret former USSR technological know-how and equipment to the West. In 2002, this was plausible but untested, and was only one of a number of possible or fanciful conspiracy theories to be considered when determining who would blow up the ship.

Carl Övberg was a surviving passenger and a veteran of some 40 crossings. Besides having some interesting observations about the dreadful maintenance of the ship (not considered a problem by the JAIC), he provided a graphic description of loading that fateful day He was a last-minute arrival himself and noticed that the dock area had been sealed as a military convoy arrived. They escorted two large trucks up to the ramp. These were the last vehicles to board.

Swedish Customs

In November 2004, ten years after the sinking, the former Chief of Customs in Stockholm came forward and confessed on television that he had wanted to speak out for too long. Lennart Henriksson confirmed that twice in September 1994, the *Estonia* had to his knowledge been used to carry former

Soviet weapons and technology. Western interests (perhaps the USA) were interested to receive sensitive technology, while other hard-liners from the Soviet days seemingly objected to the material going westward. On 14 and 20 September 1994, Henriksson had been *ordered* to wave through trucks without proper inspection in breach of usual procedures. Allegedly, this unique arrangement was known far beyond Customs and into Government circles. It seems the orders that eventually reached Henriksson came from high places. Further light will be shed on this later.

The Night Crossing

That September night, *Estonia* left dock at around 1930. The master was Captain Arvo Andresson, an experienced mariner but very much a Soviet-influenced officer. He always drove his ship hard, obsessed with punctuality and operating with what others would criticize as reckless disregard for the force of the sea that night. The Chief Engineer was Harli Moosaar.

But there was a duplication of both these officers, because also aboard were Captain Avo Piht and Chief Engineer Lembit Leiger. The curious affair of these latter two senior officers will be dealt with later. On board were known to be just under one thousand people, but with rampant people-smuggling, there may have been many more.[1] She also carried a large number of cars and trucks. This was her regular overnight crossing from Tallinn, with arrival in Stockholm due at around 0930 the following morning.

The Baltic Sea is known for being rough, especially in winter, but the conditions that autumn night were not extreme. The crew claimed to have made some preparations for the conditions by chaining down vessels including large trucks on the car deck. Passengers disputed this. As she sailed along the shelter of the coast there was a heavy swell, but as she turned west into the open sea, the waves started to batter the ship, precisely as forecast. True, it was stormy with driving rain and the conditions made many passengers sick, but the conditions were not unusual and were certainly within the ability of this large ship (if in good, safe condition) to take in its stride. The conditions were those typically encountered a few times each year and not as severe as can occur on the route. At 0030, the

---

[1]Overloading of a ship is not fanciful. The recent tragedy of the loss of the ferry MV *Sewol* off South Korea, in which nearly 300 people, mainly children, were drowned has revealed allegations that the ship, while permitted to carry under 1,000 tons of cargo, was in fact carrying 3,600 tons, a factor which may have led to the instability that caused it to overturn. It was not a Ro-Ro ferry, though it was designed to carry cars as well as cargo and passengers.

stabilisers were activated to ease the pitching and rolling of the ship, though one of these was not working correctly and needed attention.

The ship's speed had fallen in the squally conditions from around 17 knots as she encountered waves sometimes as high as 20 feet (about 6 metres). Nevertheless, she was meeting the vicious waves head-on, so that the ship was filled with the creaks, groans, stresses and strains of a ship under attack. At 0030, there was no sense of any crisis, but within 90 minutes, the vessel would be gone, capsized and sunk—stern first to settle around 250 feet down (around 70 metres)—a remarkably rapid sinking but slower than the 90-*second* capsize of the *Herald of Free Enterprise*.

The Final Hour

Around 0045, many passengers were still drinking in the bars or gambling in the ship's casino. Others were listening to music or watching exotic dancers, unaware that within 75 minutes, nearly 90% of them would be dead, drowning - or dying on liferafts.

A ship in a rough sea is alive with tormented noise as green water crashes over the bows and the screws fight both in and out of the waves. Heading into turbulent waves makes the vessel judder, shake, roll and pitch. Yet the consensus from survivors from various parts of the vessel is that above all these noises, they heard two dull bangs or crashes from the bow region—impossible to define but put down by most at the time as strikes from exceptional waves. Almost nobody thought that something catastrophic had happened, though one Swedish woman left her for'ard cabin and rushed up to the deck, fearful of what she had heard. That certainly suggests something scarily unusual.

Other passengers reported a different noise, like a sledgehammer repeatedly banging metalwork. That may have been precisely what they heard, because there were problems both with the starboard stabiliser and with the sewage system. Sledgehammers may have been used on the jammed starboard stabiliser or to repair a reported problem with the sewage tank deep in the hull of the vessel near the bow. Yet again, others later described a repeated banging noise consistent with the visor at the bow door flapping freely against the hull, having started to break free.

The vessel slowed, and at around 0045 another Swedish ship picked up a first mayday—weak and not repeated. No action was taken. Fifteen minutes, later at 0100, another loud bang was heard by survivors. The ship shuddered and vibrated with the shock. Passengers and crew deep in the hull of the vessel started to panic. Many had been in cabins, fighting seasickness and wishing the voyage was over. Some saw water escaping from 0-Deck to Deck 1, a certain sign of a serious problem. Passengers were scared by an even heavier impact sound, followed by yet another.

If these terrifying sounds were not enough, the vessel stopped suddenly while veering to port. Then in a violent motion it heeled to starboard, perhaps as far as 50 degrees before righting itself. The violent roll threw people around. Some clambered with difficulty up the stairways toward the promenade on Deck 7, as the ship rapidly tilted to about 40 and then 90 degrees to starboard. Water was undoubtedly swirling among the vehicles on the car deck as people fought to make the steep climb toward safety. For many it was just too much.

At 0122 the first official mayday was picked up, and then a second, so that 14 vessels headed for their location. Alas for most aboard, there was no happy ending as they screamed in despair as the ship settled onto its side, its funnel kissing the waves. The lights went out, adding to the confusion. Even for those who made it to the fierce winds on the sliver of deck above the sea, there was little hope. The crew had been put on action stations too late and were unable to release nine of the ten lifeboats. (As to the solitary lifeboat that was launched, more later.) Clinging to anything available on the heaving deck, the small band of survivors resigned themselves to being swept overboard any second or being fortunate enough to clamber onto a liferaft.

By this time 75% of those aboard had lost any chance of survival, trapped somewhere below the promenade in the swirling water that was rapidly bursting through the cabin areas. Perhaps two hundred and fifty people still had a chance, perched just above the waves that they must have known were soon going to swallow what little remained of the ship. Some chose to jump into the sea, hoping their lifejackets would save them and fearful of being sucked down when the ship finally succumbed. Occasionally, a wave would sweep over them, reducing the number.

It was 0130. Moments later, the starboard roll continued beyond 90 degrees. Like white mice on a slippery treadmill, the survivors had to scramble onto the hull as the promenade and much of the superstructure slipped beneath the waves. The last refuge was to cling to the upturned hull or stabiliser fin as the vessel approached a complete 180-degree roll. The keel appeared like a shark's fin, an eerie sight compared to the spanking white vessel and the flood of lights from the accommodation and bridge when the ship had sailed from Tallinn.

With a quickening pace, the 21,000 tons slithered stern first below the sea. The last refuge from the roiling sea had gone. The few remaining passengers and crew fought and scrambled to get onto liferafts and to cling to the debris that now littered the sea around them. All that remained of the ferry was a swirling patch of water where moments before had been 550 feet of ship. Cries of anguish and despair filled the darkness as young and old fought to stay afloat, one moment in a deep trough, the next cresting a wave like a giant rollercoaster.

Lifeboats

The fortunate scrambled onto the liferafts or upturned lifeboats that had broken free in the boat's last seconds. One lifeboat never broke free, but eight did. Luck played an enormous part in the survivors' stories. Some were washed into liferafts, others were washed out; those without lifejackets struggled, some naked, in the chill of the water. Only those out of the water could hope to survive for any time in the cold and angry sea—for the rest, maybe an hour or two, perhaps three at the most depending on personal factors. Even some of those under canopies on liferafts succumbed to the extremes of the ordeal and were dead before rescue came in the grey light of dawn.

The most disturbing part of these moments is the behaviour of Number 1 lifeboat. This was the one used for *man overboard* situations, always ready to cope with emergencies. This one may have even been properly launched, as it was the correct way up, but those in it were alleged to have shown callous disregard for the welfare of their fellow human beings struggling in the water. Motorman Elmar Siegel was in a liferaft when he saw this lifeboat sailing away from the *Estonia* without any interest for those fighting to survive.

A passenger called Thure Palmgren observed something like a fishing boat heading away from the ship without heed to those in the water. There is something here for conspiracy believers to get stuck into. Who was in the boat? Why were they seemingly oblivious to the cries for help?

Those who believe that persons aboard the vessel planted bombs to hole the ship deep in the hull and to damage the bow region conclude that this lifeboat was ready for launch and the perpetrators were in it. They believe that the plan was to save those who had protected Russian interests by preventing weapons sensitive to Russia from being smuggled to the West. By implication, they had planted the bombs after the safety inspection and presumably during the voyage. They had then climbed into a lifeboat and been rescued by a fishing boat that had been deliberately close by. Before dismissing this as absurd James Bond or Jack Bauer fantasy, readers are encouraged to await the concluding twists and turns of much more evidence and further events yet to be explained.

Rescue ships on arrival found few alive in the water. There were stories of heroics, of selflessness from passengers and crew alike. Others acted selfishly, reckless to the safety of others as they fought to survive. Other than regarding those secure in Number 1 lifeboat, it would be churlish to be critical of such behaviour in the black torment of the Baltic Sea on a wild night.

The sinking was in an area subject to Finnish control, and a helicopter arrived shortly after 3 a.m. but saw mainly a marine battlefield of corpses and debris, though some survivors were hauled to safety from the rafts. One rescue vessel, *Mariella*, could not use its own lifeboats in the conditions. There has been criticism that the rescue services were slow, but in those conditions it seems unlikely that arriving a few minutes quicker would have made a big difference considering how few of nearly one thousand had even managed to escape the clutches of the sinking ship. Only 95 bodies were recovered and picked up.

There were 137 survivors, although as explained later, the official passenger figures are open to suspicion and still needs to be investigated. Persons allegedly seen ashore as survivors and listed as such were later reported as missing at sea. Eyewitness testimony suggests for example that both Captain Piht and Chief Engineer Leiger (the off-duty officers) survived and were seen ashore. Captain Piht was certainly with the couple hundred or so who were perched on the capsized vessel shortly before it disappeared beneath the stormy waves. Other witnesses say he was on a liferaft.

All told, some nine "survivors" were subsequently much later reported as lost at sea. This mystery, especially involving two senior officers, has given rise to speculation that they were whisked away from hospitals in Finland and taken to the USA (or possibly murdered and dumped) because of involvement or because they knew too much and had to be silenced.

On the available evidence, it is impossible to take this suggestion very seriously, but that said, it is essential that those witnesses who saw these two officers in hospital should be cross-examined, because these two were also later listed among the nine missing. Such evidence has to be weighed for credibility. Inevitably after a tragedy like this, there will be confusion about identities, but usually the outcome is the reverse: persons listed as missing prove to be alive. Persons believed to be safe and apparently seen in hospital and listed as alive are not usually then later listed as drowned at sea.

28 September 1994

As the shockwaves reverberated through the Baltic region and then around the world, the three Governments concerned created what became known as the JAIC. Most of the dead came from Sweden and Estonia, though many other nations had reasons to grieve. Quite wrongly, Andi Meister, the Estonian Minister of Transportation, was appointed overall chairman. As he was in part responsible for the operation of the vessel, this was a crass error if an open and fair-minded investigation was ever intended. During the enquiry, in the tensions between the Commission members, he resigned both as chairman and from his ministerial role, blaming the Swedes on the JAIC for being less than frank.

Initial reports from survivors pointed to a problem at the bow with some evidence that the giant visor weighing 55 tons had broken free, forcing open the (*theoretically* watertight) loading ramp and permitting water to flood the car deck. Had it broken free due to bad design? Or due to poor maintenance? Or due to insufficient strength to cope with the sea conditions? Or due to bomb damage in an area critical to the vessel's integrity?

Bedding

Carl Övberg, the veteran of the route, knew from past trips that water regularly flooded the car deck to an inch or two. Another experienced witness once saw it far deeper. This should not have been possible with a vessel in good repair. If this occurred, the stern car door would then be slightly opened at sea to enable the water to escape, a pragmatic but wholly improper solution.

Övberg was able to describe later to other investigators how the bow ramp leaked and was always padded with bedding to stem the ingress. A rolled tarpaulin was also used at the top of the ramp when in the closed position. Övberg also described how the entire bow door entry area was distorted, and that in consequence raising and lowering the ramp was more of a problem than it should have been. When later checked, the wreck revealed that the stern door had indeed been slightly open, consistent with a policy of letting slopping water exit that way. This evidence supports the concerns expressed by the Swedish authorities on the day the ship sailed—concerns that the Estonian authorities seemingly overruled.

Foregone Conclusion

Within 24 hours of the loss, the Swedes announced that the ship had sunk because the visor area had broken off and the bow ramp had been ripped wide open, permitting the sea to rush in. This was not true. Nevertheless, from that prime ministerial announcement onward, the outcome of the JAIC investigation was a foregone conclusion based on this precept. This was the predetermined conclusion that had to be reached. Getting out a *plausible* explanation quickly, even if factually wrong, is a great technique for slanting public opinion forever after. It happened both with JFK and with the death of Princess Diana in the Alma Tunnel.

From that moment, what followed was an investigation that appeared interested only in evidence that fit this announcement. This conclusion conveniently diverted blame to the German manufacturers and away from the three countries involved. In aviation disasters, the manufacturers will typically seek to uncover pilot error or poor maintenance in the immediate aftermath to condition public thinking and to prevent loss of reputation for the manufacturer.

However, just across the Baltic in Tallinn, some different comments appear to have been made, though their provenance is a matter for a judicial enquiry. There is a fascinating dispute about a comment attributed to a very senior military figure. A German military attaché claims to have met a US army colonel called Aleksander Einseln, an Estonian, who had worked at NATO in Brussels before becoming responsible for the Estonian armed forces in 1993.

The meeting allegedly took place in Tallinn on the day the ship sank. As is known by most lawyers, courts pay close attention to what is said almost in the heat of the moment (the Latin maxim *res gestae* applies) because often admissions of truth are made that may later be regretted or glossed over by spin doctors and lawyers. When the attaché asked about the loss, he claims that Einseln commented, 'It was an attack against us.' That view was shared by the head of Estline, Johannes Johanson, who apparently also commented that '*Estonia* was sunk by an assault.'

Subsequently, Einseln said he was not even in Tallinn that day and had been in the USA. One way or the other, someone in a senior and respected position is not being truthful or is seriously mistaken. The consistency of the two alleged comments is attractive when linked to the known evidence of bomb threats against the vessel, and becomes more pertinent when fresh scientific evidence emerged of explosive damage long after the JAIC's final whitewash report.

The Joint Accident Investigation Commission's Conclusions

The JAIC produced reports over a three-year period, culminating in the final one of December 1997. Though the Commission acted in secrecy, it was known that tensions between the Estonian position and the views of the Swedes and Finns had caused great difficulties, something feared at the outset but assumed to be manageable. Assisting the Estonian team was the head of their secret police, to ensure consistency of evidence, though he left the team before the final report.

The sudden resignation of the Estonian chairman, Andi Meister, in 1996 was indicative of the cauldron in which the JAIC was operating. Based on the later revelations of 2004, it would seem that his complaint about the Swedes withholding information was fully justified. It now also seems likely that the Swedes on the Commission were being pressured by their Government, who in turn may have sustained international diplomatic pressure—an intriguing aspect in the search for the truth. Those who believe that high-value secret technology was being smuggled out believe it was to assist the USA. They contend the Americans were behind such pressure and involved in the disappearance of damaging crew witnesses. However, proof of this is scant.

The fact that the head of the Swedish team, Olof Forssberg, was forced to resign in May 1997 because of admitted lies relevant to the investigation suggests that there was more international political manoeuvring going on than had first been apparent. Despite being utterly discredited and humiliated in a radio interview, Forssberg was soon appointed as an appeal court judge. The Swedish Government evidently thought he deserved a reward, perhaps for supporting their position against heavy odds. His replacement was Ann-Louise Eksborg, who till then had been working in the legal department of the Ministry of Defence. This appointment is most interesting, as appears later.

Two fellow Swedes, Olle Noord and Bengt Schager, resigned as experts on 15 June 1997 and 8 September 1997, respectively. Allegedly, Noord had lost confidence in the integrity of the Commission's work. As mentioned earlier, two members of the Commission died during the three-year period, a Swede and an Estonian, indicative perhaps of unusual stresses from working on the investigation.

Another Estonian member was in a curious position. Enn Neidre was head of the Navigational Department at Esco, a company central to management and operations of the ship. In April 1996, he appears to have changed status from a full member of the committee to that of an expert working with the committee. In the early stages of the investigation, when he had gross conflicts of interest, he was very actively involved, especially with the very few crew interviewed, who were bound to feel pressured by this senior figure.

Wilder Speculation

Though the vessel was in relatively shallow water, it was five days before the ship (so the public was told) was officially examined. The Finns had quickly found the vessel and had marked its position with a blue buoy. It is by no means certain that the position was accurately marked, adding intrigue for those suspicious of what was happening underwater in those five days, unseen from above.

Wilder theories include that the bow had not become detached at all during the sinking, and had instead been removed in those few days after blasting it free using explosives. Though *possible* based on evidence adduced after the JAIC's final report, this outlandish conspiracy theory seems to stretch credulity too far. Other explanations of what may have been happening below the surface in the immediate aftermath may seem more likely.

Subsequent developments can only sustain concerns that there may well have been secret examinations of the vessel's interior and exterior during that time. At least there is now a potential motive for wanting to examine the vessel and perhaps seek to salvage material from the two interesting trucks. If the vessel were carrying top-secret and highly sensitive former Soviet know-how and materials being secreted to the West, urgent attempts may have been made to salvage this. But the contents of the two trucks were not the only seemingly sensitive material being carried, as appears later.

The precise location of where the ripped-off visor was found remains a hot topic. Officially it was found about one mile west of the wreck. That would mean *Estonia* had changed direction 180 degrees during her final minutes, not impossible but, in the absence of any surviving officers, at least uncertain. Some believe it was either much closer to the main hull or still attached until ripped free to support the published theory.

The Lock Failures

The final JAIC report included the assertion that the sea was *unusually* violent. This was not so. The conditions were bad but not extreme by Baltic Sea standards, and no other vessels in the region that night encountered difficulties. There has been adverse comment from other mariners that the master took the challenge of the oncoming waves too fast and added undue stresses to the bow end, but even so the ship, if in good repair and seaworthy, should have been well able to cope with the waves. The JAIC concluded that the visor at the bow took such a pounding that there was water ingress. The visor then started to break free after one and then two locks broke. The design strength of the bow area was faulted rather than the poor maintenance spotted by the inspectors on 27 September and described by the crew witness.

The JAIC concluded that after breaking free, this 55-ton weight then shifted forward, yanking out the loading ramp which was intended to be watertight, thus permitting water to enter.[2] The visor flapped free for a while, but once it fell off, the bow ramp was torn open too. The sea then poured in through the wide mouth of the opening, causing the vessel to capsize and sink. The admission of up to 2,000 tons of water into the car deck was therefore blamed for the sinking.

However, as is explained later, the two most serious *technical* defects in the report centre on these findings. Distinguished marine architects say that if water were only flooding the car deck, it would not have sunk—merely capsized and floated upside down. There had to be water elsewhere in the hull to explain the sinking. Additionally, the visor could not have moved forward as described by the Commission.

Vessel's Condition

The Commission members did not fix any blame on their own Swedish or Estonian countrymen for permitting the vessel to sail because they concluded that the vessel was seaworthy, deciding that in general it was in tip-top condition. How that measures up against evidence of such a severe leak that the bow end had to be padded with bedding material and the stern door left ajar to prevent the inflow of water becoming too deep is hard to explain.

Estonia had been built long before design changes made to the Ro-Ro ferries since 1990. This enabled her to be regarded as safe, as she complied with the law when built, despite the unlimited open space of thousands of cubic metres of car deck. She had been regarded as safe to continue operating on her earlier regular route *close to shore*, but bearing in mind that the *Herald of Free Enterprise* sank within a short distance of the harbour,

---

[2]As described later, this weight may have been up to four times greater if the visor leaked and took in water *en route*, as seems possible.

even that decision was questionable. When *Estonia* was switched to the 258-mile crossing to Stockholm, much of it on open seas, there were no searching questions about whether the ship had the strength and watertight protection to take on the more violent conditions to be expected.

Especially unsatisfactory was the way the Commission dealt with the evidence of survivors. Compared to the very public investigation (albeit still not wholly satisfactory) of the Pan-Am 103 crash at Lockerbie, the secretive operation of the JAIC should never have been permitted. Individual crew survivor testimony has been unsatisfactory and unreliable, varying from one comment to the next. The passengers proved to be a more sound source of evidence.

Key crew witnesses changed their story in vital areas, perhaps under pressure or to cover up their own failures. With the statements never being released by the JAIC and a frank admission that testimony had been paraphrased and edited to ensure consistency and to eliminate perceived errors, nobody can be confident that a full and fair appraisal of the evidence was undertaken. Dealing with witness evidence in this way is a charter to manipulate the truth. As explained later, others undertook a comprehensive witness interview programme, but the contradictions cry out for an open investigation with cross-examination to filter truth from lies or innocent errors.

The German Enquiry

The German manufacturers of the ship, Meyer Werft, had their own investigation done by what became known as the *German Group* of Experts. Just as aircraft manufacturers seek to divert attention and blame away from their aircraft, it is reasonable to assume that the shipyard owners too were intent on ensuring that the blame did not wrongly end up with them. There is nothing improper in such an understandable commercial starting point so long as the full truth emerges.

The shipyard had placed its very survival in the hands of an astute lawyer named Dr Peter Holtappels. He insisted that he and an appointed team of experts be allowed to operate free from interference from Meyer, a condition agreed to by the company and acted upon by them. Though called the *German Group*, the team comprised truly international luminaries from Sweden, the United Kingdom, Finland and Germany. Their expertise included maritime law, naval architecture, diving, explosives, video work and reconnaissance. Included was also a former master of the vessel while under previous ownership.

This team put together a far better researched and reasoned professional report than did the JAIC. Though they started work in 1994, their report was not released till 2000, long after the JAIC, the extra time being invaluable to destroy the JAIC's manipulated conclusions. It incorporated comprehensive witness statements, logic and scientific evidence that turned the defects in the official report into material for considerable mockery.

Many flaws were laid bare, nearly 30 of them highlighted below. Their work included interviewing and getting signed statements from over 120 of the 137 survivors (87%), something the Commission did not achieve. In particular, the Group took the time to proof the passengers, a segment that the JAIC had ignored. The fresh evidence was most revealing compared to some of the self-serving and contradictory comments by the crew.

Nevertheless, due caution must always be given to the conclusions of experts hired by a company under fire. The German Group of Experts has been criticised for being hired guns, but it would be a grave injustice to dismiss such a comprehensive report in such a simplistic fashion. The tragedy is that the JAIC was hostile to external evidence from *any* quarter, let alone one paid for by the shipyard. By a skilled public-relations exercise, this group's views became the rallying point for opponents of the JAIC. The German Group report never supported the wildest extremes of speculation yet provided focus for alternative causes of loss than poor seamanship and the faulty design of the bow area.

At the outset, the German Group worked closely with JAIC until they concluded that it was pointless to continue cooperating due to the closed mindset that they faced. JAIC members were not open to any facts or interpretations that were out of line with their own firmly held views. The German Group held public sessions in Stockholm before publishing their own report on the Internet. Their new conclusions on the sinking led to an outcry. However, calls for a fresh and independent investigation from a disenchanted public and from experts came to nothing until late 2004.

The ability of governments to do nothing in the face of criticism is not unique. However persuasive the arguments for a flawed investigation to be reopened, the riposte of *no* slammed shut the door to democracy. Naturally, the more flawed and criticised the investigation, the greater the incentive for governments to be obdurate—especially if, as many suspected, the Swedish Government had something to conceal. The belated and eventual fig leaf of the May 2008 reports described later served as a mere sop to continue diverting attention from the need to expose the full facts.

The Visor

The German Group of Experts confirmed that the visor itself had leaked due to the condition of the rubber seals (one of the few criticisms of maintenance in the JAIC report) and so took in water during crossings. Such ingress was a maintenance issue and increased the visor's weight from 55 to around 200 tons and therefore overburdened locks, hinges and fixings. The JAIC felt that these leaks were insufficient to add much weight or to render the vessel unseaworthy.

The Group's evidence is persuasive also that the bow visor was misaligned and had been in improper condition for months. With its weight fluctuating due to the varying depth of the water slopping inside it, this is scarcely surprising. Additionally, the bow ramp was distorted, a totally unacceptable combination. Carl Övberg's statement describes how, once the visor was opened, daylight flooded through to the gloom of the car deck—possible only if the supposedly watertight bow ramp was twisted out of true. Furthermore, he commented that when the ramp was lowered, both extremities did not touch the ground and the crew had to place a coiled rope under one corner to even out the misalignment.

The Atlantic Lock and Hinges

Inflaming public opinion were many factors highlighted in the German Group's report. For example, they had traced an amateur video by a passenger, which by chance showed the condition of the hinges on 17 September—ten days *before* the sailing. Visible was evidence of a shoddy and unsafe repair. The JAIC would not accept this as *credible evidence*.

Spoliation and loss of evidence was another factor. Following an aircraft disaster, every possible piece of debris is recovered and the plane reconstructed for expert analysis. Perhaps the best example of this was the crash of an Air France flight from Rio, which was lost with 228 aboard in the Atlantic in June 2009. Despite a depth of 3,900 metres (12,800ft) and in total blackness, the wreckage and black boxes were found almost two years later and recovery made to help explain the tragedy. Compare those efforts to the goings-on after the sinking of the *Estonia* in quite shallow water and one can only be shocked.

Even though the 55-ton visor was carried to port for the investigation, the JAIC allegedly neglected to do the same for the much smaller Atlantic Lock on the curious and flimsy ground that it was too heavy! Retrieved parts of it, including a bolt (acknowledged to be vital evidence), were ordered to be dropped back into the ocean during the JAIC investigation. An impartial observer is entitled to wonder just what the secret remit of JAIC actually was when permitting (or ordering) such evidence to be discarded.

The hinges, in the Group's opinion, had been so badly maintained that only 15% of the original strength remained. Add to that depleted strength the 400% increase in visor weight on occasions and the combined effect was dangerously unacceptable. The German Group report concluded that the hydraulics were inoperable, a view supported by other independent experts retained to investigate for the International Transport Workers Federation.

Dive-Free Zone

To add to the secrecy of the operations in the Baltic, the Governments made it unlawful for anyone unauthorised to dive within 2 kms of the hull. Sweden, Estonia, Latvia, Finland, Denmark and the UK all agreed to this law. Precisely why the UK signed up is not clear. The resting place is, however, in international waters, and so divers from non-signatory countries could still go there, risking possible prosecution if they afterward entered a signatory country. The official and ostensible reason for this law was that *Estonia* was regarded as a mass grave with many bodies still trapped inside. Retrieval of bodies was perfectly possible, though not necessarily all of them. Many families had hoped to be able to bury their loved ones. Again, with the Air France crash, some bodies were retrieved two years later, though there was back-pedalling on announcements that *all* bodies would be recovered. Declaring the site a mass grave was a perfect excuse to hinder those interested and other aggrieved parties who challenged the accuracy and adequacy of the seabed investigation. As will be seen later, when the American diver Gregg Bemis and his team went down in August 2000, they found bodies still lying on the ocean floor, a strange and distressing sight when so many families would have wished to have buried their loved ones' remains. Cynics may suggest that the bodies are those of the nine crew who were seen and reported as alive but later reported as drowned.

The Group also commented in robust terms about the video evidence made available to them by JAIC. They found it astonishing that:

- The underside of the port bridge wing had apparently been torn open when the vessel was already on the seabed. (The suggestion is that divers were later seeking something from this area.)
- Divers from "official" teams had taken time to search for, find

and salvage an attaché case belonging to a man with a reputation for being engaged in smuggling weapons.

- There had been movement of the bow ramp *after* the vessel had rested on the sea bed.
- There is evidence that other "official" divers had taken video, in particular in the car deck, but the evidence was never produced.

The Alternative Scenario

The German Group then added an entirely different scenario—that while the bow area was in a condition that *may* have caused the tragedy, use of explosives could not be ruled out. Here is the passage in Chapter 43:

"After thorough investigation of some of the underwater videos a world-renowned expert came to the conclusion that explosions have occurred on MV *Estonia's* bow. These conclusions have not been taken into consideration when establishing the casualty scenario. The sole reason was that these conclusions had to be seen in conjunction with the repeated reports about a 'big hole on the starboard side'. Whether these were explosions can only be established with certainty by a metallurgical examination of the metal affected from the wreck and whether there actually is a big hole on the starboard side can only—but easily—be established with certainty if and when the Swedish authorities release the underwater videotapes taken of the wreck by different diving teams in their original version i.e. without any tapering (sic) therewith. Only after such further investigations have been held, is it possible for anybody to establish the true causes for the foundering of MV *Estonia*."

Such a careful and astute operator as lawyer Holtappels would only have added these warning words if there had been serious reflection that this was a *plausible* explanation. He was not there to peddle conspiracy theories or to enter the wilder areas of speculation that would have detracted from the professionalism of the overall report. His comments were warranted and arose because of the lack of candour of the JAIC. Had they done their job, these facts would have been investigated and determined one way or the other. Instead of being frank and transparent, the JAIC seems to have disintegrated into a squabbling group determined to ignore unpalatable facts and perhaps above all acting to please unseen puppet masters. To quote precisely, the Group states:

"The JAIC report misleads its readers, whether purposely or due to the incompetence of its authors is left to the decision of the readers of this report."

Concerns raised by the German Group of Experts

These concerns must be read in the context that from all the evidence, the Group created a scenario that explained the sinking centred on the failure of the bow area of the vessel. However, despite the maintenance problems listed below (that had not caused a catastrophe on previous rough crossings), the vessel may also have been subjected to an attack by bombs in the frontal area that could have caused the sinking. That alternative scenario could equally explain the loss, but material evidence to discount this had either not been disclosed or had not been gathered.

1. Despite all her deficiencies caused by the way the vessel had been sailed in ice and rough seas by the operators, the vessel would probably not have sunk if the Inspector of Bureau Veritas had declined a Passenger Safety Certificate on the basis that an extension of the collision bulkhead above the main deck was essential. Without it, the vessel was automatically unseaworthy. The German Group allege this certificate to have been issued in breach of the Safety of Life at Sea Regulations (SOLAS).
2. The twisted port outer hinge of the bow ramp meant it could not be properly secured due to damage caused during 1994. In consequence, water from the filled visor (which itself should have been watertight) flowed into the car deck at sea. Water-tightness of the bow ramp is a mandatory condition of SOLAS and its breach rendered the vessel unseaworthy. The assertion by the JAIC that the ship's maintained condition was nearly like new was absurd. The witness testimony of a rolled tarpaulin and bedding being used to staunch water ingress at the bow is enough alone to discount that.
3. The hinges of the visor had lost nearly all their design strength due to fatigue cracks caused by vibration of the visor and unqualified repair work.
4. The stem-post of the visor had been cracked due to fatigue and rested on the forepeak deck, causing misalignment of the visor far exceeding permissible tolerances.
5. The hull was leaking from bad repair work even before the vessel sailed.
6. The public were informed by the JAIC that only *minor deficiencies* in the ship's condition had been found during the training exercise. This bears no relationship to reports of the findings on 27 September or from the evidence seen by the German Group.

7. Water slopping about on the car deck was a known problem from previous sailings as recounted by witnesses, including survivors.
8. The JAIC had not investigated adequately the fact that the stern ramp had been opened as on previous voyages to permit water to exit.
9. Though the deficiencies in the bow area were noted on 27 September during the training session, the Estonian authorities declined to prevent the ship sailing. Some experienced passengers on the route noted how nervous the crew seemed that evening—perhaps from knowledge of the bomb threat or from talk that the inspection that day had nearly prevented the vessel from sailing.
10. The reckless speed at which the vessel was sailed that night, consistent with previous abuse, was a causative factor in connecting and stressing the various deficiencies and creating a scenario for the eventual loss.
11. The vessel should have returned to port at 2045 due to its condition—this being before it turned into the open sea. The weight of the visor taking in water during the ship's pitches increased its weight, not slightly but by nearly four times. By then, water was flooding the car deck, yet by 2330, the vessel, now in stormy seas, was still making full speed when passing another vessel, the *Amber*. By then it was seen to be pitching heavily and taking green water onto the forecastle deck.
12. The JAIC report made no reference to the bomb warning for the voyage, and apparently no investigation of its credibility was made.
13. The JAIC knew of the hole at the foot of the hull by the sauna but made no mention of it.
14. Against interviews by the Group of 120 out of 137 witnesses, the JAIC interviewed just 7. The failure to interview passengers, many of whom had vital evidence and some of whom were able to discredit the accuracy of the main witnesses relied on by the JAIC, was a serious indictment. Only six crew were interviewed and just one passenger. The contradictions about his patrols in the various comments of Silver Linde, who was on watch, are consistent with someone feeling pressure from his employers, and perhaps of someone who may have neglected to follow orders.
15. The JAIC failed (so far as publicly known) to carry out secondary tests on the Atlantic Lock to examine molecular structure. Tests for explosives had been undertaken by JAIC on the lug area of the Atlantic Lock but the *surface testing* procedures used were never going to get the truth, as the part had been underwater for

seven weeks. In the TWA 800 air crash investigation, it was proven that one week submerged is the limit for validity of *surface* testing. Secondary tests were essential.

16. The Group had been provided by JAIC with what they were assured was *raw* video footage of the wreck. It was not raw. It had been *edited* and 40 frames had been clipped from one tape alone. The missing part was where the divers had filmed the starboard bow area—of vital importance to eliminate the possibility of bomb damage. Additionally, video evidence of another dive was never produced at all.

17. Though the JAIC had determined not to retrieve corpses or to prove who was on the bridge and in charge, they *had* ordered divers to go to considerable lengths to find and recover a black attaché case belonging to Alexandyr Vorodin, who allegedly had the reputation of being an arms smuggler. In December 1994, divers retrieved his suitcase from cabin 6230. Curiously, according to the purser, this cabin had been assigned to Captain Piht (he who was reported to have been seen ashore but later reported as a victim), fuelling suspicions of some type of conspiracy. The initial witness testimony from Vorodin's father-in-law, who was aboard, said *their* cabin was 6230, but he subsequently said it was 6320.

The nephew, who was also travelling, described being thrown out of bed and then looking out of the window after the ship abruptly made a starboard heel. If that is true, then they had to be in cabin 6230, as the other cabin had an inside view. Here is an area ripe for cross-examination to establish the contradictions and as to why this man's black attaché case was so important. *All three* survived, the statistical chances of which are for others to calculate. Interestingly, their luxury cabin was surrounded by Swedish police officers in other cabins.

18. The vessel had a serious problem from uncontrolled water ingress through a hole in the shell plating even before it left port. In consequence, the vessel had a starboard list of 10 degrees. It left port with the list reduced to one degree by a measure that was material to the ultimate disaster. The port-side hull had been totally filled with seawater as ballast. Even that was insufficient to counterbalance the list, but with this facility already fully utilised, nothing could be done in the later crisis to counter the starboard list. Maximum ballast was already filling the port side.

19. Though there was some crew testimony suggesting that the vehicles had been chained down and secured, passenger testimony

strongly contradicted this. Vehicles were moving about on the car deck in the sloshing water. (On one ferry crossing between France and England in exceptional seas, trucks and cars that were moving freely and crashing into each other had added to the risks for the safety of the vessel. Whether they had all been correctly chained or had broken free was not satisfactorily explained publicly. Fortunately, *that* ferry reached shore safely).

20. Standing orders were to lock doors to prevent access to the car deck during the crossing. This procedure was not followed and doors were frequently open, a problem that may be familiar to many who have used Dover-Calais crossings in the past.

21. An inspection of the sauna area on 0 Deck (the base of the hull) was falsified. Inspection for the JAIC took over an hour but the official dive record was altered. This part of the vessel has always been an area of concern to cynics and experts.

22. The JAIC concluded that the visor had been severely dented when, as it broke away, it had struck the bulbous bow of the vessel when making 14 knots. The paint marks on the visor are inconsistent with this. That is not how the dent occurred.

23. The first wreck position given to the media by the head of the Finnish delegation was incorrect.

24. The visor, regarded by the JAIC as core to the disaster, was allegedly found 1560 metres away from the wreck—nearly one mile away. This *fact* was fed to the public and became a readily accepted cornerstone of the tragedy. The Group only say in their statement of facts that the visor was *allegedly* found about 1500 metres away. Whether it had fallen off right by the wreck or even remained fixed to the vessel is controversial. They accept that it had come free but precisely where is unproven. It is unclear why it was found so far away and to the *west*. Conspirators contend that the JAIC positioned the visor so far away to fit with their theory that its failure led to the sinking.

25. There were delays in crew reaction and competence in the frantic minutes once the vessel started to tilt to starboard. The first mayday message was not immediately repeated. The crew received a coded alarm message suggesting there was a fire on the ship. (Suggestions have been made by others that the coded warning was consistent not with knowledge of a possible sinking but because of fears or knowledge of a bomb explosion.) Reaction from ashore could have been swifter.

26. The JAIC concluded that the bow ramp had been ripped away, leaving the ship's front gaping open, something not accepted at all by the German Group based on survivors' testimony as they watched from the sea. In its dying moments, the stern had hit the bottom, leaving only the bulbous bow standing proud out of the water. Survivors convinced the Group that the visor had fallen off but that the bow ramp was not fully open—a critical factor pointing to water ingress elsewhere. Without the bow ramp ripped open, it is unlikely that the car deck would have been completely filled with water.
27. Even allowing for translation errors, serious differences existed between original witness statements and published material in Swedish.

Explosive Evidence

It is not at all unthinkable that a hostile group could plot to sink a ship. Chapter Eleven, on terrorism, gives examples of two attempts by Basque separatists to blow up car ferries which, if successful, would have resulted in mass murder. However, just because there may have been sensitive material aboard *Estonia* does not mean that the vessel was holed deliberately by an explosive device—neither does it prove that a piece of volatile cargo exploded.

In 1996, even before the final JAIC report, rumours had spread that an explosion may have destroyed the integrity of the ship. That is scarcely surprising. Passengers, crew and others who had used *Estonia* on previous crossings could well have been aware of military vehicles coming to the Tallinn docks. In the aftermath of the end of Soviet control, former KGB officials, gangsters, scientists and entrepreneurs were known to be enriching themselves by selling data and equipment to the West and to other nations like Iraq that were keen to advance in the field of nuclear technology. Speculation that rival gangs, or alternatively the Russian Government, were seeking to prevent some of these trades spread fast.

Given that great efforts were officially made to recover the suitcase of an alleged weapons dealer and heeding the testimony of Carl Övberg about the security surrounding the two trucks being loaded that day, it seems very likely that something secretive was going on. Precisely what it was and what part it played in a possible bomb plot remains unclear. JAIC ducked this issue.

The next element for those with an independent mind was to find evidence of use of explosives or that some cargo blew up. As to the latter, there was no evidence. Had, therefore, plans been made to blast a hole in the ship? Before studying the data, it is worth looking at the work of independent experts regarding the Ro-Ro design.

Björkman

Perhaps the *bête noire* of the JAIC was Anders Björkman, a distinguished marine architect with 30 years' experience and understanding of Ro-Ro vessels, as well as an owner of this type of ship. His opinions vary from the admirably technical and well-reasoned to the highly speculative, the latter damaging his credibility on the former. JAIC spokesmen have heaped sneering scorn and abuse on an expert who understands the behaviour of Ro-Ro vessels as well as anyone alive.

His paramount conclusion is that ingress of water to the car deck from the visor and bow ramp area could not have *sunk* the vessel. He has done tests to prove it. His opinion is supported by other distinguished marine architects. He says that *below* the car deck there was 18,000 cubic metres of air. This buoyancy would have prevented sinking. Björkman's tests proved that with the car deck flooded *Estonia* would have turned turtle but still *floated upside down.*

Björkman pointed out that despite all the loss of life from Ro-Ro ships, no disaster had ever been caused by water on the car deck causing a *sinking*. His view might have been tested on *Herald of Free Enterprise* in slightly different circumstances. She capsized in such shallow water that the vessel rested horizontal against a sandbank. If the water had been deeper, Björkman says the vessel would have overturned completely and then floated upside down, as the only water ingress was into the car deck.

When a designer of Ro-Ro vessels does tests, explains them and reports on them, it behoves careful attention rather than deaf ears from the JAIC. As to why the JAIC did not want this evidence, later events may offer an explanation. Regardless, the logic is inescapable: if the ship could not have sunk from the damaged bow door region, then there had to be another leak or hole *below the car deck.* That would have reduced the 18,000 cubic metres of air by water ingress and, in combination with the flooded car deck, sunk the ship.

Unanimous Conclusions

This distinguished naval architect complained to JAIC *before* their Final Report that no stability tests had been part of their research. *He had carried them out. Why had they not?* They declined to consider Mr. Björkman's data. The JAIC diary now shows that the first stability tests made by the Commission were attempted only *after* Björkman had alerted them, 30 months after the sinking.

The two experts for the JAIC then did tests and produced two stability documents. Both proved Björkman correct. However, the JAIC Final Report *ignored* the conclusions of its own experts and thus dismissed Björkman's research too. Three experts were in consensus—two retained by the Commission and one independent expert. Their unanimous and independently reached conclusions were dismissed as irrelevant to the JAIC's conclusions.

The powerful evidence of this trio is a major pointer suggesting that there could have been a hole permitting water to penetrate and fill the 18,000 cubic feet of air space. If these three experts are correct, there *had* to be another hole in the hull below the car deck to explain why the vessel sank rather than floated upside down. The German Group had witness statements confirming that the ship *had* been taking in water *below* the car deck—evidence ignored by the JAIC, who had not troubled to seek it for themselves.

Given that there had to be a leak or hole deep in the hull, proving its existence and cause came into play.

Björkman and Conspiracy Theories

Björkman is convinced that the visor was still attached to the ferry when it sank. He believes that in the few days when the public was misled about the site of the wreck, the visor was being removed and dragged a mile underwater. To persuade most neutral observers that such an extraordinary mission could be rapidly planned and implemented without the truth coming out is hard to accept. The visor when filled with water weighed about 200 tons, so this would have been a mammoth task. In pristine condition, it weighed only 55 tons. This is not the only conspiracy alleged by the architect and such theories do tend to detract from his otherwise huge credibility as a Ro-Ro expert.

Above and beyond anything that Björkman uses to support this unlikely theory is the eyewitness testimony. Survivors reported that when the bow hovered above the waves before slipping below, the visor was gone. With more than three experts agreeing that the vessel could not have sunk without another hole, it seems better to ignore the notion of a conspiracy to remove the visor and to concentrate on the damage to the hull.

Björkman believes there may have been a leak from past repair work to the hull, but the pivotal point of many efforts outside the JAIC has been to establish that there was another hole probably caused by an explosion. That there was a hole seems an almost inescapable conclusion based on expert evidence and eyewitness testimony of water below the car deck. But the hole may have been due to bad repair work or a corroded sewage tank or damage caused during work on the hull during the voyage. Passengers *had* heard noises consistent with crew members working with sledgehammers. But then again, the evidence from other witnesses is consistent with hearing explosions.

The Independent Fact Group

Two Swedish experts reported in 1999, in justifiably trenchant but technical terms, criticising the entire central point of the JAIC investigation. This surrounded the visor. These experts reported that the Commission's conclusion was both wrong and impossible. By their calculations, the visor could not have moved forward as the JAIC found. It could not have cut its way through the massive deck beam on two sides in four cuts. As the visor could not have broken free in this manner, the ramp could never have been forced wide open to explain the ingress to the car deck. Survivors' evidence supports the fact that the bow ramp was not ripped away to leave a gaping hole.

The Swedish experts' report does not seek to explain whether the visor fitments were damaged by explosives or simply failed due to their condition. Their concern was different: they simply wanted to adopt the use of scientific calculations in an area that the JAIC had said was not practical. They at least proved that it was.

The International Transport Workers Federation

In 1998, the Federation commissioned an independent analysis of the JAIC report, prepared by distinguished UK experts Corlett, Burnett and Partners (now BCTQ). This firm concluded that the JAIC findings were questionable and called for further investigation. The Federation's report also differs in its findings of fact from that of the JAIC. The Assistant General Secretary said:

'It seems that the JAIC process was more of a political fix, concerned with appeasing vested interests rather than identifying the circumstances surrounding the loss of the *Estonia* and establishing the causes by gathering information and drawing objective conclusions.'

The Hole

Unbelievable!

Due to the JAIC's head-in-a-bucket approach to hard evidence available to them, the official report maintained a state of denial over any hole.

But without question—there *was* a hole in the hull.

How is this known?

Because it was filmed on the JAIC's behalf.

The JAIC knew all along about this hole but did not choose to mention it in their report.

Not mentioned? A hole in the hull that can explain why the vessel sank? It is beyond belief.

Its existence had even been publicly acknowledged on 13 March 1996 by Johan Fransson, director of Safety at Sea for the Swedish Maritime Administration and responsible for directing the dive teams. When asked, he confirmed the existence of the hole on the starboard side but said he knew nothing else about it. A hole in a sunken ship! Not mentioned!

The starboard side of the vessel was less accessible because the wreck lay on its right side. The German Group had cited both missing video footage of the wreck plus the 40 edited images from another official dive. Any Commission determined to expose the truth could scarcely ignore evidence of a large hole deep in the vessel's hull. But it seems the JAIC did just that. Björkman, when presenting his test results and conclusions that the ship could not have sunk without a hole, did so *before* the flow of fresh evidence that has vindicated his theory.

Swedish Divers

Mystery surrounds just what dives took place and who saw what—all due to the secretive and evasive behaviour of the JAIC. Allegedly, there was an official dive very early on. One of the team was a 41-year-old Swede called Hakan Bergmark, who was one of the first to see the wreck, and he noticed a big hole in the side of the ship. He gave a statement over 40 pages long to the German Group. Reportedly, he has now disappeared, and others apparently on the dive team do not wish to discuss what they saw. He has been quoted by Björkman as admitting back then some surprise when he read the JAIC report and saw no mention of this critical evidence.

ROV Evidence

The German Group were provided with what they were assured was raw footage filmed by the Remote Operated Vehicle on 5 October 1994 as it explored the wreck. When it was filming debris on the seabed and parts of the ship, there had been editing. Most cuts lasted up to three minutes, but sometimes up to 17. No wonder this cover-up by the JAIC has been dubbed *Under-Watergate*! Other ROV evidence has never been disclosed at all. Cuts were also apparent in the inspections of 9 and 10 October. All video footage of the area by the sauna had been cut out in frames 80–120.

The Braidwood Evidence

The German Group had been concerned that the JAIC report and video evidence provided to them had excluded any evidence of a hole, not least because they had a witness who had described hearing a *heavy shock* in the sauna area. He then saw water coming from where there should have been none, short of damage to the hull near the sauna.

There was other mysterious evidence. In 1998, the experts spotted on the video footage a package positioned on the *port* side. This image was then studied by explosives experts. Both concluded with 90% certainty that the package was an explosive charge. That degree of certainty would satisfy a British criminal court, where the case has to be *proved beyond all reasonable doubt*. This conclusion led to scrutiny of another orange cube observed in one video but missing during a later inspection of the spot.

The three experts agreed that this too had been an explosive charge. This charge had not exploded either, but due to its vital positioning by the port-side visor area, the starboard side was then checked by British underwater explosives expert Brian Braidwood. He determined that there had been an explosion on the starboard side at this point. In total, four areas were suspected of sustaining explosives damage. More bombs had failed to detonate.

Braidwood advised that the suspect package was a device containing between 1 and 3 kilograms of plastic explosive. He was satisfied that damage beside the starboard visor-side locks was caused by 1 to 2 kilograms of TNT explosive. Of the damage to the port-side for'ard on the car deck, he concluded that this was caused by a similar quantity of explosive. A round hole blown through the port bulkhead by the bow ramp was consistent with an explosive device. In a supplementary report, as evidence of damage to the starboard front bulkhead emerged, Braidwood concluded that the hole there was also caused by explosives.

The Gregg Bemis Dive

American Gregg Bemis, a colourful freespirit in his 70s, put together a dive team in August 2000. He wanted to seek out the truth and ignored the prohibition against diving to the wreck. Bemis, owner of the wreck of the *Lusitania* off the Irish coast, cannot now visit any country that has signed the agreement protecting *Estonia* from divers without risking arrest. In Sweden, a warrant is out for his arrest.

Bemis knew of the rumour of a hole by the starboard bow in the region of the sauna at the bottom of the hull. Using divers and an ROV such as was used to find *Lucona* (as described in Chapter Six), he set out to find it. And he did! A big hole was found and filmed—large enough to have been made by a bomb or a collision with, for example, a Russian submarine that some say left Tallinn at the same time as the ferry. Certainly it was large enough to admit a torrent of water such as would reduce the 18,000 cubic metres of air below the car deck that should have prevented a sinking.

The starboard side of the vessel had been partly buried, but by good fortune it had become more visible following movement of the wreck since 1994. The Bemis team brought back two samples of material from the wreck to be tested for evidence of explosive damage. In November 2000, two German laboratories tested the samples and a British explosives expert studied the laboratory reports and evidence and concluded that they provided *indisputable proof of an explosion*. In 2001, a member of the original Bemis team, German Ms Jutta Rabe, dived down again. The hull had shifted again, revealing even more evidence of starboard-side damage.

Experts reported on samples taken from the critical areas of the visor and bow and are now quoted:

Professor Neubert wrote on 16 October 2000:

'As the deformation of the investigated samples has not been created in a testing laboratory, we have to proceed that the cracking of the material was induced by a detonation or some projectile.'

State of Brandenburg Material Testing Laboratory, 26 October 2000:

'The plastic changes in the micro area, indicating an extremely strong shock effect such as occurs during detonations, are recognisable in all specimens.'

'The results obtained do allow the conclusion that the positions most affected by the detonation was in another area of the damaged material.'

The Southwest Research Institute of San Antonio:

'It is valid to say that an explosion was far more likely than a mechanical loading event to have produced the observed micro-structural features.'

The evidence now points to someone having deliberately blasted the visor and bow area and also deep in the bowels of the ship. The combination of the hole now proven (except to the JAIC) plus the destruction of the strength of the visor and bow ramp jointly led to the sinking. There may yet be other holes not accessible or visible. To an impartial observer, the obvious method of sinking a vessel of this design would be to destroy the integrity of the visor area and to blow a hole or holes deep in the hull. The combination would be a rapid sinking—precisely as occurred.

Björkman, flying in the face of eyewitness evidence, attributes the explosive damage to the work of the investigators blasting the visor free after the sinking. While possible, this seems most improbable, especially given the eyewitness evidence, the bomb warning before the ship left and the sinister, secretive material being shipped. *Before* the Bemis expedition, Björkman wrote that he could not rule out an explosion in the area of the alleged hole by the sauna—*because* (as he understood from officials) *the JAIC did not inspect the sauna*. That is *now* known not to be correct. The sauna area *was* inspected for the JAIC for over an hour, but according to the German Group, the diving records had been changed. Based on the Bemis investigation, one of several bombs had been placed in the sauna on 0 Deck—a perfect location to do real damage to the safety of the ship. A possible cause of the hole might have been impact damage as the visor broke free, but it is more probable that whoever placed the explosives with timer devices placed one in this vulnerable part of the vessel, given the expert evidence of explosive damage to the visor zone.

Despite video footage of other unexplained physical damage to the vessel, the Commission was silent on this in its report. The German Group believe this damage was consistent with post-sinking damage caused by divers searching for something sensitive.

The Bridge

There are other curiosities about who was on the bridge, but the video evidence is inconclusive. In any comprehensive investigation, it should have been fundamental to know who was operating the ship. That mystery remains. In a plane crash, it would be unthinkable not to prove that the crew were at the controls rather than partying in the passenger cabin. With two masters aboard the vessel, there is no credible evidence that either of them were or were not on the bridge.

In the movie *Baltic Storm* about the loss of the *Estonia*, starring Donald Sutherland and others, the suggestion is that more than one murder occurred that night before the vessel sank. It is hard to judge where fact and fiction intertwine in the movie, but certainly much of the core material in the movie is well-founded based on the totality of evidence now available. As it was made involving Jutta Rabe in its production, much of the storyline is likely to have been based on her dive research (and on her own theories and opinions). She was well qualified to have opinions because she was involved as a German investigative journalist from the outset. She also took part in the Gregg Bemis dive and her own subsequent dive to check out the hole in the hull...and so has been banned from Sweden.

Russian Weaponry

When I first wrote of the MV *Estonia* back in 2002, there were various indicators that on board the vessel there may have been Russian weapons or technology being secretly shifted to Sweden. Back then, it seemed to be pushing credulity to link carriage of technology or weapons to the vessel being deliberately bombed. Since then, in the next seven years especially, the tapestry has changed. Speculation has mounted that the ship was indeed carrying incredibly sensitive material required by the USA. As to what this may have been, there remains no evidence, but examples of what America coveted and dealers in Russia could offer are covered below. The first revelations came in late 2004.

The Ministry of Defence Comes Clean

Until December 2004, just over ten years after the sinking, the three Governments reacted either contemptuously or by stonewalling to calls for a fresh investigation. In 2002, a Swedish MP, Björn von der Esch, had contended in Parliament that the JAIC findings had been manipulated to conclude the reverse of what had actually happened. He wanted to know who had manipulated the report and why and for whom. He had no immediate success.

Estonia may be a fledgling democracy with a more recent pedigree born of oppression and secrecy, but Sweden and Finland are nations with a proud history of standing up for human rights and freedom of expression. The Swedish team and its Government in particular had been under the cosh for their approach to the investigation, as evidenced by the resignation of Andi Meister, the Estonian chairman on the JAIC. He had blamed the Swedes for being less than frank.

The head of Swedish Customs confirmed in November 2004 that two shipments of military material had been secretly carried on previous September days. He had decided to come clean after years of silence. He was not able to say whether another load was carried on the fateful voyage. The vessel never arrived.

In December 2004, the dam broke. The Swedish Government yielded to relentless public pressure from the Estonia Litigation Association and many others. Prime Minister Goran Persson announced a judicial enquiry after admitting that fresh evidence had surfaced from the Swedish Army that the ferry *had* been used to carry Russian military equipment—reason initially for giving three cheers until the narrowness of the investigation and its outcome became clear in January. In the end, only one cheer was justified.

A High Court judge was charged with investigating what was being carried and in particular *whether it was explosive material*. This rather sidesteps the point. Critics were not solely espousing the position that the two trucks carried explosives that then blew up the ship. Critics more generally believe that specially targeted bombs exploded in vulnerable parts of the vessel. Whether the trucks carried aboard explosives that were removed and positioned around the hull is a different issue.

It remains unclear whether this investigation was a genuine attempt to clean out the stables or merely retrenching a few metres back. In advance, it looked more like digging a different trench to stop attacks on the first failing line of defence. Judge Johan Hirschfeldt, a senior figure, reported on a very narrow basis in January 2005 that though two previous shipments of non-explosive technical and military equipment had been carried, there was nothing like that aboard this trip. In the result, it did indeed look as if the trench had been re-dug a few metres back to accommodate the fresh disclosures from the Customs Chief. The outcome in this report has all the appearance of a *confess and avoid* tactic.

What *had* been carried is, by law, subject to secrecy for 70 years, an amazing situation in these days of demands for increased transparency from governments and trends to Freedom of Information. What is apparent is that explosives *had* been smuggled aboard somehow and then positioned at some time after the bomb warning and the inspection tour that took place before the ship sailed. Someone on board after sailing must have positioned the bombs, and no doubt had a first-class seat in the lifeboat!

This Swedish bolt-on enquiry did not satisfy the many cynics and sceptics that the full facts had come to light. Bearing in mind the eyewitness evidence of two trucks being loaded after being escorted aboard, the need for a much fuller and open investigation still holds. The Estonian Government announced in March 2005 that it would investigate this aspect too.

It is hard to believe (actually *impossible*) that these shipments were not known to the Swedish Government back in 1994. It has to be recalled that when Olaf Forssberg was fired from the JAIC, his replacement in June 1997 was an in-house lawyer from the Ministry of Defence. The announcement rather explains the pressures on the Swedes on the JAIC to be less than frank with others on the Commission.

It is regrettable that the Swedish enquiry was not charged with investigating whether there *was* at least one explosion aboard. That is the essential investigation—and one still capable of being conducted by independent investigators. Just as vital frames from the Zapruder cine film of JFK's assassination disappeared, until the missing frames of the underwater video evidence are published, the pointer is that they are concealing vital evidence. Until the full truth of the hole in the hull is explained, and why JAIC went into denial about it despite evidence in their possession, no impartial observer can be satisfied.

If it looked bad already, it got embarrassingly worse!

Oops! Er...We've Lost the Film!

In August 2006, an embarrassed official from Sweden's Shipping Inspectorate had to admit that the film of the wreck taken in 1995/6 had been lost! Johan Franson explained that a three-month search had been fruitless and he could offer no explanation. The film had been requested by Sweden's State Forensic Laboratory for what was intended to be a conclusive investigation of the photographic evidence.

Russian Technology

Jutta Rabe, a constant thorn in the side of the JAIC conclusions, believes that highly important material was on board but has no firm evidence of what it might have been. Instead, she has been influenced by an article in the *New York Times* by William Broad in which he had described a virtual yard sale of unique Soviet know-how and equipment. Technology such as a space engine capable of being handheld and powered by magnetic fields instead of fuel was an attraction. The Russians had developed heat-resistant materials that would have aided NASA. Soviet nuclear reactors were of interest, besides the more conventional weapons.

Enough material was on this ferry that night to warrant two trucks plus perhaps the black attaché case. According to Rabe, hostile to this exodus of high-tech material and know-how was the Russian Felix Group. This was a fiercely nationalist body in which Vladimir Putin and Ivan Ivanov were allegedly involved. Rabe asserted that the Felix Group, had it known of the shipment, might have wanted to prevent it, though there is no suggestion that they would even have *contemplated* mass murder to prevent weapons or know-how reaching Sweden or the USA. Arms-dealing is a notoriously murky business. Other alternatives are that rival dealers may have been double-crossed or had some other reason to feud with whoever was behind this deal. Finally, the bombs may have been planted by whoever instigated the telephoned warning for reasons connected to protection rackets or port disputes.

Another Trench?

In yet a further attempt to uphold the JAIC conclusions and to discredit the German Group, the Swedish Government appointed two further expert groups, who reported in May 2008. One was the Hamburg group, known as HSVA, and the other a Swedish group known as SSPA. These two groups worked independently of each other to prove how the vessel sank without any hole in the hull. In other words, they were to work out how the sinking could have occurred in a manner consistent with the JAIC report—and thus, by implication, disprove Anders Björkman, the two independent experts hired by but discounted by the JAIC, and finally the German Group of experts under Dr Holtappels.

Both these new expert groupings concluded that it *was* possible for the vessel to have sunk due to the problems with the visor and ramp area.

But does that take matters any further in the justifiable search for the truth? The short answer is not really. ***The experts were not invited to prove how the sinking actually occurred.*** Their brief was to show it could plausibly have occurred as the JAIC had concluded—but *using the facts found by the JAIC*. In consequence, one can conclude that if their brief were flawed, then so would be the outcome.

Perhaps it *is* possible to create a scenario and conditions that explain by simulated tests how the vessel could have sunk without a hole in the hull. Perhaps every other expert was incorrect and the vessel would not have floated upside down. BUT that is not the point. There *was* a hole in the hull, to the knowledge of the JAIC, and so the expense of these investigations was pointless except as a further attempt to deflect criticism and to influence public opinion.

Here is the July 2011 comment of Dr Peter Holtappels about the brief given to HSVA and SSPA:

> *'The experts were to base their reports indeed on a factual basis determined from the JAIC conclusions, and so they did. In my humble view, every clever shipbuilding apprentice being asked whether water on the car deck of a Ro-Ro ferry would contribute to the sinking of the ship would just have one question: how much? A look into the stability booklet would then give him the answer.'*

If experts are briefed that 2 + 2 = 5 is to be used as their starting point and that they must now add 4 and they then conclude that the correct total is 9, such a conclusion cannot be faulted. But that does not make it correct! That is very much what the Swedish Government has attempted to achieve with this further evidence. The existence of at least one large hole in a critical area of the hull renders a theoretical approach ignoring the hole otiose.

Conclusion

Long before November 2006, Dr Peter Holtappels was convinced that the Swedish Government would not now broaden or reopen the investigation regarding any holes or explosion damage. He was right! That month, the Swedish Government announced their refusal to permit the raising of the wreck to ensure a proper investigation and to allay concerns. The Minister said that this would simply cause needless grief for relatives, though to what extent he accurately reflects their thinking is open to question. A yearning for truth rather than nagging doubts of a massive cover-up are unsettling and do not bring closure to those who lost friends, relatives or colleagues aboard the luckless vessel.

The body of fresh facts and scientific opinion is now so embarrassingly overwhelming that the three Governments should have a full and free independent investigation. The condition of the ship and the quality of the crew may have justified suspicions that the vessel should never have been allowed to make the voyage at all. The pre-1990 Ro-Ro design without watertight bulkheads on the car deck was a flaw that should have been righted. Poor maintenance and bad repair work meant water ingress around the visor (and elsewhere) was plausible and *may* have caused the vessel to capsize, though the majority of experts agree that it would not have sunk. But that does not mean this is what happened.

Thanks to Gregg Bemis, Björkman, Jutta Rabe, the German Group and countless other experts, the truth may yet emerge. From the scientific evidence and the sightings of unexplained holes, the probability is that bombs led to the sinking and not its poor maintenance and condition. If so, this was mass murder by organised crime in one form or another. It is shameful that it is not possible to let the victims lie in peace, but the blame for this must be placed at the doors of government.

The status of litigation filed for families of victims in a French court at Navarre remains unclear and very strange indeed. It was stalled due to the claimants' need to establish a right to sue. On 12 September 2013, the lawyers appointed to represent the victims and their relatives in the litigation that had commenced in 1996 informed the claimants through the Estonia Litigation Association that a stay of proceedings was ordered to take effect on the 14 October 2011 to allow them to disclose information and documentation proving their title to sue.

The lawyers point out that they have been unpaid for 10 years, but that in 2010 the French Supreme Court ruled that the French courts did have jurisdiction to hear the case because there was no other litigation pending in any other country. One might have thought that matters would have advanced rather quicker since then, but the September 2013 letter contains this curious confirmation of the state of affairs:

'These information and documentation are of paramount importance and cardinal to the progress of the case since the defendants dispute the title to sue of the claimants and asked the Court to dismiss the demands as non-admissible. At the moment we are still trying to retrieve the claimants and their association to update our list and justify to the court the title to sue of the victims. As we did not receive any instructions, information/documentation from you or any of the persons/entities concerned and the necessary elements to see the trial through successfully, we have no other choice to abandon this procedure and close the file. This means that victims will not recover any damages in the future and that they will be debarred from starting any new legal action on the same grounds. At the same time, we have no other choice to stop endeavours and to waive any responsibility for the consequences which may arise.'

The lawyers indicate that a stay of proceedings cannot exceed two years and that expired as recently as 14 October 2013. It is not known as yet how many relatives if any provided evidence of title by the final deadline, but if none, then the litigation will have ended forever.

Given that the Swedish-based Estonia Litigation Association was very active (and the letter was addressed to them), it is very curious that the lawyers in Paris had not been provided with the basic information they needed—seemingly from even just one claimant at *any* time, let alone in the last two years to September 2013. Providing identity cards/passports/family record books proving a relationship and therefore a right to sue on behalf of deceased parties should not have been problematic for most of the litigants. Precisely what has been happening these past 17 years regarding gathering this fundamental documentation remains unclear. After the victory in the French Supreme Court, the path to a trial in the court at Navarre outside Paris ought to have been much more rapid and straightforward. This simply adds to the mystery of the entire saga.

'The Bureau were never directly involved with this tragedy,' confirms Ellen. 'First impressions were that this was an accident. We followed events and were aware of the JAIC report and knew of the criticisms, but I would not have intervened without the clearest evidence and only then if in the best interests of members. I have no doubt that bombs could have been smuggled aboard at the port of Tallinn. Security at ports, especially where vehicle ferries are involved, is hard to achieve.

'I pass no judgment on whether the ship was sunk by bombs, as I have not seen or satisfied myself with the evidence. I am concerned that the JAIC have not seemed receptive to fresh evidence. They could easily end all speculation by transparent tests for explosives carried out with impartial expert scrutiny. These would be on all areas of the ship where unexplained damage has been caused. Until then, I do see this debate raging on.'

CHAPTER THREE
Swimming with Sharks - The Tragedy of the *Lisa Marie*

Small-time accountant David Wilson was in severe financial difficulties but thought he saw a business opportunity which promised an end to his problems. Using money borrowed from a business friend, he bought an old freighter. A good family man, he renamed the ship *Lisa Marie* after his younger daughter. But Wilson was out of his depth. This new venture was way out of his league: he knew nothing of shipping or marine freight. Worse still, he had no idea about the sharks, poised to prey on the unwary. If a deal seems too good to be true, it probably is.

Born in 1944, by 1990 Wilson was based at Olive House, Olive Lane in Darwen, a small community not far from Chorley in Lancashire, some five or six hours drive northwest of London. Wilson had not qualified as a chartered accountant but handled tax advice and accounting issues for local businesses. He operated from a modest base, a shabby, soot-blackened building tucked into a down-at-heel terrace. At one time, the building had probably formed part of a factory complex. Now it was a collection of small units rented by small businesses.

Wilson himself lived a short drive away with his wife Barbara and their grown-up daughters Lisa and Michelle in Twist Moor Lane, in the sleepy hamlet of Brinscall, in an area of small pubs, villages, rolling hills and babbling streams—rural Lancashire at its best. His home was an attractive whitewashed two-storey dwelling with a slate roof, typical of that rural community. It overlooked a tree-lined field, a rambling place, secluded but hardly isolated. In the double garage, despite his precarious financial state, Wilson kept a couple of Mercedes.

Wilson had developed a fascination with glamorous work. He loved handling offshore tax avoidance schemes. He revelled in the world of trusts and companies with untraceable owners. Setting up companies based in exotic tax havens far away from the drabness of Olive Lane was blissful escapism. Work of this nature sometimes attracts dishonest clients who wish to conceal their dubious profits through offshore anonymity. So though the daily grind of tax returns and balance sheets was part of his expertise, Wilson's business also became involved in other, more exciting fields, such as commodity trading, an area where fraud and shady dealers are legion but which offers big profits for the wily.

In London, Chicago and elsewhere there are legitimate commodity markets dealing in grain, oil, metals, tea and coffee. Prices fluctuate as speculation and rumour abound. But there is another fringe market where deals are done for cash or through offshore companies with bearer shares. Such commodities might be bogus spare parts to be sold to cash-strapped airlines, former Soviet Union nuclear spares or stolen whisky, precious metals or cigarettes.

As a heavily taxed item, cigarettes have always been big business on the black market, attractive to those who understand the no-holds-barred rules. Cigarettes are a special form of currency popular in Third World countries. Shifty-looking traders offer travellers 200 packs of Winston or Marlboro, but whether the contents are genuine is less certain. In 2005, Britain faced an influx of fake cigarettes from Eastern Europe and China. Their lead and arsenic contents rendered them especially carcinogenic.

There *is* a large parallel market of genuine cigarettes which find their way onto the black market. Investigations have been continuing into the behaviour of cigarette manufacturers following allegations that they *supported* the illegal trade. Manufacturers, stifled by import quotas in some jurisdictions, have used this parallel market to evade the restrictions.

Thus, those selling Marlboro cigarettes in bulk have a readily available cover story. There is also a mass market for smuggled or stolen cigarettes. Container lorries are hijacked and the cigarettes sold into the underworld market, one middleman after another taking a cut. The genuine market invariably operates through direct deals between the manufacturer and the legitimate receiver. The parallel market operates through chains involving agents or middlemen, all with contacts who are seduced by the prospect of cutting a lucrative deal over a glass of *Black Label* whisky.

In 1990, David Wilson needed money fast. One source claimed he had got into financial difficulties through involvement with the Polish mafia. He had debts of over £100,000 (around US $160,000 at that time), so when Graham Olliphant, an insurance broker, suggested he meet a new client, Colonel Hector Portillo of Mexico, Wilson's head turned.

The Colonel wanted offshore bank accounts opened under suitably anonymous names. Wilson's role was to make the arrangements. At the time, the creation of secret accounts or impenetrable companies was almost the norm, whereas today transparency is increasingly required. The best leading accountants and lawyers still register trusts and companies in Panama, St Vincent, the Caymans, BVI, Liberia and the Bahamas to operate tax-effective structures. Any illegality lay not in the *creation* of secretive offshore structures but in the way that their business was subsequently operated.

Colonel Hector Moretta Portillo was a stocky figure with a moustache and a good line in patter, consistent with high diplomatic office. His status as a Mexican delegate to the United Nations was an impressive pedigree. The fact that he was related to the former President Portillo of Mexico added to the aura of success, something Wilson hoped would brush off on him. To a man with humble offices in Olive Lane, the prospect of dealing with a New York–based diplomat was irresistible, especially when Wilson learned about the mind-blowing profits to be made from trading in Marlboro cigarettes. The Colonel wore his military uniform to meetings and spoke in heavily accented English.

Portillo explained that he had Marlboro cigarettes to sell—not the odd pack of 20 but millions. In fact, he had one hundred shipping containers. Portillo explained that the Marlboros, a Philip Morris product, had been manufactured in Mexico but he wanted to offer them as a genuine USA-made product. The cigarettes had been made during *ghost shifts* and deliberately labelled as US manufactured to enable Portillo to sell them on at a good price. Wilson saw himself as an honest man; he recognised the scam but did not regard it as a major crime. It was a good chance, too good to refuse on a small technicality like the place of manufacture.

Each container was offered at the bargain-basement price of $160,000. The room for profit after expenses was vast. Wilson initially agreed to find buyers for fifty containers and to set up a marketing structure, rather like a UK sales distributor. Later, he agreed to buy another three. But there was one problem. Portillo needed Wilson to buy a ship to transport the cigarettes from Mexico to Europe. Wilson was more concerned with staving off his creditors than buying a ship, but he agreed because of the profits on cigarette trading.

Giving his office address in Darwen, Lancashire, Wilson set up a company called Alamosa Limited in the Isle of Man, an offshore financial centre of the highest integrity with a renowned tax-friendly status. The beautiful, mountainous but breezy island is only a short flight or sea crossing from Liverpool, not far from Chorley, although this proximity was largely irrelevant—an offshore company could then be set up at little cost with a couple of phone calls.

Wilson contacted a Norwegian called Tore Horgen who, in return for some of the containers, was prepared to put up £1.6 million to buy MV *Gregory*. To render it suitable for carrying containers, the vessel's original design as a 3,400-ton bulk cargo carrier needed to be adapted. But £5,000 will not buy a new Rolls Royce, and £1.6 million does not buy much of a ship. *Gregory* was a *rustbucket*, long past its prime. But it only needed to stay afloat long enough to get across the Atlantic and deliver the cargo. It could then be sold on.

Ownership in the name of Alamosa was later transferred to a Nassau-based holding company called Wilson Overseas Limited. Wilson was in his element—setting up companies in tax havens, putting structures in place to conceal the profits, the multimillions, from the taxman. That kind of money would take a lot of explaining if it ever appeared on the books of his modest business, so he set up another company, Wilson Line Ltd, to operate the vessel, one step away from the ownership.

The ship was then registered as *Lisa Marie* with the Panama Shipping Registry, a routine form-filling operation. Portillo distanced himself from ownership and from any involvement in Wilson's sales structure. As befitted an international diplomat, such details were beneath him. His role was to ensure availability of cigarettes to put aboard *Lisa Marie*. Once the containers were loaded, Portillo would be paid by letter of credit and the Marlboros would then be Wilson's to sell on.

Wilson easily found buyers. He obtained orders from some tough characters in Poland, Bulgaria and Russia, none of them tolerant of failure. James MacMillan, a straight-talking Scot who lived in Dallas, Texas, put up $350,000 for part of the cargo. MacMillan was not a man to be messed with either.

Letters of Credit were opened by buyers in a bank-to-bank arrangement. The usual procedure was standard: as soon as the buyer's bank received the promised shipping documents, including the signed Bill of Lading showing that the containers were aboard *Lisa Marie*, it would then transfer the purchase cost to the seller's bank. The most essential of all shipping documents in terms of international marine trade is the Bill of Lading. This is signed by the ship's owner, the ship's master or an officer and is an acknowledgement that the goods are aboard. Supporting the Bill of Lading for this deal were documents about the cigarettes themselves—Certificates of Inspection, of Freshness and of Origin, the latter issued by the Greater

Miami Chamber of Commerce. Evidence of insurance from Lloyd's of London completed the paperwork.

Wilson, no expert in international trade, took one step that must have caused Portillo to tear his hair out in frustrated rage: Wilson inserted a clause in the Letter of Credit ensuring that no money changed hands before the goods reached the destination port—in this case, Hamburg. Portillo had expected the money to be released by the bank as soon as the cigarettes were signed off as aboard. Perhaps something had made Wilson suspicious of the Mexican Colonel.

The Certificate of Inspection had been signed by Sealand Maritime Surveyors of Biscayne Boulevard, Aventura, Florida. On 12 November 1991, they had seen and checked 50, 40-foot containers of Marlboro filter cigarettes. These were certified for transit on the *Lisa Marie*, sailing from Miami to Hamburg. Because stale cigarettes are not an attractive purchase, there was also a Certificate of Freshness confirming that they had been made as recently as between 1 and 8 November 1991.

A third document supporting authenticity was the Certificate of Origin, proving the cigarettes were *American-made* Marlboro. This false document had been sworn by Wilson before the Greater Miami Chamber of Commerce on 12 November. The precise description was:

'50 (fifty) x 40 ft containers Marlboro filter cigarettes 85mm grade "A" in flip top box hard pack of USA origin manufactured by Philip Morris Richmond VA with bar code, with health warning in English, with blue label US tax exempt for use outside the USA. 960 Mastercases per container, 50 cartons per Mastercase, 20 cigarettes per pack, 10 packs per carton.'

Wilson had travelled to Miami, seen his new ship and arranged for the crew to be paid. His daughter Michelle, who helped him in his accountancy business, had flown to New York, and in the fashionable Waldorf Astoria Hotel had personally handed over cash to Hector Portillo to cover wages for the crew.

Wilson had sold the cigarettes on. *Lisa Marie* would sail for Hamburg on 23 November. He could celebrate. Everything was in order.

If only he knew!

James MacMillan had struck a side deal with Portillo direct, cutting Wilson's profits out of the price structure. Once appointed by Portillo, MacMillan started selling Marlboro cigarettes with supporting papers showing shipment to Hamburg. In November 1991, a London businessman was approached by the Texan. A fuse had been lit. It was just a question of when the bang would occur, but Wilson did not know it. Against the shipping documents, MacMillan wanted payment to Alamosa, the Isle of

Man company Wilson had formed for Portillo. The possible buyer was a member of the Bureau and entitled to its support. On 29 November, Ellen was approached for advice on whether the IMB member should go ahead with what looked like a good deal. This man's commonsense saved a lot of people a great deal of money.

Ellen was intrigued when the man said he had been offered up to *50* containers of cigarettes, because he already knew there was a Marlboro scam going on: a banking member from Brussels had informed the IMB earlier in the month that they had been asked to finance the purchase of a large consignment. Enquiries confirmed that the cigarettes did not exist. Fifty containers was just too many, even allowing for surplus cigarettes slipped into the marketplace by manufacturers. Ellen asked for the shipping documents.

Ellen's vast experience as a police officer and then at the Bureau came into play. The documents *looked* genuine, yet he was convinced they were not because of the sheer quantity of cigarettes involved. After much careful scrutiny, he spotted what with hindsight looks like a glaring error but what was just a small point. Naively, the Bill of Lading showed that MacMillan was offering fifty containers—all with consecutive numbers. Ellen knew that there are millions of containers around the world, each with its own unique number. They are constantly in use, moving from port to port. The chances of having fifty containers numbered 440001 to 440050 on the same ship are nil. Obviously, the IMB member was going to be the victim of a con, but was MacMillan the conman or was it someone else? Ellen phoned Philip Morris, which confirmed that the goods could not be genuine. The cigarettes were stated to be *Grade A*—another mistake—gilding the lily, motivated by greed and the lure of a fast buck. Philip Morris did not even make *Grade A* cigarettes! It just looked good on paper. More Marlboro cigarettes were being offered for sale than had ever been manufactured. Another mistake was the quoted length of the cigarettes, also incorrect. Ellen advised the IMB member not to proceed with the transaction.

Ellen realised that the police should be involved but refrained from contacting Scotland Yard because of past unhappy experiences, such as an occasion when he had been contacted by a member about a documentary fraud involving petroleum on offer valued at $30 million. The central figure was a London-based Nigerian barrister. 'Our member was being asked to sign a power of attorney to buy the fuel. I was confident this was a scam and so contacted the Fraud Squad at Scotland Yard.' Ellen was informed that the Fraud Squad didn't work on weekends!

'So to get urgent action, I went to the Dutch police because the petroleum deal was to take place at the Rotterdam Hilton. A first-class sting operation was put together. A police officer posed as the banker and I went to the hotel with the police. The document produced was a forgery, an attempt to steal $30 million. The barrister was arrested and charged in the UK with conspiracy to defraud.'

Ellen's normally placid features darkened as he spoke, showing his anger and disbelief. Having retired as a chief constable to set up the Bureau, the treatment he then received was disgraceful. 'Without my work with the Dutch police, the British police had no case. However, instead of gratitude, I found they had taken offence and were seeking to prosecute me as an alleged *agent provocateur*! I was angry and upset when the police told me that I was under investigation and might be charged. Notwithstanding, they still wanted me to give evidence against the Nigerian! I arranged for dates when I was working in San Francisco to be avoided. Needless to say, that's precisely when I got called to give evidence and I had to fly back urgently. The defendant was duly convicted. In the end, even though the police did not charge me, it was a distasteful episode. With so many documentary crimes being notified to us, we had a far better understanding of this type of crime than members of fraud squads. It made for an uneasy relationship.'

His unsatisfactory experiences coloured his thinking about the best way to deal with these fifty containers of Marlboros. By coincidence, MacMillan had set up a meeting on 2 December with possible buyers, also in the Rotterdam Hilton. Ellen went straight to the Dutch police. 'The London businessman, our member, attended the sting meeting as an apparently interested buyer. As the meeting broke up, the police arrested six people, including James MacMillan, who was furious. He had put in money through Wilson *and* had become a direct sales agent for Portillo too. He protested his innocence, claiming that he believed the cigarettes existed and were in Hamburg. He blamed Wilson, justifiably, since Wilson's name appeared on the shipping documents. It soon became clear that *Lisa Marie* had not reached Hamburg. So where was she?'

David Wilson started to panic. With good reason.

Instead of sailing for Hamburg, his ship had followed a strangely unattractive course. Enquiry of Lloyd's agents in Miami suggested the vessel had sailed *empty* and bound for Nassau in the Bahamas, just a short hop across the generally placid waters of this part of the Atlantic. In a busy port like Miami, nobody would take much notice of a small freighter like the *Lisa Marie* slipping away, but it is part of the remit of Lloyd's agents to monitor movements. The ship did not dock in Nassau—or if she did, it was certainly not under that name. Nor did she head eastward toward Europe.

Instead, she had headed south. Demanding an explanation, Wilson phoned Portillo. Their conversation went something like this:

Sorry. No. Not Hamburg. She's going to deliver in Hong Kong first.

Going through the Panama Canal then?

Er, no. She's going round South Africa.

What? The long way round?

Yes.

Not Hamburg?

Not first.

Wilson was aghast. Sailing for Hong Kong, the long way round? It made no sense. The ship was adding weeks to the journey. As he tried to find out more, Portillo, ever elusive, became even harder to contact. But then came a report from the ship's master. Water had been flooding the engine room, so he had sailed for Puerto Cabello in Venezuela for repairs. Venezuela? What was *Lisa Marie* doing anywhere near South America if she had sailed for Hong Kong? Wilson wanted to believe the master. But both he and Tore Horgen were outraged. Wilson was also alarmed. The gun-toting MacMillan had paid $350,000 cash for two containers. Now he was an angry man sitting in a Dutch jail, blaming Wilson. Horgen's investment of £1.6 million was looking rather shaky too. There was only one way to find out. Horgen and Wilson dashed to the airport for the next flight to Venezuela.

After their long flight to Caracas, the important port of Puerto Cabello was yet another 100 kms west of the capital. Its attractive resort area was of no interest to the two travellers. Their only goal was the large bustling port, with its docks, terminals, and dry docks. They quickly located the *Lisa Marie* anchored just offshore and arranged to go onboard. Fearing the worst, they decided to check the cargo. Wilson ordered the master to open a container. Any lingering hope was immediately dashed. The container was empty! One by one, all fifty containers were checked. All were empty. The 25 million Marlboros that Wilson had certified were aboard simply did not exist!

As if that were not bad enough, Wilson was then told by the master that Portillo had always known the Marlboro cigarettes did not exist. Worse still, Portillo had apparently planned to scuttle the vessel with the empty containers and to claim the insurance for the fifty containers and their contents! So why was the vessel skulking around Venezuela? Wilson was told that Portillo had directed it there, perhaps to pick up drugs. As Puerto Cabello is close to Colombia, it has been used as a regular route.

After delivery of the drugs to a secret destination, *Lisa Marie* could then have been scuttled in deep water, allegedly full of cigarettes, and an insurance claim could have been made, although insurers would have been very suspicious of such a high-value cargo shipped aboard a rustbucket. Perhaps Portillo had changed his plans only once Wilson had got his buyers *to agree to pay only on arrival at Hamburg*. Though he could not explode with anger to Wilson's face without arousing suspicion, Portillo must have been furious at not receiving payment *on loading* rather than *arrival*. Wilson's additional clause had scuppered Portillo's scheme. For him, the risks of being caught by buyers checking in Hamburg to see if the goods existed were unacceptable. *No arrival, no pay* was the effect of the special clause. That safeguard had forced a change of plan. Portillo must have decided to do a drug run or sink *Lisa Marie*.

As Wilson sat at Caracas Airport waiting for his return flight to London, he was forced to face reality. Colonel Portillo had double-crossed him into selling non-existent cigarettes. He was the patsy; he had been a gullible fool. His name was on the shipping documents. He was in deep, deep trouble. The flight back to London was not happy. *Should he go to the police? Sort out Portillo? Speak to the other buyers? Convince MacMillan that he too had been conned?* There was no easy option. Every single one spelled danger, but by the time he landed in England, Wilson had decided to tell the buyers that the cigarettes did not exist.

The Dutch magistrate wanted to interview Wilson before there could be any question of releasing MacMillan. Such cross-border formalities take time. MacMillan spent Christmas in jail, blaming everyone but himself, although he could have made some simple enquiries before parting with his money.

In a brave move, Wilson decided to stand up to Portillo. He got an order preventing *Lisa Marie* from sailing from Venezuela. If the ship was worth what he had paid for it, that protected Horgen's investment. This legal step must have infuriated Portillo, especially if he had either a drug run or a scuttling in mind. But as 1991 ended and 1992 began, Wilson knew he had to clear his own reputation. His financial worries were worse than ever; he was facing a police investigation. Michelle could tell things were desperate. Wilson tried to hide his worries from his wife Barbara, telling her only that Portillo had set him up.

Telephone communication with Portillo in New York was now non-existent, so Wilson sent an abusive fax calling him 'a Mexican bastard who had set him up' and warning that Wilson was coming to get him. At some point, perhaps after the seizure of the ship, or when Wilson accused Portillo to the police, or perhaps after receiving this fax, Portillo started to lose his own cool.

Whatever prompted Portillo's next move, it was a mistake. As an experienced crook, he should have slipped quietly away. This deal had gone wrong, but he could do other deals and put it down to a bad experience. But he did not. Wilson was due to meet Scotland Yard officers on 3 March as part of the Dutch investigation. In February, he received a death threat from Portillo. If the intention was to stop Wilson talking to the police, it failed.

Portillo decided that Wilson had to be silenced. Permanently. Wilson knew enough to jail Portillo—but *that* assumed Portillo would sit around waiting for the police to call. He had ample time to escape before 3 March. Perhaps greed was his downfall. He wanted to keep his scams running, and that meant eliminating Wilson. Perhaps Portillo also naively underestimated the police. Cross-border enquiries are slow and may involve communication problems. But if Portillo thought the police would do *nothing* he was mistaken. Police around the world were alerted to watch out for *any* Marlboro deals.

Portillo engaged local private eye Paul La-Vey to spy on Wilson, to photograph his secluded home at Brinscall and to produce directions on how to find it. On 3 March, Wilson met with the police, pinning all blame on Portillo. He protested that he had genuinely believed the Marlboros existed until he reached Venezuela. The police believed him. The Dutch authorities released MacMillan from jail.

March in northern England is a bleak time of year; nights are still long, and the weather is often bitterly cold and even snowy. No doubt Wilson's worries made him feel as bleak as the weather. On the evening of 5 March 1992, two nights after his police interview, Wilson, his wife Barbara, daughter Lisa and her fiancé Mark Stephenson went over to Lisa's new home in the centre of the village, where some work needed to be done on the flooring.

Michelle, 26, decided to stay home and watch TV. At about nine p.m., she heard a knock at the front door. Unalarmed, she opened it, expecting to see one of her father's clients. At that moment, the Wilsons' life changed forever. In the darkness, two masked strangers filled the doorway. Only their eyes peered eerily through the narrow slits in their black hoods. They wore short coats and gloves. Each carried a gun, complete with silencer. One pressed his gun into Michelle's chest. Then one of her attackers bound her with tape. For two hours, the men kept the helpless, terrified young woman prisoner.

At just after 11 p.m., she heard the car returning. Wilson tried to enter through the front door. One attacker forced Michelle at gunpoint to call to him to use the kitchen door. Entering the brightness of the kitchen,

Wilson took in the horror of the situation immediately. One man had a gun aimed at him, the other still trained on his daughter. They were all prisoners now.

Wilson was silent. Lisa screamed in terror and Barbara Wilson sobbed as the gunmen immobilised all, first Wilson and then Mark, binding them hand and foot with blue masking tape. Wilson must have already feared the worst. His mind must have been churning, wondering how to escape, how to save his family, and berating himself for ever becoming involved with Hector Portillo. In disguised accents, the men then demanded to know what had happened to the money. Frantically, Wilson denied taking any money. The intruders lost patience and declared they were going to question him. They ordered Wilson to his feet and forced him out of the house to the garage.

That March night, with his family close by, David Wilson paid the price for crossing Portillo. He was forced to kneel and then shot twice in the back of the head. Death was immediate. In the house, the family heard two dull thuds and then silence. Hoping and assuming that the intruders had gone, Lisa was the first to struggle free. She freed the others and then tried to phone the police. No good—the lines had been slashed. With no sign of the intruders, the family set off by car to the village call box. There they made a 999 call to the police, reporting a *kidnapping*. Only when they returned home and their car swung back into their own driveway did the true horror become clear. The car's headlights revealed Wilson's dead body lying on the garage floor.

Though Hector Portillo had been introduced to Wilson as a Mexican Colonel, a delegate to the United Nations and a relative of a Mexican President, the truth was very different. 'Portillo' was an invention—a false name with a bogus identity and impressive credentials. The man Wilson had trusted was a hardened and highly skilled conman from the USA, sometimes called Michael Austin, though he also used many other names and identities to carry out his frauds. His real name was Michael Sporn, but he had over 30 passports and identities to go with them. The closest Austin had ever got to the United Nations was probably seeing their headquarters in New York, as he came from nearby New Jersey.

Born in 1955, Austin had previously lived an apparently modest lifestyle at home with his mother in Fort Lee, New Jersey, but his 35 years had in reality been action-packed. He now wished to enjoy some of the fruits of his criminal activities. Their apartment at Inwood Terrace was modest and unostentatious. Unusually for that neighbourhood, he drove a Rolls Royce, but otherwise he kept a low profile. One talent that was central to his new idea to create quick wealth was forgery. In 1985, he had been jailed for forging $100 notes. He had dabbled in selling non-existent sugar in the Dominican Republic. He had not been prosecuted for that scam, which had failed because of the poor-quality paperwork. It was a lesson learned. Ironically, it was his much-improved paperwork that failed him again, thanks this time to Ellen's professional acuity.

If Wilson had ever imagined he was the sole outlet for Marlboro cigarettes, he was much mistaken. Portillo had been setting up many other agents, including James MacMillan, to sell his Mexican product. Using a telephone answering service, Wilson or others could contact him on a New York number that he never answered. Austin would be notified of the call and would make contact back from elsewhere, using whatever identity was needed.

Once Austin had the signed documents *proving* the fifty containers were aboard and of the right quality, he could offer them to whomever he pleased. And he had. The containers were sold not just once but many times over to others taken in by his glib patter. The total number of containers sold by Austin's agents would never have fit on board the ship! Better still, unlike the safeguard that Wilson had put in place of payment only on reaching port, Austin's other deals favoured the more usual system of payment *on loading*, and he had the documents to prove that. The money began pouring in from others less cautious than Wilson. The profits were dispersed into many secret bank accounts.

Documents also showed that on 3 December three containers of cigarettes were loaded on the *Lisa Marie* bound for Naples from Miami! *Lisa Marie* was not the only vessel Austin used for shipping empty containers. Ellen checked just how many Philip Morris cigarettes were now on offer all over the world. He concluded: 'Austin was onto a winner. Using good forgeries, duping people into buying non-existent cigarettes was easy. So he refined his plot. Using the blueprint from *Lisa Marie*, his other agents sold five containers of cigarettes on board MV *WeiRiver* at Houston on 24 February 1992 for shipping to Antwerp in Belgium. In fact, *WeiRiver* was going nowhere. It had been under arrest since 1991 for unpaid debts. Austin had simply plucked its name out of a hat when creating his bogus paperwork.

'Another set of forgeries revealed that 20 containers of Marlboros were apparently loaded on MV *Infanta*, sailing to Bremerhaven on the German North Sea coast. Again, similar paperwork was sufficient to lure the unwary. Austin realised how easy it was. He had no need to bother owning ships—he just needed impressive documents and a vessel's name! All told, he invented at least six other ships and created documentation to match. His cool cunning was unbelievable, making it all the stranger that he muddied the waters by having Wilson murdered.'

As news of the murder spread, linking it to Wilson's involvement in Marlboro cigarettes, Austin's answering service was flooded with calls from concerned agents. He reassured them. To one caller who advised Austin to hire some good lawyers, he replied, 'I already got the two best lawyers in the world...name of *Smith & Wesson*!'

Ellen's associates were able to stop one sale to Bulgarian purchasers involving five containers allegedly bound for Antwerp aboard MV *Flemming*. SGS of Panama had issued a certificate that the cigarettes had been inspected in the containers and the Bill of Lading had been signed by Sea-Land Service Inc. 'SGS assured us that the documents were genuine. We could not believe this but accepted their good faith.'

The buyer had opened a letter of credit but payment was withheld. This was a risky and unusual step. Letters of credit are dangerous. Once issued, unless a court order is obtained, a bank must honour the terms and pay up. The consequences of wrongly stopping payment may be severe. So one treads carefully, making sure that an allegation of fraud will stand up.

The woman at Colon Free Trade Zone Panama who had allegedly *seen* the cigarettes put into the containers was interviewed and admitted that three Frenchmen had visited her and *told her* to issue the certificate! She had seen nothing. When the five containers were opened, they were empty. 'No surprise there, then! The buyer saved his millions. Nobody knows just how much Michael Austin made from selling non-existent cigarettes,' says Ellen. 'Austin's agents trapped buyers in 17 countries. He made anything from an estimated $30 million to perhaps treble that. Funds were hidden in accounts that could not be traced or accessed.'

Wilson had been found lying on his garage floor in a pool of blood. There was not much for the police to go on. The family could not directly identify the killers because they were masked. There was the evidence of Wilson's dealings. There was the information given to the police during his Scotland Yard interview. Michelle was interviewed for hours because she knew more of his complex business life than anyone else in the family. Documents were removed from his Olive Lane office. His diary, telephone records and banking details were scoured for pointers.

The police knew nothing of a Michael Austin at this stage. Their concern was Portillo. If not Portillo, who else might have paid the killers? MacMillan, a possible suspect, was brought in from Edinburgh for interview but quickly released. Detectives had no positive evidence linking Portillo with New

Jersey or even the USA. There *had been* a Hector Portillo related to the Mexican President, but he was dead.

In Withnell, the next village to where Wilson had lived and died, there had been sighting of a red saloon car on the night of the murder. Red saloon cars are scarcely unusual, but in small communities, *anything* different stands out. Then thumbprints were found on the nine feet of masking tape used to bind Wilson. This was a mega blunder by what otherwise appeared to be a professional job by specialist hitmen. But whose thumbprints were they? They did not match those of any known criminal in international databases.

Led by the highly experienced Detective Superintendent Bob Denmark of the Lancashire Crime Support Unit, enquiries were conducted by 80 detectives in this international investigation. This ruthless professional execution took a massive operation by Lancashire police, working with the IMB, INTERPOL, the US Customs and the FBI until the mesh of fraud and murder began to unravel.

Though Denmark quickly suspected Portillo of hiring hitmen, it was over four months later, in July, that the mystery of Michael Austin's secret life was cracked. The painstaking and unglamorous task of trawling through telephone records revealed a pattern—a web, at the centre of which was Mr Big. There was sufficient proof that 'Colonel Portillo' was in reality Michael Austin, late 30s, of New Jersey. US Customs started investigating his background. As Austin went to close on a deal to buy a $3 million apartment at the luxurious Trump Tower, Central Park in Manhattan, one of the Big Apple's most fashionable addresses, he was snatched off the street by US Customs. They found he was using yet another name, Michael Bond, and for his purchase had chosen as his company name 'Universal Exports'—one invented by Ian Fleming for the James Bond books!

The arrest was just the beginning. Austin fought extradition to the UK all the way to the US Supreme Court. He lost and was flown to England for the criminal process, but it would still be five years before the biggest murder and criminal investigation in the history of the Lancashire Police came to an end. Det. Supt. Denmark later confirmed that Austin had checked out the likely media and police reaction to a murder. But he underestimated the ability and determination of the police.

The police found that money received by Alamosa had been sent to various secret destinations; most of it had then passed into an account in Zurich and thence to the Caribbean. Besides the *Lisa Marie*, there were all the other *bogus* ships and cargoes and the profits earned from those scams. Denmark explains that Austin used fifty different identities all over the world—stolen passports, passports belonging to dead people. Austin cleverly manipulated people but made it impossible for them to contact him. It was as though he had invisible tentacles all over the world.

Fortunately for Denmark, once Austin had been identified, telephonic evidence linked him to an Englishman called Stephen Schepke, a 49-year-old from Oldham, also in Lancashire. Intense police work revealed that Austin had engaged Schepke to arrange Wilson's murder. Schepke was the middleman. But who were the killers? There was still no positive lead.

At Carlisle Crown Court, Austin denied any part in setting up Wilson's murder, despite strong evidence put to the 12 members of the jury. He was convicted and sentenced to life imprisonment in January 1995. But a witness in the case sold his story to a newspaper and so Austin was granted a retrial at Liverpool Crown Court. This trial was presided over by a senior and distinguished High Court judge, Sir Oliver Popplewell, who had chaired the enquiry into safety at football stadiums following the Hillsborough disaster.

Popplewell, very much a man of the people despite his first-class education and privileged background, had no truck with the defence put forward by Austin's Queen's Counsel that he was involved in fraud and not murder. The defence tried to convince judge and jury that the hitmen had been hired by others, perhaps the Polish mafia, whom Wilson had crossed, or by some 'violent' American brokers. Following the judge's summing-up, a second jury returned their verdict of guilty of murder. Popplewell sentenced the conman murderer to 20 years minimum in prison. In childish defiance, Austin gave him the finger.

Sadly for the tragic Wilson family, Barbara Wilson died of a brain haemorrhage before Austin was jailed. After his second conviction, Austin lodged an appeal. Michael Hill QC, defending, alleged that Popplewell's summing-up had been unbalanced in the way he had presented the issues to the jury. But the three Appeal Court judges were having no truck with Austin either. His conviction was upheld.

Stephen Schepke had been convicted of aiding and abetting murder and sentenced to life imprisonment. Lesser figures had also been convicted of fraud or deception offences, but Denmark was determined to pursue the hitmen. In April 1996, after Austin was convicted for the first time in Carlisle, two men from the Kent-London borders were taken into police custody. Stephen Playle, 34, was arrested at his flat in Longlands Road, Sidcup, Kent. Playle was a veteran of the Falklands war. After leaving the army, he had begun working as a chef in the Black Horse pub, close to his home.

Michael Crossley, 34, was an ex–army corporal from the Thames Estuary town of North fleet, a nondescript type of place. He managed the Six Bells pub. He and Playle used to meet up at the Black Horse, as did Schepke. The links were falling into place. But acquaintance was not evidence of a murder hundreds of miles away in Lancashire. What else could be put to a jury?

Crossley's wife Alison owned a red Vauxhall Chevette similar to the vehicle seen in the village on the night of the murder—interesting, but flimsy. When Schepke was arrested, his wallet was found to contain scraps of paper bearing the phone numbers of Playle and Crossley—again interesting, but in a murder trial with skilled legal representation, lightweight. There was also scribbled information about Austin and Wilson, certainly enough to get Schepke convicted.

When Playle and Crossley's fingerprints were taken, Playle's thumbprints matched those on the blue tape used to bind Wilson. It was a bad mistake, irrefutable evidence of a link to the murder. The police had their man. Playle and Crossley were both duly convicted of murder.

Eric Ellen, thanks to whose astuteness the great Marlboro fraud was uncovered, has no doubt that justice was done. 'Wilson was a pawn in Austin's game. He may have intended to pass off Mexican cigarettes as American, but no more than that. He certainly did not deserve to die the way he did.' Wilson's tragedy was that he had neglected to ask the right people the right questions. Had he been as prudent as that London businessman, he might have ended up bankrupt, but he would not have died kneeling on the cold stone of his garage floor.

Again, if you swim with sharks…

CHAPTER FOUR
Poverty in Port - A Tale of Two Guns

The saying *any port in a storm* has connotations far beyond the maritime sphere. No doubt it once had practical validity: riding out severe weather was more dangerous than entering a strange port. Today, though, for those entering ports in many countries, another phrase is more apposite: *caught between the devil and the deep blue sea.*

Ever since its creation, the IMB has viewed with alarm the increasing levels of violence involved in attacks in harbour. Brazil, East and West Africa and the Far East have been festering thorns in the IMB's side; far too many ports are still hotbeds of robbery and violence. Some ports are total no-go areas. In others, a visiting vessel, to feel secure, would need at the very least the combined forces of Schwarzenegger and Rambo patrolling the decks, and a dash of James Bond's luck into the bargain. Ports are a breeding ground for crime: muggings, pilfering, armed robbery, container theft, drug-smuggling, people-smuggling and *apparent* theft from containers to underpin bogus insurance claims or money laundering. This chapter discusses armed attacks against ships in harbour or anchored just offshore and the special issues relating to sailing boats and pleasure cruisers.

Ports such as Oslo or Felixstowe are relatively safe, whereas Djibouti is a no-go area and many African ports and much of the Indonesian coastline are best avoided. But despite the dangers of West African ports, ships have to go there to make money for their owners and charterers whatever the risk. Nigeria, for instance, has a huge oil industry, but the Gulf of Guinea, alongside Nigeria, is now replacing Somalian waters as the hotbed for violent attacks on merchant shipping.

After 2012, when international action, better protection and precautions began to be effective against booming kidnap-and-ransom activities off

Somalia, crime in Nigeria and the Gulf of Guinea, already rife, became rampant. The only way of reducing the risks to seafarers is through strong political action on land, backed up by greater vigilance aboard ship. The IMB Piracy Reporting Centre in Kuala Lumpur publishes a weekly update of dangerous ports, so there is no excuse for crew ignorance. The IMB supplies this information out of their conviction that prevention of crime through information is far better than the thrills and glamour of dramatic arrests.

The gangs depend on *surprise*, *speed* and *violence*. But being aware of the dangers and deciding how to fend off or prevent an attack remain the subject of debate. Especially dangerous ports include Luanda (Angola), Conakry (Guinea) and Dar es Salaam (Tanzania). In Brazil at one point, *reported* attacks in port or at anchorages reached one per day, with many more unreported. In Latin America, the number of reported attacks has ebbed and flowed, but poverty breeds crime. Any laxness in security will be exploited. Attacks around South America and in the Caribbean have yet to develop into the realms of kidnap and ransom like the situation around Aceh Province in the early 2000s or piracy off Somalia or Nigeria. Attacks usually take place in ports, but violence has occurred during robberies.

All reported figures are a gross understatement of the problem. For every incident reported, masters and owners keep quiet about many more. Ellen estimates that only one in five attacks around ports is reported, and usually only if death or severe injury is involved. Mostly, masters hush up incidents to avoid criticism by their bosses. Owners need speed of transit to make a profit. A ship lying idle is a liability. Port delays while local police make a meal out of an incident, achieving very little, is a central problem. Accurate data would give the trades unions, the United Nations and governments the best weapons with which to fight back.

The MV *Cape Georjean* was lying at anchor in the territorial waters of Sierra Leone when she was attacked. Sir Peter Blake, international yachting hero, was murdered near the mouth of the Amazon River in Brazil. These attacks fell within the Bureau's definition of piracy and armed robbery, which does not differentiate between attacks on the high seas or near port:

'An act of boarding or attempting to board any ship with the apparent intent to commit theft or any other crime and with the apparent intent or capability to use force in the furtherance of that act.'

Whether the attackers are called thugs or pirates is all one. Armed men, ready to kill or maim, are boarding ships to steal whatever they can. These vicious attacks are reminiscent of the so-called *golden days* of piracy 300 years ago, when cross-dressing pirates like Anne Bonny and Mary (Mark)

Read plundered Caribbean shipping with Captain Jack (Calico) Rackham. In port or out of port, they stole whatever and wherever they could. Today, only the prudent and the lucky can expect to avoid death or violence while visiting the most dangerous ports, as John Bailey would confirm from his own dramatic encounter. Tragically, Sir Peter Blake cannot.

PART ONE
The Superintendent's Tale - Sierra Leone

One October night, *Cape Georjean* was anchored off Sierra Leone, West Africa. This nation of five million people lies north of the equator, sandwiched between Liberia to the south and Guinea to the north. As a major registry for shipping, Liberia's port of Monrovia could not afford an international reputation as unsafe. By contrast, Conakry, in Guinea, poses a significant risk of violent crime. Armed gangs rule the quays unchallenged by compliant or intimidated security forces.

At the time, in the early 2000s, Sierra Leone was not a high-risk destination, but like many places in the Third World, its port of Freetown can never be regarded as safe. On shore, there was an uneasy peace after 10 years of bloody civil war. Tens of thousands had fled to neighbouring Liberia to avoid the violence. Two million people had been displaced, 40% of the population. Earlier in 2001, a peace deal had been brokered with help from the UK Government, and thousands of weapons had been surrendered. Countless more had not. Life had become cheap, values debased; weapons remained plentiful.

Bauxite, diamonds and cocoa should have made this a wealthy nation, but for too long hatred and war had held sway. A country rich in resources had been bankrupted; over 50,000 were dead, and tens of thousands had been raped and deliberately mutilated. Endemic tribal hostility and lust for power on the part of political leaders had destroyed both quality of and respect for life. The most tragic aspect had been the involvement of children barely into their teens, abducted and turned into soldiers. Lads who should have been kicking footballs were armed and brutalised for 10 bloody years.

The war officially over, these young men faced even bleaker prospects. They still had weapons; they were still fuelled by memories of forced sex and the blood-rush of slaughter. In Freetown, burned-out cars littered the streets, rusting in the sultry heat. Trash lay rotting alongside dusty tracks that served as roads. Dogs scavenged for scraps while men without jobs or futures lay about in the shade amid the garbage. Against such a backdrop, the only surprising thing is that attacks on visiting ships had not already become a *mainstream* pastime for armed gangs. Ships with a safe, food, valuable watches, alcohol, cigarettes and high-tech goods offered a unique opportunity.

At nightfall, *Cape Georjean*, a 5,200-ton tanker, lay at anchor three miles offshore by Cape Sierra Point, swaying gently. The distant lights of Freetown twinkled across the dark waters and the sickly smell of effluent polluted the steamy atmosphere. It was the rainy season; the damp air hung heavily. The ship's 10-member crew, mainly Russians, were mostly below decks. One was Marine Superintendent John Bailey, 52, an Englishman from Yorkshire, a county known for its doughty characters. Blunt and forthright, John Bailey epitomised that breed.

Unseen, a small boat approached, speeding out from the harbour. It carried eight locals, all heavily armed with Kalashnikovs and clubs. Nobody spotted them clambering aboard. Encountering no resistance, they took command, surprising and taking hostage the Chief Mate before starting their looting rampage through the accommodation. In the scuffle leading to his capture, the Chief Mate received a number of savage blows to his body.

Their next victim was the Ukrainian Captain. Seconds later, he too was held prisoner so that the safe could be ransacked. Usually, except around Indonesia, most local gangs have no interest in the crew, the cargo or the boat itself. At that time, especially around Lagos or Bonny River, West African pirates *might* break into the containers on deck and steal cargo, but the crew's valuables were the main attraction. Youngsters might be satisfied with paint, rope, a ladder or a coil of wire—useful for later bartering. However, today most attackers want more. For the locals lacking sufficient experience to steal entire cargoes, the *supreme target* is the safe, usually located in the captain's cabin or office. This gang was no exception. They were after money.

In his cabin, John Bailey had been asleep. In the darkness of the early hours, he awoke to the sounds of shouting. A veteran of the sea, he was well aware of the dangers of attacks in port—indeed, his ship had been attacked only a few weeks previously. Beside him he had a pump-action shotgun. Thoroughly alert to the dangers but conscious of the threat to his shipmates he approached his cabin door, ready to use his weapon if need be. His priority was to save the crew.

He paused by the door. From the other side, he heard movement. The attackers had reached him first—*not good news. He was trapped*! Worse still, he heard the sound of automatic weapons being cocked. The distinctive sharp clicks were both chilling and unmistakeable. Bailey could imagine the scene on the other side of the door and did not like it one bit. But he never wavered, even though he knew he was taking an irrevocable step into a frightening unknown.

Surprise was his only friend; he flung the cabin door wide, hoping his sudden initiative would catch them off guard. He was out of luck. A menacing black figure thrust a Kalashnikov towards his chest from a short distance. Before Bailey could do anything, the attacker pulled the trigger. That should have been end of story—John Bailey, deceased, another victim of global piracy, another statistic to be used by the IMB but ignored by the world at large.

But the Kalashnikov jammed.

Bailey seized the initiative; he opened fire, his own shotgun spraying pellets in the confined space. Bailey fell to the floor as the pellets ricocheted around him, but as he fell he fired again as the man retreated and disappeared around the corner. Bailey coolly grabbed more ammunition and gave chase. He followed the trail of blood, unaware that he was confronting not just a couple of robbers but a gang of eight. The attackers did not at once leave the ship, no doubt still ransacking the crew's quarters, but Bailey managed to get out a radio alert. This was picked up by UK Coastguards in Falmouth, a small maritime community in Cornwall. Bailey also used a satellite phone to call Neil Thornton, a director of the owners, Atlantic Bunkering Limited, in Newcastle upon Tyne, northern England. Thornton also called the coastguards and found that Falmouth had already swung into action. In Freetown, the military, the police and a special adviser from the British forces had already been alerted and mobilised.

But they were three miles away and the armed thugs were still aboard. With no thought for his own safety, Bailey took the fight to the enemy. He took up the chase, blasting off about 17 more rounds. How many he killed or injured he had no idea. In the shadows and confusion, he could not see. His intent was not to kill but to terrify the gang into leaving the ship, and in that, he was totally successful, gaining the satisfaction of seeing the attackers jumping and diving over the side. The attack was over.

Though Sierra Leone forms part of the British Commonwealth, there was no Royal Navy vessel on hand. In the old days, before the world became superficially safer with the end of the Cold War and politicians slashed their defence budgets, Britain would have had warships in the area, useful as a deterrent and to provide support. Those days have gone, leaving merchant fleets more exposed in consequence. Bailey was later questioned by police and freed without charge. The surviving attackers, who had expected quick spoils, may now think twice about repeating the attack. But as the IMB statistics show, reported crimes are already up. Social unrest and poverty make it ever more dangerous to visit Freetown—factors that were also to play their part in tragic events which would take place two months later in Brazil.

Ellen, both irritated and sorrowful, reveals that he had long ago warned that port management needed to accept that most crime is employee-based and that corruption is rife even at the highest levels, including the police. 'Nothing has changed my view. Corruption is a way of life, ineradicable; but paying a decent wage would be a start, as would making individuals with mundane, repetitive jobs feel they are important and valued—building esteem and self-worth. But if the example set at the top is rotten and the chances of being caught remote, active involvement or taking money to turn a blind eye will continue.'

Perhaps trades unions like NUMAST could increase pressure by getting ports blacklisted, with their members refusing to sail there unless security is increased. That extreme action has been taken in the past. 'Much port crime is preventable,' adds Ellen. "But action has to come from governments. Crews, for their part, must be more vigilant in repelling attackers—preventing them from boarding is the best way.'

But what if a gang does get aboard? Ellen is adamant that arming the crew is not the answer. 'The pirates come in such numbers, usually with heavier firepower, that one man, say a security officer, has no real chance. Letting the whole crew have firearms would be disastrous. To be effective, they would require training in the use of weapons and would need to keep up their skills. In attacks in port, the sensible response is to show no resistance.'

Ellen gives cogent reasons for this apparently defeatist attitude. A distress call from the ship to the local police in dangerous ports will be ignored. If the crew repels the attackers by force, they tend to regroup and attack again, perhaps with reinforcements or better weapons. In general, attacks on ships in harbour are not random. Port officials have tipped the gang off about a good cargo or valuables. 'For those who are still resolved to resist, believe it or not, bows and arrows worked well in Lagos, straight back to the days of the Battle of Hastings nearly one thousand years ago!'

Captain Mukundan agrees. 'Merchant crews are not trained to use weapons. Crews are often short of sleep and outnumbered. Ships are not ideal battlegrounds. Bullets will ricochet everywhere. Anyway, who do you arm? You can't arm everyone. If you arm one or two, they will need regular practice and may find themselves up against anything from 5 to

30 pirates, perhaps with automatic rifles and the advantage of surprise. Is it really worth provoking a one-sided gun battle and increasing the stakes all round?'

Arming the crew would not be worthwhile in the case of low-level attacks where equipment and personal valuables of relatively little worth are stolen. In a major hijacking, the pirates are armed to the teeth and unrelenting. A few crew members with handguns will not deter them. The occasional heroic incident, like the brave John Bailey's actions, cannot overrule the dangers of confrontation.

The debate continues, driven especially by the ongoing risk of hijackings and attacks in and around too many ports. As explained later, shipowners are now hiring armed security guards for routes that may expose the crew to a hijacking risk.

PART TWO
Murder of a Hero

In the world of international sailing, the America's Cup is the ultimate trophy. Originally a challenge between the UK and the USA, the rules were changed so that Australia, New Zealand and other nations may now compete against the skill and financial resources of the American boat designers. To win this Cup requires huge financial backing, but beyond that, it takes a crew able to master seamanship at the supreme levels of human endeavour. Sailing experience, cunning, courage, determination and team spirit all combine to create a world-beating crew.

In 1995, New Zealand, a country perhaps better known for its legendary All-Blacks rugby team, produced just such a world-beating crew to win the America's Cup under the leadership of Peter Blake. Overnight, Blake, already renowned for his seamanship, became a national hero. To gild the lily, in 2000 he won the Cup again for New Zealand. Along the way, he competed in the first five Whitbread Round-the-World races, winning in 1989 and 1994, and also won the Jules Verne Trophy.

Blake—'Blakey,' to his mates—was a big rugged man with a commanding physical presence, a generous moustache and piercing eyes; he had star quality stamped on his forehead. His thick mop of flaxen hair and moustache were turning a distinguished grey. He was a born leader, ready to accept the life-and-death challenges of the elements in some of the world's cruellest oceans.

His personal courage and his innate sense of right and wrong were at the forefront on the night of his murder. He died a hero, trying to protect those on his yacht from people who threatened to murder them.

Blake, born in 1948, had spent long voyages surrounded by empty seas. He had learned to love and respect the bounty of the ocean and had grown increasingly concerned about preserving the world's water resources and their quality. He founded Blakes Expeditions. With support from the United Nations Environmental Programme, whose special envoy he became, he established a five-year research and educational project about water conservation and maintaining water quality.

In 2001, after a spell in Antarctica, he and his crew had sailed their yacht *Seamaster* northward from the frozen wastes up to the Amazon River in Brazil in the tropics just south of the Equator. The *Seamaster* was rather special: her aluminium hull was reinforced so that she could operate safely in the pack ice of the polar regions. With a shallow draft and well-crafted base to the hull, she could even operate on top of the ice!

Seamaster measured 36 metres and had twin 27-metre masts. Additionally, there were two 350-horsepower motors. Resplendent in silvered aluminium, with the logo *blakexpeditions.com* written in blue on the side, she looked like a rich man's toy. With financial sponsorship for the expedition from Omega watches, she had been adapted on arrival in the tropics to cope with the intense heat and humidity after the icy blasts of the southern hemisphere.

To poverty-stricken Brazilians from the sprawling city of Macapá, she was an obvious target. A single glance had the local *ratos de agua*, the river-rats, dreaming of the wealth on board. In provincial Brazil, that nation of contrasts, life was cheap, murder a run-of-the-mill occurrence, and the lure of riches irresistible.

For most Brazilians, for many of whom life has little to offer, idolisation of local heroes like Pelé, the world's greatest footballer, or Ayrton Senna, the greatest-ever Formula One driver, is understood in a way that is almost unimaginable elsewhere. Heroes are *super-gods* in Brazil. When Blake was murdered, the nation reacted with the passion of those who know what it is to lose a hero.

Brazil is full of so-called *rats* of many kinds, and not just river-rats around the Amazon. *Court-rats* are peddlers of bribes to the judiciary, scurrying furtively around with cash from litigants. Judges in the lower courts are bought as a matter of course. The same applies to the Brazilian police—whether Federal, State, Military, Civilian or Municipal. In Rio, the poorest slums or *favelas*, *shanty towns*, cling to the hillside, lying cheek by jowl with luxury hotels and million-dollar homes. The slum-dwellers can see the comforts of wealth so near and yet so impossibly far. Starvation or theft is their stark choice. Forty million people live in Sao Paulo, a city of drab grey tower-blocks, where there are 14 murders on the streets every day. The criminals are young; many 14-year-olds have knives, some have guns. Life is so cheap that anyone offering resistance is likely to be savagely attacked. Every year rich people are beaten up, robbed and sometimes killed. One early morning, a BBC journalist was stripped naked, robbed and abandoned to hide his embarrassment on a Rio beach. Even Formula One world champion Jensen Button only escaped an armed attack on his car in Sao Paulo in 2010 through the skill of his local chauffeur.

Macapá has a population of around 250,000 people. Not far from the luxurious heavily walled or guarded villas with their lush greenery and bright flower gardens are the *favelas*, corrugated iron and pieces of wood providing makeshift homes, a breeding ground for river-rats and street fighters.

Brazil has another serious problem: drugs, some imported from Colombia, others coming from the vast hinterland. Children, especially those from more wealthy backgrounds, get sucked into marijuana and cocaine abuse or heroin addiction. The availability of drugs and lack of police enforcement have led to a drug culture that seems to be spiralling out of control. Drugs played a role in the death of Peter Blake, too.

The Amazon is not the world's longest river. At over 4,000 miles, it is the second longest. It is, however, the largest and most powerful. Its outflow of water into the Atlantic in northeast Brazil represents 20% of *all* water entering the sea from rivers. Cruise liners sailing across the mouth stay over 50 miles offshore to avoid the strength of the surge of dirty brown water. Indeed, the river was first discovered because an explorer tasted fresh water two hundred miles out to sea and traced its source.

Inland, the Amazon is up to six miles wide, flowing with enormous force: Blake reported that they made three times the speed sailing downstream as they had managed during their two months sailing upriver and around the interior. Here, they had met the locals, seen entrancing sights and gathered material for two special television documentaries about the environment. Scientists interested in vaccine research and antidotes to poisonous venoms had been invited aboard for research purposes. Ecological expeditions into the jungle and visiting primitive communities had been undertaken. The Amazon is home to deadly piranhas, six cm of teeth and pure aggression. Swimming in shoals, they will strip a human body to its bones in seconds. Giant anaconda snakes lie in wait in the water, only their dead eyes glinting above the surface as they watch for suitable prey—including humans.

Toothpick fish, which enter every human orifice, are also a risk. Caimans lurk on the banks; coral snakes writhe through the undergrowth.

Helen Clark, then Prime Minister of New Zealand on an official visit to Brazil, fitted in a couple of days working with the *Seamaster* team in the hinterland. Little did she know that within a short time she would be giving the eulogy for Blake at an English church, the Church of St Thomas à Beckett in Emsworth, Hampshire. This church was named for the archbishop murdered in Canterbury Cathedral in 1170 by four knights in the service of King Henry II.

The *Seamaster* was safe enough for most adventures, although a lookout was posted to watch for unlit craft and logs. Blake had learned that the locals were no respecters of wildlife if it posed any threat—*get it before it gets you* was their watchword. Snakes and insects were slaughtered with no second thought. But Brazilians living in remote rural areas face an even more deadly menace, one which colours attitudes to life and death not just in Brazil but throughout South and Central America: the sinister, deadly Chagas disease. This disease was named after the Brazilian physician who first identified it in 1907. There is still no cure. In South America, it affects one in five people. Of Brazil's population of around 170 million, some 30 million may die prematurely from this intractable killer. In rural areas or *favela* communities, the disease is more prevalent than AIDS, which is also widespread.

By sailing up into the Amazonian rainforest and visiting the small communities along the banks, Blake and his crew had risked infection, which typically occurs in one of two ways: either from a contaminated blood transfusion or from an insect known as the *kissing bug*. *Seamaster* doubtless carried blood supplies to avoid any local transfusions. But in remote villages, the chances of being bitten by this one-inch-long bug were unpleasantly high.

The bug, especially hungry at night, thrives amid communities living in mud-and-stick homes. From the crannies in the dwellings, the *kissing bug* emerges to bite its unfortunate victim—the kiss of death, although death is not immediate. The insect, partly the colour of maple, partly mahogany, drops its faeces into the wound. In consequence, the disease spreads throughout the bloodstream of the human or animal.

With the steady movement of people from the interior to the cities, Chagas has followed, so that what was a rural issue has become a problem even in urban communities. There is no antidote. Two decades may pass before the fatal effects kick in—usually heart failure. In adults, the immediate effects of the bite may appear insignificant, but those who know they have been bitten are aware that the poison is working its lethal way into their system—their colon, oesophagus, and ultimately the heart. Blake's team had taken some unpleasant risks, but thus far had seemingly avoided the worst of the hazards, though Chagas has a lengthy time lag.

With such a high rate of infection, Chagas may already have taken many a Macapáriver-ratin its insidious grip. For those already doomed to die from Chagas, the risk of jail for killing a rich foreigner for his watch or camera appears negligible. Two months before, while John Bailey was seeing off the attackers on *Cape Georjean*, Blake and his crew were upriver amid the toothpicks, anacondas, crocodiles, piranhas, poisonous snakes and Chagas. Now, the end of the trip was at hand; the worst dangers had been overcome. All that stood between the *Seamaster* and the ocean was an overnight stop near Macapá. It was December 5 2001. The trip had been a great success and the mood was relaxed and celebratory.

Blake had logged a message on *blakexpeditions*' website, emphasising his commitment to the environment, concluding: 'We want to make a difference.' Blake had planned that *Seamaster* would stop near Santana by Macapá, until well-meaning help intervened. Unimpressed by Blake's celebrity, Claudio Lira, Harbour-Master, was simply doing his job. Aware that river-rats operated around Santana, Lira suggested they should moor the yacht near him in the safer area at Fazendinha instead. Blake accepted Lira's advice and dropped anchor in midstream several hundred metres offshore. A lengthy routine customs inspection followed. The crew then plotted their next routing: northward to Venezuela, past the infamous Devil's Island.

The heat of the day was over. The brilliant orange and red of the sunset had long gone. At 1800, black night had descended over the swirling grey-brown water. The chatter of birds that had drifted over the river gradually died away. The moon would not appear till much later. In the early evening, the crew—comprising New Zealanders, two Britons, a Frenchman, an American and a Brazilian chef—had gone ashore to dine in the beachside community of Fazendinha, enjoying *caipirinhas*, the strong local liquor made from sugar cane braced with lime, served in a sugared glass. A big soccer match that evening was on everyone's minds, and most of Brazil's population was glued to the television.

After returning to *Seamaster*, eight crew stayed on deck playing music and enjoying a few beers as the relentless river surged beneath them. From the shore now came the endless chirrup of insects. An occasional vessel passed, red and green lights twinkling in the blackness. Otherwise, all was quiet, enveloped by the inky dark.

Blake was still on deck, but cameraman Leon Sefton and another crew member had gone below. The remainder were sharing a few laughs, their minds not on any imminent danger, though they all knew of the risk of pirates. They had no formal lookout posted. Nobody had a clue that murder lay just round the corner. An elderly launch piloted by 20-year-old Rubens da Souza was approaching *Seamaster*. His passengers were an unsavoury bunch, heavily disguised. The gang had come up from the city, some 10 kilometres away. It seems unlikely that they had been cruising the river at night on the off chance of encountering prey. Somebody must have seen *Seamaster* by daylight and tipped them off.

They were veterans of river crime, and the valuable yacht meant just one thing: money, lots of it. *Only rich people had vessels like this. It would be a pushover. Probably a bunch of elderly millionaires. Quick surrender once attacked. There would be no trouble.* Silently, black-hearted as the night, they glided closer to their quarry, needing the advantage of surprise. They had donned balaclava hoods and facemasks. At least one had put on a motorcycle helmet. With a skill born of long practice, they drew alongside, concealed from where the crew were relaxing by a tarpaulin. Suddenly, they were aboard, brandishing guns, seeking to impose their authority through shock tactics.

Rodger Moore, British but a resident of New Zealand, was first to sense something was wrong. Glancing up and seeing the terrifying sight of disguised figures waving firearms, he hurled his beer at the nearest thug and was rewarded with a severe blow to the head. Anthony Bullock was pistol-whipped across the head and knocked unconscious.

In a flurry of activity, Blake, as befitted a natural leader, reacted at once and instantly took charge. He rushed down the companionway to the cabins below, yelling, 'We're being attacked. This is for real.' No shots were fired, but within seconds the crew were being pinned to the deck and restrained, guns to their heads. Blake had only one thought: protecting his crew. He had a pair of .308 rifles and ammunition in his cabin.

From his cabin, Leon Sefton heard the racket on deck but was unsure just what was happening. There was violent movement, the sound of things being knocked around. As he peered out of his cabin door, he saw Blake in his cabin, the door ajar, and assumed that the skipper had been there all along and was retiring to bed. He decided to go up himself to see what was going on.

He had barely started up the stairs when a figure in a balaclava blocked the exit and advanced toward him, gun raised. The man shouted: 'Money! Money! Money!' Instinctively, Sefton raised his hands. It was no contest.

But then *Blakey* appeared. Sir Peter had grabbed his rifle and ammunition, planning to go back on deck to control the situation. But it was too late. He saw Sefton, arms raised in surrender, being threatened by a man later identified as Israel da Costa.

'Get off my effing boat,' Blake yelled, aiming his rifle. Though the intruder did not speak English, no doubt he got the message, but he did not back down. Sefton heard the exchange of shots, though who fired first was unclear. Among his many talents, Blake was a useful shot. His bullet struck the gunman, shooting away a finger and wounding his arm up to the elbow, a blow calculated to incapacitate but not to kill. The intruder's gun hand was useless. Undoubtedly Blake's brilliant shot had saved his own life—for the moment—and also spared that of the attacker whom he could more easily have shot in the chest. Da Costa's shot had missed—Blake himself was uninjured. The intruder retreated up the companionway to the deck, no doubt to inform his leader.

Then the dead hand of fate intervened. Blake's gun had jammed, probably from lack of maintenance in a humid climate. Had this not happened, events might have turned out very differently. Blake could have been able to go on deck and stamp his authority. As it was, he was once again unarmed.

Sefton, no longer facing a hooded gunman, snapped into action, planning to grab the second rifle from Blake's cabin, but Blake ordered him to go through to the bow to clear the hatch and prepare an escape route. Blake himself re-entered his cabin, where he was struggling to get his rifle working when another assailant moved in—now known to be Ricardo Colares Tavares, 23, and the gang leader,. He fired at least twice and then from close range pumped another two bullets into Blake's back, fatally rupturing his aorta.

Slain, the great man slumped to the floor by his cabin door. This was a needless vengeful killing by Tavares; he shot in the back a man who offered no immediate threat. After da Costa's injury, the gang could have fled, but Tavares was hell-bent on revenge. He ripped Blake's Omega watch from the dead man's wrist and grabbed his rifles. When Sefton returned and saw his friend and skipper lying dead, he tried to resuscitate him but it was hopeless. A man who had sailed thousands of miles, faced such dangers, run such risks and achieved so much had ended his life's journey in a cowardly and pointless attack by a *river-rat.*

Up on deck the robbery continued. The rats were in total control, seizing anything valuable. His shipmates had to restrain Don Robertson, who was desperate to get at the gang. As it was, he took a slight bullet wound to his back as he lay on the deck. An inch lower and there might have been a second murder. Cameras, watches and a couple of rifles: not much of a haul, without the expected load of cash—especially with a corpse on their hands as well. As suddenly as it had started, the attack was over, the thugs tumbling into their launch and speeding away, taking with them one of *Seamaster's* rubber dinghies.

Across the water, on-duty Harbour-Master Claudio Lira lounged in his dilapidated wooden hut, watching the match on television, cheering on his favourite team. Using the remaining dinghy, two of the crew reached shore and galvanised Lira into action; soon the emergency services were racing to the scene. Local bureaucracy took over. The crew were relentlessly interrogated as the furore grew, eventually reaching the Brazilian president himself far away in the capital, Brasilia.

To those who deal daily with maritime crime, the news of Blake's murder came as no surprise. The number of attacks, not all of them fatal, on yachts, cruisers and commercial ships annually runs into the thousands. The IMO and IMB had been calling for greater crew awareness and more effective local action for years. The murder of an international celebrity certainly added impetus to calls for action, quickly echoed by diplomats and politicians. But if the underlying problems of poverty and local corruption are not addressed, the reality is that such attacks will continue.

The Brazilian Government faced a barrage of international criticism. Prime Minister Clark's recent visit to Brazil added focus to the calls for the gang to be caught. For Brazil, which has a constant battle to protect the stability of the *real*, its national currency, such a high-profile incident was bad news. Media coverage about the murder drew attention to the robberies, the kidnappings, the corruption and violence in Brazil. The risks of sailing up the Amazon were highlighted. The horror stories were detrimental to the tourist industry and discouraged potential investors in the Brazilian economy—no international corporation wants to set up a company where its directors will live in constant fear of being mugged or kidnapped or where corruption is widespread among police, politicians and the judiciary.

The local police protested that they were hampered by lack of resources. But an order from President Cardoso himself that the killers must be caught led to the type of determined action that achieves results.

Blake may well have known that another ecologist had been murdered up the Amazon. In 1988, Chico Mendes had campaigned to save the rain-forests, but farmers near Manaus had murdered him. One man's ecology campaign is the loss of another man's livelihood. Blake had received many death threats, even days before his murder. Those who advocate ecology are unpopular with local communities and big companies. The New Zealander had shrugged off much of the hate mail and cranky stuff that follows most celebrities with his customary robustness. But recent warnings had been sinister and even Blake had been sufficiently concerned to report them, commenting, 'We've always got crank mail but it has been going beyond that recently.'

The Brazilian Secret Services confirmed that they had already been investigating the threats, but as events in Macapá unfolded, it seems that the wishes of whoever had wanted Blake dead had been fulfilled by the hands of others.

The murder of such a heroic figure caught the imagination of the Brazilian people; the public were hungry for arrests. Israel da Costa himself handed the police a vital clue: his finger had been left aboard the boat. When he went to the local Macapá hospital, it was the breakthrough the police needed. He was arrested. A taxi driver then came forward and confirmed that he had been hired to take a group of men to a house in a poor part of town on the night of the murder. He had been paid 40 *reals*, plus Blake's stolen rifle.

Within 24 hours, arrests were made, and in late January 2002, a mere six weeks later, six men charged with robbery resulting in murder went to trial. Throughout, rumours circulated about civil police brutality. A photograph of one of the accused was alleged to show injuries sustained in police custody, intended to extort a confession. It was claimed the prisoner had been handcuffed from hand to foot, causing him to be doubled over. A plastic bag had then been placed over his head and he had been viciously beaten. Tavares, through his lawyer, also publicly declared that his confession had been extracted by torture. The police denied this, but in a surprising comment on a matter attracting global coverage, the Secretary of Justice, Elizabeth Sussekind, confirmed: 'Torture by the police in Brazil is common.'

Da Costa argued that Blake had attacked him and he had fired in self-defence. Tavares admitted firing but denied any intent of killing Blake, and through his lawyer spoke of his grief. Tavares had apparently been a long-time fan of the French marine explorer and conservationist Jacques Cousteau and could not believe he had killed his successor.

Nielson Amaral, the lawyer representing Tavares, prepared the groundwork to keep his client out of jail. In frank public statements, Amaral explained that his client had never had a chance in life. Born into a dysfunctional family where his father had been violent both to him and his mother, he had become addicted to drugs at the age of eight. His addiction had led to a life of theft to feed his habit. At the time of the murder, Tavares was already awaiting trial for another crime.

This is a tale familiar to police in Marbella, Manchester or Milan. Youngsters hooked on drugs are a major part of the crime statistics; kids high on drugs not only steal but are often intensely violent. If what Amaral said was true, then Tavares did not have much going for him in his first 23 years: he was a typical drifter, living from hand to mouth to needle. On that fateful night he was apparently high on heroin and marijuana.

But was it true? Or had Tavares devised this fiction to enable his lawyer to plead for him to be *treated* for drug abuse rather than punished? His cousin, who was sister of another of the accused, Jose Irandir Colares Cardoso, nicknamed *Junior*, had little doubt and came forward. Her portrayal of Ricardo Tavares was very different. She alleged that all three of them came from middle to upper-class homes. Tavares was well educated, making it through to high school and only afterward turning to crime. She painted a picture of a youngster slipping from a prosperous background into the seedy world of drug addiction and theft.

After the murder, Tavares's mother had flown nearly 2,000 miles to Sao Paulo to get herself treated in a clinic, giving the lie to heart-wrenching stories of poverty. Such clinics are exclusively for the moneyed classes. An impoverished family could never even afford the airfare.

The other men accused represented a cross-section, including an electrician, a bricklayer and a fisherman. After the arrests, Blake's team quickly gave their evidence and were released to get on with their lives. The formalities were then adjourned till June 2002, when the gang were convicted. Tavares received over 35 years and five others received between 20 and 35 years. Three other men received suspended sentences.

Santana and Fazendinha, where Blake was murdered, were both, sadly, listed as high-risk ports by the IMB's Piracy Centre. Brazil is dangerous *anywhere* near the conurbations. Corruption among port officials makes combating crime frustrating. Ellen concludes: 'Any master taking a vessel near or into these ports is dicing with death.'

Both Bailey and Blake were fearless, concerned only with saving others. Both dared to take on armed attackers. One won, the other lost. A jammed AK-47 saved Bailey's life but a jammed rifle cost Blake his own. At the Kuala Lumpur Piracy Reporting Centre, Noel Choong added brief details of the two attacks to his weekly reports and annual statistics. The IMO in London did the same—just a record of the cold, hard facts, like thousands of others. Every entry reflects an unacceptable personal tragedy.

Ellen's views apply to vessels of any size. Those chartering a yacht or small cruiser need to take security seriously and have a clear action plan ready if attacked. 'Though many thugs do carry weapons, only the minority of crews get injured. Retaliation, however heroic, is risky.' There are examples where crews fought back and the attackers were killed. But the best advice is to surrender and hope the gang will only rob and then leave. Frank Pentti, from the US Maritime Administration (MARAD), produced guidelines for those under attack. This was his advice: ***DON'T BE HEROIC IF THE BOARDERS ARE ARMED.***

'I do not approve of arming crews save for one caveat,' explained Ellen. 'On small boats around the Caribbean, there have been enough murderous or violent incidents to justify considering self-defence in a dire situation—perhaps to prevent a wife or daughter being raped or killed in front of you. If you are going to carry a firearm, then you must be prepared to shoot to kill. There is no room for any sympathy for an intruder with a gun. If you want to raise the stakes by being armed, then mere wounding is a mistake. During the attack on the Israelis at the Munich Olympics, the German police did not shoot to kill. It was a lesson learned. The American police are trained to shoot to kill.

'Sir Peter only wounded his attacker. It was a big mistake, neither being effective as a deterrent nor a meek surrender. I hope others who sail will get the message. If he had shot the man dead, then the rest might have fled or he might have had to take them on too. The tragedy is that Blake *was* acting heroically, attempting to protect his crew. It sounds harsh to say it, but the unfortunate fact is that if he had not wounded the first gunman but had raised his hands in surrender, in my view he would not have been mown down so ruthlessly. Leon Sefton, who was first confronted on the stairs, surrendered at once and no shot was fired at him. None of the others on deck were shot at till shots were fired down below.

'Conversely, if you do kill an attacker, then don't expect sympathy from the local police. I've come across decent people flung into the local jail for alleged murder, where they suffer intolerably.'

PART THREE
Pleasure Craft

Over the past 10 years, public awareness of piracy has risen dramatically, especially because of the plight of the Chandlers and the movie *Captain Phillips*—both attacks involving the Somalia region and the Red Sea. The dangers of sailing near Somalia and in the Red Sea have been known to the Bureau and the IMO since the early 1990s,but until the nightmare ordeal suffered by the Chandlers, the risks were not taken seriously enough by sailors, politicians or the wider public. Today, any sailor in a small craft trying to navigate through that region is running an unacceptable risk of being kidnapped or worse.

Giant supertankers and even warships get attacked by pirates with rocket-propelled grenades and Kalashnikovs. Small craft like yachts are especially vulnerable. When Ellen created the Bureau, small craft were not its true focus, but the constant influx of data about attacks could not be ignored. Typically, a bunch of youngsters will charter a yacht to sail around the Caribbean for a couple of weeks. They might know how to sail but aren't geared toward security, dozing happily after a boozy dinner as the yacht sways at anchor off some white palm-fringed beach. Few even contemplate actually *keeping watch* overnight.

For local thugs around Antigua, Barbados or Trinidad, they're sitting ducks. Whereas most attacks on moored yachts are motivated by greed, in these waters, rape is also frequent. *Be vigilant* urge the IMO, IMB and the US Coast Guard. Attackers count on surprise. Preventing them from boarding makes the personal dangers far less. Once aboard, what happens next is a lottery. Too many times, holiday sailors have been callously killed.

Ellen recalls the *Comptacenter Challenger* tragedy, where two crew and an elderly American couple were all shot dead while moored off Barbuda. This caused an international outcry, threatening tourism, and the killers were hunted down and convicted. 'Crack cocaine has taken a grip in the Caribbean,' explains Ellen. 'Violent attacks have increased for this reason—but there is another, less well understood, cause of crime down there.' The American Government repatriated some of its most hardened criminals, unleashing them into small island communities without the resources to combat their malevolent influence. This has introduced the vicious underworld expertise learned in American big cities and jails and strengthened the drug trade.

Techniques for smuggling drugs are always changing. As one channel is closed by the authorities, ingenious criminals open another. Yachts and cruisers may still be hijacked for drug-running, especially in the waters southeast of the USA. A favoured ploy around the Bahamas and the Exumas has been for drug-runners to approach an unsuspecting crew and steal the boat. *Without taking prisoners.* Too much is at stake.

These small low-lying islands, where wind-bowed trees and shrubs brush the sandy beaches, are still undiscovered by mass tourism. At night, they are a haven for luxury yachts and cruisers, usually moored in the tiny harbours or sheltered bays on the leeward side. Inhabited or visited by only a few wealthy and scantily dressed people, these secluded islands have proved a godsend to the drug trade and presented risks to the unwary. Narcotics would leave Colombia by air for Panama, Nicaragua, Cuba, Kingston or George Town on the Caymans and then proceed toward the USA by boat, island-hopping via these dots on the map.

For many years, Norman's Cay, about 30 minutes' flight from Nassau and just 200 miles from Florida, was a drug cartel headquarters. The island had been taken over by Medellin Cartel boss Carlos Lehder. His partners were the notorious Pablo Escobar and the Ochoa family. The small island's few residents were *invited* to leave. In their place, a bevy of beauties appeared, ready to entertain the drug barons in the small beachside hotel. Armed guards patrolled the beaches and Dobermans guarded the narrow runway cut from between the trees as King-Air turboprops and old DC3s flew in, heavily laden with cocaine and *Colombian Gold* marijuana. Tons of drugs arrived in large quantities but the cartel would ship them to the mainland or Nassau in smaller quantities so that a boat riding low in the water would not arouse the suspicions of the authorities. The boats used were small cruisers or yachts stolen from harbours or hijacked at sea. A Fort Myers couple were murdered on their pleasure boat close to Norman's Cay island.

This smooth-running racket was dramatically killed off long ago. Despite the huge bribes that had allegedly been paid to the ruling Pindling family in Nassau to secure their silence, the American Drug Enforcement Agency got its way. Norman's Cay was closed down by the Bahamian Government. Carlos Lehder fled. The runway remains today but the small terminal hut is now derelict, still showing signs of the final shootout with the authorities. A crashed DC3, half-submerged in the water just short of the strip, is another lingering sign of the Medellin days.

Ellen warns that, although that time has gone, crews should still be careful. Drug smugglers are at work anywhere in the Caribbean or that part of the Atlantic. 'One technique is for drugs to be dropped into the sea around these islands with pinpoint accuracy. A speedboat or other craft will pick them up. GPS and mobile phones have made this transfer method so much more reliable. Just don't be a witness when it happens.' Death threats are real.

In November 2003, HMS *Manchester*, a Royal Navy destroyer on duty in the Caribbean gave chase to a speedboat and secured a haul of cocaine worth $42 million. The drug-runners also had a craft filled with extra fuel for the voyage. Using a Lynx helicopter to harass the crew with the downdraught from the rotors, they watched as the 42 bales of drugs were tossed overboard. The naval team retrieved the one-ton haul despite difficult sea conditions, but when they tried to arrest the crew, the speedboat escaped to Colombia, where it was found abandoned near a truck with another ton of cocaine apparently ready for transit.

The chance of unwittingly being caught up in a drug transfer cannot be discounted, as I know only too well from an experience when working on this book on Highborne Cay, just a hop from the former drug centre.[3]

Due to UK Government cutbacks, HMS *Manchester* was withdrawn from fighting the Caribbean drug war, but both the American Navy and US Coast Guard are present to keep drugs out of the USA. USS *Stump* had two victories with hauls totalling over $100 million—once in the Pacific and the other off Jamaica. In the latter incident, the crew also ditched the cocaine, some 82 bales, before trying to escape. In the chase, *Stump*'s crew opened fire and disabled the boat by destroying the outboards. Arrests followed.

Pleasure-boat sailors run grave risks in many regions of the world. Off the Indonesian islands, sailors, many of them Australian, have been robbed, raped, murdered or kidnapped and held to ransom. Piracy, sometimes linked to drug-running, is a global problem. Drug-running by sea is widespread and Customs and police fight a never-ending war against professionals or amateurs tempted by seemingly easy money. Scottish police caught a yacht, *Red Scorpion*, with three Dutchmen aboard who were trying to smuggle in cannabis valued at £43 million. Another slick operation in Jersey led to arrests of a team trying to import a record amount of cannabis by small boat.

In Europe, the eastern Mediterranean is the most dangerous. A Canadian moored at a jetty in Crete was attacked by an Italian gang who tried to board, but he beat them off with an oar. They then used their vessel as a battering ram and deliberately slammed into his boat. They were determined to sink her, and positioned their boat to ram again at speed when he let rip with a shotgun. One attacker died. The Canadian was held in jail for nine months awaiting trial, accused of using excessive force. Ellen was most unhappy

---

[3]After a stormy night, I came across a speedboat with powerful twin Evinrude outboard motors beached in a sandy cove. The island's harbour was just around the headland and so it was clear that this discreet bay had been a preferred spot to take sanctuary.

Remembering Eric Ellen's warnings, I was intrigued but wary, especially when I spotted that where tourists would have stored six-packs and food, there were only extra containers of fuel. The boat had been prepared for an especially long journey, typical of a Caribbean drug run. Three fit-looking thugs appeared from the scrubby trees, where they must have been resting. I scuttled away like a spider crab, counting myself fortunate that I had not seen anything incriminating by peering more closely into the boat.

about his treatment. 'He then got bail and asked for my advice. The Italians had past convictions for GBH, other acts of violence and drug offences but were not to be called as witnesses. He was not going to receive justice, yet he had been in real danger of being murdered. I could think of nothing better than for him to skip bail. This he did.'

Corfu, with its usually calm waters and Mediterranean climate, is a popular holiday destination. But Corfu's close neighbour, Albania, is a poor country with a pedigree of violence. Albanians are now probably the most widespread and significant gangsters in the UK. There have been shootouts between Greek Coastguards and Albanian pirates. The charterer of the yacht *Carenia* was murdered off Corfu, one incident among many. Albanian gunmen were blamed.

Attacks on holiday sailors may be opportunistic, sparked off by visitors flashing money and jewellery in local bars. Especially if the tourists appear the worse for drink, locals may later pay them a visit and quickly hunt out their valuables. Another mistake holiday sailors make is to sleep under balmy skies with the hatches open, fondly imagining their boat is as impregnable as Fort Knox. The need to lock doors at night is no different than back home in Dallas, Glasgow or Frankfurt.

The Red Sea and the Gulf of Aden are fraught with dangers for vessels of all sizes. Somalian piracy has substantial links with Al-Qaeda, but the IMB has known for years that a voyage to Mogadishu or Djibouti, its neighbour, was an invitation to be robbed, kidnapped or worse. Somalia is largely ungoverned, its economy woeful. Crime is out of control. For two decades, the IMB's Kuala Lumpur Piracy Centre website has been publishing blunt warnings. Originally, these were on the lines of ***Don't sail within 50 miles of the Somali coast and preferably keep 100 miles away. Use of radio communication including VHF in all these waters should be kept to a minimum.***

Now, using mother-ships, pirates can operate even 500 miles from land. The latest warnings reflect this, as is explored later.

'Nobody in their right mind wants to enter Djibouti,' Ellen says. This explains why over 10 years ago British security agencies stopped and searched the cargo ship MV *Nisha* in the English Channel. Nothing was found. The vessel had been in Djibouti and had then disappeared for a while. The fear was that Al-Qaeda were using it for some terrorist purpose. Djibouti is in a key position close to the Gulf of Aden and opposite Yemen, a country close to the heart of Middle East terrorism. Every ship that uses the Suez Canal heading east or west must pass through the straits between Somalia and Yemen.

In June 2004, the British yacht *Alcor*, which should never have ventured into such perilous waters, was attacked off Somalia by nine armed pirates. They approached in a fishing boat, waving in a friendly manner but, when close, opened fire with machineguns. The yacht's crew were armed and returned fire, forcing the gang to retreat. Quickly, the yacht hauled anchor and sailed away before the pirates could return with reinforcements.

'It really is vital to know who you have aboard,' explains Ellen. 'We've had examples of yachts being stolen by a stowaway. Before sailing, the vessel should be thoroughly searched as a matter of routine. Most people won't bother—and will get away with it. But others will be awoken at sea to find a gunman leaning over them and the nearest land miles away. The stowaway, acting perhaps on orders from a drug cartel, will commandeer the vessel. The owners will rarely survive. A tragedy which could have been prevented by the simple precaution of checking the boat before casting off—yet people won't do it.'

The lure of the sun, excitement, and an easy life attract many young people. They join a crew, sail to another port and then move on. They come and go, drifting aimlessly from place to place, bumming rides or working their passage as crew—usually harmless and a lot of fun. But some of them are criminals waiting for the right opportunity to mutiny. They hang around bars in small ports like St John's or English Harbour in Antigua, keeping their ears to the ground, putting it about that they are looking to join a crew—and of course, something always turns up.

Once at sea, they make their move, taking over the boat at gunpoint, perhaps as another boat draws near. The real sailors are robbed, probably murdered, and a new crew are then put aboard from the support craft. The yacht or cruiser is then available for the drug trade, or renamed and sold. The lesson for yacht-masters is to verify the reliability of the crew before sailing, especially checking out any last-minute additions or changes. Such a precaution can save lives.

Only a minority of vessels get attacked, but because of the sheer numbers of holiday sailors, the tally of victims is worrying. Adverts for exciting boating vacations in exotic places will hardly draw attention to the downside. The Bureau and the International Maritime Organisation try to keep these crimes in the public mind; greater understanding of the genuine risks would mean less crime.

Small boats at sea provide the ideal context for murder. Proving murder when one of two people on a boat claims the other was swept overboard is difficult. Ellen has come across a number of examples where he was convinced a crime had been committed but had no sufficient evidence to lay before a court. Crimes in international waters are always costly to investigate. If there is a seemingly credible explanation for *man overboard*, the file will quickly close. Only if there is careless talk or there are other clues, such as motive, will boating accidents be treated as possible murder.

In one example in the Indian Ocean, Alan MacLean, a young Scotsman, had been enjoying a carefree existence in the Seychelles. He now wanted to reach Egypt at the northern end of the Red Sea, so he joined the *Correlation*, a yacht skippered by Frenchman Philippe Sorel. This seemed an odd choice, since, on a previous voyage from Australia, the relationship between the two men had been stormy. During one bitter altercation—possibly over drugs, according to a third person aboard—MacLean had locked himself in his cabin.

This time around, the 43-foot yacht was headed for Aden, sailing through waters known to be infested with Somalian pirates. There were three aboard—Sorel, his Moroccan mistress, and MacLean. According to Sorel, the boat was attacked by pirates. Men armed with Kalashnikovs came aboard, forcing the three to take refuge below decks. MacLean grabbed his didgeridoo (*yes—seriously!*) and rushed onto the deck, swirling it to confront the armed pirates.

The likelihood of a pirate attack was real enough, yet the story sounds weird and improbable. MacLean was shot and killed by a Kalashnikov. The attackers left. Sorel cleaned up the boat and buried MacLean at sea, apparently because of the speed of decomposition in the tropics. What Ellen finds odd is that pirates in this region would not usually murder just one of the crew, as allegedly happened. With little fear of being arrested and tried, pirates here murder at the drop of a hat. Why allow the victims to live to tell the tale? They are simply murdered and dumped overboard.

The Yemeni authorities investigated inconclusively. A further report highlighted the absence of any traces of blood or bullets. Sorel retorted that he had cleaned up the mess; he denied that he had delayed in reporting the murder. The IMO's investigators put Sorel back under suspicion. The results of a French investigation, launched because the ship was French-registered, have not been made public.

Ellen's warning about knowing your shipmates is too easily ignored! Alan MacLean is far from the only sailor to die in curious circumstances. All too often, the sea buries its secrets.

CHAPTER FIVE

Shipping Fraud of the Century? -The *Salem* Scam Unravelled

Piraeus, Greece, 1979

Though it took place over 30 years ago, this crime is so fascinating that the story still intrigues. The *Salem* fraud has been called the shipping crime of the twentieth century. Most shipping crimes never make the front pages, but for months the twists and turns of this drama about the giant supertanker captured the public imagination.

To understand how this audacious fraud came about, some background is needed.

With so much of Greece comprising small islands dotted about the Aegean and Ionian Seas, it is not surprising that the Greeks have a strong maritime tradition. One quarter of the world's shipping is Greek-owned. Ships may be managed from London or New York, registered in Panama, Liberia, Honduras or Cyprus, but the underlying ownership is indisputably Greek.

The Greeks' unparalleled maritime reputation is matched only by their renown for shady dealing, usually at the expense of London insurers. Over the past 50 years, reports about Greek shipowners have featured accounts of sharp practice, outright crime and ferocious double-dealing. The epicentre of this particular crime was Piraeus, the port of Athens, but the ripples were felt thousands of miles away in London, Rotterdam, Africa and the USA. Piraeus is always noisy and vibrant, bustling with freighters being loaded and passengers disembarking from cruise ships and ferries. In summer, temperatures can soar to 100 degrees, and the swirling dust and pollution from trucks make a cool beer in a dockside bar a welcome relief.

The *Salem* affair was like a kaleidoscope, its shape always changing. The International Maritime Bureau had yet to be formed—indeed, this fraud was the catalyst that speeded its creation in 1981. To investigators from the FBI, Interpol and national police forces, the *Salem* case was like an onion: there always seemed to be another layer to peel away. The full story may never now be known, so devious were the criminals, so contradictory were their actions and explanations. They forged a plan so subtle, so full of complexities, that even now the truth lies hidden. If the result was not a total triumph for the criminals, then the stolen multimillions must have been some comfort to the masterminds who escaped scot-free. Their identities are still not spoken of publicly, but Eric Ellen, who then played a central role as Chief Constable of the Port of London Police, has a pretty shrewd idea of who was behind the plot. *Knowing* and *proving* are frustratingly different!

Some of the greatest personalities in the world of shipping have been Greek. In the second half of the twentieth century, wealth, women and wheeler-dealing had led to bitter rivalry between two tycoons: Stavros Niarchos and Aristotle Onassis. At one time related by marriage, the contest between them for domination of world shipping and the tanker market filled the gossip columns. The deaths of Onassis and Niarchos spelled the end of an era of glamour, intrigue and wild parties. Dynasties like theirs with enormous wealth, a reputation for living on the edge and abuse of power grew up around Piraeus and among the tiny Greek islands. The supremacy of the inner circle of powerbrokers was known in the media as the *Piraeus mafia*. The tiny island of Chios, a mere dot on the map measuring 14 square km, produced tycoons like the Pateras, the Laemos and the Hadjipateros. Their names may be less familiar but their power and influence was immense. Other small islands—Andros, Kassos and Ithaca—have bred over a hundred families who have made Greek shipping the power it is.

For the mightiest magnates—Niarchos at his peak, or Latsis—life involved constant travel. They might be at home on private strongly guarded islands only a flight away from the mainland or aboard their yachts—floating palaces bearing little or no resemblance to sailing boats where the crew duck heads to avoid the swinging boom! Onassis too luxuriated in these blue waters, his yachts as big as cruise liners, helicopter pads and all. In the state rooms, champagne and Beluga caviar were served on ice. The barstools, covered in the foreskins of whales, would be brushed down in readiness for guests who, when regaled about this feature, squealed and squirm with delight.

In Onassis's heyday American presidents like JFK and Nixon enjoyed the high life in this fairytale world of fabulous wealth along with

Hollywood stars like Marilyn Monroe, Frank Sinatra, Elizabeth Taylor and Grace Kelly—all pampered even beyond their expectations. The wedding reception of Prince Rainier and Grace Kelly was held aboard the Onassis yacht. Having met Onassis through her late husband President Jack Kennedy, Jacqueline Kennedy herself eventually married the tiny but charismatic billionaire.

In 1979, when the *Salem* plot was being hatched, the dynasties of Onassis and Niarchos dominated the tanker market. Others had acquired large fleets but none could match them. Around this part of the Mediterranean, knowledge of loopholes in insurance practice or having valued shipping contacts were worth their weight in gold. Whether in bars along the quay, in colourful cafés offering the morning's catch, or in state rooms furnished with precious metals and objets d'art, people planned and plotted. In an industry where the concept of integrity was unknown, Interpol and insurers were objects of scorn.

Around Piraeus, shipping agents could hire crews from a smorgasbord of crooked mariners ready to steal cargo or secretly scuttle ships that had become a liability. Perhaps a vessel was due for an expensive inspection or had become uneconomic. *Sink it and send the bills to Lloyd's of London!* Specialists could sink a ship without trace, the maritime equivalent of *convenient* fires in the North London rag trade. But activities went far beyond scuttling. Diversion of valuable cargoes to small, secretive ports where they could be sold was another lucrative pursuit in the placid azure waters of the eastern Mediterranean.

Poorly paid crews could earn generous sums for risking a voyage on a vessel they knew would never again reach port. For these so-called *scuttling crews*, the risk of being arrested was negligible. Lloyd's Marine Insurance Market in London had too rarely undertaken more than superficial investigations. They might *suspect*, but suspicion counted for nothing. Hard evidence was needed to call wealthy and powerful policy holders to account.

In 1979, despite this volume of criminal expertise, nobody had ever tried to scuttle a supertanker. But there were those who were ready to accept the challenge. The audacious notion of tackling something so huge with such mind-blowing financial profits acted like a magnet on the criminal mind. Just as the arrival of the Boeing 747 represented a watershed in aviation, the launch of the first VLCC tanker was a milestone. These *Very Large Crude Carriers* ranged from a *mere* 200,000 tons up to 350,000 tons. To the public, the Boeing 747 became the *jumbo* and these crude carriers became *supertankers*.

Seamen hang about on the Piraeus waterfront, sipping ouzo, watching football or eyeing up attractive women, like a row of taxis waiting to be hired. They have no sense of direction till *an agent* hires them, perhaps to sail to Harwich with a legitimate cargo or to man a ship bound only for the bottom of the sea. In turn, that agent is without direction until hired by somebody else, an owner or charterer of a ship needing a crew to take a ship from Trieste to Singapore or from Piraeus to Le Havre. Piraeus has plenty of agents awaiting instructions to supply a crew.

If the owner wants a *scuttling crew*, he knows which agent to contact. But the identity of *the owner* is more elusive—and this vagueness underpinned so much maritime crime. The true owner sheltered in anonymity behind a shield of secret offshore companies, obscure trusts, discreet lawyers. These companies or trusts had nominee directors, nominee shareholders and local laws guaranteeing that the true owner's name remained concealed. Back then frauds like this were so much easier, but despite so many reforms to achieve transparency in commerce, opportunities still exist for the cunning.

Most ships are owned by reputable companies like Maersk, Carnival or Evergreen. Transparency abounds and the ships, as assets, appear on the balance sheets for debate at the AGM. At the other end of the spectrum are the singletons, where an owner has a single vessel, or perhaps many vessels but each hidden in a separate offshore company—one company, one ship. Before 11 September 2001, Intelligence agencies reportedly suspected that Osama bin Laden's Al-Qaeda network owned more than 20 vessels. But the shipping owners' register would hardly have read: '*O. bin Laden Esq. c/o The Caves, Tora Bora, Afghanistan.*' With the passage of time, doubts have grown that bin Laden in his lifetime ever possessed such a fleet.

In 1979, money laundering was rife. Little effective legislation was in place for another 10 years, when governments started to tackle the flow of hot money pouring through these anonymous corporations. It took 9-11 to accelerate much more stringent but not foolproof controls. In 1979, bulk oil was a buzz commodity. Producers from OPEC nations had recognised their power to earn millions by controlling oil production. Prices spiralled. Ownership of oil cargoes changed hands in rapid wheeling and dealing, even during transit from the Gulf states to Europe or the Far East.

The world had become a giant monopoly board where speculators could make a quick buck by buying cheap and selling on a rising market. Timing was everything. In this market, some wealthy Greek businessmen, specialists in tankers and the oil business, found the challenge of stealing a *basic* $50 million (hundreds of millions in today's money!) irresistible. Once the idea had been formulated, they used their knowledge about chartering ships, offshore companies and Swiss bank accounts to their advantage. Such was the audacity of their plan that it is almost inconceivable that anyone other than *Piraeus* insiders could weave a web of intrigue like the dramatic *Salem* affair.

Eric Ellen has no doubt that *the mastermind* behind the plan was Greek, but three or four powerful figures well known around Piraeus were also involved, each a specialist in one essential area. Bar talk suggests each man put up $250,000 to finance the crime—pin money to shipping millionaires. However, these men were shadowy figures, staying in the background, careful to keep a distance between themselves and the dirty work. The front man, or, as some would say, the *fall guy* was American.

Fred Soudan was smart enough but in shipping matters he was an inexperienced babe in arms. He would take the rap but he did not have the experience to dream up the plot or the essential contacts, nor did he understand the oil business or have the knowledge about how and where to buy and sell ships and their cargoes. That was the stuff of small talk in Piraeus.

Soudan was born in Lebanon in 1943, a beautiful country still struggling back to normality after years of civil war. Soudan had matinee-idol good looks, charm and an easy manner. Once an American citizen, he lived near Houston, Texas, a city synonymous with the oil industry. In the '70s, though, he was a life insurance salesman with an attractive Spanish wife and a longing to get rich quick. Did Soudan, who had no real money, really wake up one morning and announce to his startled wife: *Honey, I won't bother selling insurance today. I'll buy a supertanker for $12 million and fill it with oil, steal the cargo and then scuttle it?*

When the frauds were later investigated, Soudan's fingerprints were over everything. If, as the prosecution and media proclaimed at the time, he was *the* mastermind, he did nothing to cover his tracks—quite the reverse! Everything seemed to point toward him, suggesting that the real conspirators were happy to let him take the rap. Fred Soudan was not *the* mastermind. He was not even in the inner circle.

In 1979/80, South Africa's apartheid policy meant that most countries treated South Africa as a pariah, especially in terms of import and export. Sanctions in force forbade OPEC members to supply oil. An embargo can be an entrepreneur's charter to riches. The oil embargo was a severe but surmountable problem for the South African Government. The main inconvenience was that sellers, knowing that South Africa was desperate for oil, extracted what could be politely called a *premium* on top of the current spot price—virtual extortion. The South African Government encouraged both illegal exports and imports, ignoring inconvenient details; the end justified the means. Indeed, the Government passed a harsh confidentiality law concerning international transactions so that sanction-busting could not be publicised in the media.

Soudan formed a company in 1978 called American Polomax International, with premises in Houston on Bel Air Boulevard.. The idea was to jump aboard the oil bandwagon but it was not his own idea. In 1979, he bought a dormant Liberian company, Oxford Shipping, from a New York company called Northern Ships Agency, owned by two Greek-Americans, John Avgerinos and Andrew Triandafilou. Their future role was to be crucial.

Soudan had approached them in his search for a ship. However, they decided they could not regard him as a serious buyer of a supertanker. Instead, they sold him Oxford Shipping as a company that could be used for ship ownership—if he were ever able to afford it. Control of Oxford Shipping was vested by shareholding in American Polomax, his company.

But Soudan could not meet the sellers' terms—he had difficulty even raising the funds to buy this shell company, let alone a ship. He needed time to pay and had little choice but to confide in the sellers. They saw at once that he had devised a potentially lucrative plan and decided to turn it to their own advantage. As astute businessmen, they negotiated a high price for the shell which had neither assets nor liabilities.

Under clauses 3 and 14 of his legal agreement to buy Oxford Shipping, payment was deferred and the share transfer would only occur on payment. The way matters later developed, these clauses proved critical. Payment would be due on or about 27 December 1979 on the sale of oil in South Africa. If the oil sale proceeded, Soudan owed $300,000 and the controlling shares in Oxford Shipping would become his. If the deal failed, then the shares became his for only $25,000. Until then, the attorneys for Northern Ships Agency would hold the shares for safekeeping.

Between close friends, terms specifying an illicit delivery to South Africa would have been unwritten. Plainly, in this case, neither side trusted the other to that degree. Their written agreement was to prove crucial. There were so many vested interests, so many different versions of the truth, from conspirators, governments, oil companies, shippers, their agents and crew that it is impossible to be sure of the facts. As with the assassination of JFK and the death of the Princess of Wales, truth and perceived truth have become blurred. History has been rewritten, tracks have been covered. An insurance salesman in Houston might have been aware of an embargo on trade with South Africa. Whether Soudan would have known how to *supply oil secretly* is doubtful. He must have been supplied with insider information.

One man who did understand the oil business was Dutchman Anton Reidel. He was based in the important Dutch port of Rotterdam, central to the import of Middle East oil into Europe. Reidel, in his mid-40s, had long operated on the fringe of shipping. Mature, suave and well-dressed, he commanded respect. Although described as a broker, he had no *known* connections with oil trading. However, in the circles he moved, he could well have picked up tales of easy money from oil sales to South Africa.

Cigarettes, alcohol and duty-free goods were Reidel's stock in trade, and the Dutch authorities suspected him of conducting borderline illegal operations. One unsubstantiated claim suggested that he had been convicted of smuggling in Naples. As an intelligent man who lived by his wits, Reidel played an important role in the conspiracy, but whether he knew the identities of the principals is unclear.

How did an insurance salesman in Houston chance upon a cigarette broker from Rotterdam—both wanting to get rich quick? Possibly Reidel and Soudan's paths had crossed at some point over dealings in cigarettes. Or perhaps somebody facilitated an introduction? If so, it was probably a Greek, Captain Nikolaos Mitakis, who ran an agency in Piraeus.

At a meeting in June 1979, Mitakis had offered Reidel six oil cargoes of 200,000 tons each—with the added bonus that, through some deft sleight of hand, it could go to South Africa. Reidel had been quick to seize this potentially lucrative opportunity; he tried unsuccessfully to place the oil himself in South Africa.

Insofar as Soudan and Reidel became a team, Reidel was the senior partner. He had brought Soudan into the project, an alliance of convenience rather than friendship. Reidel regarded the grand design of the oil sales to South Africa as his own, because Mitakis had approached him, but he had failed to clinch a deal, where Soudan later succeeded.

Somebody must have prompted Soudan to chuck insurance selling: that someone may have instigated the meeting. Reidel knew enough to be able to convince Soudan that there was huge profit and nothing illegal in a deal to provide South Africa with much-wanted oil. Following his conversation with Reidel, Soudan acquired Oxford Shipping, the preliminary step toward ship ownership without money.

In October 1979, Soudan flew to South Africa to meet two people *apparently* previously known to Reidel who could open doors in the South African oil business. Another version claims that Soudan acquired his contacts through a meeting with a British trading agent called John Day, who in turn introduced him to a Parisian trader, an acquaintance of Jim Shorrock, a South African commodities trader.

Soudan lied to Jim Shorrock and the other South African, Jack Austin, telling them he was in the oil business. He explained that he owned an oil refinery in the USA and owned or had access to millions of barrels of Middle Eastern oil, on the precept., 'If you are going to lie, make it a big one!' When, years down the line, Soudan was eventually brought to justice, the American prosecuting attorney quipped: '*The only petroleum he owned was in the tank of his car*!'

Whoever arranged the introductions, Shorrock's wife then contacted the crude oil manager of the Strategic Fuel Fund Limited (SFF), an oil-buying agency for the South African Government charged with the difficult task of outmanoeuvring the oil embargo. She informed them, in good faith, that Soudan owned available oil.

The door to a confidential oil deal was now open. Shorrock and his wife had completed their immediate mission. Now it was up to Soudan. He had no oil, no ship, no money and no oil refinery. He owned the right to the name Oxford Shipping, but not the shares. But to fulfil his burning ambition to become a millionaire, Soudan *only* had to sweet talk the SFF into clinching a deal to sell them oil he did not have. A meeting was arranged for 15 October in South Africa at the SFF offices in Sasolburg.

Soudan, in debt, even using borrowed money for his airfare, naturally presented himself as a man of substance rather than an impecunious chancer. Soudan could spin a yarn. When he met the top SFF representatives, including Fanie Naude and Jan Bredenkamp at their headquarters, he told them he had six shiploads of crude oil available, an interesting number for various reasons.

The SFF had cultivated a reputation as a combination of the CIA, FBI and KGB rolled into one. Their public image presented a standard uniform—khaki safari suit with short trousers, comb in left sock and a line of pens in the top pocket! Perhaps Soudan's salesman's patter helped him captivate the SFF top brass with details of the Dallas-Fort Worth Oil Corporation (which, naturally, he owned) and of another Soudan-owned refinery in Louisiana. His problem, so he explained, was that he had bought *too much* oil for his refineries to process, hence he was in a position to offer them the surplus. This could be delivered in six shipments of 200,000 tons each. From each shipment, he would retain 10% to go to his own refineries so that the 90% imported into South Africa would be concealed.

They had swallowed the bait. Now for the tricky bit: Soudan needed to get them to part with the money to buy a ship; he had no money to buy even a rowing boat, let alone a giant tanker. Ironically, there he was, sitting in the SFF boardroom, boasting to the meeting about his wealth, yet he needed their money to buy a boat. In his elegantly cut suit, crisp shirt and tie, he certainly *looked* the part of an oil tycoon.

So, Mr Soudan, as a man of substance, with your own refineries and millions of barrels of oil in the Middle East, how come you've got no money to buy your ship?

Soudan was well prepared for the question.

My money's all tied up in the oil. And at this time, my own tanker has engine trouble. I want to be sure I can deliver on time.

He glossed nimbly over his lack of a vessel to their satisfaction. Now for the big one. He needed to get their money to buy a supertanker. Payment in advance for the oil would have suited Soudan. He would then have the cash to buy the ship. Cheekily, he put forward the wholly fantastic proposal that they should pay for the oil upfront. The South Africans politely declined, despite the fluency of Soudan's shtick. After more discussion, a solution was found. Naude and Bredenkamp agreed to issue a Letter of Credit for the first shipment. It would be due on delivery of the oil. No doubt Soudan's heart fluttered at this moment. While not as good as cash, a Letter of Credit from the SFF would give him credibility with a local bank, who otherwise would have laughed at a request to borrow $12 million to buy a ship. Supplying 200,000 tons of oil to a blue-chip buyer was a good point of reference. He was nearly there.

The next day, supported by the Letter of Credit, Soudan, with Austin and Shorrock, struck a deal with MercaBank in Johannesburg to lend him $12.3 million to buy a ship and sufficient fuel for the trip. Reimbursement was to be made directly by SFF from the cost of the oil due to be delivered on or about 27 December in Durban. That guaranteed source of payment was crucial.

In this agreement, negotiated by Soudan, Reidel's name also appears as an authorised signatory in dealings with the bank. However, Reidel and Soudan's relationship had been growing cooler, even though Soudan's smooth talk had set up a hugely profitable deal. Reidel may have felt uneasy that Soudan was becoming so central, while he himself was becoming marginalized.

The price for the oil was $34.70 per barrel, making the deal worth $43.4 million. The South Africans must have been delighted by the price. It was lower than the going spot price! The oil business, hugely profitable for those who succeed, breeds hard men. The SFF usually paid *more* than the spot price; they were, in a word, held over a barrel. Soudan was offering a real bargain.

Why didn't alarm bells ring then? Shouldn't the South Africans have been suspicious when an American tycoon offered fuel at *discount* prices in an overheated market—especially when the overall circumstances of the deal were rather odd? Evidently, they were unconcerned; no status checks were made.

Soudan's gamble that they would not check up on him had paid off! The South Africans were in no position to be too pernickety in their choice of contracting partners. Law-abiding companies and individuals would not deal with them because of the embargo. No doubt Naude and Bredenkamp reasoned that Soudan would not be paid until the oil was delivered. So there was *no risk*—or so it must have seemed.

Soudan's trip to South Africa had been full of champagne moments. Buoyed up with his own importance, he began to throw his weight about. Reidel was resentful. But Soudan had won a huge contract to deliver 200,000 tons of oil to Durban. He had an unsecured loan to buy a ship guaranteed by the South Africans. Buying a ship was the next item on his agenda, but time was short—delivery was due on 27 December.

Until one has seen supertankers at close quarters, it is hard to envisage their bulk. *Salem*, built in Malmö, Sweden, in 1969,was a vessel of 214,000 tons. She was over 300 metres in length and 25 metres in height. She could travel at around 13 knots. Her shortcoming was that she was powered by a steam turbine driving an increasingly outmoded single-screw propeller, making her costly to maintain and operate.

Salem was 20 times bigger than most of the cargo vessels referred to in this book. In 1969, when launched, she had been a striking example of the trend to build giant ships for bulk carriage of goods. Her first name had been *Sea Sovereign* but she became the *South Sun* in 1977 on change of ownership. The buyers, Pimmerton Shipping, then chartered the ship back to the previous owners.

In 1979, Pimmerton decided to sell, perhaps because *Salem* was costly to operate. Soudan first tried to charter the ship from them on a *bareboat* basis. A bareboat charter can be compared to a long lease of a property. The vessel is still *owned* by the same person or company but the ship is used by the charterer as if it were his own. The owner may not see the vessel again till the charter ends, maybe 15 years or more down the line. Equally, the owner is not responsible for how the ship is used. The charterer assumes all responsibility; he hires the crew. He also has to keep up the payments to the owner.

No sensible owner would lease their valuable home for 20 years to a stranger without being sure of the person and their ability to pay. Pimmerton was wary of a bareboat charter with a person like Soudan who had no track record in shipping circles. Oxford Shipping was an asset-free zone providing little reassurance.

The risk was unacceptable.

Pimmerton insisted Soudan buy the vessel outright. Their stance worked. Soudan was desperate: the ship needed to be loaded and in Durban by 27 December, and so on 29 November 1979 Oxford Shipping purchased *South Sun* for just over $12 million using MercaBank's money. The name was changed to *Salem*. Now a new figure appeared on the scene: the mysterious but influential Bert Stein.

Who was Bert Stein? Soudan later claimed he had never met him. But, even if that were true, there had to be some link between them. Oxford Shipping entered into a *bareboat charter* with Stein, or more accurately his Liberian company, Shipomex Management, which then hired the crew. In return, Oxford would receive $285,000 per month for the charter, signed by Stein and also by Wahib Attar, a relative of Soudan's who was acting as his lawyer. Attar never met Stein, and Shipomex's office in Zurich was no more than a brass plate with a telex.

At the end of November, Shipomex took control of *Salem* in Dubai. A bareboat charter leaves an owner vulnerable in one way but protected in another. He has no management role. Oxford Shipping now had no direct control over the vessel but was at risk if the monthly payments were not made. Soudan was unconcerned about that because Stein was part of the team, providing a useful buffer between Oxford Shipping and anything that later occurred on *Salem's* voyage.

Whatever he knew of the planned sanction-busting in South Africa, Soudan's Oxford Shipping was now legally distanced from it. Where the vessel went was at the (apparent) whim of Shipomex. If Stein had declined to carry the oil, Soudan could not have protested. It is plain that Soudan, Reidel and Stein all knew just what was going on.

Where did Stein get the funds to pay $285,000 per month? For starters, he was not Bert Stein. His passport was a fake. The British and Greek police were later satisfied that Stein was probably a Frankfurt businessman called Locks, although he denied this. The photo on Stein's passport appeared to be of Locks, a man with abundant fair hair and glasses. At the Zurich offices, the photo of Locks was later identified as Bert Stein.

Other suggestions are that Bert Stein was never just *one* person but that various people used this name to fulfil different functions. People who claimed to have met Stein gave graphically different descriptions. That could be because they had met different people or because they wanted to add to the confusion. A Greek court later actually convicted a man called Thomas Jürgen Locks on the basis that he was Stein, but in his absence.

Shipomex already had a crew lined up for *Salem*. Earlier, Stein had *chosen* Mitakis, the Piraeus agent, to hire the crew. Who told him to appoint Mitakis will never be known, but Mitakis was a wise choice for the shady dealing to come. As usual, the key players were all making the right moves, dancing to the tune of their unseen puppet masters. Mitakis is the *one man* who probably knew *at least* one man who was pulling the strings: the *person* who had nominated him. It was not Reidel, Locks/Stein or Soudan.

In his sleazy circles, Mitakis enjoyed a reputation as a wheeler-dealer. His love of the sea and shipping had led to a successful career on the Piraeus waterfront. Now in his middle years, he was sunburned with wide eyes and a helmet of silver hair. When later interviewed on the BBC Panorama programme, he appeared evasive and an inept but profuse liar. Despite the conventional appearance of his shipping agency operations, vessels he was involved with seemed to have an uncanny knack of suffering mishaps at sea—a track record that qualified him for the *Salem* plot.

A long-time Piraeus insider but certainly not one of the principals, Mitakis was hired to obtain the oil, to find a willing buyer for it and to supply a crew. From his busy, untidy office overlooking the docks at Piraeus, he achieved all these goals. Indeed, he was in the odd position of having organised a *suitable* crew even before the *Salem* had been identified. This was because a previous attempt to fix a vessel had fallen through.

Stein had met the senior officers during the hiring process. As the would-be charterer, this was reasonable but knowing the *right* officers for the project was critical, and here Mitakis's experience came in. The sea was his life, either aboard ships or operating his agency. His contacts were endless and he knew the special qualities the officers would need. As master he selected Captain Dimitrios Georgoulis.

By now, the vessel had been lawfully registered in Liberia as *Salem*. The change of name and control were duly recorded, but the Liberian Registry made no inspection of the vessel. At the time, Captain Alister Crombie was Deputy Commissioner-Marine Safety for the Liberian Registry, based in the USA. 'I had been in office for about a year or so,' Crombie, who had been a Trinity House Pilot before joining Liberian Services, recalls. 'On the Register then were all kinds of vessels and owners, some of which did not appear to be sound business. I had started a clean-up operation. I was trying to ensure that vessels using our flag were inspected as part of the registration process. This would have ensured a better standard of vessels and crew.

'*Salem* was registered without any knowledge on my part and there was no inspection. The purpose of an inspection is to check seaworthiness and to check on the crew and in particular the senior officers. Had an inspection been made, we would have declined to accept the registration because Captain Georgoulis had no licence to sail such a vessel.'

Such an inspection would not have prevented the fraud. The gang would merely have approached another flag-of-convenience Registry eager for fees. So long as owners can register their vessels in Registries with little interest in anything but the dollars earned, vessels that are unsafe or operated by unqualified crews will sail on.

Georgoulis and his crew made their way to the United Arab Emirates to join the supertanker. The master, aged 43, had a pleasant elf-like appearance with small, deep-set eyes and a full pointed beard. Forty-two Japanese crew left the ship but only 24 Shipomex crew, Greeks and Tunisians, plus perhaps a wife or girlfriend, arrived in Dubai to take over. The departing sailors watched them arrive and noticed something odd. *The new crew seemed to be travelling very light. Where were all the usual personal items that a crew takes aboard for a long trip?*

In December 1979, for Soudan, matters were forging ahead on all fronts. All that was lacking was a cargo of oil, but he knew that was in hand. The only unresolved issue was his increasingly uneasy relationship with Anton Reidel. From underdog, he had become topdog through his success with the South Africans and Reidel found this hard to take. As yet their mutual distrust had not manifested itself in any damaging way, but it would soon take a sinister turn.

To bolster his own status in Johannesburg, the Dutchman was cosying up to the SFF. Aware that through his relationship with Mitakis he could get five more cargoes, he wanted to ensure that he would not be side-lined by Soudan. In commerce, there is often friction when one middleman wants to guard his contacts and claim ownership of exclusive deals. Jealousy seems to fatally cloud their judgement.

Mitakis was Mr Fix-It, but he needed frontmen like Reidel and Soudan for the SFF deal and to purchase a ship. Such was his own dubious reputation in Piraeus and even in London that Mitakis could never have bought a ship for himself and expected to get insurance cover. Furthermore, he had no experience or credibility in selling oil to the South Africans (nor, of course, had Soudan, but that had not prevented him from inventing an impressive CV for himself!)

Allegedly involved with Mitakis in selecting the crew was a Greek shipowner called Gregarios Makrygiorgos. He too had a questionable past, especially as the owner of the *Alexandros K*, a vessel that had been engaged in fraud; its master, the same Dimitrios Georgoulis, was later convicted and sentenced to four years imprisonment. Mitakis later pleaded that it was *Stein* who had suggested names for the crew, including Captain Georgoulis. This appears highly unlikely. It is easy to blame a fictitious person, especially one not present in court.

It was certainly *desirable* to distance oneself from a master like Georgoulis: he had commanded three other vessels in what bore all the hallmarks of shipping crimes. Though he denied any wrongdoing, he was later convicted for his part in one fraud. His Liberian master's licence was also invalid and he held no licence under Greek law.

To choose such an unqualified man as the master of a supertanker was such crass negligence that it must have been deliberate. Georgoulis had never been in charge of such a huge vessel; hiring a captain with no relevant experience and no licence would have been unimaginable in a legitimate shipping business. His qualifications lay solely in his aptitude for crime.

Other crewmen hired include a Radio Officer, Vassilios Evangelides, who had served aboard another ship, the freighter MV *Brilliant*, that had got into distress and then sunk in curious circumstances after a belated distress call for help. Two other senior crew hired were Chief Engineer Antonios Kalamiropoulos and a Chief Mate nominated by Mitakis, Andrea Annivas.

The involvement of a shipowner like Makrygiorgos in hiring a vessel in which he had no apparent financial interest is noteworthy. The true extent of his involvement will now probably never surface. In the subsequent Greek prosecutions, he was charged but acquitted. Was he one of the masterminds, yet only charged with a walk-on part? There is insufficient evidence to substantiate any allegations.

Mitakis had represented to Reidel that he could access six cargoes of oil. Now it was time for him to deliver. Deadlines were pressing, especially because of the hiccup over the first ship selected. One obvious way forward was for Mitakis to buy the oil, but there was a snag. Buying oil means *paying for it*. Far better to let *somebody else* buy the oil!

Telling reputable brokers that he represented the ship's managers, Shipomex, Mitakis explained that he had a tanker looking for a cargo of oil, preferably from Saudi Arabia—a term stipulated by SFF in the deal with Soudan. Why the SFF wanted Saudi oil is unclear. Both Saudi Arabia and Kuwait had agreed to an embargo against South Africa.

The brokers identified Pontoil, a major force in the market. This large Italian company needed some *Kuwaiti* oil to be shipped to Italy. Soudan was asked to assist. The glib salesman persuaded the South Africans to waive the Saudi clause. To meet the deadline, he told them, delivery would *have to be* from Kuwait. His excuse was *overcrowding and delays* in the Saudi port. The deal was struck.

Soudan, through Oxford, insured *Salem* for $24 million and she sailed from Dubai to Mina-al-Almadi in Kuwait, where she took on 196,232 tons of light crude oil on 10 December. The paperwork was completed. The Bill of Lading was signed, confirming the oil was aboard.

Pontoil, the owners of the insured oil, were to take delivery in Genoa. Mitakis, Reidel, Soudan and Stein knew better. Captain Georgoulis had his instructions: deliver this huge cargo to Durban—in short, steal it. No doubt Mitakis looked across the port from his Piraeus window and imagined the supertanker slipping away, exulting that his part was done: he had delivered, got them a ship and cargo with no financial outlay, and provided a scuttling crew. Now for the big payday! Nothing could go wrong now!

As the ship sailed down the east coast of Africa, there were two developments, one planned, one unforeseen. The sanction-busting crew painted over the name *Salem*. She was now the *Lema*; no official paperwork was filed. This was just a *lick of paint* job. The second development was *seemingly* unexpected.

Eric Ellen has studied the oil dealings. 'Shell had been interested in chartering *Salem* before Pontoil came on the scene and so had a previous interest in this oil,' he commented. 'In negotiations with Mitakis, Shell even persuaded him to load the ship in Kuwait rather than Ras Tanura in Saudi Arabia. Then, just when the deal was advancing well, Shell backed off, but then once the vessel was at sea, they decided to pay much, much more to Pontoil for the same cargo.'

Selling a cargo of oil at sea is commonplace. In the overheated oil market, Shell was short and paid top dollar—$56 million for the entire cargo. Pontoil had paid $30 per barrel and sold for $40 within days. In later court proceedings, it was alleged (under cover of legal privilege against defamation) that Shell *must have known* that this oil was always heading for Durban and that is why the company paid such a high price for it. Shell has always dismissed this theory, claiming they planned to deliver to France. No convincing evidence of complicity against Shell was found.

As Christmas approached, the *Lema* dropped anchor over a mile offshore from Durban and was moored to a buoy used by Shell and Mobil. The Durban port authorities knew better than to subject paperwork to undue scrutiny. The Bill of Lading showed that SSF was buying the oil from owners called Beets Trading, a company owned by Reidel in Switzerland. On the Bill of Lading, there had been an amateurish attempt by Reidel to exchange the names of Pontoil and Beets—explainable, allegedly, because the true owner would not want to be seen to be delivering to South Africa, even assuming that Pontoil had not sold on to Shell.

The paperwork was superficially in order and probably consistent with a regular *modus operandi* used to bust oil sanctions. Reidel himself always maintained he had no intent to deceive and thus no criminal offence was committed; in other words, the alteration was not *to deceive* the SFF but *to assist* them.

Beets Trading was a shell company (having no assets or liabilities and little more than a registered name) established by Reidel in Zug, Switzerland. In English the name chosen seems an ironic play on words: Beets Trading could mean *it beats working as a trader*! This deal certainly did! Stealing and then selling Shell's oil for over $40 million was a classic heist.

Shell naturally knew the tonnage of oil aboard *Salem* and its likely position at sea, yet their suspicions were not raised when a vessel with a similar name—*Lema*—and an identical quantity of light crude oil dropped anchor at Durban. Ironically, the company involved in the secret discharge operation at Durban was none other than Shell! Furthermore, Shell then actually purchased some of the oil via SFF!

These coincidences were certainly sufficient to enable a lawyer to draw the court's attention to Shell's involvement, but no evidence of any crime has ever surfaced. It remains an amusing twist that Shell, in discharging the oil, were helping to steal *their own cargo* destined for France. More twists in the Shell story only came to light over 10 years later.

On 2 January 1980, having offloaded nearly all the oil, the *Lema* sailed from Durban. After another quick paint job, she was renamed *Salem*. Only 15,000 tons of oil needed for the next part of the plan remained aboard. A supertanker riding high in the water heading round the Cape and up the west side of Africa would have attracted immediate attention. Vessels heading to Europe are invariably fully laden. To conceal the cargo theft, seawater was pumped in as ballast. Even then, her height above the water was later to arouse suspicions.

Discharging had lasted several days, but at last Soudan could now buy the shares in Oxford Shipping. Shell's cargo had been stolen. SFF had its oil as promised by Soudan and had paid $43.5 million to a Reidel bank account called Beets Trading in Switzerland, less the $12 million or so due to MercaBank for Soudan's loan repayment.

Oxford Shipping now owned the vessel free of the loan, but Soudan had still to pay Northern Ships Agency in New York for the shares in the company. Until the shares were his, Soudan had no claim to ownership of the vessel. Payment for the shares to the two American-Greeks at Northern Ships became his urgent preoccupation—turning, indeed, into a dangerous obsession.

From the Beets bank account, Soudan was due a fee of $4.5 million—a hefty sum, but over $30 million was payable to others wittingly or unwittingly engaged in the crime. The *Salem's* crew had to be well paid for their role and their silence. Another $3 million left the Beets account to pay commissions to Austin and Shorrock, the South African middlemen; $8 million went to secret bank accounts in nominee names in a number of jurisdictions.

The identity of the ultimate beneficiaries is not known, although Soudan's $4.5 million was one of the transactions. Others may have included Makrygiorgos and Stein/Locks. Reidel's own money went as well even though he controlled the account. This was to prevent anyone trying to recoup the money later.

After these transfers, there remained a balance of some $20 million in the Beets account. Ellen had no doubt that the money went into the account of a man seemingly called *Nicholaus Trilizas* on 29 December 1979, but the name was false. The American FBI, in their investigation, used fingerprint evidence to identify *Trilizas* as none other than Nikolaos Mitakis. But he did not keep it. There were others behind him wanting their cut.

Within two weeks, the Trilizas account had been emptied, the money moving on in three separate tranches, destinations unknown. The principals got their generous cut, a good return for putting up $250,000 each. Perhaps even Mitakis himself did not know to whom he was sending the money. The recipients were concealed behind numbered or nominee bank accounts in various jurisdictions.

Someone made a vast profit, but it was not Soudan. Had Soudan conned his way into getting a bareboat charter from Pimmerton he would perhaps have been due an extra $12 million rather than having to buy an unwanted vessel. As it was, he had to pay Northern Ships urgently to get ownership of *Salem* in order to get a bigger share of the profits.

Mitakis, when he was later prosecuted in Piraeus, played what lawyers call the *violin defence*—ill health and poverty—but it seems certain that his central role earned him a generous cut. He admitted he was Trilizas and that he had received $20 million, but he gave no evidence as to how that sum had been divided. He was no doubt well rewarded for his inability to identify anyone.

As soon as the *Lema* had discharged the oil, Soudan owed $300,000 to Northern Ships Agency in New York for the shares. It should have been a simple matter: he had the money now. But the already uneasy relationship between Soudan and Reidel now exploded. At the very moment when the two men had just gained enormous wealth from stealing oil belonging to Shell, their behaviour was absurd. They were rich, even without further deals. Instead of celebrating and working together for the next deal, mistrust consumed them. Their moment of triumph was also the moment of their greatest folly.

On 28 December Soudan phoned Northern Ships about the payment. *No pay, no shares, no ship*—a powerful incentive for urgency! Triandafilou, one of the directors at Northern Ships, stalled, suggesting Soudan phone again in the New Year. However, each subsequent attempt to make contact failed. Soudan, already suspicious that he was being given the run-around, panicked. His was not a happy New Year. He was worried sick. As the days passed, his fury grew, sure he was being double-crossed.

In desperation, he spoke to the lawyer for Northern Ships, who was holding the shares pending payment. There was no good news. 'You're too late to pay now,' he was told. 'Your rights under the agreement have expired.' In horror at being duped by Northern Ships, Soudan complained to Anton Reidel, his co-conspirator. Presumably, he expected a sympathetic ear for his complaints about the agency and its directors.

But far from it. Reidel claimed *he* had now paid $300,000 to Northern Ships to buy the shares—presumably because Soudan had failed to pay on time, despite his best efforts! Soudan suddenly realised how he had been neatly shut out. Reidel could now claim ownership of shares and thus of the *Salem*.

Reidel and Soudan, who had cleverly enriched themselves with a stolen cargo of oil, now fell out over ownership of a ship that legally should have belonged to Soudan. Was it pre-planned, or a spur-of-the-moment double-cross?"

Salem was now on a voyage to nowhere, apart from the bottom of the Atlantic, the remaining part of the scheme to conceal the theft of the oil. Did Soudan intend to benefit personally from the planned scuttling by making an insurance claim for $24 million? Or did he know nothing about it? Did he believe that what was supposed to have been his ship was to be used in further deliveries to South Africa? Was he expecting to earn a tidy income from the monthly charter payments from Shipomex—assuming that the elusive *Bert Stein* paid up ?

His next actions strongly suggest that a red mist descended over Soudan's eyes. He retained New York lawyers, who issued proceedings against Northern Ships for an injunction to prevent them transferring the shares to Reidel or to anyone but him. Taken alone, that does not sound too foolish. The problem came when affidavit evidence, sworn testimony given in written form, was needed.

Recklessly, Soudan produced his contract with Northern Ships. The document was both his trump card and the joker in the pack! It proved he could buy the shares for $300,000 after the sale of the oil but it also revealed the conspiracy to steal. Clauses 3 and 14 confirmed the plot to divert the oil to South Africa! Soudan's publication of this evidence was to blow everyone out of the water, not just himself.

Refusal by the judge of an injunction on this evidence was not an option and so Soudan won—a Pyrrhic victory. On these applications, the court only decides whether the *status quo* should be maintained pending a full trial. Soudan had not won the war; he had prevented it from being lost. The real court battle was set to resume later.

It seems crazy that Soudan pressed the *self-destruct* button or that he and Reidel let the fact of the South African delivery become a matter of public record! After the decision, much too late, both men seemed to recognise that a damage-limitation exercise was essential. Despite their mutual mistrust, they settled their differences in New York on 11 January as the *Salem* ploughed on through the ocean off the Cape of Good Hope, heading north up the west coast of Africa.

Soudan got his 500 shares and ownership of *Salem*, but at the cost of revealing the crime in court documents! The sweetener in the settlement for Northern Ships was a clause whereby both Reidel and Soudan agreed that Triandafilou and Avgerinos would receive a further $300,000 on each of the five further oil runs the Salem would make! Northern Ships, being ignorant of plans to scuttle *Salem* any day now, must have thought this a fine deal. But were *both* Reidel and Soudan laughing up their sleeves? Did they *both* know *Salem* was to be scuttled? Or did just one of them know? Or did *neither of them* know that ,at that very moment, Captain Georgoulis was training his crew for the sinking?

Why did Soudan think it was worth pressing the self-destruct button? Did he believe he was going to remain the owner of *Salem* for further trading even though he had never paid for it? Was ownership part of his reward? Did he believe *Salem* was going to make further voyages? Did he know nothing of the scuttling crew hired by Mitakis? How did he think the theft of the cargo could be concealed once the vessel reached Shell in France? Or was the vessel, in his mind, bound for Houston?

Perhaps both Reidel and Soudan knew about the planned sinking but had underestimated the furore it would cause. Soudan always maintained he wanted *Salem* for further lucrative voyages. Though Soudan always denied any such knowledge, he was later to be convicted of knowing of the plan to scuttle. So had he planned to claim on the over-insured hull? Had that been the attraction for Reidel too? Soudan later maintained that he had always planned to conceal the theft, but not by sinking. How did he expect to conceal it? There were only 15,000 tons of oil aboard. The truth of who knew what about the scuttling lies somewhere in the complex relationship between Soudan, the Dutchman Reidel, the fictional Bert Stein and the wily Greeks.

Subject to any arrangement Soudan had made through his company with any of his co-conspirators about division of its value (presumably none at all), he had an asset worth $12 million. Oxford Shipping could sell it or borrow against it. But scuttling the ship to conceal the crime had the big attraction of opening up an insurance claim for $24 million for a hull for which only $300,000 had been paid. Or so it seemed. Insurance would not prove the goldmine Soudan naively believed—or was led to believe.

To add to the confusion about exactly who knew about the scuttling is that, just too late, Soudan did in fact seek a mortgage from a Houston bank, secured on the ship. Reidel's actions had queered the pitch for Soudan, because the news that *Salem* had sunk beat him to the bank. Had he got there in early January as owner, he would have got his loan and thus cash well before the scuttling.

The shenanigans in New York had caught the attention of Frank Wiswall, at the time Admiralty Counsel to the Bureau of Maritime Affairs for Liberia and President of Liberian Services. *Whatever was going on, it seemed to him to make no sense*. Whatever it was, he did not like the look of it.

'I was so concerned and intrigued by this dispute,' explained Wiswall, 'that I sensed something strange was happening. So I phoned my colleague Alister Crombie and asked him to keep a special watch on events with *Salem*.' Wiswall, an eminent global figure in shipping laws, laughs at his foresight. 'Alister Crombie did not have long to wait, and neither of us could have missed what happened just a day or two later.'

Experts can calculate in a few seconds how long a vessel like *Salem* should take to travel 8,500 miles from Kuwait to Senegal, West Africa. At a steady 13 knots, this was a journey of 27 days, yet the *Salem* had already taken about 38 days to reach the deep Atlantic waters near Dakar, the capital of Senegal. A cover story was needed to conceal the lost days while the ship was discharging the oil in Durban—time Captain Georgoulis had personally spent rather comfortably, meeting people and making telephone calls, while based ashore at the Royal Hotel Durban.

During the later BBC Panorama investigation, he denied he had even been ashore, despite being confronted with his signature in the hotel's guest-book. The wife of another crew member whom he had sent home had been at the same hotel! Despite his shifty denials on camera, it seems conclusive that he was there.

Georgoulis and his senior officers planned to explain away the lost days with a story of maintenance trouble. The Liberian Bureau of Maritime Affairs later investigated and found that Georgoulis had to report when his vessel passed both Cape Town and Gibraltar, a normal procedure. The day before reaching Cape Town, the vessel had reportedly developed a leak 'in the tubing in the port boiler.'

Such a problem is repairable, and the Chief Engineer's team apparently set to work. The Liberian investigation discovered that the repairs took 15 days at sea because the Chief Engineer claimed to have found three leaks. Reportedly, it was not until 14 January that the ship could even get up to 12 knots. During the works, the port boiler had to be shut down and the ship operated on reduced power. Whether *in fact* the ship was deliberately marking time is unclear, but it seems a racing certainty.

This suggests that *Salem* was dawdling after 2 January, perhaps awaiting further instructions about scuttling. The wrangling between Reidel and Soudan was a needless sideshow. It must have ruined any plan to sink the vessel as soon as it reached West Africa, where it was due to arrive while their dispute was still raging. Dawdling would be consistent with more than one factor, not least an intention on the part of Soudan to approach a Houston bank for a loan. Perhaps both Reidel and Soudan had made a deal with their Greek co-conspirators that they could borrow against the ship before it was scuttled in deep Atlantic waters. If so, Reidel's attempt to damage Soudan was an aberration. Regardless, the ship was sunk before any loan was obtained.

A plausible explanation is that, because of the lawsuit, the masterminds agreed to delay the ship until credibility was threatened or their time or patience expired. They may have been thoroughly exasperated at the squabbles in New York. Indeed, if they found out, as they may have done, that Soudan had disclosed the South African involvement, they would have been justifiably furious. That sworn evidence meant they would all be suspected of being party to the crime of scuttling.

The Atlantic Ocean on the tanker route off Senegalis vast, often seemingly empty, and, at around 4,000 metres, far too deep at that time for any attempt to be made to examine sunken evidence, though later this was unsuccessfully attempted by the Liberian investigators. Taking to a tiny lifeboat in preference to remaining on a comfortable ship that towered high above the ocean with a deck long enough to use as a runway as a desperate measure. With the threat of mountainous seas and the potential of not being rescued, it is unsurprising that the crew wanted every safeguard. Captain Georgoulis, for his part, wanted to make the operation as foolproof as possible.

Ordinary human greed was responsible for the failure of the operation. While the crew prepared to abandon ship at one of the deepest parts of the Atlantic, the seeds of their downfall were sown. In a *genuine* disaster, such as the *Titanic* or the cruise ship *Costa Concordia*, which struck rocks off Italy in 2012, or MV *Sewol* in which around 30 youngsters died off South Korea in 2014, getting people into lifeboats as the ship starts to sink is not easy. Those aboard the MV *Estonia* had the same problem. With no power or lights, a ship starting to plummet bow first like the *Titanic* or listing dramatically like the *Costa Concordia* or *Sewol* creates confusion, terror and pandemonium. 'Even abandoning a genuinely stricken cargo ship is no orderly disembarkation,' explains Ellen. As it lists or starts to sink, lowering the lifeboats and getting all the crew into them is fraught with peril. Abandoning a supertanker that has truly suffered explosions and is perhaps blazing like an inferno from end to end is a fearful prospect.

A *scuttling crew* want the best of both worlds: to *appear* to have been panic-stricken but actually keep risks and discomforts to a minimum. If the South African part of the plans rated ten out of ten for organisation, the scuttling rated more like zero. So many mistakes were made that the truth about the scuttling *and* the South African oil deal were revealed. Other oil tankers and cargo ships had regularly slipped secretly into South African ports. Details of those deals never became public knowledge. Diversions to the beleaguered regime had functioned well because *genuinely owned cargoes* were delivered. However, Soudan and his associates had sold *stolen* oil. Soudan always maintained that he thought *Salem* would sail to Corpus Christi, Texas, where the missing 196,000 tons would be concealed by a deal at a friendly refinery. How that fits in with Shell expecting delivery in France is impossible to reconcile.

Another curious fact was that spare parts for the vessel had been ordered for delivery to Texas. Was this a clever ruse by Soudan, or did he genuinely believe the ship was going to Texas? To Ellen, it seems more likely to have been window-dressing. A scuttling in deep water, if well executed, was a realistic option to conceal the crime.

Soudan and possibly Reidel might well have believed that after a scuttling, extracting insurance money from Lloyd's underwriters in London would be easy. Far from it. 'The chances of getting money from Lloyd's for the insured hull value were unrealistic,' Ellen continues. 'The Greek end would have known that. Captain Georgoulis had no licence to command a supertanker. Moreover, he had a dubious reputation. He was the marine equivalent of a learner driver! 'Insurers would have refused to pay out.

After rounding the Cape and sailing northward through the steamy tropics, the *Salem* passed Liberia, home of more ships' registrations than any other. The officers, if not the crew, knew *Salem* was registered there. Sinking the tanker close to Monrovia, the capital, would be foolhardy. Rescue, when it came, would probably mean being taken to the homeport—a place with legal jurisdiction to hold searching enquiries and to prosecute. If the crew were held for interrogation, they feared Liberian prisons would be stinking, filthy and dangerous.

So they sailed on until they were so far north that any rescue ship was unlikely to take them to Monrovia. But the Nigerian port of Lagos was scarcely more attractive, having a reputation for violence and corruption. At that time, demands for bribes and shipping frauds involving cement were rife. Even if there were no *legal* grounds for holding a crew in Nigeria, Georgoulis would not have wanted to risk being slammed even temporarily into some dreaded Lagos jail.

Dakar or Banjul were better options. Banjul, formerly Bathurst, was the capital of the Gambia, a former British colony. Dakar, the very cosmopolitan capital of Senegal, previously French, was even better. Besides, the Atlantic off Senegal is especially deep. These considerations probably went through the minds of the conspirators on land and sea. The charade of the alleged 15 days of engine-trouble to conceal much more than the Durban delay strongly suggests that Georgoulis was killing time, probably awaiting instructions to scuttle after the lawsuit was settled on 11 January.

Arranging a scuttling of a tanker is complex. Georgoulis needed to keep the crew onside. One of the Tunisians had heart trouble and at least one other was reluctant. Agreeing to join a *scuttling crew* for $10,000 in cash may seem fine in the comfort of a dockside bar. But when the moment to abandon ship approaches, some will have second thoughts.

A *sudden* sinking of a full oil tanker is not possible. This ship was quite full, although mainly with seawater. Taking on *more* water will not send it rushing headlong to the bottom. The ideal method is to reverse the pumps. Instead of pumping out water, water is taken on to flood the engine room. If the crew are safe, the quicker the ship can disappear the better—so long as rescue is on the way. Freighters with an engineroom well below decks and close to the stern will sink quite rapidly if flooded. The *Salem* was a different proposition, and Georgoulis had never scuttled a ship before. It proved harder than expected. What he achieved was a triumph of ingenuity but still not worth the fees, perhaps running into six figures, that he and the engineer probably received.

The sinking of the *Salem* was neither slick nor dignified. Since leaving Durban, the Chief Engineer and the master, the key conspirators aboard, had been planning the method and orchestrating the crew's cover stories. The Japanese sailors who had left the ship after its previous voyage had thought the new crew had come aboard with remarkably few personal belongings. This, in retrospect, was a clear pointer that the new crew knew they were on a voyage to nowhere, although Georgoulis denied this in court.

The crew gave various fictional explanations. Just before dawn, they told their interrogators, there was an explosion. At 0355 am, the fire alarm sounded, waking Georgoulis in his cabin. Naturally, he had rushed to the bridge to take command. There, he had heard a muffled explosion. The crew claimed this was in the pumproom and had caused water to be taken aboard. Georgoulis told the Liberian investigators that, in the early morning light, he had seen smoke coming from the bow of the ship some 300 metres in front of him.

Captain Alister Crombie later led the team of three investigators. Georgoulis was asked whether the smoke was black or white, or perhaps grey. He wasn't sure. Chief Engineer Kalamiropoulos gave contradictory evidence: he told Crombie that when he was woken by the explosion, not only was it still dark but it was still dark when the ship was actually abandoned. Sunrise some 90 miles out from Dakar was at 0626 local time. Clearly, Georgoulis had foolishly invented his story.

The fiction continued. The Chief Engineer reported that when he dashed to the engineroom, he found the First Assistant had stopped all power on his own initiative, without orders. If anyone expected dramatic details to be forthcoming—this unfortunate man being terrified, blackened, burned or deafened by an explosion so loud that it had woken others far above water level—they would be disappointed. The Chief claimed he was told there was water ingress to the engine room from the forward section, where a bulkhead divided the pump room from the engines.

After a hurried visit to the bridge to report the problem, Kalamiropoulos raced back below. The situation in the engine room was dire! He reported to Georgoulis that, although all available pumps were working, the battle was being lost—the water had risen by a metre in his brief absence. The master feared further explosions and decided it was hopeless—the ship was doomed. To save the crew, he gave the order to abandon ship.

The crew took to the lifeboats. As dawn broke (but in darkness!), the crew huddled in the two lifeboats close to the giant hulk, surrounded by empty ocean. Georgoulis and Kalamiropoulos were in one lifeboat with nine others, while the Chief Mate commanded the other with ten men. To their horror, as they bobbed not far from their monster ship, it continued to tower above them: *Salem* showed no signs of sinking.

According to the officers, it had been impossible to grab the vital ship's log in the emergency...yet the Chief Mate had conveniently managed to salvage all the essential passports. As he told investigators, he had gathered these in readiness for a bunkering stop at Tenerife in the Canaries! The explanations about the log and passports just did not ring true.

In 1975, Radio Officer Evangelides had been involved in the previous loss of the cargo vessel *Brilliant*, where calls for assistance had been curiously disputed and delayed. Evangelides now said his mayday distress call positioning *Salem* 120 miles southwest of Dakar had produced no response. He claimed he had then put out further distress calls from the lifeboat, which was distinctly improbable. The last thing the crew wanted was to be rescued while *Salem* was still afloat.

Nobody answered their alleged calls for help, and still the tanker stubbornly refused to sink. Fortified by endless rounds of sandwiches, the crew sweltered beneath the tropical sun, temperatures soaring to over 30 degrees centigrade. The boat was crammed with their *packed* suitcases and personal belongings, wholly inconsistent with a terrifying order to abandon an exploding oil tanker in the middle of the night. Had there been explosions, the crew would have abandoned ship in haste, leaving behind clothes, family photos and other personal effects.

Day became night. Night became dawn. It was now 17 January—nearly 24 hours later and still the 212,000 ton vessel refused to surrender. The official investigations proved that parts of the ship's frame had been removed to flood her but the officers had miscalculated how long it would take.

Crombie remembers visiting Lloyd's Register of Shipping to retain experts on scuttling. They confirmed how difficult it would be to sink a vessel like *Salem* just by flooding the engine room. Their opinion was that 'in no event could the vessel sink without substantial flooding of her *cargo* tanks.' But these were allegedly full of oil destined for Shell. This expert opinion uncovered the lies of the officers, who had persistently denied ever stopping at Durban. The storage areas, allegedly already filled with oil, had to be flooded to capacity to sink the ship.

Crombie decided to investigate elsewhere. 'These experts told me that in *their* Registry, their interests were in keeping ships afloat, not in deliberately sinking them! So I contacted Captain Alec Thompson, a Senior Superintendent at Gulf Oil in Houston. This friend permitted me to recreate a sinking of a supertanker like this one. I borrowed a stability book and managed to achieve a *scuttling* by pressing up the cargo tank and by opening up the main circulation system into the engineroom. The process involved opening an inlet with a wheel valve at the bottom of the hull towards the stern.

'I was surprised to be able to achieve it but when I did, it was a very slow process, with the stern sinking first.' Sadly, Crombie was never asked in court about his tests. Court reports from Houston show that his calculations on how the vessel sank were produced during testimony and were described as *impressive*.

Clearly, the master and Chief Engineer had expected the ship to sink more quickly. As it was, they could have stayed aboard safely for a further 24 hours. Around dawn on the second day, as they sat reclined among their televisions, transistor radios and other salvaged personal items, the young sailors must have realised that their payoff was not easy money. Those in the lifeboat who were asleep at four a.m. on 17 were apparently awoken by yet another explosion. The master reported to investigators that the navigation lights then went out. *Salem* was in darkness.

On the second day, the rising sun revealed a most welcome sight! The stern was sinking at last—but as the fiery sun rose over Africa, they saw a much less welcome sight. Rescue was at hand, but it was premature—they did not need rescue until *Salem* had sunk. From the vast Atlantic, a tanker, MV *British Trident, was* approaching. She had been cleaning her tanks when an officer on watch had spotted the *Salem*, obviously distressed, though he had heard no distress calls. *British Trident's* Radio Officer eventually got a response from the lifeboat. Evangelides had been cornered. He had no option but to respond. For the first time, he used the radio transmitter.

A few hours more and the *Salem* would have been on the ocean bed. Some very suspicious seamen were watching from *British Trident*, puzzled by what they saw: the rescued crew were all dressed in civilian clothes and had suitcases. They looked more like a group going on a charter-flight holiday than distressed sailors who had cheated death on an exploding tanker.

A month later, junior members of the crew were interviewed by Crombie with an interpreter. The crew's version of events was lurid—they spoke of flames, of smoke and fire in the bow. Yet when *British Trident* drew near, there was no sign of fire nor of structural damage. *Salem's* Second Mate described a 'great explosion' at around 10:00 a.m. on 17 January. None of the crew of the *British Trident* witnessed this.

Aboard *British Trident*, Captain Robert Taylor reported how at 10:50 a.m. on 17 January, *Salem* was first sighted and seen to be sinking by the stern. Taylor was a highly experienced mariner, a soft-spoken Ulsterman in his 50s who had seen a thing or two but nothing quite like this. *His* ship had taken the initiative of trying to make contact. Eliciting a reluctant response from the lifeboat had taken 20 minutes. Presumably, Georgoulis had been hoping that if no request for help were broadcast the British tanker would speed away. Such hopes were dashed as the *Trident* approached and rescued them from the water, still close to the abandoned ship.

Only after Robert Taylor's crew had ample time to study the ship did *Salem* tilt ever sharper, the bow rising from the sea, before slipping backward under the surface on its 13,000-foot dive to the ocean bed. The crew and their belongings were taken to Dakar. While they were there, *somebody* from Greece arrived and paid them off in cash bundles. All but two were then permitted to leave Senegal and flew back to Europe. Only Georgoulis and Kalamiropoulos remained. They were wanted for questioning by the Liberians. 'We were angry and disappointed that the crew were able to leave Senegal. It left us without key witnesses for the type of show trial that we at Liberian Services wanted to put on,' said Crombie.

The loss of *Salem* on 17 January 1980 was the first loss of a supertanker, and it was big news. In the case of a hull insured for $24 million with a cargo worth $56 million, the need for investigations was urgent. Reports of such a giant ship exploding and sinking with a valuable cargo of Shell's oil hit headlines far beyond the simple entry in the Daily Diary kept at the Lloyd's Building in London. Insurers, cargo owners, lawyers, brokers and investigators swung into action.

Besides the US-based Liberian team, the FBI, Scotland Yard, the Dutch police and the Greek authorities all had an interest in seeking the truth. Eric Ellen, too, was quickly involved. The media portrayed him as the central crime-buster, which put a few British noses out of joint. A young *Daily Telegraph* journalist, Barbara Conway, asked for his views on *Salem*. He obliged with a controversial headline-grabbing opinion. Conway's story brought her the *Young Journalist of the Year* award. 'From that moment onward,' Ellen says, 'I became pivotal in media eyes on the issue of maritime crime, something that did not endear me to some of my professional colleagues at New Scotland Yard. They were doing the slog of detective work while I was epitomised as a central figure.'

David Bruce at the London offices of Liberian Services interviewed the crew of *British Trident*. Captain Taylor had ordered an inventory of the items found in the lifeboats. 'There were 151 unusual items rescued from the ship, irrespective of the suitcases,' said Eric Ellen. 'No wonder Taylor was suspicious of what Georgoulis told him. He and his officers saw no massive oil slick. The 15,000 tons deliberately left aboard may have created an *illusion* of a major slick, but nearly 200,000 tons of escaping oil would have covered the ocean for miles and created a pollution disaster. Besides that, valuable navigation equipment like a sextant had been saved, as had paint brushes, a pair of crowbars, screwdrivers, wrenches and some hose clips. Even a grapefruit knife had been rescued! It was all absurd—unthinkable! Following a fire or explosion on a tanker, escaping with your life is the sole priority.'

This jackdaw's nest of trinkets had probably been pilfered in anticipation of the scuttling. Georgoulis should never have permitted this. It was a cardinal error. Perhaps his previous ventures had made him overconfident. He had certainly underestimated Captain Taylor's thoroughness.

As for Soudan, until the sinking, he had a good track record as far as the South African SFF was concerned. That the oil he was selling had been stolen from Shell was still not known in early January when Soudan negotiated with SFF about delivery of another six cargoes. Reidel did not feature in Soudan's plans; their New York litigation was rumbling on. But once the sinking started to look like a scuttling, no doubt the South Africans got the wind up. It was now clear why the oil had been so cheap! In March, detectives from Scotland Yard had evidence that *Salem* had stopped in Durban. Their travels took them to Switzerland and on to South Africa, where they received no help from the authorities. Requests to see documents were refused. Officialdom closed its doors on an unsavoury episode. The Scotland Yard team were even suspicious of all things Liberian—'even of the Liberian Investigation Team,' recalls Crombie.

London solicitors representing hull insurers had also been at work gathering evidence. One crew member described how large plates and manhole covers on deck had been removed to enable water to flood the engine room, though Crombie knew that this alone could not have scuttled the vessel. The ship's cook, denying any knowledge of an impending scuttling, let the cat out of the bag: He said: '*I was unaware of any planned sinking. The only odd thing was when I received orders from the bridge not to bother cooking dinner but just to make sandwiches. I only saw the reason for this when I was sitting in the lifeboat eating them!*'

Theoretical expert evidence of how the ship had been sunk was now supported by actual testimony of pre-planning. Then matters moved on apace: the fateful New York affidavit about the intention of selling oil to South Africa came to light, despite the confidential terms of settlement. Once it was proved that the cargo had been stolen, the motive for the scuttling was clear.

Soudan denied knowing the oil was stolen. He could properly deny having any control over his ship, as it had been chartered to Shipomex. But faced with his sworn affidavit, he could scarcely deny sanction-busting. The document was a severe embarrassment to the South African Government, which did not relish the global headlines. But there was another aspect that must have constantly bugged Soudan, besides regretting his affidavit. As the months rolled on, he never lodged an insurance claim for the hull. Oxford Shipping had paid a large premium, but an insured event had allegedly happened while the vessel was under the control of Shipomex, for whom he was not responsible.

Soudan, not for the first time, was caught between the devil and the deep blue sea. An honest owner would immediately put in a claim. Failure to put in a claim would make him look guilty of complicity in the scuttling. But that presented a problem: criminal charges for attempted fraud on underwriters could only arise if he were involved in the scuttling plan *and* if he made a claim. In London, underwriters, police and brokers watched and waited in vain. No claim came.

Despite no fraudulent claim on hull insurance, Scotland Yard obtained warrants from the Guildhall in the City of London for the arrest of Soudan, Reidel, Johannes Locks (alias Bert Stein) and Captain Georgoulis. The allegations involved conspiring to scuttle the ship and conspiring to dupe such UK persons as might use the vessel for the carriage of oil. There is one additional noteworthy aspect to the warrants. Besides also naming Beets Trading, Oxford Shipping and American Polomax as parties to the second charge, the warrant alleges a conspiracy with '*other persons*.' No doubt the British police had in mind the secretive *masterminds*, but they had insufficient evidence. The proceedings never went further, as the defendants avoided arrest by staying out of the UK. Perhaps this suited Scotland Yard.

Beating sanctions had been crucial to South Africa, but how they did so was so confidential that publication of details was a criminal offence. An excellent investigation of *Salem* had been made by Jeremy Paxman for the BBC Panorama programme in 1980. Some insurers then invited Ellen to go to South Africa to show this programme and to lecture on maritime crime. He got permission from both the South African Embassy and the police.

Following his presentation, there were newspaper headlines and an uproar! The Minister denied Ellen had any permission and the Vice Squad were ordered to seize the film. At the time, Ellen was still a Chief Constable and supporting a stand against organised crime. Despite assurances by friends in the South African police that there would be no problem, he had copies made of his letter of consent to broadcast and escaped from Johannesburg to the country for the weekend. But on his return he surrendered the film to the police and left the country. The pressure was just too great.

'Back in London, I protested about my mistreatment and obtained a breakthrough: if I went back and repeated the lecture, the Pretoria Government would admit its role. I agreed but on the precondition that they would give evidence and cooperate in any subsequent prosecutions. Scotland Yard and other investigators had not got the help they needed there. I kept my part of the bargain, but when evidence was needed from South Africa to support prosecutions, especially in Holland and the USA, they still did not help.'

In South Africa, as the unpalatable truth became public, the SFF were floundering. The team saw themselves as something like an intelligence agency but now they did not look very intelligent at all. Apartheid had left the Government in Pretoria with few friends internationally, especially in the media, so when Shell started legal proceedings in London concerning the theft of its cargo, journalists everywhere sharpened their pencils with relish. Techniques for sanction-busting had become big news globally, although censorship had prevented South Africans from knowing the truth. Those troubled days were recalled by a local lawyer who still preferred anonymity. 'We once ran a different legal claim over an oil spill from a tanker *that was not there* during discharge of a cargo *that did not exist* into oil tanks *disguised as sand dunes*!'

Stealing a cargo was one way to break sanctions. However, a more usual way was to choose an OPEC member with a *flexible approach*—a nation that *publicly* upheld sanctions while secretly doing what was best for itself commercially. Assuming that paperwork showed 20 tankers had been filled with 200,000 tons of oil, if in fact there were a 5% shortfall in delivery on each one, another 200,000 spare tons would then become available to go on a 21st vessel. This secret hoard pilfered from other buyers never passed through the exporting nation's books. This and other schemes involving the transfer of oil from one ship to another undoubtedly happened.

None of this public scrutiny was helpful to the South African Government. It made securing further shipments that much harder. Ellen produced a book and pointed to a marked paragraph. 'These words of Rudyard Kipling have always served me well. I use them when educating people about fraud:

I keep six honest-serving men

They taught me all I know
Their names are What and Why and When
And How and Where and Who.

'If the South Africans had applied Kipling's words, they would not have fallen for a conman. They ended up the losers because they had to pay Shell over $30 million damages on top of what they had paid for the oil.'

In their English High Court lawsuit, Shell claimed $56 million from Lloyd's for the money paid to Pontoil but gave credit for the damages paid by the SFF. The proceedings started in February 1981 and Shell won the first round on the interpretation of the policy. The claim went to the Court of Appeal, where the senior judge was none other than the Master of the Rolls, Lord Denning. Arguably the most distinguished English jurist of modern times, he and the two other sitting judges were unanimous: Shell *lost* on policy interpretation and were not entitled to recover from Lloyd's. They ruled that the insurers were liable to pay only for the oil *still on board* when the *Salem* was scuttled, not for the oil discharged in Durban.

Shell appealed to the House of Lords, the highest court in the land. At that time, there was an uneasy relationship between the Court of Appeal and the judges in the House of Lords. Legal observers sensed a readiness to overturn decisions from Denning's court because too often he had tried to achieve *justice* (the right result) without due regard to the law of precedent that governs the English legal system.

But Shell's hopes were dashed. Portraying Shell as the innocent victims of fraud cut no ice. The House of Lords upheld the decision of Lord Denning's Court, leaving Shell with a black hole in its accounts.

In South Africa, the costly fiasco simmered on even through the 1990s. Questions were then raised in their Parliament. The performance of the Strategic Fuel Fund came under particular scrutiny. Whistleblowers emerged. Allegations of corruption and incompetence were rife and mainly wide of the mark, but with apartheid over, there were still old scores to be settled. Scapegoats had to be found. The spectre of *Salem* resurfaced from the depths of a murky past that many would have preferred forgotten.

Despite the disclosures during the 1990s, full details of the South African role have yet to emerge. A probe by the then-minister, Penuell Maduna, into *post-1992* SFF operations led to the Fund's chief, Kobus Van Zyl, being suspended and subsequently fired in circumstances that were to cause public concern. Initially, it was said that there were some 180 allegations against him, including fraud. Nearly all the allegations were groundless. However, this serious attack on a senior figure included a reference to *Salem*.

Maduna claimed a report he had commissioned into the affairs of the SFF would "embarrass" certain people. Addressing Parliament, he quoted from a handwritten note written in October 1994, 14 years after the sinking, by Kobus Van Zyl to Roy Pithey, CEO of the Central Energy Fund. The 'John Drake' referred to was CEO of Shell South Africa. As reported to Parliament, it read as follows:

> 24/10/94
> ROY. *Salem.* We (Shell and myself) had agreed on the following:
> 1. They will write you a letter explaining the matter. This letter will be hand-delivered.
> 2. We will then advise them what to do with the money. In view of transparency, we must find a way which will not disclose the origin of the money.
> 3. We again agreed on secrecy. No one will disclose anything.
> 4. If you agree, we can inform Minister Botha. He can then thank (or whatever) John Drake over the telephone. Nothing in writing. In doing it this way, Shell gets acknowledgement from the top that we have the money, but we do not have to disclose the origin in the books.

Anyone reading this note is bound to be intrigued by the cloak-and-dagger dealings at such a high level. What did the handwritten letter *explaining the matter* actually say? Why was this so secret that an acknowledgement of receipt of the money had to come from Minister Botha? The inference is that a large sum of money was to pass from Shell to SFF, since the matter was treated in such a delicate and sinister fashion.

At the time, Shell had publicly received some $30 million as compensation from the South Africans for the stolen oil. Why then was Shell now giving *any* sum, large or small, back to the SFF in a *secretive way*? The oil company had not done well—the theft had cost them millions. That answer became clearer, yet raised even more unanswered questions.

A subsequent report by the Auditor-General dealt with allegations against the SFF, including the *Salem* issue. When, in 1980, Shell told SFF that it had owned the oil, the Fund disputed this. Negotiations led to a written compromise. In the deal, Shell received only $30 million, though they had paid $56 million to Pontoil. However, under Clause 6, in the event of future receipts paid by any *outside* party, they agreed to *share the proceeds* equally.

In the context of 1980/81, this still seems perfectly reasonable. There were various ways for both sides to obtain money from elsewhere as compensation or damages. Whether it was worth pursuing legal remedies was another matter. Shell made only a small recovery from its insurers, but whether there was much left after legal costs, having lost on the major part of the claim in the House of Lords, is not public information. But this secret payment *by* Shell, first uncovered 14 years later, was *not* insurance money.

According to the Report, this payment from Shell was a recovery made 'from the perpetrators of the deception.' Who paid Shell? Soudan? Reidel? That seems most unlikely, although Soudan's secret accounts were traced and frozen by the FBI. The amount paid by Shell to meet the Clause 6 obligation was not large for a multinational—R6,784,754,33, in effect only about $1.9 million, small beer in the context of the losses suffered by the two parties.

The receipt was recorded in the official records as *Saldanha Strategic Sales*, and included in the 93/94 accounts on that basis. So why the secrecy? Pithey explained that the idea not to make full disclosure was *so as not to embarrass Shell* while nevertheless making sure that the SFF got its money. The Auditor-General's Report comments: Pithey 'averred at the time that Shell was anxious to avoid the issue becoming a matter of public debate because of the *Salem* history.' That is the SFF/CEF explanation of the secrecy, and presumably accurately reflects Shell's position.

The Auditor-General *deprecated* that the receipt had not been correctly recorded, but there was no fraud, just a mis-description. Van Zyl, in seeking to assist John Drake's wish for utmost confidentiality, was the fall guy for the innocent sleight of hand. The SFF claim *they* had nothing to conceal. If Pithey is right, then Shell's wish for secrecy ironically led to *much closer* public scrutiny than this small receipt would otherwise have warranted.

Why would Shell allegedly nurture a desire for secrecy bordering on paranoia? It was a small sum being paid to meet an obligation under Clause 6 of an agreement presumably drafted by lawyers. Would Shell's shareholders have protested? It seems unlikely. Alternatively, was there a fear that Shell's role, already unfavourably alluded to in court under legal privilege, would again come under scrutiny from the new regime in South Africa?

Eventually, in October 1998, Van Zyl was dismissed after an internal disciplinary panel found him guilty of four out of five charges, none of which involved fraud. Van Zyl did not accept the ruling, but so far as concerns the *Salem*, the panel found him in breach of his duty. Meantime, for Shell, the hope must be that the files on *Salem* remain permanently closed as a difficult chapter in its history. Those historic problems, though, pale into insignificance compared to the scandal that rocked the company in 2004 concerning alleged overstating of oil reserves by around 40%.

In Dakar, just two men remained from the crew: Captain Georgoulis and Chief Engineer Kalamiropoulos. Their passports had been confiscated, not because Senegal was interested in how or why *Salem* had sunk, but because if there were oil pollution damage, it wanted compensation. However, with Salem's cargo being mainly seawater, the Senegalese coastline of sandy beaches and small fishing communities was spared any serious problems.

Until 1980, Liberia had enjoyed a stable political history with strong American connections; English was the main language. Ties between the USA and Liberia had been strengthened by President Roosevelt's trip to Monrovia in 1943, which led to finance for the creation of a major port. The main source of national wealth was fees paid by shipowners for registration in this remote backwater.

Though Liberia was an unlikely country to have won pre-eminence as a Shipping Registry, it had worked hard to create a slick operation. In the USA, the Office of the Deputy Commissioner for Marine Affairs for the Republic of Liberia operated to great effect from New York and Reston, not far from Washington, D.C.

The problem for nations like Liberia providing ship registrations is the need to strike a balance between registering all-comers, however suspicious and poorly inspected, or, as a Third World economy, to concentrate on profitability, or to operate to the standards of Germany and the UK.

The sinking was a blow to Liberian pride and increased accusations that Liberia was a *flag of convenience* jurisdiction. To counter this, the Crombie team wanted both truth and prosecutions, and so the Liberian President and his Minister of Justice obtained an extradition order, requiring Captain Georgoulis and Chief Engineer Kalamiropoulos to be sent to Monrovia.

Captain Chadwick has long been an eminent figure in marine administration. He had been in the D-Day landings in 1944 as a young sailor on a battleship at Omaha Beach, rising in the US Navy to the rank of captain. In 1977, he joined the administrative arm of the Liberian Bureau and had a special interest in the transportation of petroleum. Since leaving Liberian Services in 1995, he has remained active as Maritime Adviser to International Registries.

At the time of the loss of *Salem*, he was the Chief of the Investigation Division at Reston. Chadwick well recalls the determination with which the Liberian investigating team carried out its obligations. 'At that time, the scandal of crime at sea had been given focus by the FERIT investigation concerning scuttlings in the Far East. Now, Liberia was faced with what appeared to be an audacious attempt to steal oil and bury the evidence in the Atlantic. As the *Salem* was flying our flag, it was our obligation to apply considerable energy and expense to show that *our* Registry was not prepared to stand back and do nothing.

'But despite our best efforts, events did not quite turn out as planned. We appointed a first-class team of the Deputy Commissioner of Maritime Affairs, Captain Alister Crombie, Captain Tzamtzis, a Greek national from our Marine Safety Office in Piraeus, and an American attorney called Kenneth Volk. They were scarcely the only people out there seeking the truth.

'You had people chasing everywhere for the apparent fraudsters and for their statements. Our own work was thorough and we were greatly helped by Scotland Yard. We worked quickly. The charade of a genuine sinking was quickly pierced.' The Crombie team recommended prosecutions, and but for a dramatic turn of events the two men would have been tried and convicted.

Crombie recalls visiting Monrovia and interviewing the two officers. 'I was convinced the two men were lying and evasive in their denials of any scuttling. But we needed *evidence*, and the release of the rest of the crew from Senegal had been a setback. Our interviews were constantly interrupted by lawyers wanting to represent them because rumours abounded that the men had plenty of money!'

Georgoulis had no master's ticket, so that was an easy charge to bring. The Minister of Justice, Joseph Chesson, also accepted the advice to prosecute for the scuttling. Events then took a dramatic twist—nothing to do with the *Salem*. A young soldier, Master Sergeant Samuel Doe, organised a coup in Liberia. Everything changed.

All the work came to nothing. President Tolbert died in the coup. Needlessly, on a Liberian beach, on orders from Doe, several government ministers including Justice Minister Joseph Chesson were tied to stakes and executed. Chadwick relived the hell of those troubled days. 'Our Interim Report was never turned into a Final Report. The *Salem* investigation was officially closed.'

Coups in Africa are unremarkable, but Liberia had been a stable country. Master Sergeant Doe proclaimed himself president and thence forward the credibility of Liberia was compromised, and in shipping terms, it was undermined. Its asset of an orderly Government had gone. Foreign banks became nervous about lending against the security of Liberian-registered ships. Doe unwisely raised taxes on ships to boost the national economy—a counterproductive move and a deterrent to shipowners.

On the precise events surrounding the release of the two ship's officers, neither Chadwick nor Crombie would comment, as they had no first-hand knowledge. Those were dangerous times in Monrovia; even in faraway Virginia, people were prudently distancing themselves from the bloodbath.

President Doe pardoned a large number of jailed prisoners. There was confusion as to whether the two Greeks would be prosecuted or not. A well-known Greek lawyer, George Alfantakis, representing his fellow countrymen, successfully lobbied the new president. In June 1980, President Doe not only went to the jail *personally* but he arranged for the two men to be released and to receive his televised apology for their *illegal detention*. They were later to boast that they had been acquitted, but this was incorrect. There had been neither formal trial nor acquittal.

For Chadwick and those who had worked so hard in Reston and New York, there was disappointment. No evidence suggested that anyone, let alone Alfantakis, paid any bribe, but such rumours circulated at the time.

Alfantakis was one of 21 persons later arrested in Piraeus in a major swoop against what the media called the *Piraeus mafia*, but that does not mean he even *offered* a bribe to President Doe. In 1990, Doe was himself overthrown and violently tortured. His ears were cut off before he was killed. Allegations against him included corruption while in office.

For the two officers, release from Monrovia was not the end of their legal problems. The legal circus moved on to the USA, Holland and Greece. After some initial hesitation, the FBI had taken up the challenge of investigation. There was no sense of outrage in America over the sinking of the *Salem*. No Americans had died. No American investors had lost money. The president never mentioned it. Most Americans knew nothing about it. The FBI's only real interest was in Soudan, the insurance salesman turned shipping tycoon.

To their credit, once the FBI's evidence justified charges, matters were effectively handled. Eventually, four years later in January 1985, Soudan was indicted in Houston on charges of theft of the oil and of masterminding the scuttling.

Since he earned a fortune in January 1980, Soudan's behaviour had invited scrutiny. He received over $4 million (nearer $12 million in today's money) as his share of the oil sale, yet failed to mention his newfound wealth to the Internal Revenue Service. He could scarcely admit to receiving this money from selling Shell's oil, but some cover story could have been devised by the right kind of accountant. But that was not Soudan's style. *Soudan had it, and he was determined to flaunt it.* He bought a big house, an expensive car and spent lavishly.

James Shorrock, one of the brokers retained by Soudan in South Africa, was also charged by the FBI in regard to the theft. This was a clever move. Their sights were on Soudan but charging Shorrock created a pressure point.

To the FBI, he was a *bit player*, a pawn to be sacrificed to get the king—one of their favourite strategies. They offered Shorrock a deal to escape jail if he gave evidence against Soudan. Faced with the likelihood of a conviction and a lengthy jail sentence, Shorrock agreed. The FBI's case was boosted by this cunning ploy. The South African pleaded guilty and was freed based on time already spent in prison plus probation on release.

In October 1984, a whiff of a plea bargain had also been in the air for Soudan. The trial was scheduled for three months from January, involving some 60 witnesses. The attractions of a deal made sense for both sides. There was speculation in the papers that Soudan would plead guilty to the oil theft only and not the scuttling. In return he would get six years, though in reality he would be imprisoned for only three.

The plea bargain deal went before Judge Carl Bue behind closed doors at the Federal Court in Houston. Bue rejected whatever bargain was put to him. All deals were off. Soudan had to face a full trial on all counts in front of a judge who had shown where his instincts about Soudan's role lay. In January, the tough US Department of Justice prosecutors painted a picture of Soudan *the mastermind* who had conjured up the greatest marine fraud of all time.

In all, 17 charges were proved. Captain Crombie, who gave evidence for over five hours, was able to observe both the Judge and Soudan. 'I was at Court for about 10 days. As an expert witness on the scuttling, I was permitted to remain in court. The Judge was tough, very much no-nonsense with a strong control of his court. Soudan created an image of being mild and inoffensive—and rightly so, but frankly my view was that he was in it up to his eyeballs.'

Interestingly, in view of their *hot and cold* relationship, Reidel gave evidence on Soudan's behalf, another twist in the complex relationship between the two men. In Judge Bue, Soudan was unfortunate. The judge, a former admiralty lawyer, was keen to send a tough message to marine criminals.

For those who believed Soudan was the ringleader who had gained most from the crime, the sentence received was perhaps justified. For those convinced he had been used or manipulated by the European masterminds, the 35-year jail sentence seemed excessive.

However, nobody needs to shed tears for Soudan: he is no longer serving *any* sentence. In 1988, just three years after being jailed, he was being held in a low-security prison at Fort Worth, Texas. He phoned his Spanish wife. Her humble pickup truck attracted no attention when it pulled up close by. Soudan walked out, climbed in and disappeared. He has never been seen since.

His wife had purchased two tickets to Madrid. Did he go to Lebanon or remain in Spain? On the Spanish coastal regions of Costa Blanca and Costa del Sol, there are so many foreigners that another couple like the Soudans would not be noticed. In the cosmopolitan town of Marbella, an hour north of Gibraltar, Americans, British, Germans, Scandinavians and Spaniards rub shoulders with thousands of Arabs. The King of Saudi Arabia had a palace there, modelled loosely on the Washington White House. Oil wealth is richly spread over the multimillion-dollar homes. In this community, Soudan, equipped with a false passport, could easily live in quiet prosperity without attracting attention.

Officially, the American attitude was that Soudan should be caught and returned to jail, though it was evidently not a priority. Texan observers reckoned Soudan believed his plea bargain should have been accepted and that three years in jail was enough and so had decided to go walkabout. No doubt his wife had orchestrated the escape under his direction.

Soudan was not fined by the court but what he had hoped were untraceable offshore bank accounts had been frozen and forfeited to repay Shell and the insurers. But most of the money had gone anyway. Even after expenses, Soudan probably cleared about $3 million, but this was never traced. Whether funds in some traced accounts went to South Africa under Clause 6 of Shell's contract of settlement is not known. The *secret* payment that brought problems for Van Zyl did not apparently appear until the '90s.

As a Dutch national, the Dutch police had an interest in prosecuting Anton Reidel, if their evidence was strong enough. They too faced all the problems of cross-border litigation—delays, language barriers, missing witnesses, confusions about the evidence, difficulty in establishing facts and challenges on jurisdiction. The failure of the South African Government to support the Dutch police despite their promise to Ellen was a significant disappointment. The fact that Beets Trading was a Swiss company did not help. With so many different investigators and investigations in various countries, it was difficult to achieve and present a coherent image in legal terms.

Curious behaviour or apparent sleight of hand is insufficient to prove guilt in presenting a criminal case. The Dutch police wanted to prove that Reidel was the *mastermind* of the fraud—a mistake, in Ellen's eyes. Soudan had *already* been portrayed as the mastermind and convicted in Houston, despite Reidel's evidence that he and Soudan were merely brokers for *a Greek mafia*.

The world's press swallowed this, depicting Soudan as the mastermind. However, evidence suggesting Reidel got $8 million infers he had played an important part, although it is most improbable that he was the mastermind.

Ellen found him an elegant, cultured man—impressive, well dressed and distinguished, even though his background had been smuggling cigarettes—but the evidence that he was the brains of the outfit did not stack up. *Neither* Soudan nor Reidel was the mastermind, in Ellen's view. The Dutch team failed to prove even criminality involving the altered Bill of Lading, central to the scam. Reidel's defence was that he was fooling nobody in South Africa. The paperwork had been altered but the South Africans at SFF were not fooled. This was just an essential charade to conceal illicit supplies.

The Dutch proceedings were a failure. It was now up to Greece—some key players and people with vast wealth, power and influence who had the connections and knowledge to set up the crime were Greek. 'There was uncertainty as to whether Greece would ever prosecute,' recalled Ellen. 'Once the IMB had been established in 1981, I was acting as a sponge in this affair, soaking up information from many sources and squeezing out droplets when appropriate. We worked closely with a number of forces and agencies and did our best to encourage prosecutions. In Greece, there was a great opportunity to arrest and proceed against a number of individuals.

'Following the Liberian debacle and the failure in Holland, I thought it vital to get convictions in Greece. The apology from President Samuel Doe to the two officers had been an insult to world shipping. We lobbied and petitioned the Greek Government and I flew to Athens on a number of occasions to provide information and encouragement. Eventually, after a difficult and long process, arrests and charges were made.'

In Piraeus, the mass prosecutions of the so-called *Piraeus mafia* hit the headlines. The list of those eventually charged filled pages—naming officers, crew and businessmen. What followed, though, were deals, appeals, non-appearances and all the drama of Greek theatre. In the end, there *were* both convictions and acquittals, some of the accused being dealt with *in absentia* under the local law.

SeaTrade Week announced the charges in May 1983. Various thefts of cargo were alleged along with other frauds besides *Salem*. Besides naming Georgoulis, the owner Gregarios Makrygiorgos, who had allegedly helped select the crew, was included, but, interestingly, so was the peripatetic lawyer George Alfantakis, cited in connection with the *Poseidon* prosecution. One of his co-defendants had already testified as to the lawyer's alleged role in a series of previous cargo frauds. Those attempts to secure prosecution were baulked when 174 pages of vital court papers were *lost in transit* on the short journey from Piraeus to the prosecution office in Athens! Neither Alfantakis nor Makrygiorgos were ever convicted.

Foreigners like Reidel and Locks (Bert Stein) were both tried in their absence. 'I spoke to Locks several times by phone as part of my investigation,' Ellen confirmed. 'He stonewalled me and denied any involvement.'

Captain Georgoulis, Chief Engineer Kalamiropoulos and Radio Officer Evangelides were convicted, as were nearly all the Greek crew. Nikolaos Mitakis, the man who had fronted so much of the brilliant organisation, was convicted despite his violin defence of heart trouble and poverty. In court, the Greeks blamed the foreign non-attendees for the scuttling—a clever way to divide and rule.

Reidel was convicted in his absence but then won his appeal, alleging that had better efforts been made to bring him there, he could have been at court and would have refuted the allegations. It was an audacious and brilliant move by his lawyers, who argued that if the Greek prosecutors had wanted him there, they could have brought him there. His address had been no secret and he had not tried to evade arrest; he had simply not made it easy by flying into Athens. Some charges were left on file to use against Anton Reidel if he entered Greece, but now, after so long, it is unlikely that he will ever be tried.

Frank Wiswall had also played a key role in the affair from his standpoint of Admiralty Counsel. 'I have no doubt that Fred Soudan was rightly convicted but equally agree with Eric Ellen that he was never the key figure. Others were the real masterminds. I have no evidence to support this—call it *my little whimsy*. I think Soudan knew or found out who the real organisers were. I think he feared for his life. There was the danger of an attack on him in jail or the alternative of an escape. I think, *like to think*, that he had warned the people behind the crimes that he had left a message in an envelope *naming names*. This had been secreted in a safe place to be opened in the event of any sudden or violent death. That bought his safety.'

Is this more than mere whimsy from a distinguished lawyer who knows how to pick his words? Either way, the theory, coming from someone so close to the action, deserves serious consideration.

Incomplete justice had been done in Greece. The criminal process was over.

One very positive consequence of the scuttling was that it proved there was a need for a new body such as the International Maritime Bureau. *Salem* was the catalyst. 'By 1979, I think the momentum for a Bureau was irresistible,' commented Ellen. '*Salem* simply demonstrated just how urgent the need was.' The size of the scam and the involvement of eight countries advanced his argument. On 1 January 1981, the ICC-International Maritime Bureau started operations from Ellen's home before expanding to an unprepossessing grey tower-block in Barking, near London. More recently, it has moved to an impressive HQ in Wapping High Street, in east London. Ellen's own personal ambition for a broader platform from which to fight crime had been fulfilled. He retired from his position of Chief Constable to become its inspirational director.

Achieving credibility from a standing start is not easy, but Ellen's own credentials ensured that the Bureau swiftly penetrated to the heart of the *Salem* intrigue. Had the Bureau existed in 1979, history might have been different. Pontoil, Shell, MercaBank and even friends of SFF (but obviously not the SFF directly) could have checked out with the Bureau the names and backgrounds of Mitakis, Georgoulis, Kalamiropoulos, Bert Stein, Soudan, Reidel and others. These were the men to whom the safety of a valuable ship and its cargo were to be entrusted.

Captain Mukundan, Ellen's successor, adds: 'The Bureau's database has confidential material about many personalities in shipping to assist members who choose to use due diligence. That is critical. Much of our work continues to be educating the shipping community to take more care about who they are dealing with. The Bureau has saved so many members from being defrauded.

'Also, a recent technological development could have made *Salem* very different. In 1999, we approved a new commercial device, the satellite-inspired system *ShipLoc*.' This is increasingly playing a major role both in acting as a deterrent to crime and in aiding with the capture of criminals in the act. Shipowners conceal the transmitting device on the vessel.

'It only costs a thousand dollars or so. Messages transmitting the precise location of the vessel are sent out frequently. Owners ashore can monitor progress. It is not intended for a cargo owner such as Shell, but there is no reason why cargo owners should not *contract* with owners and charterers for an entitlement to receive precise daily reports on location. Salem's unexplained lost days and the diversion into Durban would have been spotted.'

Ellen is confident that the main players escaped jail. But for the difficulties of proving it in court, he could name them. As so often happens in police work, the identity of the leaders of organised crime are known but convictions are only secured with time, information from informants and sometimes a lucky break. John Gotti, the New York Mafia don, was known for years before the FBI secured convictions to jail him for numerous crimes.

Was the *Salem* truly the maritime crime of the century? It might have been, if the fraudsters had sunk the ship secretly and had also been successful in borrowing millions against the vessel or in extracting $24 million from the insurers for the hull. As it was, it was an audacious near miss, marred by feuding between Reidel and Soudan and miscalculations about how difficult it was to scuttle a laden supertanker.

Did the *masterminds* strike again? Tempting though it is to assume that most of the *Salem* story is known, an oddity is the loss of the tanker *Irene Serenade* five weeks later on 23 February 1980. She, too, had slipped into Durban before sinking. She, too, left only a small oil slick though reputedly carrying 100,000 tons of crude oil. Were the same criminals involved? Was it a copycat crime, or not a crime at all? Yet no positive link could be made between this loss and *Salem*. As Ellen points out, 'Suspicion is not enough. Proving what may seem obvious can be very difficult.'

Author's Footnote

Just as the *Salem* was a catalyst for Eric Ellen, this single crime also shaped my life. That is no overstatement, though I did not know it then. Without the events of January 1980, I would not now be writing this book at all.

In early January 1980, the month of the scuttling, I had arrived in Dakar to use the port as a great setting for a new novel on shipping crime, to be called *Undercurrent*. An earlier meeting with two London shipbrokers had been the launchpad. Over lunch in the *Boot & Flogger* pub, I had asked them to suggest a good place to scuttle a ship.

'Nowhere much better than the Atlantic Ocean, old boy. Just off Dakar, West Africa. Bloody deep there! Your feet certainly wouldn't touch the bottom! Around 4,000 metres, I'd say. Nobody likely to be looking either. Bury the evidence. Just make sure you get the right crew aboard—ones who know how to sink a ship and who'll keep their mouths shut. We could tell you a name or two; Greeks are specialists. Masters and Chief Engineers who'll do the business. Reverse the jolly old pumps. Open the hatches. Get a load of seawater in instead of out. Then bingo, down she goes! Just guarantee the crew won't get their feet wet when the old tub goes down.'

'What type of ship do you suggest?'

'A big one. A *supertanker*. Plenty of them sail up the West African coast. Too big for the Suez Canal. They have to go from the Gulf to Rotterdam all the time, round the Cape of Good Hope.'

Six weeks later, as the winter temperature pushed 33 degrees, I met Lloyd's shipping agent in Dakar. His unglamorous office, close to the harbour gates, was filled with the latest reports of everything moving off West Africa. He is the eyes and ears of the shipping community. His reports are vital to trade and to insurance interests. 'No,' he said. 'Nothing suspicious has gone down here. But 100 miles out—it's deep out there.'

At the Dakar Port Authority, I received similar confirmation before returning to London. Within two weeks of my return, the *Salem* had been scuttled. Reality had overtaken fiction and I put my novel on ice. It was more than ten years before *Undercurrent* was written and published, the plot much changed. The true story of the *Salem*, even though not fully known, had been too good, killing off my original plot, but West Africa still features prominently, as does the Malacca Strait.

I often wonder what the Lloyd's agent and the Dakar Port Authorities thought of the Londoner who had been asking *if there had been any good scuttlings recently*. Perhaps they decided that I was involved, that I knew what was about to happen or what *should* already have happened. After all, but for the New York litigation, I might have been there just when the vessel sank!

And those shipbrokers at lunch in the *Boot & Flogger*? Had they picked up a buzz of a big crime being planned? In the gossip of the tight-knit shipping community in London with its tentacles in Piraeus, it is certainly possible, for I know now that rumours of a big scuttling had circulated. How right they were! If they *knew* nothing, then as palm readers or soothsayers they could make a fortune. They had predicted the location, type of vessel, the scuttling and key players in what the media called the maritime *crime of the century*!

CHAPTER SIX
Death Doesn't Matter -The MV *Lucona*

Vienna, the capital of Austria, is a city of magnificent architecture, the epitome of culture and elegance. Tourists flock to see the carefully preserved reminders of the Habsburg Empire, queue to visit the Spanish Riding School and admire the white Lipizzaners. Others visit to delight in Vienna's gastronomic delicacies: the rich chocolate Sachertorte, Viennese cream cakes and coffee. Vienna's legendary cafés, with their walls adorned with grand oil paintings and their fine china, encapsulate the style of a bygone era. Locals are proud of their coffeehouses and their *Geműtlichkeit*. It is all so *civilised*.

One such temple of luxury is *Demel* in Kohlstrasse, only a few steps from the Austrian Parliament. Hedonistic delicacies had once been created here for royalty. Yet upstairs during the 1970s was hatched one of the most ruthless shipping crimes of all time. Too many acts of piracy involve violence, sometimes because a crew resist the attackers or because the bloodthirsty gang relish slaughter. The *Lucona* fit neither category: this was cold, calculated, premeditated murder in pursuit of profit.

Unlike Hong Kong, Piraeus or Manila, Vienna, landlocked and far from the sea, is an unlikely cradle for maritime crime. Yet here at *Demel* a group of powerful men, including lawyers and politicians, would mount the winding wooden stairs to the small meeting room. These were members of the exclusive Club 45, with connections and power sufficient to control events as they pleased, wielding such influence in Austria that some members believed themselves above the law. Admission to the Club was strictly controlled. Leading members of the ruling Social Democratic party dominated membership; powerful figures like the Austrian Chancellor might be chatting over pastries with the Minister of Defence.

Demel was owned by Udo Proksch. His list of friends and contacts was legion. Movie stars, Formula One legends, royalty and world leaders were all charmed by the extrovert bonhomie of the man. Short, corpulent and sporting a shining bald head, Proksch strutted through the city's elegant social occasions. In *Demel*, his photo, giving a Churchill-style V sign for victory, dominated one wall for many years but has now been removed. He knew Leonid Brezhnev, the Russian president, and was able to talk to King Hussein of Jordan as an old friend. He was always at the centre of fun; beautiful women like Imelda Marcos flocked about him. He partied with Formula One world champions like James Hunt and Austrian Nikki Lauda, who later founded Lauda Air. He was a scene-stealer, a headline-grabber. He jumped from aeroplanes as an act of bravado, once parachuting into a friend's party bearing a cake!

But there was another, darker side: Proksch was also well connected in the shady worlds of espionage and arms-dealing. Proksch was born in 1934 and came from a humble background in East Germany. Among his many talents, he was a trained pilot and flew a jet Vampire. Toiling in the kitchens of *Demel* was not his scene. Much more likely to be true are stories that while managing *Demel* he was a spy for the East German Stasi.

Where Udo Proksch got his inspiration for what became known as *Der Lucona Skandal* is unclear, but in this upstairs room Proksch and his associates plotted a giant insurance fraud. Murdering the crew was regarded as acceptable collateral damage. Proksch knew about guns and explosives and, presumably through his friends, had learned how to get rich through shipping crime. Though the *Lucona* plot was planned in about 1976, the saga only ended over 20 years later in 1997 with the final conviction of Peter Daimler, one of the leading participants. That there was a prosecution of anyone owed everything to advanced high-tech developments and the end of abuse of power and corruption in Austria's ruling party. All along, until belatedly charged with murder, Proksch could rely on the influence of his friends to protect him. As the truth gradually unravelled, heads rolled. Politicians were disgraced, people died—scarcely part of *Demel's* traditional *Geműtlichkeit*.

One of the buzz issues of the '70s in Austria had been nuclear power and the problems of radioactive waste. In 1960, Austria had planned its first nuclear power plant at Zwentendorf. But as the building work continued into the '70s, opposition grew. By 1976, the plant was ready, but with public resentment mounting, the Government, fearing electoral consequences, postponed the opening. Café talk was of uranium, its value, its availability and the problems of its management.

In 1976, the Bundesländer Versicherung Insurance Company of Vienna received a request from a German called Hans-Peter Daimler to insure some high-tech machinery to be exported from Austria to Hong Kong via the Italian port of Chioggia. Daimler had known Proksch since teenage days. A stern-faced, bespectacled businessman, he possessed a deceptive gravitas. His commercial knowledge was essential in setting up the paperwork in the plan to steal from the insurers.

This appeared to be just another routine request for the protection of goods to be carried at sea, though the value was substantial. The policy was issued to cover the transit of plant used for treating non-ferrous metals, and uranium in particular. The uranium ore dressing plant, previously used at Pisting, had an insured value of 31 million Swiss francs or about US$20—impressive sums even today, but not so extreme as to be obviously bogus.

The paperwork showed that the Swiss-registered exporting company, Zapata AG, had a contract to supply this valuable plant to a company registered in Hong Kong, North Pacific Trading. (Neither company has any connection with any other company existing then or now using those names.) North Pacific Trading was another company without assets, tailor-made for the Proksch plot.

Proksch was an officer of Zapata, which had been formed in 1970 in Zug. This small Swiss town seems to have been a popular location with fraudsters, as it was also selected by those involved in the *Salem* affair a year or two later. Zapata was a typical *shelf company* with neither style nor substance. Such companies were convenient for those sheltering hot money or needing a corporate shield to protect the owners against legal liability. Now, as banking and corporate secrecy is steadily eroded, the hot money element has been curbed, if not killed off completely. These companies can be quickly formed and as readily dissolved when their usefulness is spent.

The original plan was for Zapata to despatch the valuable cargo by container in August 1976, but loading was delayed. The crew hired for that trip probably never knew what a lucky escape they had. The ship, MV *Beatrix*, sailed without the cargo. It was not until January 1977 that container number 083737-9 was loaded onto a different vessel, the *Lucona*, at Chioggia, along with 16 others. This small port, a few miles south of Venice, lies on the Adriatic.

That the container went aboard is beyond question. A witness to the loading, in the unlikely setting of an Italian dockside and far from Vienna, was no less than Leopold Graz, the then-mayor of Vienna and a member of Club 45. Graz, born in 1929, had a distinguished political career until he was disgraced in the backlash of the *Lucona* affair in 1989. A lawyer by training, he had entered Parliament in 1963. He had been mayor of Vienna from 1973 to 1984 and was then appointed foreign minister. At his peak, he was president of the National Council. A fine-looking man with abundant grey hair, he was the ideal person to call upon to give evidence that he had been on the quay and witnessed the loading of valuable goods onto the ship.

However, standing on the quayside waving farewell to containers was hardly part of Mayor Graz's official functions. Those of a suspicious nature might wonder what such an august personage was doing there. The *Lucona* was a Panama-registered freighter. At the stern, her fo'c'sle with the white bridge and hooped funnel rose above the engine room. In front of the bridge were the derricks for loading and unloading cargo. *Lucona* was 175 metres long and weighed 1,200 tons. Aboard were 12 persons. The Dutch skipper, Captain Jacob Puister, 35, was an experienced mariner with 20 years at sea behind him. He was travelling with his wife Adriana as a passenger. The First Officer, Jacobus Nicolaas van Beckum, 31, was also Dutch, from The Hague. The crew were the usual blend of nationalities, including Portuguese and West Indians.

After leaving port, *Lucona* sailed through the warm and generally calm seas of the Eastern Mediterranean. The master was ordered to report position every 12 hours. The route to Hong Kong was through the Suez Canal. The ship docked at Port Said on the North African coast, at the mouth of the canal. The mixed cargo was below decks, and, though laden, the ship was photographed riding quite high in the water. The sailing was delayed because of non-payment of dues for use of the canal.

After navigating the canal, the ship sailed southeast through the Red Sea and the Gulf of Aden. After an unscheduled stop at Djibouti, a port that features in other dubious maritime episodes, she proceeded uneventfully southeast ward through the vast expanse of the northern Indian Ocean toward Colombo. After Sri Lanka, it would be the long haul across 1,500 miles of the eastern Indian Ocean before the next landfall near the Thai-Malaysian border.

By Sunday 23 January, the *Lucona* reached the Maldives, an archipelago of small subtropical islands whose white sandy beaches and hot climate have made them a popular tourist destination for sun-worshippers. But the crew were not planning on stopping. Proksch and his team had checked that, although shallow around the islands, the sea in this part of the Indian Ocean is from two to three miles deep. In 1977, any ship sunk here was its own tomb, a resting place never to be disturbed by mourners or investigators—ideal for burying uncomfortable evidence.

The weather was good as the freighter passed the Island of Minicoy in a position 08.50° north and 70.30° east. The seas were calm, the skies sunny, and there was a light north easterly wind. The temperature was nudging 38° centigrade as the freighter sailed uneventfully toward its far-distant final port of Hong Kong. At 1400 hours local time, van Beckum took over the watch from the captain.

Puister remained on the bridge for a while, relaxing on a sunbed with his wife. Later, he went down to his cabin but his wife remained on the bridge. Other crew members were sunbathing too. Down below, engine function and readings were normal. Ahead, the sea was clear of hazards. Everything was routine as the bows sliced through the emptiness of the ocean. But *Lucona's* fate had been decided by Proksch in that smoky room at *Demel*.

By 1600 hours local time, there was still nothing untoward to report in the ship's log. This would be another night under a sky filled with an endless vista of stars, clearly visible in the unpolluted atmosphere. The sea was calm as glass. Occasionally, they had glimpsed another ship on the horizon or fishing boats from the islands. *Lucona* was its own little island, a cocoon of safety in the infinite sea, accompanied only by the occasional flying fish performing escort duty beside the ship.

It came out of nowhere in the late, lazy afternoon. Two mighty explosions rocked the ship. They twisted, rolled and tore her apart. Filthy smoke and a fireball enveloped the deck; the deadly menace billowed from somewhere below decks and rolled back toward the bridge. The crew who had been enjoying the sun were killed as the ship erupted and shards of metal and flying debris were dispersed by the massive blast. It was scarcely surprising that they were unprepared for the sudden disaster. Ships rarely blow up in mid-ocean. The six dead, mere collateral damage to the criminals, were unlucky to be on the wrong ship and in the worst places when the deck exploded beneath them with a fiery roar and a mass of acrid black fumes. The survivors owed their lives to luck, certainly not to Proksch, who intended to leave no witnesses.

Ships *do* sink, tragedies *do* occur, but usually there is an explanation, such as a violent storm, a leak or a collision. Badly loaded cargo may shift, making the ship unstable, but generally there will be time for a mayday distress signal. Sometimes, as in the controversial loss of the bulk carrier *Derbyshire*, an entire ship disappears with all hands. But the *Lucona* was not involved in a collision. Conditions were perfect. Had all 12 aboard died as was intended, probably Proksch and Daimler would have escaped justice, even if the high-value cargo would have aroused suspicions.

The *Lucona's* Radio Officer had no chance to put out an SOS from the ruins of his small cabin as water poured into the front and middle sections of its hull. The blast had penetrated the bow region. The damage was irreversible. The stricken ship listed and then began to sink in a shroud of thick and deadly smoke, fires roaring at the site of the explosion. Water swept through the cargo decks and filled the companionways. The acrid smoke reduced visibility aboard to almost zero.

Below decks, the lights failed. Captain Puister, lying in his cabin, had been hurled by the blast into the ship's saloon; here he came round, bemused but aware at once that something catastrophic had occurred. He raced to the deck. Realising his ship was doomed, he gave the order to abandon ship.

As the survivors fought to save themselves, the bow was already beneath the water and the stern was riding high, the propeller already above the water. Through a mixture of good luck and courage, the survivors either swam to a lifeboat or clung to liferafts. There they watched as their ship disappeared on its long final journey to the seabed. In three minutes *Lucona* was gone. All that remained was an oil slick and floating debris.

Bearing in mind the lack of a distress call, the six survivors were fortunate to be picked up quickly by a passing tanker, MT *Sapem*, and taken to Aden.

As the crew struggled to survive or lay dead, shattered by the explosions, thousands of miles away, in Vienna, it was lunchtime. No doubt Proksch and those who had planned this outrage were enjoying a relaxing day with friends or family. Proksch, at least, must have imagined the drama out on the ocean, as the massive bomb had been detonated by a timing device. He must have known to the minute, indeed to the second, and must already have been planning his next move—claiming for the loss of the uranium treatment plant loaded in container number 083737-9.

Both Puister and his wife survived, as did the First Officer van Beckum; the victims included a young Dutch woman, two men from Barbados, two Portuguese and the Chief Engineer. Their lives were callously ended by wealthy crooks in the name of profit. Daimler and Proksch's euphoria that they would soon be able to put in a claim for the loss of Zapata's cargo must have been dampened when news came through that there were survivors who had reported that *Lucona* exploded and sunk—the words entered in the Day Book at Lloyd's of London on Lime Street on 24 January.

A traditional hub of marine insurance, Lloyd's was started in 1696 by Edward Lloyd. He ran a coffeehouse in Tower Street in the City, near the

Tower of London. There he received and dispensed news of shipping. Wealthy Londoners drank coffee with Lloyd, gossiped and agreed to risk their money and to accept *the perils of the sea* in return for payment. Thus was born the world of marine and other insurance.

Piracy abounded then, too. There was no technology and the sea charts were less sophisticated. But these men wrote generally profitable business. Thus the world of marine insurance had started, and by 1977, Lloyd's, now run from an ultra-modern metallic building close by, though far from the biggest insurer, was still a key player in marine underwriting. Fortunately for Lloyd's, they had not insured the Zapata cargo. This problem rested with Bundesländer Versicherung Insurance Company, although reinsurance by the Austrian company had been placed in London.

Captain Puister described a gold and red fireball almost amidships, but there were reports of two explosions. Had the bomb or bombs been placed at the bow, or had Puister identified the location of the main explosion? Whichever, for all the explosives expertise that Proksch had mustered, it had proved to be a total miscalculation. The accommodation, while badly damaged, had not been destroyed, and neither had the vessel sunk quickly enough to take all aboard with it.

Had another bomb beneath but adjacent to the bridge failed to detonate? Proksch had ready access to explosives. There would have been no problem with overkill by planting too much on board. Almost all the containers were stowed on two decks in front of the fo'c'sle, but two were positioned immediately beneath the for'ard part of the bridge—ideal for causing mass destruction in that area. Synchronised bombs exploding fore, amidships and aft would surely have doomed everyone aboard. Perhaps one failed to detonate, though there is no evidence of that.

But what if there *had* been a loss with all hands? How would the investigators have reacted? There would have been no evidence of a bomb, just an inexplicable disappearance. A sinking in open seas can be explained if the ship starts to leak, but a mayday call will summon help and the crew will survive. If cargo shifts, a vessel can capsize, but this, too, would probably give some time for an escape and a mayday.

In calm seas, cargo movement is unlikely but in any case a distress call would be put out. Despite the prevalence of deliberate scuttlings at that time, this would have been regarded as a longshot—a crew does not sink its own vessel only to drown themselves. So the investigators would have had to consider piracy involving the entire ship either being stolen or sunk by the attackers. With a highly valuable insured cargo aboard, stealing ship and cargo might just make sense. They would also have been suspicious about the high-value cargo. While a payment to Zapata might eventually have been made, it would have been delayed pending enquiries about the probity of the owners and the pedigree of the cargo.

What debate took place between Daimler and Proksch at this point is not known. But they must have weighed their options. Failure to put in a claim would have been an obvious indication of guilt. Zapata would never have bought insurance and then made no claim. Equally, they must have appreciated that putting in a huge claim after the ship had apparently exploded would inevitably trigger investigations into the history of the uranium-cleaning plant and would invite speculation that the cargo owners, as opposed to the ship's owners, had never wanted the vessel to arrive in Hong Kong.

Faced with a large claim in curious circumstances, any insurer will sniff around the background before paying out. The ship's hull was separately insured and experts investigated who stood to win by blowing up the ship. The value of the uranium-cleaning equipment meant its owners had the biggest interest in getting cash for the goods insured, *especially if the goods had never even gone aboard.*

Though the Austrian insurers had less experience with marine fraud than Lloyd's of London, they quickly reasoned that if the cargo had never gone aboard, Zapata would get 31 million in cash for nothing. Suspicions and proof are poles apart, but Bundesländer Versicherung decided to play hardball. The background and identities of the crew were checked to see if any had a suspicious past. But that seemed unlikely.

In the early days, nothing could be ruled out. Lloyd's local representatives in relevant ports were asked to check for sightings of vessels similar to *Lucona* but sailing under a different name. They were asked to watch out for suspicious quayside transactions—just in case the ship had not sunk but had been diverted in a plot by the crew, or hijacked to sell off the high-value cargo for cash. They noticed nothing significant.

On 25 January, within 48 hours of the explosion, Zapata claimed payment of its 31 million Swiss francs. The big insurance company was unimpressed. Something was fishy. The decision was made to investigate Udo Proksch, Hans Peter Daimler, Zapata and the valuable cargo.

The investigation team were suspicious about the insured value and the size and weight of the uranium plant being carried. Zapata, in support of its position, produced the invoice addressed to North Pacific Trading. They managed to obtain sworn testimony from Leopold Graz, mayor of Vienna, that he had witnessed the loading at Chioggia. The Bill of Lading, the document that represents the goods in transit, was produced. The paperwork was signed on behalf of the ship's owners acknowledging that the cargo had gone aboard.

Bundesländer Versicherung were unimpressed. Zapata initiated a lawsuit to recover the insured value. Interest on the 31 million allegedly wrongly withheld by the insurers was mounting. The stakes were getting higher—but so was that smell of fish. The investigators had become increasingly unhappy about the evidence of the contents of container number 083737-9. Their painstaking research took them back years. The fact that the registered office of Zapata proved to be in a rural farmyard hardly inspired confidence that this was a legitimate shipment of multimillion-dollar goods.

It was the first breakthrough, though it was scarcely enough. Zapata's shareholders were men of substance: men like Steven Low, born in 1932 in Poland. Low had become a successful and well-connected businessman in Canada before involving himself in European deals, but he remained a man of mystery. Karl Lütgendorf, the Austrian Defence Minister, had a penchant for big cigars. Proksch, too, was a powerful and respected figure in Vienna. You can't go calling such men fraudsters or murderers without solid evidence.

Owning shares does not necessarily give control, still less mean that shareholders are aware of any wrongdoing. Many shareholders in big and small companies have been duped by those in daily control. In the case of a small company like Zapata, though, suspicions were aroused as to just how much these influential people knew. Steven Low was interrogated in Paris in 1986 based on legal process from Vienna concerning Proksch and Daimler. He was quick to point out that he had no directorship or management role in Zapata. Tactically, he sought to distance himself from the incident. Nothing was ever proved against him, although, as a shareholder, he had an obvious vested interest in claiming the insurance money.

Proksch had many strings to his bow, so it may not have come as a surprise but it was an intriguing triumph when the investigators uncovered that a number of years previously he had bought an Austrian coal mine in Grosshöflein. Proksch had sold off the old coal-mining equipment as scrap to a Swiss businessman called Leo Tannaz, also known as Jean Mardin. Tannaz was certainly at a meeting with Daimler and Proksch at about the time that North Pacific Trading was established in Hong Kong with nominal share capital.

Evidence was uncovered that, before the sinking, Proksch had been indulging another interest. His friend and Club 45 member Karl Lütgendorf was a leading military figure and politician. Proksch had a keen amateur interest in matters military. That summer, the cafe proprietor had amused himself experimenting with explosives at Hochfilzen military camp. Also at around this date, Zapata signed the insurance application for the uranium plant to be shipped. It was a further 12 years before more details of this military involvement emerged when a former member of the Austrian Army alleged that in 1976 he had been ordered to assist Proksch by supplying him with a large quantity of explosives and detonators. Allegedly, this order came *from the top*—from none other than the then Minister of Defence Karl Lütgendorf, a shareholder in Zapata!

The investigators decided it would be prudent to check out the premises where the uranium plant had operated before being taken out of service, ready for export to Hong Kong. The trail led them to the small hamlet of Pisting. If they had expected to find the remains of a high-tech treatment plant, they were to be disappointed. The premises were nothing more than a former carpenter's workshop and a yard full of scrap metal and rubbish. Could valuable equipment suitable for working with uranium have come from here? The investigators were unimpressed; one wrote: 'It was impossible to enter the pigsty.'

During this urgent search for the truth, the insurers had continued to resist the Zapata claim. Their original decision to deny liability under the policy was becoming increasingly vindicated. Proksch, using his powerful friends, tried both litigation and influence to obtain the payout, but to no avail. The battle dragged on into the 1980s. The courts were not satisfied that Zapata's claim was genuine.

Getting payment from the Bundesländer Versicherung was not Proksch's only problem. In Austria there was increasing outrage. There had been calls for a prosecution and for a full independent investigation, but here the political clout of the Club 45 members intervened. The judicial process of investigation was perpetually outmanoeuvred. Graz and others were able to stall any serious attempt to uncover the facts in any criminal process. Later, state prosecutor Wolfgang Mühlbacher testified in a parliamentary enquiry that police efforts to get matters moving had been baulked by Ministers and other influential figures. Proksch, adopting attack as the best form of defence, lodged a complaint of alleged police harassment with his friend Karl Blecha, the Interior Minister. Unsurprisingly, Blecha's brother was also a legal adviser to Proksch.

It was not until 1983, six years after the sinking, that the façade of probity started to crumble, but even then the wall of silence was by no means breached. Formal complaints were filed against Proksch and Daimler for various offences including suspicion of murder. But no serious charges were preferred, thanks to the corrupt abuse of power by Proksch's supporters. The most irrefutable evidence lay unavailable at the bottom of the Indian Ocean.

Evidence at the later enquiry into the political scandal heard that, in 1983, Karl Blecha, the Interior Minister, had helped Proksch by preventing police enquiries from being run from Salzburg, where it would have been harder for Proksch's corrupt friends to exert their influence. Instead, Blecha had the file sent to the State Public Prosecutor in Vienna, where later evidence showed that the investigation was constantly impeded, though it never ground to a standstill.

In 1984, Blecha ordered that the police take no further action on the *Lucona* files. This should have been the trump card, but instead the police raided a number of addresses including that of Peter Daimler, a man as close as any to Proksch in the build-up to the ship's departure. The raid was a success; fraudulent documents were recovered. The police knew they had a breakthrough and asked the Public Prosecutor to arrest both men. They were baulked again. Somebody—somebody very powerful—prevented this.

Now the police were on fire. Defying Blecha's orders to drop the case, they raided *Demel*, with even more remarkable results. Why incriminating evidence should have been kept here for seven years is a mystery—it seems the height of folly. It should at least have been concealed elsewhere. Perhaps Proksch overestimated the power of his friends...or underestimated the determination of the police to prove what they so strongly suspected. With his connections, one might also have expected Proksch to have been tipped off about the raids. One can only assume that the decision to storm *Demel* and seize documents was known only to a very few people.

At *Demel*, behind the elegant round tables and glass cabinets filled with rich cakes, files and papers were found dumped in the yard and upstairs at Club 45. At last the police had evidence linking Proksch with the crime, material to be added to the dossier from the insurers. Lists of contents were discovered for 16 containers sent to Chioggia—and they certainly did not tally with the claim put forward by Zapata.

Based on the information, ten Italian jobbing workers were traced and questioned about their activities at Pisting in the so-styled *pigsty*. They admitted that back in 1976 they had been hired on a cash-in-hand basis to clean up some old coal-mining machinery. The investigators were convinced that this had come from the Grosshöflein mine originally bought by Proksch. They reckoned the machinery had been transported to Chioggia after cleaning so it looked superficially better than scrap. Under questioning, the transport company admitted that the certified number of boxes of freight apparently transported had been false. On the night of 4 January 1977, this old scrap had been placed in container 083737-9 with an insured value of 31 million Swiss francs. The case for fraud was building up, but still there was no evidence of murder.

Graz's evidence that he personally witnessed the valuable plant being loaded was obviously false and sufficient for him to be charged with perjury. But matters did not advance as quickly as they should have. There was still only talk of a possible prosecution—perhaps for 'an attempt to defraud an insurance company,' a much lesser offence that did not satisfy the mood of a public, who suspected murder and cover-up. One man in particular was keeping the suspicions alive. Hans Pretterebner acted as a sleuth and journalist to keep the story prominent. To him must go enormous credit for his persistence. Proksch dismissed the allegations against him as rubbish, maintaining there had been no explosion and that the ship must have struck a reef or some obstruction.

However, the Austrian authorities still felt there was insufficient evidence to prosecute—conveniently, after Proksch's complaint about harassment to Interior Minister Blecha. The Minister of Justice, Harald Ofner, attracted a chorus of derision by refusing calls for a prosecution, saying, 'The soup is too thin!' In 1985, there was another surprising twist.

The main concern of Proksch and his accomplices was how to extract a large sum of money from the insurers. The possibility of criminal proceedings was an irritant, but one which, with the Social Democrat Government in power, could be delayed, obstructed or probably quashed. Succeeding in the claim would, he believed, kill off the criminal enquiries.

In 1985, fresh evidence emerged about the authenticity of the cargo. The first claim had been based on the plant coming from the Pisting pigsty, but even in the year of the sinking Zapata had substantially altered their story. Then it had been claimed that the uranium-cleaning plant had been supplied by a Swiss company called Decobul. Allegedly, it had been only *delivered* to Pinosa's premises at Pisting. The civil court was unimpressed by this evidence and the supporting testimony from Decobul and rejected Zapata's claim for payment from its insurers.

1985 saw yet another sideshow with even less credible facts. The new *evidence* came from the Rumanian Embassy in Vienna. Proksch had always enjoyed a good relationship with members of the former Eastern bloc and it seemed now to pay dividends. As a reputed spy, he could probably call in a few favours. At the time, the tyrant Nicolae Ceausescu was still in power. His bloody dictatorship would not end until his trial and execution on Christmas Day 1989.

Under the *Old Pals Act*, Proksch managed to obtain the superficially impressive support of the dictator's son. It was suggested that Leopold Graz may also have used his connections in the Embassy, something he always denied. That denial must be judged against his role in asserting the integrity of the cargo loaded at Chioggia.

The sudden appearance of new documents from the Rumanian Government eight years after the ship had sailed was always going to arouse interest and scepticism—especially when a new variation of the uranium plant's pedigree was now put forward.

We had it wrong when we went to court on two previous occasions saying the plant had been used at Pisting or had been supplied by Decobul. Now...the real origin of the uranium-cleaning plant was...Rumania. Thank goodness the correct original documents have now become known and released by the Rumanian Government! The new set of invoices proved delivery of the costly plant to Udo Proksch. So...Bundesländer Versicherung, please just send Zapata a cheque for their goods lost at sea plus interest plus costs. And please Judge stop these futile enquiries into this absurd notion that Zapata sank a ship carrying coal-mining scrap.

Just as at the insulting meeting when the claim was first made, the Viennese insurers remained unmoved, even now when confronted with apparently authentic invoices from a neighbouring government. They investigated the authenticity of the invoices. The truth quickly emerged: these were forged documents, though the identity of the forger was unknown—possibly someone connected to the Rumanian Embassy. The original invoices showed the sale of...coal-mining machinery! Despite Graz's denial of any involvement, at the subsequent enquiry into the scandal evidence was given that the Rumanians had provided the documents to Graz, who had taken them to the Judge in charge of the criminal proceedings.

By October 1986, the charges had not really progressed despite three years of mounting evidence, not to mention the debacle and embarrassment of the feeble forgeries from Rumania. Proksch, though on bail, was still free to travel. His passport had not been confiscated. Meantime, the Austrian public were baying for blood. The Government was finding the pressure intolerable. Then, in another twist, at the national elections the Social Democrats lost power. Eleven years after the sinking, in 1988, a new coalition took control, though some former Ministers survived. The new Government were determined to resolve the *Lucona* problem.

Proksch recognised that he was about to be stripped of his small remaining shreds of respectability. Some of his ministerial friends were yesterday's men and could no longer protect him. After talking to them, he accepted that proceedings were inevitable. It was time for a change of scene. He had used a false name before when it suited him. Under the name of Serge Kirchhofer, he slipped out of Austria, planning never to return.

His former friends included President Ferdinand Marcos of the Philippines and his wife Imelda, but they had fallen from grace in 1986. Proksch still went to Manila and stayed in Marcos's former presidential palace before moving to Japan. Somewhere he obtained another identity, using plastic surgery and obtaining a passport to match. While in seclusion in Manila, unsubstantiated rumours claim he was involved in making pornographic movies.

In 1989, the parliamentary investigation ended Graz's high-flying career that had taken him to Speaker of the Parliament. He resigned. Nevertheless, he maintained his denial of any wrongdoing or abuse of his position. The investigation found Blecha guilty of judicial interference; still protesting his innocence, Blecha, too, resigned, but only under pressure from Chancellor Vranitzky. Much more recently, his name has cropped up through his presidency of the Society for Austro-Arab relations, a group that allegedly received a voucher in the programme now called the *Iraq oil-for-food scandal* engulfing the United Nations. No impropriety is suggested, but Blecha is clearly a survivor.

And Proksch might have continued living as a wealthy, well-connected fugitive until he died. Other fugitives from justice have successfully evaded arrest using false identities. The notorious Lord Lucan, for example, is rumoured to have lived in new surroundings, protected by wealthy friends, rather than facing charges of murdering his children's nanny in London's Belgravia. But Proksch's luck ran out.

Ellen explains that Proksch travelled once too often under a false name. He was in transit through London's Heathrow Airport en route from Hong Kong to New York for some unknown reason when a sharp-eyed Immigration Officer became suspicious about his passport. Proksch, in keeping with his reputation as a ladies' man, was accompanied by a girlfriend. He was also carrying $250,000.

The official studied the passport with increasing interest. On leafing through the official stamps, he found one that was puzzling. Apparently, the gentleman before him had passed through Terminal Two at Heathrow on a date when it had been shut! This tiny flaw in an otherwise convincing document started Proksch's downfall, although his conviction was still a long way off.

The Immigration Officer had no idea he was dealing with Udo Proksch. The traveller was detained for further questioning. Instead of being permitted to fly on to the USA or able to make a run for it to Germany with his girlfriend, as they attempted at Heathrow, Proksch was put on a flight to Vienna. His girlfriend travelled to Vienna as well—amazingly still carrying the money in a case, nearly managing to escape seizure.

The Austrian police did not know that the man was Proksch, but they had their suspicions and these were confirmed. The irony about all Proksch's efforts to delay and escape justice is that, had he been tried in 1977, there is a chance that, with a good lawyer, he might been acquitted on the charge of murder. The burden of proof is heavy. There would have been suspicions, some ominous pointers to crime, insinuations that he had a motive. But suspicion and convincing evidence are very different things. But when Proksch was arrested at Vienna Airport, 10 years' dogged work by a private detective hired by the insurers had built up a convincing case.

Part of this concerned the manipulation of the ship's voyage. Before leaving port, Proksch had miscalculated the weight of the cargo. It was far lighter than expected. Reports from the ship every 12 hours had been disturbing. The vessel had made quicker progress en route than he had intended. Through quick thinking, he slowed it down. The delayed payment for canal dues at Port Said and the unscheduled stop at Djibouti had been clever ways of delaying the vessel so as to ensure that *Lucona* was over deep water when she sank. But a smoking gun was needed, and this is where modern technology had overtaken him. The judge ordered an investigation and search of the ocean bed, something not possible in 1977.

In 1980, speaking in New York at a conference on prevention of maritime fraud, Eric Ellen predicted that the day would soon come when criminals could no longer expect to conceal their crimes in deep waters. He was right. So it proved with *Lucona*. Experts started work in August 1990, nearly 14 years after the sinking. This part of the seabed was sculpted by volcanic activity. A smooth seabed would have made the task easier. The craggy features masked the ship's profile.

By now a new line of defence was being put forward: the vessel had not been under Proksch's control at the time; it had been sold by the crew or stolen, and was on a mission of its own. In effect, the vessel had not sunk but had become a *phantom ship*. Yet Lloyd's agents had found no evidence of any sightings nor of the cargo appearing in any port. Had there been no survivors, this argument might have been plausible but it contradicted testimony from the six crew who had not been murdered.

The company charged with the daunting task of finding the evidence was Oceaneering Advanced Technologies (AdTech). They had won the contract for recovering the remains of the Space Shuttle *Challenger* after it exploded just after take-off in 1986. That search off Florida had been successful, though it had taken seven months, even in shallow water. AdTech collated all known data and then hired Daniel H. Wagner and Associates Inc. to assist them.

Dr Joseph Discenza takes up the story. 'At Daniel H. Wagner, we specialise in providing consultancy services in operations research, mathematics and software development. For legal reasons laid down by the Austrian Court, I am not permitted to describe the details of how, together with Oceaneering, we found the wreck. I can, though, explain the principles involved.

'The starting point is to study any known navigational details. These are the clues of a likely location. We are looking for intended sailing direction and any emergency message giving position. In the event of working from last previous known position, we would dead reckon, meaning predict motion from last position using speed and course.

'In some investigations we have clues like floating debris. We can use that data after estimating wind and current effects to take account of drift. Oil slicks can be used too. However, if there is *fresh* oil bubbling to the surface, then we need not take account of drift. Once every possible bit of data from this evidence and from survivors has been gathered, we use statistical techniques to combine time-of-incident locations into one distribution. This we call a *probability map*. This is a process not many people get right. From the probability map, we create a search plan. This is through a computer programme that takes the amount of available search resources and computes an optimal area.'

The computer is programmed to evaluate how much money is available to carry out the search on the ocean bed. If there is a large budget, more hours on location means a larger area can be searched and perhaps the use of longer-range sonar systems, which would speed up the search and cover a larger area.

'The in-the-field search guys like to plan the search to get double coverage by the sensor with 100% overlap. If resources are limited, relative to the problem, then it makes sense to reduce the overlap to gain extra square miles of coverage.'

For the *Lucona*, a search plan was put together as described by Dr Discenza. Using computer software later known as the *Melian II Search and Recovery System*, the probabilities were pinpointed. The search zone centred on an area nearly 15,000 feet deep. In effect, the *Lucona* was nearly three miles down. The spot had been well chosen! The delays Proksch had engineered had worked well.

On site, an ROV (Remotely Operated Vehicle), a type of unmanned mini-submarine, was used to explore the depths. An Ocean Explorer 6000 was used, towed on a cable over six miles long. It trundled along in the dark depths about 1,200 feet above the bottom. A bathymetric chart was created. Sonar returns were analysed in real time by a Triton QMIP Simage processing system. With full technological support, after six days the wreck of the *Lucona* was found. The searchers cheered: for Proksch, it was a chilling moment.

The ROV was then activated to take video film and still pictures. The photographs captured irrefutable evidence of crime, though Proksch still did his best to defend the indefensible. There *had* been a massive explosion near the bows. It had started inside the for'ard portion of the hull, tearing the ship in two. Proksch's phantom ship defence was blown to pieces, just like the *Lucona.*

For centuries, probable frauds by scuttling against insurers had been impossible to check. Suddenly, insurers had a powerful new weapon at their disposal. The word was out: *Don't imagine deep waters will hide your crimes.*

The photos and video were used in the criminal trial and provided deadly evidence against Proksch and bitter and emotional memories for the survivors who had lost friends. The blast had come from *inside* the vessel. Any notion that the ship had sunk from striking a reef or other obstruction was laughable. The photos showed jagged shards of twisted metal forced *outward* from the powerful explosion. And, more damningly for Proksch, the explosion had occurred just where the Zapata cargo had been loaded. As for the insured goods in transit, the photos showed them for what they were: useless scrap, never worth shipping at all.

Proksch denied any guilt but was duly convicted of the murders and for his part in the fraud and sentenced to life imprisonment. Lütgendorf, the Minister of Defence who had authorised the provision of the explosives, *apparently* committed suicide. He was found in his car, shot through clenched teeth—scarcely the clearest indication of a voluntary death.

Hans Peter Daimler was charged with insurance fraud and as an accessory to murder. Although deeply implicated in the plot, Daimler denied his involvement, but he was brought to trial in Germany in 1992. The proceedings lasted a staggering five years and only in 1996 did he admit to any role. In 1997, 20 years after the *Lucona* had been so callously sunk in the name of profit, justice was done, and this co-conspirator was condemned to 14 years in jail.

This crime would never have been resolved but for the dogged persistence of the Bundesländer Versicherung, and perhaps also the determination of journalist Hans Pretterebner, who dared to challenge the powerful Viennese establishment. He never wavered despite intimidation. To their credit, despite the legal battles and the political pressures applied to them, the insurers never faltered either.

Eric Ellen had been monitoring the *Lucona* story for years. Confidential sources fed him information that he passed on to the Austrian police. Like the Austrian public, he felt frustrated by the slow progress toward any legal actions against Proksch and Daimler. 'We had an Austrian chairman at the time, and through him I passed on information that I did not think the Austrian police knew. We also wrote to the authorities complaining about the delays in bringing charges against Proksch and Daimler.'

Ellen declined to acknowledge that he had been tipped off about Proksch passing through Heathrow and had alerted Immigration, and thus Immigration must take the credit for spotting an apparently insignificant discrepancy in Proksch's forged passport.

Today, Café *Demel* on Kohlstrasse continues to serve up its magnificent cakes.[4] However, Udo Proksch, *bon viveur*, entrepreneur, spy, arms-dealer and adventurer, no longer greets his customers. He died in Graz following heart surgery in June 2001 while still a prisoner. Among many Austrians, Proksch has attained the undeserved status of a folk hero or cult figure. In 2004, he was the subject of a musical produced in Vienna, entitled *Udo 77*.

Proksch does not merit celebration as a hero, although his life had its fascination. Those who now revere his legend might like to recall that he provided a delectable chocolate cake from *Demel* to the crew of the departing *Lucona*. Perhaps this kind gesture eased his conscience: the unsuspecting crew had also sailed with about one-third of a ton of explosives and his intention had been that none of them should live to tell the tale.

---

[4]I can vouch for the cakes because I was permitted to give a lecture about the *Lucona* in the upstairs room where the conspirators met—a strange and moving experience.

CHAPTER SEVEN
The Chinese Enigma

In 1998 alone, of some 78 murders at sea, most occurred in Chinese waters. Some traumatised crews survived only to suffer permanent mental damage, haunted by disturbing flashbacks to their time as prisoners of often drug-crazed thugs. For them, the prospect of returning to the sea was too terrible to contemplate. *Anna Sierra* and *Cheung Son* are only two of dozens of examples of life and death on cargo ships sailing these waters. These two attacks have been pivotal in shaping exciting changes in China. The shipping world watched how they were handled. Tumultuous events occurred as the last century closed; the enduring implications are now more clearly visible.

Hong Kong–September 1995

The slight Singaporean made his way down in the express elevator, his thoughts on the meeting ahead. A regular visitor to the high-roller rooms of Macao's casinos, he was a pillar of the community and also a fabulously wealthy crime boss. His luxurious penthouse suite on the 67th floor offered magnificent views across Hong Kong's bustling harbour to Kowloon.

His armed chauffeur greeted him with friendly respect and opened the door of the black bulletproof Lexus. The boss slid into the deep leather seating, and after a swift journey through the flyovers and underpasses, the car pulled up at the entrance of the swanky Mandarin Oriental Hotel.

A meeting room had been booked in the name of an untraceable company. His own penthouse would have been more convenient, but the anonymity of a hotel meeting room was essential. There was no point holding meetings where the authorities could bug the discussions or monitor comings and goings. Secrecy was paramount. The agenda was full but the ground had been prepared.

The hotel room overlooked the Star Ferry Terminal. Below, the green and white ferries criss-crossed the narrow harbour, but he had no interest in such frenzied action. Big money was at stake. As he took his seat at the head of the oval table, he exchanged pleasantries with the three others present. Tea was served with a platter of tropical fruit as a centrepiece. The other men had flown in for the meeting, one from Bangkok, another from Batam Island in Indonesia, the other from Shanghai. They were all staying in different hotels in Hong Kong.

The chairman called the meeting to order. 'Item One is the *sugar problem*. Where do we stand on that?' The question was addressed to the man on his left, who had flown in from Shanghai. After a nod of the head acknowledging his responsibility, the chubby Chinese businessman ran down his manuscript list of items for discussion. 'All in order. The vessel is *Anna Sierra*. She will sail from Ko Si Chang in Thailand on 12 September. Aboard will be sugar worth US $5 million and a crew of 23.'

'Destination?'

'The Philippines, but we will take her to Beihai.'

'Attack time?'

'Soon after midnight on 13 September, a few hours after leaving port, in the China Sea. Captain Bekas, an experienced operator, will run the action. There will be two speedboats.'

'Name change?'

'All fixed. As soon as she has been captured, *Anna Sierra* will disappear. The ship's new papers are all organised.'

'And a crew?' The chairman reached across for more green tea, the monogrammed cuffs on his cotton shirt emerging from his tailored suit.

'We have a strong experienced team to go aboard, carefully selected. Some will leave with the valuables after we've taken control. The remainder will sail the ship to Beihai and, of course, will deal with the *crew problem*. Somewhere off Vietnam a day or two later.' He saw that his listeners understood and moved quickly on.

'Price of sugar for the, *er*, buyers?' The chairman's smile was wolfish.

'$4.2 million. An exact fit.' Everyone laughed.

'Excellent.'

'Port Authorities?'

'All fixed. Border Police, Customs—all our usual contacts. No problems there.'

'False papers for cargo?'

'In order. Bill of Lading and the rest. Shows the sugar was loaded in Brazil.'

'Thank you. Just one detail, then. Cover stories for the crew?'

'All briefed. They don't bear scrutiny, but with our friends in Beijing and the port, not a problem. They will believe *any* story put forward—assuming that the owners can even trace the ship.'

'Thank you. All very satisfactory. Then we can move on to Item Two on the agenda. Our next shipment of immigrants to the USA. What is arranged? Please be brief. I have to chair a meeting at the bank at 1100.' He turned to the man on his right. 'Please proceed.'

Gulf of Thailand–13 September 1995

MV *Anna Sierra*, a bulk carrier, was owned by Skate Shipping Company Limited of Limassol, Cyprus, where the vessel was also registered. The Cyprus Registry has an undistinguished record in looking after the interests of owners who pay the fees.

In September 1995, *Anna Sierra* was in the Thai port of Ko Si Chang loading 12,000 tons of sugar worth about $5 million, owned by the Indian State company MMTC. The destination was Manila in the Philippines. Aboard was a crew of 23 of mixed nationality. Loading concluded, she weighed anchor on 12 September and sailed eastward.

The criminals' informant, perhaps someone in the shippers' office, had confirmed the details of the cargo, crew and time of sailing. Perhaps a member of the gang had been planted aboard as a crew member, able to pass information secretly by mobile phone.

MV *Anna Sierra* did not get far. At around 0030 next day, the crew realised they were under attack. As usual, the mantle of darkness was used to conceal a swift and unseen approach. Thirty pirates approached in two fast boats, probably from the stern, bouncing and riding through the vessel's wake. They clambered aboard, one team from either side.

Ellen explains that it is surprisingly easy to board a merchant ship. Some ships, such as big cruise liners, travel fast and ride high in the water; their sides are too tall and sheer to be a soft target. Others, perhaps smaller or heavily laden tankers, ride much lower, their decks perhaps six feet above the water line. For skilled and fit young men, such vessels are an open invitation.

'The syndicates pay them well to grapple their way aboard. Ships making 12 and even 18 knots are no problem. A trick used by some attackers, though not on this occasion, is to position themselves in two small boats a distance apart. They straddle a shipping lane with a cable between them. The unsuspecting target vessel hits the cable and pulls the attackers into each side of the ship and at the same speed. The pirates can then get aboard.

'More usually, the attack will come by small and swift speedboats or rubber dinghies with powerful outboards. They approach from the stern to reduce the risk of being detected by radar. Unless the crew are patrolling the deck 24 hours a day watching for possible attackers, the odds are stacked in favour of the gangs.'

Once aboard *Anna Sierra*, the masked or hooded pirates opened fire with machine guns. In a terrifying show of force, they shot away the door to the accommodation where most of the crew were sleeping or relaxing in their quarters. Those on the bridge were overpowered. Surprise had made it easy. Within minutes, the pirates were in control. Forced from their bunks or from the engine room under threat of instant death, the crew offered no resistance. Fearing for their lives, they were forced into two cabins, handcuffed together in lines, and left.

There they remained, awaiting their fate, without food or water for two days. There were no facilities for bodily functions. In those cramped and locked cabins the atmosphere was appalling, the stench of fear, stale sweat, and excrement overwhelming. Escape was impossible. Their best hope had been that they would be freed quickly after the pirates finished their looting. The hours dragged on. Any hope that the raiders would leave quickly evaporated.

The steady throb of the engines reverberated through the ship. Laughter and excited chatter was heard as the attackers rampaged through the cabins. As the second day dawned, the crew's spirits were low. Some knew of pirates who had dumped crews on remote islands. They had all heard of crews that had simply disappeared, presumed murdered. Unseen by the prisoners, 14 pirates sped away, taking their loot with them, leaving behind enough men to control the situation and run the ship.

The sound of their cabin doors being unlocked aroused mixed emotions. After two uncomfortable days, the unshaven, dishevelled and starving crew were freed from their makeshift cells. There was no offer of food. Instead, they were driven at gunpoint to the deck. The shabby group shuffled along, their wrists aching from the handcuffs. The smell of the salty air was like wine. It was a relief to be freed from the cramped confines of the two cabins. Their clothes were filthy, they stank and were demoralised by their ordeal and traumatised by the ferocity of the attack. They shuffled forward, fearful, wondering what these brutes would do to them. Each man's thoughts were of family and friends. Their imaginations ran riot when they saw the hooded men, machine guns at the ready.

Some had heard of the *Jump Buddy* Pirate Gang, notorious for making crews *walk the plank* at gunpoint with the command *'ambak pare'—jump, buddy*. This was just one of 36 Filipino gangs operating in these waters, some believed to have military connections. Their victims rarely survived. Were they to share the same fate? Balaclavas were being removed by the pirates, revealing young faces with dead eyes and hard mouths. Sullenly, hearts full of dread, the crew stood in a line, wary, studying their captors for clues as to their intentions. The deck heaved and pitched as the *Anna Sierra* rode the swell. Silently, the gang surrounded them, machineguns poised, life and death in their hands. The leader of the pirates, Captain Bekas, an Indonesian, had other plans than murder. The frightened group was divided in two. A makeshift liferaft lay on the deck; the pirates had used oil drums and wooden planks. It was lowered to the heaving waters and the first group were forced over the side. The prospect of being abandoned on this raft, barely seaworthy, without food or water and so far from land, was a terrifying prospect.

Though the crew had no means of knowing where they were, *Anna Sierra* was now some 60 miles from the Vietnamese coast. The second group watched them. Fear of death was written on their shipmates' tired, weather-beaten faces. On their makeshift raft, they were reluctant to leave the vicinity of their ship for the uncertainty of the black empty ocean. But they were not given a choice. As they bobbed and tossed on the turbulent waters, the pirates machine-gunned around them, forcing them to allow the raft to drift away into vast empty seas.

Nobody was hit by a bullet—perhaps not surprising, in view of the sea conditions. On board *Anna Sierra*, the remaining crew were then forced overboard, this time onto a proper liferaft, and also abandoned to their fate. The cries of the dumped crews died away as *Anna Sierra* sailed north. In the warm accommodation, food was prepared for the pirate team. It was a time for celebration. They had completed the first part of their contract with the crime bosses: stolen a ship plus a cargo worth $5 million. The fate of the crew was of no concern to them.

The two liferafts drifted apart, mere corks bobbing about in the vastness of the rolling sea. The fate of the 23 men was a lottery. Many honest seamen have died by cold-blooded execution; others have been dumped overboard and never seen again. This crew was luckier. The eight men on the oil drums were picked up later the same day by Vietnamese fishermen and taken to Condao Island. The other 15, including the master, were also rescued later, having drifted another 40 miles away from land.

The master and his crew were taken to Vung Tu, where on 18 September he was able to brief the owners on Cyprus. The Cypriot Registry contacted authorities including Interpol, the American Regional Search and Rescue (ARSR) and the IMB. Immediately, the American Mutual Vessel Research (*AMVER*) team started a search. This system, sponsored by the US Coast Guard, assists in rescue coordination. Ships in the area using the voluntary system are notified of the missing vessel and directed to watch out for her or, in cases of sinking, to provide emergency help. Underwriters for the hull of the ship announced a reward for information. The IMB's Regional Piracy Centre in Kuala Lumpur started enquiries in every possible port from India to Japan.

Unbeknownst to the searchers, the *Anna Sierra* had even now, on 20 September, put into the Chinese port of Beihai, some 350 miles from Hong Kong, in Guangxi Province, just west of Guangdong Province in the southeast corner of China. The *Anna Sierra* arrived unannounced under the name *Artic Sun*. Instead of the Cypriot flag, she was now apparently registered in Honduras, a Registry favoured by criminals.

Ellen decided to try a different tack to find the ship. Having a good relationship with several intelligence agencies, he asked one to use their satellite to trace the ship. The feedback was that the vessel was moored off Bangkok. They were able to pinpoint her position. When Ellen gave the owner the good news, he was overcome with emotion over the phone and promised Ellen a holiday on his yacht!

'There had been some typical publicity about the hijacking and the reward. This led to a call from an Australian who ran a mission. He explained that his father knew a Thai admiral who could help. I asked him to find out if the pirates were still aboard and he reported back that they were, saying she was moored about 40 miles offshore. Furthermore, it would be seized by the Thai Navy at 2130 that night. Success seemed assured.'

The intelligence officer was passing through London, so the owner, who was not in town, treated Ellen and the officer to a celebratory dinner at the five-star Savoy Hotel overlooking the Thames. There was every reason to believe they had succeeded. They had traced the vessel. The cargo was still intact and the ship was about to be seized. Success did not usually come so swiftly. Now, with ShipLoc technology, tracking stolen ships is much easier.

The celebrations were premature. Ellen took a call expecting more good news from Thailand, but the Australian reported that the Thai Prime Minister had refused permission for the seizure because the vessel was outside territorial waters. Ellen's request for his phone number was refused.

He was told it was a very busy line. Ellen contacted his Kuala Lumpur office and asked them to pull out every stop. A flight over the ship's apparent position brought even worse news.

Ellen's man reported that the ship had never been near Bangkok. The intelligence agent had got it wrong! A phone call to the Australian police revealed that the informant was a known hoaxer who had probably been attracted by the published reward of $100,000 for information! Breaking it to the owner was not easy, either. He had been landed with the bill for an expensive dinner—and no ship either! Ellen never got the holiday on the yacht.

'Fortunately,' he says ruefully, 'later, better information from our Far Eastern contacts led us to the vessel in Beihai, China. The informant was positive that the so-called *Artic Sun* was *Anna Sierra*. We asked the authorities to hold the vessel and on 25 September we got confirmation that she had been taken under the control of the local representatives of the Chinese Frontier Defence Authority. The pirate crew was still aboard. We had found the ship but it was another false dawn.' Never again would anything about the *Anna Sierra* give cause for celebration.

The IMB Regional Piracy Centre at Kuala Lumpur, which had opened in 1992, was then being managed by John Martin. He flew to China to investigate, arriving there on 8 October. Identifying the vessel moored at Quay 4 was straightforward. The words *Anna Sierra* were still visible, as was its original name, *Diagara*, which was welded on both the bow and stern of the vessel. The name *Artic Sun* was just a splash of paint. In discussions with the Chinese Frontier Defence Authority, Martin was satisfied that there was clear evidence for action against the pirate crew who had sailed her into port. Only one of them had a certificate of competence. Additionally, the Bill of Lading was a forgery, stating that the sugar had been loaded in Brazil.

Martin was able to demonstrate the truth without difficulty. The sugar had been loaded in Thailand and was owned by MMTC. But, as he reported to Ellen in London, each fact proven was dismissed. The officials were unreceptive and adamant. Against overwhelming evidence, the pirate gang maintained their innocence and were believed.

'John Martin's evidence was never going to move the authorities, no matter how convincing. From past experience, I was not surprised. We knew of the corruption in China and of the close relationships between gang leaders and the Chinese authorities.' Nonetheless, after a promising start with the arrest, this was another setback after the Thai episode. The *apparent* owners of *Artic Sun* produced further explanations and false documentation. However feeble their claim to ownership, it was sufficient. The Chinese authorities made sympathetic noises but did nothing to assist. Meantime, the vessel lay in dock, the sugar still aboard along with the pirates, who should have been in jail awaiting trial.

Martin then played his trump card: he produced further evidence of the crew's part in the crime. Their passports showed entry into Thailand at Bangkok Airport on 7 August but lacking exit stamps—precisely as might be expected from a gang of pirates. However, their leader, Captain Bekas, stuck to his story: *We sailed from Thailand to Manila in a vessel called the Polaris. There, we were hired to join a ship in need of a crew. Its name was the Artic Sea. Anna Sierra must have been before our time. Nothing to do with us. On 16 September, we sailed from Manila and reached Beihai four days later to deliver the Brazilian sugar. Sorry. End of story. Not our problem.*

The plausibility of this fiction did not bear scrutiny. Firstly, the ship could not have sailed from Manila to Beihai in four days unless she were rocket-propelled. The *Anna Sierra* was only capable of making 11 knots. She would have needed to travel at 33 knots, three times faster than her top speed!

It was becoming evident to the Bureau that Bekas had been assured by his paymasters that any old story would do. The criminals had good friends in Beihai. Bekas knew he would never be jailed. Certainly the Chinese Frontier Defence officials accepted this obvious hogwash!

The Bureau rethought their strategy. Martin made further enquiries. There was no record of a vessel called the *Polaris* either leaving Thailand or arriving at Manila. Bekas was blatantly lying. Cypriot Registry officials made representations in Beijing; it did no good at all. The locals in Beihai did precisely as they pleased.

The Bureau tried again, exposing another lie: the Honduras Registry confirmed that there was no registration for a vessel called the *Artic Sun*. The Bureau really had won this—game, set and match—but the local officials preferred the lies and forged papers, including the bogus Bill of Lading. The criminals knew better than to waste money on legal formalities and expense like a temporary ship registration. They had something far better: the *complicity* of the authorities.

Luckily, the false papers were still very helpful: they revealed an involvement in a previous crime. The forged Honduras registration incorporated the registered number of a vessel involved in a previous operation, linking these pirates with organised crime, a view which further evidence would support. The false ownership papers had been prepared onshore but, when the *Artic*

Sun sailed towards Beihai, a speedboat had delivered the necessary paperwork to give the crew some semblance of credibility.

Any reasonable Government would have freed the ship and arrested the pirates. But in China in 1995 the opposite happened. The *Anna Sierra* remained under arrest, and upkeep and maintenance onboard was ignored. In December 1995, after two hard months of talks, research, and more talks, the Chinese Public Security Bureau gave a millimetre. They admitted what had been obvious all along: the *Artic Sun* was the *Anna Sierra*! But she could not be released to the owners. There were more enquiries to be pursued.

With this stalemate, the Public Security Bureau then took an extraordinary step. They authorised the release of ten members of the pirate gang. Worse news still for the interests of law-abiding seamen, insurers and shipowners everywhere, they allowed them to leave China. The message was plain: *Criminals win here. As for the rest of you, tough!*

Ellen and the Bureau felt badly let down by the Chinese, but things would get worse. A few weeks later, in February, the owners received both good and bad news from the authorities in Beihai: they could have their ship back. They were delighted. The sugar needed to be delivered urgently and the ship needed urgent maintenance.

Just pay us $400,000 to cover our expenses—then your ship is free!

Perhaps not surprisingly, this deal was rejected by the owners! It was neither the first nor the last outrageous ransom demand. Pathetic rates of pay meant the temptation to make a fast buck at the first opportunity was irresistible. 'So if you were faced with problems, you could never be quite sure of the vested interests,' explains Ellen. 'You have the Chinese Navy and Border Patrols operated by the military. Then there is the PLA, the People's Liberation Army, and less powerful than these are the police. The National Security Bureau runs the police.'

Each province had its own police, scarcely surprising in a country of this size. Significantly, powerful members of the PLA used to set up trading companies to run commercial ventures, probably, but not inevitably, linked to smuggled or stolen goods. That factor was potential dynamite. Additionally, the mighty Public Security Bureau wielded corrupt influence locally from Beijing. Corruption flourished at all levels.

As the days went by, the remaining gang members were treated with agreeable hospitality. They left the discomfort of the neglected ship as its condition deteriorated and were accommodated in a guest house like visiting sailors rather than the local jail, more appropriate for ship-stealers who had dumped a crew in the sea.

Perhaps refusing to pay $400,000 no longer seemed such a good idea, because over a year went by with more wrangling. Then officials from the Public Security Bureau brought the type of news that owners dread. Unfortunately, the engine room had flooded. The holds containing the sugar didn't look too good, either. 'We've tried to salvage some cargo by removing it from the ship.'

Salvage! A predictable euphemism for theft! The Indian owners of the sugar refused to take this lying down.

Infuriated by this double-talk, they flew to China, intending to inspect their cargo wherever it might be. The mission was doomed to failure before it started. They were denied access to the ship! Enquiries led them to conclude that half their cargo, some 6,000 tons, had already disappeared up country.

In February 1997, in another predictable move, the Public Security Bureau reported that the now listing vessel was a danger if left at Quay 4. *Anna Sierra* was towed away and dumped, stranded on a sand bank at a nearby beach, where, no longer seaworthy, she reposed for years. Perhaps she is still there!

The remaining pirates were later repatriated to Indonesia, despite a legal basis for action under the 1988 Rome Convention (of which the Chinese Government were signatories). No doubt some of them returned to their piratical trade. As for the cargo, the Bureau learned that the PSB planned to sell it to a local buyer at cut-price rates. The Bureau intervened but only succeeded in getting the sale postponed. No sugar was ever recovered.

There is a fascinating background to this hijacking. The *Anna Sierra* was not hijacked as a random act of piracy. Ellen is sure this was a carefully planned crime with a sinister background. The pirate crew, though Indonesians and Malays, were controlled by a criminal gang operating from Hong Kong. The bosses had entered into a deal with some Chinese businessmen who represented a Chinese state-owned company. The Hong Kong gang had then defrauded the Chinese, who lost $800,000.

'Reneging on such deals or failing to meet obligations can be dangerous. With a *state-owned* company involved as a loser, the Chinese authorities might have intervened officially and taken action against the fraudsters,' Ellen said. 'Or the Chinese businessmen in on the deal might have taken justice into their own hands.'

He continued, 'To prevent such reprisals, a new deal had been agreed: the Hong Kong gang was to deliver sugar to Beihai at a bargain price, $800,000 below its true value. The local buyer would pay $4.2 million for a $5 million cargo. The books would then balance. And of course the best thing to do is to steal the ship and the sugar. Then both sides win. The losers are underwriters and the owners of the vessel and its cargo. That's what happened here. *Anna Sierra* was *stolen to order*, specifically targeted to repay a debt. This explains why the false documentation showing a sale of the sugar to the Chinese buyer was prepared even *before* the *Anna Sierra* sailed from Thailand. It also explains why the ship was wrongfully detained, the pirates released and the sugar delivered locally instead of to its rightful owners. The entire operation was pre-planned.'

The unfortunate crew who had been dumped in the ocean endured a terrifying ordeal. Some never returned to sea. The master was hospitalised for a year. Riding the waves on the high seas perched on bits of wood and oil drums, perhaps with killer sharks lurking, would haunt anyone. But these highly organised gangs had no respect for human life—only profits and deals counted. This crew was lucky. They survived.

The *Anna Sierra* case was a gross injustice to the owners and to the entire shipping world, but it was not an isolated incident. By releasing pirates, a Government encourages others to seek easy pickings; the criminals themselves are free to return to the line of work they know best! The names of some have been linked to subsequent attacks.

Ellen closed his file with a resigned shrug. 'Sometimes the law is unclear, but here the Rome Convention had been signed by China and it had a legal *obligation* to act against the pirates.' During an unrelated investigation, Captain Mukundan had uncovered a contract between gang leaders and pirates promising a quick release or good legal representation if captured or arrested. Such a contract is far more valuable than the Rome Convention.

What had being going on in and near Chinese waters had fascinated and frustrated those seeking truth and justice. That ships were being attacked, stolen, diverted, phantomised or just robbed was clear. That crews were being attacked with cannon, automatic rifles and rocket-propelled grenades was evident from the rising number of reports. Beyond that, the truth was confused by cunning crime bosses and by political denials and evasions.

Before the frightening *Cheung Son* incident, the traditional approach of the Government in Beijing had long been to wash its hands of piracy. During the '90s, the shifting sands of Chinese politics subtly changed this standpoint. The full extent to which attacks were beyond Government control or how far Government employees were implicated may never be fully known. But much of the mystery of the attacks, the *modus operandi* and the type of figures behind them, can now be explained through the help of the Bureau, especially since the outrage over *Cheung Son*. Ellen helps to put legend and fact into perspective.

'Around 30 years ago, the Bureau reported that the majority of phantom ship crimes were organised in China by gangs with connections in Hong Kong, Singapore, Thailand, Malaysia and Indonesia. More distantly, they worked with connections in the USA and Japan. In such crimes, once the initial cargo has been stolen, the vessel is put to work with a new identity. China had been central to the activity. Probably there was Triad involvement. The crime may not have been organised during meetings in China, but Chinese crime bosses were in on the deals and were probably the prime movers.'

Corruption in the big ports made them a safe haven where stolen ships could be disguised or stolen cargoes sold. 'Take MV *Tenyu*,' Ellen recalls. 'She was pirated in the Strait of Malaccain 1998, just before MV *Cheung Son*, but ended up in a Chinese shipyard, where she was discovered being disguised to become a phantomship. Her 15-man crew were less fortunate. They were never seen again. What happened next is almost unbelievable. In a repeat of the *Anna Sierra* experience, the pirates were all freed, even though probably guilty of murder. No doubt they all returned to their old ways, perhaps using new identities.'

Despite official denials from Beijing, crews who were attacked were the victims either of local warlords or of warlords working with powerful influential politicians or central Government officials. For too long, Beijing failed to impose its will to quash regional corruption, oil smuggling and piracy. This was because powerbrokers in the Beijing Government knew that the tentacles from the ports might ensnare them too.

The problem for the Japanese merchant fleet, Ellen believes, is that to reach Japan, ships have to run the gauntlet of these waters from the Gulf states, India, Malaysia and Singapore. For years, the Chinese authorities totally failed to police their waters properly. As often as not, attacks on ships involved pirates who operated with the knowledge of corrupt Chinese officials or who were actual officials abusing their powers.

Japanese vessels, often carrying valuable cargo such as oil, were first exposed to the significant risks of the Malacca Strait. Then the vessels headed northeast toward Hong Kong. These hours in the South China Sea were dangerous. The risk of an attack could continue right up the east coast of China between the port of Xiamen and the island of Taiwan. Japanese merchant ships were attacked 66 times in five years, the majority around here. Owners, the Japanese Government and insurers grew increasingly angry as losses mounted. Representations were made to the Bureau to assist. Despite using their influence and contacts, for years they achieved very little. Much of what they attempted was ignored by the Chinese

Government. Yet despite the lack of *obvious* progress while he was director, Ellen's persistence, like the drip of water on stone, was having an effect.

Captain Mukundan continued the campaign, but it was not until 2004 that the scourge of wanton piracy was seriously tackled in the Malacca Strait. Patrolling was commenced, plus aerial surveillance under arrangements between Thailand, Malaysia, Indonesia and Singapore. In 2006, the Indian Navy became involved too. But suppressing crime simply drove the pirates into the less risky waters of the South China Seas. Around 140 reported attacks there around the turn of the century fell dramatically in the mid-2000s but then later rose again to over 70 per annum. However, thanks to naval patrolling, better procedures and increased awareness of crews, the number of incidents in the Malacca Strait has recently dropped to almost nil.

One catalyst for the increased determination to be effective in the Strait was the backlash from 9-11. With around 64,000 vessels passing through the Strait annually and Singapore being a key pro-West port, fears mounted of a terrorist incident occurring in or around the port. Indeed, in 2002, the Singapore Government thwarted an intended attack on US Navy vessels in harbour—something along the lines of the attack on USS *Cole*, discussed below. But the greater fear was of a vessel with a toxic or dangerous cargo being pirated by terrorists and then used as a weapon around Singapore.

Ellen observed: 'Problems for shipping around these waters went beyond the high seas, right into ports, law enforcement and justice. In Fujing and Guangdong Provinces in southeast China, corruption was so rife that it coloured everything. Community leaders greedily pocketed extorted money.' Commands from the top brass in Beijing, Xiamen and Guangzhou filtered through to every aspect of trade—to the quayside, to Customs and to the Border Patrol Police. Wherever they had power (and in this region that was *everywhere*), the Chinese warlords imposed their will on merchant shipping, either through power and influence or by force of arms.

By 1994, the Chinese Government was aware of the deep concern of international bodies such as the IMO, the Baltic and International Maritime Council (BIMCO) and the Bureau. In Beijing, diplomats had regularly delivered strongly worded complaints about maritime robbery and murder. These complaints were met with *apparent* horror and indignation that anyone should blame the Chinese authorities—whether for ineffective action to catch the criminals or for active participation in crime.

'The first sign that our message was getting through to the Government in Beijing came in 1994,' confirmed Ellen. 'Chinese ministers admitted a need to improve the safety of their waters and ports. In a paper presented to the International Maritime Organisation (IMO), they accepted that *yes, there was a problem. Some* official law enforcement officers *had* been involved in smuggling and other incidents. It was denied, however, that they were involved in acts of piracy. It was pointed out that some attacks had probably been carried out by *black ships—look-alike craft* masquerading as Chinese official vessels.'

In 1994, in a further attempt to distance officialdom from pirates, the Chinese Customs changed the appearance of its anti-smuggling vessels, but to little lasting effect. The gangs were still able to impersonate the Customs or to use their vessels to launch an attack. Almost imperceptibly, the official Beijing position changed as the turn of the century drew close. Beijing no longer met protests from people like Ellen or shipowners with bland assurances and flat denials. Instead, there was an admission that *in certain regions*, matters were indeed *out of control*! This was a major concession, subtly expressed. But could Beijing impose law and order on its unruly provinces?

The uncontrollable problem in the regions was smuggling. Ironically, a well-intentioned new law from Beijing aimed at curbing this only led to a marked *increase* in shipping crimes. Beijing introduced a *reward scheme* for those like the police and customs: 50% and more of the value of contraband goods seized would belong to the captors. Ellen continues the story. 'The aim was to encourage local officialdom to crack down on crime, rather than to accept bribes or share in the gangs' profits. Oil, perfume, watches, Marlboro cigarettes and whisky were among items taxed heavily. The higher the tax, the greater the incentive to smuggle.'

Smuggled goods sold tax-free meant big profits for the smugglers. But the gangs took it further, *stealing* the smuggled cargoes, especially oil. The rich profits had to be shared with corrupt local officials, but the biggest slices were reaching the bosses, whether in ports like Xiamen or in distant Beijing.

Regrettably, the good intentions backfired. Law-abiding ships carrying attractive cargoes were seized by Chinese authorities both inside and even far *outside* their waters. They forced the vessel into port, claiming the ship had been caught smuggling, and demanded their reward of half the value of the goods! The innocent shipowner then had to pay a virtual ransom to get his ship released.

These unjustified arrests amounted to piracy and hijacking, yet sometimes the ship's master faced absurd charges of smuggling. The crew would be forced to sign confessions and money was demanded for their release. Sometimes they were even charged with illegally entering port, having been forced there at gunpoint from as far as 1,000 miles away! The warlords' rule was totally out of control.

Hong Kong shipowner William Tay faced this problem. He owned two ships, the *Hye Meiko* and *Hye Prosperity*. Both were hijacked by Chinese Customs and forced into port. The former was carrying cigarettes worth $2 million. William Tay tried to get his ship freed and was arrested for smuggling. His other ship was targeted within a year. The total cargo stolen was valued at $4 million.

Disturbingly, and a sign of the decline in traditional standards at sea, distress calls went unheeded, even though the attack on *Hye Meiko* occurred 1,000 miles from port, providing ample time for intervention. These were not Chinese territorial waters. The British Navy in Hong Kong wanted to intervene but was ordered not to do so. The UK Government wanted no confrontation with China. No doubt Chris Patten, the last governor of Hong Kong, did not want to sour delicate relations leading up to its return to Chinese rule.

Many countries, including the USA and the UK, protect their interests outside their territorial waters. 'So one can't jump to the conclusion that the Chinese were behaving disgracefully in arresting ships. What changes the position is the knowledge that such arrests were often not *bona fide* and were just piracy attacks. But to intervene with a British warship would mean you had to be very *sure* the victim was not a smuggler.'

Customs Patrols sailed ever further to find innocent ships to seize for rich rewards. Through their local contacts, they knew which vessels to target and technology helped track their targets down out on patrol. At the same time, Customs Patrols were still accepting bribes from the gangs to ignore the *genuine* smuggling that continued unabated. Their activities, under the cloak of officialdom, created havoc for merchant shipping.

Imagine standing on the bridge of a 3,500-ton vessel far out in the South China Seas. You are carrying a lawful cargo of perfumes or cigarettes, mobile phones and whisky bound for Japan. Suddenly on the horizon a vessel appears, speeding towards you. As it approaches, you note that it is flying the Chinese flag. The vessel is grey with a white bridge. It seems official and thus has the authority to stop and search. The crew, wearing black uniforms, are heavily armed. *It's the Chinese Customs! But we're outside their waters. But if they say different, who would believe us in a Chinese court? And if we disobey, they can open fire. But what if they aren't genuine? Suppose they are pirates? And even supposing they are genuine, are they going to rob us all and steal the ship? Will they kill us all?*

Such were the thoughts running through the minds of honest, law-abiding seamen. And with good reason! In one year alone, 98 crews went missing or were murdered in this region. 'Some attackers *were* customs officials, on or off duty, abusing their status,' explained Ellen. 'Others were Border Patrol officers or members of the People's Liberation Army, which included naval personnel. Additionally, criminal gangs did deals to borrow the official boats or uniforms—or even to buy them outright. *Someone*—someone high up in Beijing—*must have known* what was happening. But it was impossible to prove anything. Not every attack involved Chinese officials directly. Crews from elsewhere—Burma, for instance—masqueraded as Chinese in some attacks.'

Just before the attack on MV *Cheung Son*, the IMB and BIMCO had written a joint letter of complaint to Huang Zhen Dong, the Minister of Communications in Beijing. BIMCO is the world's leading private association of shipowners and other companies, with representation in over 100 countries. 'We hoped that the letter would open a dialogue with the Chinese Government,' recalls Ellen. 'High on the agenda was the conduct of the Chinese Port Authorities, the Public Security Bureau, the Police, Navy and other maritime authorities. A number of examples of disturbing attacks and failures to investigate or take action were listed, including the *Anna Sierra*.

'The *Vosa Carrier*, a container ship, had been hijacked by what appeared to be a Chinese Patrol boat in November 1997 and taken to Hui Lai. The attackers had been dressed in what appeared to be military uniforms. There the police allegedly forced the master and crew to sign confessions of smuggling. After signing, the crew had then been forced to sail the vessel to a port in Shentou, where containers worth $2.5 million were offloaded by the police. Having been forced to pay them $100,000, the vessel was freed to go. The cargo was stolen.'

The *Asian Friendship* had also been boarded without justification in November 1997 at Guangdong and forced to sail to Shanwei. Complaint was made also about *Petro Ranger* and *Tropicana*, but the core complaint was the shabby way that the *Anna Sierra* situation had been handled.

'I regret to say,' concluded Ellen, who was a signatory to the letter, 'that we had neither acknowledgment nor a reply. That was perhaps to be expected. Whether our letter did any good behind the scenes is harder to judge but I believe it did. It may have started or encouraged a radical overhaul of the problems.' Subsequent events support him. The drama of *Cheung Son* was the opportunity for Beijing to take heed of the complaints.

Cheung Son was targeted from behind closed doors during secret meetings by crime leaders, probably Triad societies. A suitably vicious bunch of thugs were hired for the attack. Their seafaring credentials were less important than their ruthlessness and the ability to use a machinegun or to slit a throat without qualms.

Ellen explains that in planning an attack, bosses leave no stone unturned. They get hold of the target crew's names and the addresses of wives and families of senior officers. At gunpoint on a darkened ship, threatening a man's family, showing they know the home address, provides a powerful incentive to cooperate.

Once the Triads or other criminal syndicates have stolen a vessel, they have many options. After the cargo has been sold at a suitable port, they may then change the crew again, distancing both themselves and the pirates from the original attack. Their new phantom ship might then carry legitimate cargo designed to be stolen, or the vessel may be used for people-smuggling or as a mother-ship from which to launch further attacks.

The shipping crime bosses are Teflon-coated, impregnable in their apparent respectability. The crew would have no idea of the identity of their paymasters. A middleman would know something of the boss above him but such dangerous knowledge would never be revealed. The penalty would be death, and probably a painful one.

The criminal masterminds mingle in polite society, chatting around the baccarat table, meeting politicians and socialites in exclusive clubs on Singapore's Tanglin Road or in boxes at Happy Valley Race Track in Hong Kong. Many made their fortunes in the 1970s by scuttling ships, usually with an *apparently* high-value cargo, for insurance payouts. Such crimes were then in vogue; in most cases, the insurers paid up.

So concerned were authorities and insurers about ship scuttling that in 1979 a high-powered international maritime team was established. The *Far East Regional Investigation Team* (FERIT) was based in Hong Kong. Their task was to investigate suspicions about crimes in Southeast Asia and discover who was behind them. FERIT scrutinised a cross-section of suspicious losses or dubious claims. Their report startled maritime society from its complacent slumber. *Of the ships lost and claims investigated, a large number were probably fraudulent. Organised crime was indeed behind the sinkings; the gang leaders could be identified; the profits made were mind-blowing. Notwithstanding, there could be no immediate prosecutions.*

Before this report, the attitude around London EC3, where the Lloyd's insurance market is centred, was that the occasional unusual sinking was not really worth the cost of a probably fruitless and expensive investigation. Bitter experience had blunted London's reactions. Suspicions might be raised or even confirmed, but expecting a strong enough case to decline payment or prosecute was unrealistic. Underwriters could only adjust future premiums to reflect the risk.

FERIT shook them up, but in more than 30 years, little has changed. Deliberate scuttling of ships for insurance is a trend that comes and goes, depending on the state of the market. If the cost of keeping an ageing rust-bucket afloat became too much, the owners (who often belonged to Triad gangs) would create false paperwork to show a valuable cargo when the reality was very different. The ship would then be lost at sea. Underwriters in London would shrug their shoulders, smile through gritted teeth, and pay up.

In the 1970s, a Hong Kong syndicate operated out of Singapore hotel rooms. Discretion dominated their behaviour. As captains of industry, they did not appear out of place attending closed-door meetings in the Shangri La Hotel in Singapore. The Chinese members were as likely to be based in Hong Kong. By using their own unique cashless transfer system involving vouchers and nicknames, the value of money was transferred between participants in these crimes, far beyond the reach of police or others trying to secure evidence of crime. Scrutiny by authorities clamping down on money laundering was avoided. This private system operated totally outside lawful banking. Use of nicknames concealed true identities—even if the individual were known. *Mr Wong*, the Singaporean operating the Indonesian end of a syndicate, is a case in point. Though he has been caught and jailed, his true identity remains a mystery!

These were the *Mr Bigs*: smooth-talking, sophisticated men with black limousines and gold cigarette cases. Men with political connections; men who knew Chiefs of Police and Prime Ministers. Men who put personal greed before the lives of innocent sailors. Men who might even attend a meeting in London or Hong Kong about how to combat piracy! These were the men who masterminded the notorious pirate attack on the *Cheung Son*.

MV *Cheung Son*, built in 1997, seemed an unlikely vessel to become a milestone in modern piracy. There was no obvious reason for this Panama-registered bulk carrier, managed by Waibert Steamship of Hong Kong, to be selected for attack. Perhaps the attack was opportunistic. But it is far more likely that she was targeted with meticulous care because she fitted the needs of the ringleaders. At 17,000 tons, she was quite large but she was carrying nothing more attractive than furnace slag—no whisky, no oil, no cigarettes, no Rolex watches. The value of her cargo was only $750,000—small change in maritime crime circles. The attraction must have been capturing a valuable new ship for future use as a phantom.

In November 1998, *Cheung Son* was moored in the huge Chinese port of Shanghai when the decision to mount an attack was made. With 23 Chinese crew aboard she sailed for Port Kelang, a Malaysian port close to Kuala Lumpur, some 400 miles north of Singapore. To reach its destination, the vessel first had to brave the dangers of the South China Sea, then run the gauntlet of the Philip Channel by Singapore before entering the Strait of Malacca, all areas teeming with pirates. IMB statistics show that at that time attacks had been reported every two days.

Only three days after *Cheung Son* left Shanghai, while it was still steaming southward through the Taiwan Strait in the South China Sea, the attack came. The crew were busy about their duties on the bridge, in the engine rooms or galley—just another routine day at sea. In the distance a fast-moving vessel appeared, heading towards them. As the speck took shape, it was evident that this was the Chinese Customs. Their patrol boats were always active in the region, ever watchful for smugglers or other opportunity to make a fast buck.

There were 32 personnel on the patrol boat, an unusually large number. They wore the uniform of Chinese Customs or paramilitary police. The Chinese officers on *Cheung Son*, seeing what looked like officials approaching, must have pondered three possibilities. Were they genuine Government officials going about their lawful duties? Were they genuine officials abusing their boat and uniforms to seek private gain on a day off? Or were they a bunch of pirates who'd acquired a patrol boat?

Patrol boats owned by the Chinese Government had been bought by gangs and syndicates. For gangsters able to forge papers and organise ship stealing, acquiring uniforms to look like military or customs personnel was easy. Piracy was an *industry*, with a regional turnover estimated at billions of dollars every year.

As the order was given for the *Cheung Son* to be stopped and searched, the officials in the black Customs uniforms gathered on deck, sinister and intimidating in their sunglasses beneath their caps, machineguns at the ready. But *Cheung Son* was not engaged in smuggling. The more optimistic among the crew relaxed. They had nothing to hide. There would be a routine search and they would be on their way again. On the grey and white patrol boat, the Customs Officers, the apparent representatives of the Chinese Government, tied up alongside *Cheung Son*, boarded and swarmed everywhere, rounding up the bewildered and terrified crew. Too late came the realisation: they *had* been duped. This was no Customs Patrol. This was a pirate gang in disguise on an official boat.

Now prisoners, the fearful crew of the *Cheung Son* stood silently on the deck. Soni Wee, the Indonesian leader of the attackers, strutted about, barking out commands to his excited team. The prisoners' fate lay in his hands and that of a Chinese called Weng Siliang, a central figure in what followed. The captors relished having the power of life and death over the cowering crew.

Ill-educated, impoverished and just trying to earn a basic wage at sea, *Cheung Son's* crew's lives were now at stake. If they had refused to stop for searching, they would have been arrested if the officials were genuine. If criminals, they were doomed to be invaded anyway: Soni Wee and Weng Siliang had their orders. *Cheung Son had to be taken*. She fit the bosses' bill.

Forget the glamour, the *frisson* of the Jolly Roger fluttering in the breeze, the chink of gold doubloons, the swigs of rum. There were no parrots on their shoulders—just automatic weapons. These pirates were hardened criminals, hired by the faceless bosses ashore. They were ready to kill if necessary, even delighting in their victims' terror. Scenting blood, their faces were alight with anticipation. Some were high on drugs and alcohol. Soni Wee was no exception.

Around the freighter stretched the rolling emptiness of the South China Sea. For the crew, there was no fairy godmother, nothing and nobody to end their nightmare. This was no film, no pulp fiction. The glinting machineguns, the rocket-propelled grenades, the curses of their captors were all horribly real. So was the mocking laughter as Soni Wee's brain raced, his drugs kicking in. The plan was brilliant. His shifty little eyes blazed at the prospect of what lay ahead. He saw it all in glorious Technicolor. Grinning, he snapped out the order and beckoned. The first crewman in line stepped forward…

On 26 November the IMB put out an alert. MV *Cheung Son* had disappeared. Ships in the area were asked to look out for her. No *known* crime had been committed, but she had disappeared some 200 miles east of Hong Kong. The area was notoriously dangerous. No mention was made of hijacking but the worst was feared. A few days later, the first evidence emerged. Fishermen from Shantou in Guangdong Province hauled in their nets, hoping to have caught enough fish to sustain them for another day. But their haul was unexpected and gruesome. In the net lay a rotting corpse of a Chinese male bound to a heavy metal weight, his mouth taped. Soon, the nets brought up five more bodies. All the men had been murdered. Some had been bludgeoned, some stabbed, others shot. Post-mortems would show it was unclear whether some were even dead when they were thrown into the sea.

In contrast to their usual reluctance to take effective action against organised crime, the Chinese police acted decisively. Identification of the mutilated corpses became a priority. Once they had been identified as members of *Cheung Son's* crew, instead of the usual fudge and hypocritical assurances, urgent efforts were made to trace the attackers.

The authorities were relentless—and fortunate. By chance, during a separate investigation of a theft on land rather than at sea, the police stumbled on devastating evidence: sickening photos of a party on the deck of the *Cheung Son*. The murderers were seen drinking and laughing in triumph, a grotesque celebration of the murder of 23 innocent men. The mystery of the crime quickly unravelled—at least on one level. In January 1999, 20 men alleged to have been involved were arrested. Soon, that number rose to nearly 40. The apparent leader, the 27-year-old Indonesian Soni Wee (also known as Wei Suoni), was carrying 156 grams of narcotics. While he was widely reported and regarded as the leader, the criminal court later decided after a six-day trial that although Soni Wee had put the team together, it was in fact the Chinese Weng Siliang, also aged 27, who was the leader. But not one Triad paymaster was arrested. The traditional silence had not been broken.

The full story started to break. The pirates had each been paid $11,000, a very large sum for poor Asian seamen when overtime rates for a police inspector were only 60¢ per hour! Once aboard, the terrified prisoners had been lined up on deck and forced to watch helplessly as each in turn was murdered by the method *chosen by the killer*: a crowbar, a blade, a gun or a length of rope.

The leaders wanted to bloody the hands of their accomplices, to ensure their silence and loyalty. But the celebratory photos had scuppered the plan. Each pirate being ordered to kill a victim explains why some had been bludgeoned with metal bars, others stabbed or shot—all 23 slaughtered to satisfy expediency and bloodlust.

Their murders were unnecessary. Many successful pirates have left the crews unharmed, perhaps dumped on a remote island or forced onto liferafts. The crew of *Anna Sierra* could count themselves lucky compared to the hapless victims of *Cheung Son*. One of the disturbing trends since the '90s has been the increase in violence, with drugs used by captors playing a significant role.

No incident compares to the gratuitous wanton killings on the *Cheung Son*, although the *Jump Buddy* gang also revelled in cruelty. Drink and drugs played a significant part in the exultant behaviour of this murderous gang. Who knows what horrors were endured by the other 78 murdered and missing crew lost that year? The Chinese People's Supreme Court decided that the death penalty was appropriate. Most of the men had been convicted of ship robbery, mass murder, drug smuggling and the illegal possession of firearms. *Cheung Son* was only one of their targets. Evidence revealed they had been involved in at least three other attacks, including that on the *Loishan*, an oil tanker from Singapore. Following the trial, 13 of the 36 accused were executed in Shanwei in Guangdong Province amid an orchestrated fanfare of publicity. Nineteen received jail sentences; six were acquitted.

An appeal from the local court in Shanwei was turned down. The Supreme Court ruled that the facts were clear, the evidence complete, the convictions correct and the punishments appropriate. Those executed reportedly went to their deaths drunk on rice wine, bawling out the Ricky Martin hit *La Copa de la Vida*. The Chinese Government had acted throughout with ruthless efficiency—a line had been drawn in the sand. At last a message was given to the pirates: *China would no longer tolerate such crimes*. It also marked another significant first. The corrupt influence of their paymasters had not sheltered the thugs, nor helped them avoid arrest and execution.

Among those executed was the supplier of the vessel they had used to give the impression that this was a Customs visitation. The same man had provided the uniforms. Those executed were no saints, but no *Mr Big* was charged, convicted or executed. Yet even the masterminds must have been shaken by this turn of events. One selling point when they hired gangs to steal ships had been their ability to protect the pirates from prosecution. In future, there would be fewer volunteers, since they could not rely on promises of protection.

The Chinese Government had wasted many opportunities to clamp down. They could have started over 10 years earlier, or in 1994, or after the *Anna Sierra* saga in 1995. Sharp action then would have saved those 23 sailors on *Cheung Son*, the crew of MV *Tenyu*, and hundreds of others. Many unsolved murders were probably committed by the *Cheung Son* killers.

Neither the ship nor its cargo of furnace slag has ever been traced, but according to the Chinese authorities, Soni Wee and Weng Siliang, the two ringleaders, had sold looted items for $300,000. '*Cheung Son* became too hot to handle. It has completely disappeared. Nobody wants to be associated with it for obvious reasons,' explains Mukundan. Perhaps it now lies deep in the South China Sea.

'*Cheung Son* was a watershed, a hijacking too far,' Mukundan added. 'Since *Cheung Son*, the People's Republic of China has acted firmly on two other attacks. MV *Marine Master* was later stolen by 20 Burmese pirates dressed in what appeared to be Chinese military uniforms. *Marine Master* was later found under another name but recognised and the crew were arrested. The real crew had been forced onto makeshift liferafts, all but one of which had broken up. Somehow, this crew survived by clinging to the debris. Again, the legal process was swift and decisive. The pirates were convicted, although only the leader was in fact executed.

'The Chinese Government also acted forcefully following the theft of MV *Siam Xanxai*. The 10 Indonesian attackers who had stolen the ship and cargo were caught and sentenced to long-term imprisonment. The crew had been dumped on a remote island. The vessel was promptly returned to its owners and, though the cargo of oil had been stolen, some compensation was paid by China.' Changed times indeed!

Whereas before 1999 the waters around China were highly dangerous, crimes like *Anna Sierra*, *Tenyu*, *Hye Prosperity* and *Cheung Son* have now been stamped out by decisive Chinese action in securing convictions and clamping down on corruption. Mukundan confirms: 'China is no longer causing difficulties. It has shown that however in-built is the corruption, the menace of piracy can be resolved. Actions taken involved big changes in the Public Security Bureau and were central to this welcome new environment. Now, our efforts are centred on assisting the Indonesian authorities to meet their obligations.' That said, perhaps around 2005 was the moment of greatest security for these waters; since the end of open-season piracy in the Malacca Strait, the open seas here once again present increasing dangers, but nothing to match the callous brutality of the murderous gang who killed so many.

Captain Hartmut Hesse, formerly Head of the Navigation Section in the Maritime Safety Division of the International Maritime Organisation but now Special Representative of the Secretary-General for Maritime Security and Anti-Piracy at the IMO, added a cautionary note. 'The action of China was effective in its waters and ports. The problem is that the criminals then shifted the focus of their activity away from the penal risks in China for other parts of the region where law enforcement is lax and corruption still operates.'

However, in the years since the crackdown, the big drop in murders suggests that the gratuitous bloodlust that drove some gangs has been curbed. The Chinese action has had lasting effects as the ripples of its ruthless purge have spread. The IMB's report of October 2013 records no incidents in the region classified by them as 'China.' There still remain problems in the South China Seas, but nothing compared to the days before MV *Cheung Son*.

The Indonesian tsunami of 26 December 2004 interrupted the shocking wave of crimes round northern Sumatra and the Strait of Malacca, but after just a few weeks the lull ended. Hopefully there will be no return to the regular hijackings and ransom demands around Aceh, and certainly no return to the days of stealing ships for changed identities. But the problems of Far Eastern waters have not gone away.

In November 2013, pirates attacked a small tanker off Malaysia and held the crew captive while they used a pipe to offload the cargo of gas-oil into their own vessel—just one example of the many crimes that still concern the IMB's Piracy Reporting Centre in Kuala Lumpur. In the first nine months of 2013, there were 91 attacks or attempts in this Far Eastern region alone. Globally, the total in the same period was 188. The overall figures are dramatically down from 2011, when there were 130 attacks or attempts around Somalia alone. The IMO initiative to ensure that vessels of over 300 gross tons carry an Automatic Identity System (AIS) that provides details of speed, position, cargo, etc. has been a significant factor, as has the (still underused) ShipLoc system favoured by the IMB. Some masters believe that use of AIS around Somalia is a danger and they are permitted at their discretion to switch it off in the interests of crew safety. However, the IMO still expect it to be left on in the region.

For observers like Eric Ellen, the major disappointment had been the failure to destroy the real powerbrokers. As it turned out, *Cheung Son* sparked off more than just a 'safer seas' policy. It triggered the internal purge against corruption in Chinese officialdom that has continued to date. Curing endemic corruption is a long and difficult job in so vast a country, where 46 million officials work for the government. But relentless efforts by the previous and current regimes are helping to eradicate crime both at sea and around the ports.

Attempting to stamp out or at least curb regional corruption was a bold and risky strategy akin to stirring up a hornet's nest. Just which powerful figures might be implicated was the worry. Most Asians understand the concept of *face*. International businessmen working in the region are briefed on local etiquette. A Chinese will not insult you by saying *no* in the brusque manner that might command respect in a Detroit boardroom. There will be subtlety, grace and dignity in his refusal. During the '80s and '90s, *face* played a part in Chinese attitudes to complaints from outsiders about shipping crime The Chinese Government was coming under fire from other Governments and from world bodies like the IMO, the IMB and BIMCO—and rightly so. They were still on the back foot from the public relations disaster of Tiananmen Square in 1989. A siege mentality informed ingrained resistance to criticism. In those days, for Beijing to admit point-blank that central government was powerless to control its regions would have been unthinkable.

After 1994, the tone changed slightly: there just *might* be a few problems in some coastal regions. With local warlords so obviously dominating both the quaysides and cities from Shanghai through Xiamen to Guangdong Province, this was the barest of admissions. Yet for the Government to acknowledge it was the first sign that external pressure and the realisation of their own impotence could no longer be ignored.

Cheung Son had presented Beijing with an opportunity. *Chinese* fishermen had dredged up *Chinese* corpses from a vessel in *Chinese* waters that had sailed from the *Chinese* port of Shanghai. This was a *domestic incident* of shocking atrocity. A clean-out of the Augean stables commenced at once, with implications far beyond shipping.

One mastermind behind many smuggling crimes was Lai Changxing, a prominent and fabulously wealthy businessman who had developed a web of contacts in the Xiamen area in Fujian Province and beyond. Born in 1958, he had become a popular Robin Hood figure, having helped redistribute wealth from his smuggling empire by funding community projects. He drove a bulletproof Mercedes (previously owned by President Jiang Zemin himself). Smuggled oil, cars, cigarettes, electrical and other luxury goods had produced profits of over $6 billion between 1996 and 1999 alone, and he had been operating long before that. One-sixth of China's vast oil requirements passed through his hands. After his downfall, the price of petrol rose sharply—he had been popular for providing it locally at cut-price rates! It could be said without exaggeration that, in Xiamen, his black economy had become *the* economy! The region's local and central Government servants were virtually doing two jobs: their legitimate duties and their work for Lai Changxian's illegal operation.

His influence and power penetrated every area of community and business life—the Communist Party, the Public Security Bureau, key local politicians, the police, the Police Border Defence Force, bankers and customs officers. The former Director-General of Customs, Yang Quinxian, was a splendid contact. He would later testify in court how, in return for a Lexus car and the cost of maintaining his lover, he had turned a blind eye to what was going on. Condemned to death, his sentence was commuted. He was fortunate. Another Customs official, Wu Yubo, also based in Xiamen, was executed.

Xiamen is an important coastal community with a major deep-sea port. The city, which has a population of over one million, is situated in Fujian

Province, southeast China, opposite the island of Taiwan. Significantly, it is far from Beijing. This city was the power base for Lai Changxing until he and his wife were forced to flee the country to avoid arrest. Armies of residents viewed the destruction of Mr Lai's empire with regret. He had been revered as a man who had done more to assist them and improve their quality of life than Government ministers in Beijing.

During the '90s, Xiamen had been modernised and the typical pollution problems of Chinese cities had been tackled. In 1999, the US Embassy's website attributed the success of Xiamen to a wide variety of possible causes, including *cultural differences* and approaches, but unless cultural differences was an intended euphemism for corruption, the assessment was wide of the mark. One man above all had transformed the city. His *Yuan Hua* company dominated the economic prosperity and controlled the way the city was run. It had even been suggested that Xiamen be renamed Yuan Hua!

Stung by the *Cheung Son* murders, influenced by the regular complaints from the IMB, the IMO and BIMCO, and knowing the extent of regional corruption, the Government decided on a thorough investigation. President Jiang Zemin appointed Prime Minister Zhu Rongji *personally* to take control. Publicly, they announced that the investigations would spare nobody, but they knew they were walking on thin ice: the scandal from Xiamen and the Provinces could topple senior figures both in the Communist Party and in Government. Skeletons in cupboards have been at least as plentiful in Chinese politics as elsewhere—and probably much more so.

The Prime Minister acted decisively. Instead of local police, dozens of agents from Beijing swarmed into Xiamento investigate the crimes. They formed a command centre in a local hotel (subsequently bugged to keep Lai Changxing informed!). At one point, over 150 Government officials were being held. The evidence showed that the Xiamen smuggling syndicate reached the core of the Government's power base. A picture emerged of a region operating like a private fiefdom. Involved were senior party members in Beijing and local powerbrokers; Mr Lai stood out as the kingpin.

The extent of the clean-up was staggering. In Fujian Province, 600 Government officials were charged with involvement in smuggling through Xiamen. That should be seen in the context of a nation with nearly 50 million civil servants! Li Jizhou, Vice-Minister of Public Security, was the highest figure in the Beijing Government to be disgraced. He was sentenced to death, suspended for two years for taking bribes from Lai Changxing. Around the equivalent of $50,000 was involved. His official duties had included acting as Deputy-Head of the National Anti-Smuggling Group!

The evidence against him suggested he had accepted bribes in return for manipulating both police and border security. He was luckier than seven others, executed in February 2001 following convictions for tax evasion, smuggling and associated offences. Investigations also suggested that the Prime Minister's own wife may have been involved in corruption, having held a position of influence in Xiamen. No proceedings have been taken against her, so the investigations either cleared her or were inconclusive.

Li Jizhou's life may have been spared in return for his silence in taking the rap for other, more important figures who were not charged. Their exposure would have made the collapse of the Government itself a real possibility. As it was, the scandal was the largest in 50 years of the Communist Party's rule. Also convicted of corruption in Beijing was a former Deputy-Chairman of the National People's Congress, while a Lieutenant-General was charged with providing protection for local criminals. With such well-placed friends, small wonder that local criminals were able to steal ships or cargo and to smuggle goods with impunity.

Despite the Prime Minister's promise that the investigations would expose wrongdoing right to the very top, and although some big fish *were* arrested, it is most unlikely that all the major figures were implicated. One close friend of the President, whose wife was under close scrutiny and who himself had been Governor of Fujian Province, was later promoted to China's Standing Council. Some say *that* friendship saved *both* husband and wife, though both deny any wrongdoing.

As the investigation gained momentum, Lai Changxing still thought he was safe, until an urgent message from Zhuang Rushun, former Deputy-Director of the Public Security Bureau, tipped him off to leave at once. The deputy mayor of Xiamen, Lan Pu, and his wife were also warned to leave. Taking $600 million with him and travelling on an illegally obtained Hong Kong passport, Lai went to Canada. However, Lan Pu was later arrested and convicted of taking bribes, and was sentenced to death with a stay of two years. Lai's two brothers only avoided the death penalty by cooperating with the investigation.

If press and court reports are accurate, Lai Changxing was Mr Big in southeast China, though he denied this. There is no suggestion that he was *immediately* connected to any shipping incident (although his oil import business was central to his fortune). By the time he was forced to flee, he was certainly *Mr Everything* in Xiamen, if not the *Mr Big* of the criminal fraternity as the Government contended. His company, *Yuang Hua* (Fair Well), was reportedly used to remove any obstacles in his path. Though he always denied paying *bribes*, others since dead or in jail have admitted accepting money or favours from him or his company. He used his wealth to achieve his goals. He claims there was no intent to corrupt or bribe—just a wish to be generous with friends and business associates.

The alleged payments were large, sometimes running into millions of dollars, but even small sums seemed large in a poor society. For less important services, he allegedly presented gifts—small cash sums, alcohol or chocolate, or paid for children to be educated abroad. He also invited useful people to parties at his pleasure palace, the Red House, from the outside a deceptively unprepossessing seven-storey building. For these privileged contacts he provided old wine and young girls who catered to every desire of his favoured guests in the *fun area*, with its karaoke, dance floor, sauna, footbaths and luxurious Jacuzzis.

Those who had enjoyed their frolics at the Red House were taken aback by the later revelation that their benefactor had been videotaping the action! The extent to which Mr Lai may have used the footage to pressure the businessmen caught *in flagrante* is not clear. Ironically, some of those arrested were only identified by being caught on camera.

Central to the regional shipping crimes was the repeated hijacking of oil tankers where the oil was stolen. The Government believe that Lai's smuggling, especially oil, where the profits were greatest, enabled him to buy the local soccer team (renamed Yuang Hua). He also built a 30-storey hotel, launched brands of Yuang Hua cigarettes, sold Yuang Hua wine and created the Yuang Hua Entertainment City, modelled on the Forbidden City. This alone cost $17 million. At the time he fled, he was building an 88-storey skyscraper, the tallest in the region, presumably to be called the Yuang Hua Tower. The building site became a gigantic puddle.

Lai became a corpulent married man with dark close-cropped hair and a prominent moustache, though later his physique and face showed the stress of a fugitive's lifestyle in Canada as he fought to stay out of the Chinese judicial system. He had come a long way from his peasant upbringing, when he had collected garbage. Dubbed China's *Public Enemy Number One*, he fought for years to dodge extradition. Back in 2000, Chinese secret agents masquerading as businessmen had slipped into Canada, offering him a deal to return voluntarily in exchange for no death penalty. Lai nevertheless suspected that he would be executed. For around 12 years, he battled against extradition in legal proceedings that cost Canada millions of dollars.

In 2004, he had been ordered to be returned to China, but constant legal manoeuvring kept him in Canada. If Chinese assurances were to be believed, Lai Changxing would get a fair trial and would not face the death penalty if returned, factors that would ultimately influence the Canadian position. In November 2006, adopting a major shift of strategy, Lai alleged that back home he had a close relationship with a number of the topmost Communist Party officials, all of whom would fall from grace were he to be forced to volunteer their names. As a teaser, he named Jai Quingin, a member of the Politburo Standing Committee, who in the '90s had been the Communist Party chief in Fujian Province. Whether there was anything improper or corrupt in the relationship is of course unproven.

Canada faced mounting pressure and eventually, in mid-2011, an order was made for him to be extradited after 12 years living near Vancouver. To the end, Lai Changxing maintained that even though he might not be legally executed, if repatriated, he might still end up dead in sinister circumstances, from an apparent fatal illness or mysterious sudden death. Throughout his fugitive years, he and his Canadian lawyers were well aware that a Chinese computer expert charged with fraud had been deported from Canada following assurances from Beijing that he would not face the death penalty. After trial in China, he was sentenced to death. A similar fate befell a former planning official extradited from Thailand. The Thai authorities had been assured there would be no death penalty. He, too, was executed for corruption.

Lai Changxing therefore had good grounds for fearing that he would face the death penalty. Some eight lesser figures in his extraordinary empire had already been convicted and executed. The angry comments of Premier Zhu Ronghi in October 2000 reflect the official views of the damage he did to the interests of central Government. 'If Lai Changxing were executed three times over, it would not be too much!'

Though Lai initially lived the life of a casino high roller in Canada, everything changed during those 12 years. Lai Changxing lived (apparently) impoverished in Vancouver but continued to resist extradition until the order was issued against him. At times, he had been held in custody, at other times free to live in the community. He had also been under virtual house arrest, his vast fortune inaccessible in frozen bank accounts.

In May 2012, he was convicted in his own town of Xiamen for running a multibillion smuggling operation involving cars, cigarettes and oil, and sentenced to life imprisonment, still fearing an unexplained death in custody rather than one from natural causes. His Canadian lawyers had pointed to the deaths in prison of Lai Changxing's brother and his accountant, both of whom allegedly died in strange circumstances. Now, in his prison cell, the tycoon can only dream of bygone days when he had houses all over China, luxury cars and the power and wealth to achieve anything he wanted. Now, he can only hope that a sinister death does not await him. Two years later, he is still alive and in prison. Right up to the time of his dramatic escape by speedboat to Hong Kong with a false passport, he believed that he would manage to avoid arrest, but, just as the pirates of *Cheung Son* discovered, Beijing's steamroller of justice had started on its juggernaut course.

In other parts of China, too, the war on corruption has been ongoing. The practical effects of the tough line on marine crime, plus clipping the wings of the local warlords, has been of enormous help to bodies like the Bureau, who knew that corruption was rife in the ports and far more out of control than the sanitised comments from Beijing suggested. The hundreds of arrests bear witness to the scale of the problem the Bureau had been up against. Seatrade is now booming. Freight rates are high. Part of this boom is due to the explosion of Chinese exports. However, Captain Mukundan does not think that ownership by Triads or gangs explains the drop in crime. In his opinion, it is the clean-up on corruption, and in particular sweeping changes in the Public Security Bureau, that have ended the glut of attacks that formerly plagued this area.

What Triad bosses and other gang leaders will now do in the context of shipping crime is unclear. Stealing ships and cargoes was just one way to make huge profits. Loansharking, prostitution, counterfeiting Western goods and smuggling are still mainstream activities. The syndicates will turn to whichever crimes are most profitable and offer least risk. People-smuggling has now become one of the most lucrative crimes; despite occasional arrests, too many illegal immigrants reach *Golden Mountain*, as the Chinese call the USA. Meantime, while it is too soon to say that Beijing's iron-fist approach has permanently stopped hijacking of ships, there have been no more incidents like *Anna Sierra* or murderous attacks like *Cheung Son*. Killing for fun is no longer a viable hobby in the China seas.

CHAPTER EIGHT

People-Smuggling and Human Trafficking - And the Shame of *Rape-Island*

Where there is poverty, repression, war or loss of hope, many people will seek a new start elsewhere. Dreams of a better life far across the sea are irresistible. Nowhere is that dream better exploited by organised crime than in parts of Eastern China. Gangs are estimated to be earning $8 billion a year peddling false hopes to those who aspire to a better life in the USA, Europe or Australia.

To the Chinese, America is the land of riches and opportunity. They call it the *Golden Mountain*. Some aspirants never live to see it, dying during terrifying ordeals en route. Many wish they had never tried to find the rainbow's end. Only the most fortunate find their pot of gold. Only the Triad gangs like the notorious *Fuk Ching* who run the operations get rich quick.

Though the Chinese Triad gangs dominate this evil trade, illegal people-smuggling is rife. Would-be immigrants come from Afghanistan, Haiti, Turkey, Indonesia, Mexico, the Middle East, Africa and the Balkan States. Russian Mafiosi and other groups have muscled in on this lucrative trade. Events in 2013 around Italy have shown that death in transit is a special risk for immigrants crossing the Mediterranean from North Africa. But death stalks all those who put their faith in people-smugglers.

There is a fine line between *people-smuggling* and *human trafficking*. What starts as one may end up as the other. People-smuggling is a business run for profit. People are paying for a new life abroad. Human trafficking often involves people, usually women and children, snatched from their homes or the streets of Thailand, Hong Kong or other Oriental cities, never to be seen again, or people hoping to be smuggled to a fresh start but who are snatched while in transit.

Kidnapped, these victims reappear in prostitution the world over, often having been forced into drug addiction. Many young children are exploited to satisfy the perverted needs of paedophiles. Even Dublin has been receiving a steady influx of enforced prostitutes who are controlled by Chinese *snakeheads* or other criminals. Gangsters from Eastern Europe operate a similar type of business, seizing women and children from the Balkans and elsewhere and forcing them to work as prostitutes in cities as far away as Sydney or Sao Paulo.

Peter Schatzer, when Director of the International Organisation for Migration (IOM), confirmed just one aspect of human trafficking: 'The Council of Europe organised a Budapest conference on sexual exploitation of children in cooperation with the United Nations Children's Fund. Delegates painted a grim picture of as many as one million children who are sexually exploited around the world. The trafficking of minors from Europe's former Communist countries is increasing at what delegates said is an alarming rate.'

Schatzer also commented that the incidence of illegal immigration into Europe had become so serious that the EU has to contemplate visas—not, in his view, an infallible solution to the problem. He sees *prevention* as the prime focus, with a need to improve job opportunities and rewards in those countries from which people emigrate. Interestingly though, in the case of China's Fujian Province, extreme poverty is less of a problem than in other parts of China. Here, it is a cultural tradition of travel, fuelled by genuine success stories from those who *lawfully* migrated, that feeds the process that has led to an estimated ten million risking the perils of being smuggled to a new land.

As expanded later, the International Maritime Bureau has been concerned about people-smuggling since the days when thousands of Vietnamese boatpeople were attacked and abused as they fled their war-torn country toward a new life in Hong Kong or elsewhere.

Fujian Province, China

It is early evening in the narrow, jam-packed streets of Fuzhou City on China's eastern seaboard. A snakehead is busy on his rounds, one of hundreds of hunters operating in the region. He is the first link in a complex chain headed up by the ultimate crime bosses. He is responsible for signing up the unfortunates who wish to escape illegally to a promised better future. Part of a Triad operation like *Fuk Ching*, *Sun Yee On* or *Sai Fong*, he is answerable to his superiors, the true snakeheads who make their millions from trading inhuman misery. The proceeds of crime are good. This *small* snakehead, a young man in his late twenties, has a smart house, a Jacuzzi, a home gym and his own car. He has material assets and suffers no pangs of conscience about the deceit and lies he peddles to get people signed up. Today, he has a list of families to contact.

The name *snakehead* comes from the words *She-Tou*. The epithet originated from the serpentine routes these men follow to smuggle the brave and the gullible into foreign countries.

Dodging the bicycles, he hurries between the shabby tenements, where caged birds and washing hang outside the windows. Next, he will visit rural villages, where other hopefuls will sign up for the voyage. A few days later, he will return to his comfortable home far away across the sea, near Changi Airport in Singapore.

He is meeting a young man who wants to abandon his life in the suburbs of Fuzhou to travel to *Golden Mountain*. Once there, he wants his wife to follow and then to start a family, giving them a great start in life. Ying Xing Kuihas worked as a kitchen hand in a restaurant and his wife is a machinist. They could earn more in the big city of Xiamen, but only if lucky enough to find or bribe their way to a job. But messages from friends who made it to America suggest big opportunities—high wages, 20 times higher than in Fuzhou; people over there had washing machines, televisions, high-tech goods and were free to travel.

What the naive Ying Xing Kui did not understand was that these friends had entered the USA *legally* and not by the snakehead route, or else they had been forced to write glowing testimonials. America accepts many immigrants ever year under a variety of schemes. But Ying Xing Kui did not know how to apply, so he turned to the snakeheads—*well-connected and clever people* who could get you to the USA by boat *and* set you up in jobs.

The snakehead climbed the stairs to the one-bedroom apartment where they sat round a dimly lit table. Excitedly, the couple listened to the plan. He showed them an album of photos from New York and London. Flipping over the pages, they saw snaps of happy smiling families beside big houses and cars. These people had allegedly taken the snakehead route to wealth and happiness in the West. Chinatown in New York was Ying Xing Kui's dream. He was told he would probably leave by fishing boat to Taiwan. There, well offshore, he would join a larger vessel. Maybe they would go to Hong Kong and join others. Maybe they would travel to Hong Kong by road, a journey of many hours. Maybe they would cross the Pacific direct, heading for Seattle or San Diego. Then there would be transport to New York and the new life. *But bring nothing at all. Not even a suitcase with belongings.*

How much?

$38,000. But all you pay now is 10%. That includes a false passport from Singapore.

Ying Xing Kui was not surprised. He had even heard of $50,000 being paid. *Perhaps this will be a smaller ship, a bit less comfortable*, he reasoned. From his bedside he produced cash—loans from their parents and all their savings for this big moment. He handed over the down payment and was given a formal contract. In ignorant expectation, he signed away his future. The balance was to be paid in instalments from his earnings, his *big earnings* in *Golden Mountain*, or by the family here.

Eight weeks later, in December 1999, bidding a fond farewell to his wife and promising that she would join him soon, Ying Xing Kui set off to the meeting place in Xiamen. He took no belongings, nothing to identify him. Here the snakeheads, as sales representatives for the Triad gang running this voyage, knew that leaving in a fishing boat would be trouble-free. Bribes paid to the local police and navy meant that nobody would be interested in the boat slipping her moorings to enter the Strait of Taiwan with a human cargo of 20.

Early the following morning, huddled against ropes, with nets for a pillow, Ying Xing Kui was aroused by an order to make a move. He saw the vessel that would be taking them to their next rendezvous. He knew little of ships but could see it looked quite big, certainly compared to the boat he was in, jammed against the other hopefuls. *Perhaps he would have a cabin. That would be better.*

Their next carrier was a small cargo vessel of 1,500 tons, stolen to order by pirates down in the Philippines and now operating as a phantomship with a new name and an apparent registration in Belize. Once aboard, he found hundreds of others like him—men, women and children, all pushing, shouting and jostling as they were herded in the cramped space. There were no cabins, no suitable washing facilities, only a scramble for the rice and noodles. He found himself locked into a dark hold that stank of fertiliser. They were packed in and ignored.

None of his fellow passengers seemed to know what lay ahead. Some had heard from friends who had taken the snakehead route and had phoned to say how they should do the same. *Life in America was good. Big money, big cars, lots to eat.* What they did not know was that all these calls had been made under coercion. Once in America, new arrivals quickly realised that they had sold their birthright to the gang. Their future would be working as slave labour, perhaps for over 100 hours a week, most of the money going to pay off their debt for the journey.

The local snakeheads forced them to write home to encourage their friends to make the trip. Violent deaths silenced the occasional brave soul who tried to warn others in China. In protecting their interests, Triad gangs have no qualms about inflicting violence. In London, three young people were locked in a basement, doused in petrol, set alight and left to die. One survived, badly maimed and disfigured. Only the brave or foolish risk crossing the paths of these gangs.

The rusting ship sailed south and entered Hong Kong harbour, its human cargo hidden below decks slipped in unseen; people had been paid to turn a blind eye. Shiao Lin knows, from her life in Taiwan and from working with the Bureau, that people-smuggling into Taiwan from mainland China is rife. In 2003, four men were jailed for murdering six illegal immigrants being taken to Taiwan. About to be caught, they threw the women overboard to hide the evidence of their illegal trade. 'Often, to go to the USA, they are brought to Hong Kong by road. If Europe is the destination, then gangs take them over land as much as possible. That's cheaper. Generally, the method of carriage to the US is by dumping the emigrants into the holds of a cargo ship, 20 to each one. Previously the cargo may have been coal, iron ore, grain or whatever, so you can imagine the filthy conditions.

'The vessel crossing the Pacific is always a rust-bucket—an accident just waiting to happen and virtually unseaworthy. Only the rust and a few rivets keep the show afloat. Sometimes old fishing boats are used, and who knows how many of them have sunk en route across the Pacific. The money for transit probably purchased the vessel—sometimes for a one-way voyage only. The boats are often abandoned near the American coast. The food, water and toilet paper are rationed precisely. The food is measured precisely to last the voyage and not a minute more. There is no margin of error.'

Ying Xing Kui and the rest on this Triad package tour from hell found no bunk beds, just a dirty hold. Some immigrants are now paying $60,000 for no more comfort. Prices have risen since 9-11 as the problems of getting into the USA and Europe have increased through tighter security, better intelligence and heat-seeking technology used to find immigrants concealed in containers.

In the shadows around Hong Kong harbour, under cover of darkness, Ying Xing Kui was led with a handful of others to the container depot. Here, giant gantries shrieked and groaned as they picked and dropped containers in relentless cacophony. Groups disappeared in different directions, all entering separate containers. Finding himself crowded into a 40-foot container was not what Ying Xing Kui had anticipated. A snakehead led the party in. Eighteen hopefuls looked around: there was some basic food and water and a slop bucket in the corner. This was their *cabin* for their voyage to *Golden Mountain*.

They had been told that it would take 14 days and were assured that they had ample water and food. The container doors were slammed shut. They were now prisoners, the doors bolted and the seals put in place. Ying Xing Kui was frightened now. It was dark and the container jolted and creaked as it was grabbed for transit. The immigrant hopefuls felt themselves being picked up and then lowered, expecting that soon they would feel the vibrating throb of the ship's engine.

But it never came. What was happening? They had been told they were sailing at once. Even the snakehead was anxious. Something had gone wrong. As fear mounted, Ying Xing Kui had to fight a desire to scream out his terror of dying here in the darkness. He knew he could never see his wife in New York. He could never permit her to endure this hell. He would have to return to Fuzhou once he had the money.

Day after day passed. The water and food was the bare minimum for a 14-day voyage. It was disappearing in the silent gloom as fast as the snakehead rationed it out. At last, after a week standing on the Hong Kong dockside in December 1999, the container was again lifted and this time lowered below decks on a ship bound for the USA. They were now in the hold of a cargo ship called *Cape May*, bound for Seattle.

The seas were heavy as the ship approached the American coast. Not that those in the container cared much about the weather or the sea condition by that stage. There were other, more urgent problems. The quayside delay had been disastrous for those in the stinking container. Their sparse rations had long been exhausted. They had paid $680,000 for the journey. The snakeheads had no contingency plan. They didn't care.

Ying Xing Kui felt delirious, lightheaded, his mouth dry and painful. They were starving to death. Dehydration was setting in. He was short of breath and his heart was racing. As he listened to the rustlings of others around him, all now too weak to move around, he sensed his life was slipping away.

Ying Xing Kui was lucky to survive. *Cape May* moored at Harbor Island, Seattle, on 11 January 2000. The container was raised from the bowels of the ship and dumped on the quay, then shifted along with some 35 others to the Container Terminal. The next phase was to transport them to New York. A van would arrive, ready to take them on the long journey from coast to coast.

Ying Xing Kui and the others in this container were spared that trip. In winter, when the icy winds from the Canadian wastes sweep across the northern part of the USA, bitterly cold weather grips the route, usually dumping a great deal of snow. Ying Xing Kui never got to feel those freezing temperatures. A tip-off from Hong Kong had led to a massive security operation in Vancouver and on seaports on the USA's West Coast. On 2 January, a container had been seized and opened by Immigration and Naturalisation Service officials. Inside they found 12 hopefuls like Ying Xing Kui. They had travelled on another container ship, and had been more fortunate in their choice of *tour operator*, as they had sailed from Hong Kong on schedule on 19 December. Agents from the Immigration and Naturalisation Service had waited. They were not disappointed. A van arriving to collect the immigrants was stopped for questioning. Two Chinese from New York were arrested. Charges followed and the two men, Yu Zheng and Sheng Ding, pleaded guilty to a smuggling conspiracy.

Another 25 frightened Chinese were found on 3 January in a container offloaded from *California Jupiter*, which had arrived in Vancouver, just the other side of the American border. She had sailed from Hong Kong on 20 December.

On 11 January 2000, long shoremen were instructed to open the container from the *Cape May*. They choked on the stench of decaying corpses and accumulated human waste.

Ying Xing Kui survived, but four others who had paid their money also paid with their lives, dying from heart failure caused by starvation and dehydration. Following enquiries in New York, arrests were made and charges preferred against three Chinese, two men and a woman. The charges included *wanton disregard for human life*. In 2002, the ringleader was jailed for nine years.

In the American successes, besides the INS officers, the FBI, US Coast Guards, Port of Seattle Police, and the Organised Crime and Triad Bureau of the Hong Kong Police were involved. Since 9-11, the US has restructured its approach and the operation became coordinated by US Immigration and Customs Enforcement (ICE), part of the Department of Homeland Security. In November 2004, 51 alleged organised crime figures were arrested in New York, charged with alien-smuggling, attempted murder, money laundering and illegal gaming.

In the period between January 2000 and April 2001, some 200 smuggled persons were seized by INS, a mere tip of the iceberg of the many who succeeded and still succeed in reaching *Golden Mountain*. The precise figure is unconfirmed, but experts believe that at least 25,000 Chinese enter the

USA illegally every year by boat, besides those arriving by air or across the border from Mexico. In Miami in November 2003, a couple were arrested and charged with having allegedly succeeded in bringing in thousands over a 20-year period. The route from China was via the Philippines, France, the French Caribbean islands and then Miami to New York City.

Ying Xing Kui claimed political asylum. But back in Fujian Province, even as news broke of the deaths and the inhuman travelling conditions, the flood of immigrants did not stop. Many in the Province see it as a matter of family pride to accept the challenge of going abroad to become a big breadwinner. Fuzhou City, with around 1.5 million people, is, by local standards, reasonably prosperous, but many are still tempted by the tales of a better life and the dream of reaching *Golden Mountain*. On one occasion, a US Coast Guard cutter intercepted a rust-bucket, the *Wing Fung Lung*, bound for the US. When this 200-foot Russian freighter was stopped about 300 miles offshore, it was crammed with 249 Chinese. When challenged, the master initially claimed the vessel was Taiwanese, had only six aboard and was carrying plywood and rice. Identity checks soon proved this was false.

The Coast Guard then had a legal entitlement to check a stateless vessel. More than six faces could be counted peering through portholes. The master refused permission to search. The crew launched a liferaft and started to scuttle the ship. This prompted a naval cutter to deliver a boarding party of 25, which forced its way aboard.

Taking on a crew plus a mob of angry and frightened immigrants is a tough proposition. The passengers had paid huge sums and were nearly at *Golden Mountain*. They would not be thwarted by the US authorities. The master released the passengers from their noxious dungeon, the main hold. Suddenly the deck was swarming with starving, thirsty, confused people, among them the controlling snakeheads and the crew, blending in to avoid arrest.

Aboard the freighter, the Americans found 12 inches of water in the engine room—the valves had been opened to let water in. 'I'm not at all surprised by this cynical attempt to drown the immigrants and save themselves. Each passenger is just a disposable commodity. Their disdain for human life is limitless,' confirms Ellen, adding, 'These Coast Guards could have been lynched.' Once the ingress of water had been reversed, the snakeheads tried to set fire to the ship. While trying to control the throng crowding the deck, the Americans were assaulted and attacked with wire rope. One snakehead arm-wrestled a gun from an officer and fired it. Nobody was hit. Eventually, pepper spray and batons subdued the mob.

'One of the problems is identifying the guilty from the passengers,' confirms Shiao Lin. 'You look for clues. Which ones seem better fed rather than wasting away. Tattoos are another giveaway. You may notice some people giving rather than receiving orders. If you're lucky, some passengers might assist in identification, but most are too scared to do so. Understandably.'

Wing Fung Lung made it to land and the 249 were repatriated, lucky to be alive, unlucky to have been caught. Arrests were made and charges brought against the ringleaders.

In the never-ending battle against organised crime, the story is not all negative. The police in the USA and Europe have arrested two snakehead bosses—very big cheeses indeed. The most important one is called Chui Ping Cheng, known as *Sister Ping* or sometimes *Big Sister Ping*. She was New York based and her name differentiated her from her namesake, *Little Sister Ping*, the leading snakehead in Europe masterminding immigrant-smuggling there. Her real name was Jing Ping Chen. *Little Sister Ping* is alleged to have smuggled over 200,000 people into the UK alone. Her husband was the reputed head of the 14K Triad gang in Rotterdam, where she lived behind the façade of a Chinese restaurant called *The Orient*.

When 54 illegal immigrants were found dead crammed into a container at Dover Docks on the English southeast coast, all hell broke loose. *Little Sister Ping* was not originally named as the mastermind of the operation in Europe; indeed, a Turk was cast as the mastermind of the illegal shipment and sentenced to 10 years. Only when his girlfriend then volunteered that he was not the leader at all and that it was *Little Sister Ping* did the real snakehead boss get arrested. Despite trying to avoid arrest, she was caught and convicted. Cleared of any direct responsibility for the deaths, she was jailed for a derisory three years. Others moved in to fill the vacuum she left.

The International Maritime Bureau know that people-smuggling has been increasing globally, despite the deaths at Dover docks. Al-Qaeda has raised money for its terrorist activities by involvement in this trade. Some Chinese have even been routed through the hotbed of Fallujah in Iraq to reach Europe. The divide between rich and poor has increased in many nations so that the gangs can easily exploit the market, charging huge sums. No wealthy nation is immune from illegal immigration. Japan also has a constant battle to keep out Chinese.

The IMB's Transit Fraud Department said: 'Ship operators have little control over the contents of containers they carry and can be unaware of the presence of stowaways, yet they can be held legally responsible for the safety of the people found in the cargo. There is a growing need for a central body to quantify all illegal immigration worldwide and provide centralised assistance to organisations dealing with the problem around the globe.'

Few would disagree. But beyond that is the need to crush the gangs. But people-smuggling is a multibillion-dollar business organised by captains of industry and obscured by opaque, impenetrable structures. These big bosses are shielded from prosecution by intimidation and an *omerta*-type silence.

Most successful prosecutions are against small-league players or middle management in the complex chains. Even when a big fish like *Little Sister Ping* is caught, a three-year sentence is hardly a deterrent. The ultimate powerbrokers who benefit every time a hopeful signs away thousands of dollars are protected, far removed from the front line. Their influence in high places is too strong, and their resources, whether from people-smuggling, from ship stealing, from drugs or prostitution, are ample to protect them.

The CIA and US Border Security estimate that there are around 11 million illegal immigrants in the USA, around 1.5 million of them from Asia. *Big Sister Ping*, Chui Ping Cheng, has reportedly been involved in many instances of arranging to transport Asians to the USA. She was first indicted in 1994 and again in 2000 on charges of money laundering, kidnapping, hostage-taking and alien-smuggling. As the alleged Godmother of all snakeheads, her arrest was the biggest coup to date. Above all the rest, this tiny, matronly Chinese woman, born in 1949 in Fujian Province, dominated the illegal immigrant scene since her own arrival in New York's Chinatown in 1984.

Until she fled to Hong Kong in 1994 to avoid arrest, she operated her empire of private money transfer and immigration from the *Yeung Sun* restaurant in Chinatown on New York's East Broadway. The Hong Kong police arrested her in 2000 at the airport with three false passports. Eventually, after a three-year battle, Sister Ping was extradited from Hong Kong in 2003. In 2005, she was convicted, and in March 2006 she was finally sentenced to 35 years in jail for her role in people-smuggling on a grand scale, including involvement in the *Golden Venture* fiasco.

Back in 1994, Sister Ping had been identified as the Mother of Snakeheads by members of a panel put together by Eric Ellen for an IMB meeting in California, which I chaired. Dr Peter Unsinger and Ms Charlotte Shiang-Yun Wong from San Jose University presented an excellent paper on people-smuggling, later published by the Bureau. Based on her first 10 years in the USA, Sister Ping was even then a legendary figure, as they described: 'The business (of smuggling aliens) has become so lucrative that...Sister Ping, who was smuggled out of Fujian about 10 years ago, may have earned more than $30 million in the smuggling business and recently purchased a building for $3 million in cash.'

'In 1993,' confirms Eric Ellen, 'we knew of the apparent role of Sister Ping. Proving it was another matter.' The unprovable knowledge back then involved the first well-known people-smuggling tragedy. It happened off Long Island, New York, in June when the cargo vessel *Golden Venture* had almost reached its destination from Fujian Province. Poor navigation led to the vessel running aground with 300 illegal immigrants aboard. It was a nightmare scene for the rescuers, who watched hundreds of terrified Chinese jump into the water, despite shouted warnings and encouragement to stay aboard. In the event, only 10 drowned—a tragedy, but it could have been far worse.

'We were confident from our informants that Sister Ping had a key role in this shipment. Our contacts in Taiwan, Hong Kong and Fujian Province convinced us, but getting evidence was another matter. We also knew that she had not acted alone and so were delighted when Guo Liang Chi was extradited from Hong Kong to America for the *Golden Venture* tragedy. It was a start. In 1998, he got 20 years for criminal conspiracy. Routes into the USA were not simply cramming the hopefuls into containers or holds of cargo vessels. Sister Ping also used planes and trucks as part of the transit methods.

'When arrested, Sister Ping's assets, including much real estate around New York, were estimated at $40 million. She was charged not only over the *Golden Venture* disaster but with some unsavoury crimes of kidnap and ransom.' However, the latter charges were not proven.

Shiao Lin adds: 'Kidnap and ransom is a well-known means of extortion in the Chinese community. Sometimes it is used against the arriving immigrants, who have paid their 10% deposit. They still owe, say, $35,000, but are then held prisoner on arrival. Their families back home are threatened and forced to put up yet more money to secure their release, or themselves be tortured.' Interest rates may be a wicked 5% per month.

Once the Chinese reach their destination, they are typically kept by force in safe houses, known by some as '*hell-houses*' because of the overcrowded conditions. There was evidence of beatings by hammer or knives and burns. Those able to get relatives back home to pay off the debt quickly might be freed into the community to get jobs, but the big snakeheads might continue to extract money from them on various flimsy and illegal pretexts—and who would dare resist?

Despite all this history known about Big Sister Ping dating back to 1994 and earlier, justice was not done for a further 12 years. The maximum sentence was handed down. To the end, the diminutive Mother of Snakeheads denied guilt, contending that she had acted under duress from Triad figures, something US District Judge Michael Mukasey dismissed as *simply incredible*.

As in the smuggling businesses and ship thefts, people-smuggling could not go on without active support or blind eyes from persons of authority. Probably, according to US Government officials, there has been participation by members of China's powerful Public Security Bureau. As was seen in the clampdown on corruption, if the Beijing Government had the will to prevent this mass exodus, the 25,000 who arrive by ship each year in the USA would be staunched. There have been sweeping changes in the Public Security Bureau, but as yet there has been no sign that the flood of immigrants has stopped.

Justice in China can be a swift and effective deterrent. Snakeheads in China are aware that they can face the death penalty if caught. Unlike the USA, where inmates of Death Row can survive for decades by raising all manner of legal technicalities, in China the time from verdict to execution may be only 14 minutes. The Government has introduced *death vans*. These vans park outside the courthouse and the guilty are escorted in and killed by lethal injection, replacing execution by single bullet to the back of the head—the cost of the bullet having been charged to the family! Speedy justice can be a deterrent, but the lead must come from Beijing. Greater efforts to crack down on the Triads seem unlikely when the exodus of emigrants suits China rather well.

New procedures have been introduced at international container-terminals to spot containers crammed with illegal immigrants. Heat-sensor checks and trained sniffer dogs can be effective. But as one opportunity is blocked, the gangs seek out alternative means to continue their profitable trade. Detective Superintendent Suzanne Williams, as she then was, grew familiar with the kidnapping problem as part of her work at Scotland Yard. Until retirement to undertake specialist work in piracy negotiation and advising on hostage situations, she was head of the Hostage and Crisis Negotiation Unit. 'Kidnap and ransom is far more common in the United Kingdom than is generally realised, but most of it involves ethnic communities, and the Chinese in particular. One snakehead gang may import an immigrant, who is working to pay off the debt when he is kidnapped by *another gang* and a ransom demanded. This is then paid by the first gang on behalf of the victim. On release, the unfortunate person then has an even greater debt to repay at high rates of interest.'

Usually, an arriving immigrant will be taken to a *safe house*—more like a prison—and held there till the entire debt is paid off. Even in rural Norfolk, UK, a three-bedroom safe house that caught fire was found to be crammed with 18 Chinese. Such safe houses are run by the snakeheads all over the UK and USA. The safe-house system in the UK is similar to the *hell-houses* of New York City. 'Once in the prison-like *safe house*, the families back in China are terrorised unless the debt is repaid all at once,' confirms Williams. The amount demanded, excluding the extortionate interest rates, is the equivalent of about 24 years' salary around Fuzhou.

The new arrivals, whether in New York or Manchester's Chinatown, may be put to work washing dishes or other menial jobs for pitiful wages, which are then mainly withheld to pay for accommodation and to clear a debt which never seems to reduce because of the punitive rates of interest. The cowed, terrorised immigrants are powerless to resist; those foolish enough to cause trouble may well be brutalised or murdered.

'The system is barbaric,' concludes Ellen. 'London's Metropolitan Police have raided some of these *safe houses* and freed people who have been held prisoner for years. How many immigrants have been murdered is unknown, but tales of torture and abuse are plentiful. Slicing off fingers and extracting teeth is a speciality.

'The Chinese Government was directly supportive of this trade, or at the very least not concerned to prevent it. With such a massive population and so much poverty, they seemed content to see their people depart. There are reckoned to be some 10 million people around the world who have left Fujian Province alone. The savings to the Chinese economy are obvious.' On the other hand, the cost lays a hefty burden on other taxpayers the world over. Such is the scale of the problem that all major police forces are now devoting ever greater resources to prevent this trade and to fight the criminal gangs. In 2013, the UK Government started a major drive to tackle the problem.

Part of prevention, according to Peter Schatzer of the International Organisation for Migration, is educating communities about the risks of trusting the snakeheads. This makes sense, but the numbers still lining up after the Dover tragedy proves it is not the whole complete answer. In 2003, 19 immigrants died while being transported across Texas by container. The inside temperature of the refrigerated unit had reached 173 degrees. The driver, who had been paid $7,500, ignored the shouts for help; he only narrowly avoided the death penalty. When the container was opened, the bodies were piled up in pools of vomit. People had clawed, thumped and ripped the walls in their desperation. The Internet is a useful means of warning the unwary of the perils, but encouraging messages from friends still sway the undecided. 'Until governments unite to fight this domestically,' concludes Ellen, 'and support international initiatives to prevent people-smuggling being so lucrative, it will thrive. The gang leaders are able to use their wealth and corrupt influence to continue this exploitation with little or no risk of being caught.'

The seeds of this multibillion *export industry* may have been sown in the aftermath of the Vietnam War, when the unscrupulous moved in to *assist* those wishing to flee Communism. In the following years, the suffering of the Vietnamese boatpeople was a harrowing story of both people-smuggling and human trafficking.

The Shame of *Rape-Island*

One man's tragedy is another man's pension fund. In Vietnam, until 1989, dread of the new Communist regime drove millions to flee over a 14-year period. Initially, the refugees were escaping from political oppression, but in the latter years their motive was mainly economic. The desperate exodus saw the rise of dishonest entrepreneurs and gangs ready to extort huge sums, guaranteeing *safe* passage to Malaysia, allegedly avoiding the dangers of Thai waters. Four ounces of gold, then worth $1,000, equivalent to many years' wages for peasant farmers whose *annual* income was less than $150, bought the promise of *a safe passage* away from war-ravaged Vietnam. Of course, no *safe passage* was ever arranged. No safe transport was provided either.

In one typical instance, Ellen remembers, the overfilled boat set sail with a schoolmaster who had never sailed before at the helm. 'All that counted was the chance to profit from poor, desperate and naive people. What then happened at sea was a disgrace, as was the fate that met many refugees on Koh Kra, which we called *Rape-Island*. The victims were the fleeing Vietnamese; the villains were the Thai fishermen who saw them as easy prey for rape, theft, and increasingly for satisfying a lust for domination and even murder.'

The Bureau received many distressing reports. One of dozens of escapes recorded at that time is typical. On 12 February 1987, a small group of Vietnamese set sail from Camau, Minh Hai, in a tiny boat. Their intended destination was Malaysia or Thailand, where transit camps had been set up for them. Ahead lay a long and hazardous sea crossing. Within ten hours, they were attacked by the crew of a fishing vessel. Armed with two rifles and a pistol, the pirates conducted a body search before dragging the women and children onto their boat. There the women were repeatedly gang-raped.

After 12 hours they were returned to their own boat. A few hours later, another two fishing boats attacked them. Three women and one child were again abducted, but this time the refugees' small boat was rammed and sunk. The four men were picked up from the water by the crew of the second boat. Their hands were bound. The crew then threw them into the sea. Half-drowned, they were again picked up, hands retied and dumped in the fish hold. One of the women had her hands tied. She was thrown overboard, discarded as of no further use. Fortunately, she freed herself and was picked up by some kindly fisherman. The fate of the other seven members of the little group is unknown. Ellen guesses that the women and children were taken to Koh Kra Island or given to a crime syndicate for the sex industry, or were simply murdered when the attackers had no further use for them.

Ellen's concerns as Director of the Bureau were not just focused on protecting commercial interests and fighting organised crime. Between a hectic schedule of meetings and frantic phone calls to assist in release of ships or find stolen cargo, heal ways found time to campaign for more assistance for the boatpeople. The humanitarian disaster had started in 1975, before the launch of the Bureau, but continued long after. 'There was piracy, corruption, people-smuggling and human trafficking. There were so many atrocities involving the escaping Vietnamese that I couldn't stand back once the Bureau provided a suitable platform for me to act.'

The core of the problem lay in the Gulf of Thailand. Once at sea, stormy weather and rough seas led to many drowning. The vessels were top-heavy with people clinging to every inch of space. Others, inexperienced sailors and concerned only to escape the certainty of danger at home, took on the long crossing with inadequate food and water, thus starving to death. But there was a greater and much more evil danger—piracy. Throughout the '80s, too little was done to prevent attack after attack on defenceless, desperate men, women and children seeking a new life, clutching a few cherished belongings. Of the hundreds of thousands who left in overcrowded, unseaworthy vessels, Ellen believes the majority in the early days never made it. The precise number of murders or deaths is not available for obvious reasons. There was inadequate policing of the Gulf of Thailand to prevent piracy. Shipowners failed to rescue passengers from sinking boats. Predators, mainly Thai fishermen, robbed, raped and murdered.

'It was mass piracy with the authorities unconcerned to act. It was racist too. The Thais resented the Vietnamese; disputes over fishing rights and historic territorial disagreements went back 300 years. But nothing justified the brutality of one of the most nauseating eras in maritime crime.'

The only explanation for the repetition of these ghastly crimes was that the Thai Government's response was woefully inadequate. They did not care about the fate of the Vietnamese. Filmed evidence revealed the Thai attitude to the boat people. The Red Cross and United Nations agencies set up camps in Malaysia, Thailand, Indonesia and Hong Kong. The last six of the hundreds of thousands of refugees were sent to France and the last camp was closed only in 2001. The main aim had been to repatriate the majority to Vietnam without reprisals—forcing a return to what refugees saw as a hostile regime. Though it had its critics, a human tragedy of immense proportions was averted by the humanitarian endeavour. Generally, those returned were not persecuted.

Some refugees had sailed north toward Hong Kong, but the more common route was to head for Thailand and Malaysia to the west, sailing around the southernmost point of their country. Thai territorial waters extend more than halfway across the Gulf, the stretch of sea that most refugees entered. The crossing was around 160 miles once the boat entered the Gulf. At the northern end lies Bangkok, a major port, so that the refugees were crossing waters busy with merchant shipping able to assist, but too often not willing to get involved.

The attitude of shipowners operating in the Gulf was generally both brutal and heartless, though to an extent understandable. 'Hundreds of commercial ships sailed these waters daily, yet stories of 20 and even 40 vessels ignoring the distressed people were rife. Crews did not wish to get involved in the delays, costs and dangers of mounting a rescue. Beyond that, political wrangles can follow a rescue at sea.' Ellen recalls the example of a newly registered vessel in Bermuda, where the master rescued some refugees. The Bermuda Registry threatened to cancel the ship's registration to prevent him taking the Vietnamese to that island paradise. This incident and the furore over the Bermudan reaction led to the end of the Registry.

'Rescued boatpeople should be carried to the next scheduled port of call. Now if a vessel were heading north for Bangkok, the problem of caring for them was short-term. If the vessel were heading south, next stop Dubai, thousands of miles away in the Emirates, the problem of catering for, say, 70 people, some perhaps needing medical help, was not an attractive proposition. The second option was that, if the next port were unsuitable, then the burden fell on the flagstate. Well, Bermuda was not prepared to take on the burden, but others like Liberia, Honduras and Belize were also ill-equipped to cope with an influx of refugees. Countries like the UK, France, the USA, Germany and Norway were better able to manage, but they had few ships registered compared to *flag-of-convenience* nations.

During the '80s, Ellen felt there was a crying need for better organised initiatives and took every chance of saying so to anyone who could make a difference. The US Government set up a fund to compensate shipowners whose vessels stopped to assist, but it was poorly publicized. The United Nations High Commission for Refugees published guidelines for masters about what to do when faced with a rescue.

Ellen lobbied for better piracy prevention. He resented the Thai attitude. There was a need for more effective patrolling of the Gulf and for air cover. Deterrent by arrest and conviction was ineffectual in the early years with a reluctance to press criminal charges, partly due to lack of convincing evidence and partly to lack of zeal. The fact was that, despite the soothing words of the diplomats, the Thai Government lacked the political will. Furthermore, little was done to tackle the root cause of the mass exodus from Vietnam: the intimidating and abusive Communist government. For geographical reasons, the sea was the only practical escape route.

From 1980 to 1984, around 250,000 refugees reached another country. Of these, about one in five had been picked up by a passing ship. In the early '80s, around 65% of their small boats were attacked, often more than once. The average number of persons aboard was around 70, although many carried twice as many, thus endangering stability. Typically, a boat measuring a mere 30 feet long by 10 feet wide would carry around 40. Initiatives taken with the financial backing of the USA involved a well-meant joint programme with the Thai Government, but that quickly ended when the Thais insisted on more money—another $30 million. During that initiative, decoy boats were used to lure pirates into an attack and thus arrest. A patrol boat was also established, manned by the Thai Navy, but this was a gesture rather than an effective way to police the Gulf. There were 14,000 Thai fishing boats at work, many of them prepared to attack the helpless refugees.

Open season for murder was free to continue. Ellen reckons every conviction cost around $1 million. It was hopeless. Despite incessant lobbying, seminars, and meetings with the main agencies, the best efforts of outsiders could not solve the fundamental problem: the Thai authorities' complete indifference.

The second initiative through the United Nations was to introduce night patrols and computerise the registration of fishing vessels. An anti-piracy centre was set up to coordinate information, and a commando unit was established to tackle the problem at sea. Gradually the constant pressure from many quarters, including the Bureau, led to a decrease in the number of attacks and a few successful prosecutions. At one special meeting the

Bureau set up, Ellen had the chance to discuss his concerns with a most distinguished group of interested parties, including the Thai Ambassador to the United Nations, who maintained that more effort was needed, even then in the late '80s, to stem the flow from Vietnam. He, like other Thai officials, was not prepared to accept the truth of allegations against the authorities. Ellen adds: 'It is only when you encounter the abrasive and ungoverned views of the fishermen that you can see why the Government was so ineffective.'

The glib assertion is that local Thai fishermen were responsible for these piracy attacks, and there is some truth in the claim. But it seems clear that, as news spread of the delights of this sport of robbing, killing and raping, other opportunists joined in. Of course, not all Thai fishermen joined in the savagery and many boatpeople owed their lives to them, but the accelerating tide of boats led to a rapidly escalating problem. The chance of easy pickings from defenceless people was irresistible. Evidence suggests that even the Thai Police may have joined in the killing spree on occasions.

Ellen remembers one example of an atrocity of which they had notice but could not personally confirm. There were suggestions that the Thai authorities covered up some of the pirates' activities. On one occasion a UNHCR representative witnessed an attack at Songkhla on the east coast of Thailand. He claimed the Thai Police opened fire on a boat full of refugees, killing several.

'In another incident, 19 refugees successfully defended their boat from an attack by pirates, presumed to be fishermen. Some pirates were killed and the Vietnamese then boarded the fishing boat. Three surviving pirates complained, and the Thai Navy arrested the refugees, who were prosecuted and sentenced to death. By contrast, severe sentences were rarely given to convicted pirates (and in the earlier years most were never caught or prosecuted anyway). Later on, some stiff sentences, like 50 years, were handed down as the international community pressured the Thai Government to clamp down on the crimes.'

It seems likely that organised criminals increasingly dominated crimes in the Gulf. Initially, though, the Thai fishermen nursed their own historic hatred of the Vietnamese. Many had been arrested for fishing in disputed waters off Vietnam. Some had spent years languishing in jail there. Bitter memories festered. Additionally, there was some irrational fear that these boatpeople were some form of invasion, a threat to Thailand. It was palpable nonsense but grew into a multi-headed monster, fuelling racial intolerance.

Nothing, however, could justify what happened between 1975 and about 1989—14 years during which an orgy of sexual depravity and bloodlust was allowed to continue because of the indifference of society as a whole and the apathy of powerful nations that could have intervened.

Koh Kra is a tiny, idyllic islet in the Gulf of Thailand west of Vietnam and lying some 80 miles southeast of Koh Samui, the popular holiday destination. It measures only one half a kilometre square. Isolated and empty, Koh Kra became the ideal secluded retreat where a giant pleasure ground was created for sadistic visitors. Safe from prying eyes, it was here that the pirates delivered captured boatpeople. Thus Koh Kra became known at the Bureau as *Rape-Island.*

This was no safe haven for the Vietnamese. Here Thais fulfilled their fantasies of lust and violent depravity—rape, bestiality, child abuse and murder. It was one long-running communal gang-bang. Details still vivid in their minds, both Ellen and Shiao Lin speak passionately about these atrocities. 'I dealt with the United Nations area representative, Ted Schweitzer,' explained Ellen. 'He did everything in his power but still never succeeded in getting this island safe during those years. Ted told me that sometimes as many as 500 pirates would gather on Koh Kra to abuse the refugees. He explained that the fishermen who had brought the women there quite often had by then murdered the men, and the children too. Sometimes women were forced to have sex in return for the life of a child. Ted visited the island often with the Thai Navy and saw the atrocities and saved as many people as he could. But you'd have thought the UN would have sent in some show of force to close the place. It was no time for diplomatic niceties.'

Yet few today have heard of the atrocities carried out in this tropical paradise. Indeed, visiting divers are now encouraged to explore the blue waters around the islet. They are warned of the dangers of cruising sharks, which, so it is said, are attracted by the absence of humans in the area. A far more likely explanation for the sharks' presence are the hundreds of Vietnamese corpses dumped into the sea here.

The small island resounded with screams of victims, its placid waters littered with bodies of children surrounded by desperate and dying women, driven mad by abuse and grief. There is no memorial to those who suffered and died here. The island is now exploited by the Thais themselves. Little over a decade after the end of the atrocities, *Rape-Island* became a playground for trippers. The notion of running discos and barbecues at Auschwitz would rouse a deafening outcry—yet now tourists frolic and dive in what was once a sea of blood. Nothing stands in the way of making a quick dollar.

Perhaps the very fishermen who once gang-raped women are even now ferrying tourists to the sandy bays. Tourist money is too important. Anyway, the Thai Government never acknowledged the extent of the problem. Yet those who suffered should not be so easily forgotten, nor history so easily rewritten. It is a disgrace.

Rape-Island: One Woman's Tale

The small boat, only measuring 30 feet by 10, slipped away from Phu My, Vietnam, under cover of darkness. Seventeen-year-old Nguyen Thi Thuy, like the others, was silent, terrified of being caught and attacked by a Vietnamese Patrol boat. It was 1979. The Communist authorities took pride in preventing escapes. Like everyone on board, she knew stories of these flimsy boats being deliberately rammed by patrol boats and the occupants left to drown.

The single Yamaha engine slowly carried the 38 passengers through the gentle swell; three days and nights of extreme danger lay ahead. Food was short, water too. All spare space was filled with fuel and a mixed bunch of strangers. The young girl had left her widowed father behind; he was too infirm to travel. Only her uncle and cousin had joined her.

After the boat rounded Vietnam's lowest point, the swell picked up. They all felt queasy from the smell of the diesel and the lack of food. But the journey was uneventful. They saw some passing ships, some tankers, and a container vessel all heading north up the Gulf. None appeared to have any interest in their shouts and waves of articles of clothing. Many of the younger children started to fret, crying and clutching their parents for comfort.

More than halfway across, the engine failed and there was silence except for the frantic sounds as a young man struggled to get the diesel fired again. It was then that two small craft appeared over the horizon, heading toward them. The fishing boats pulled up alongside; within seconds there was chaos as the women, including Nguyen Thi Thuy, were dragged into one of the boats. The last sight of her relations was of them being clubbed with metal bars. What became of them or the other 20 or so still aboard is unknown.

For the next several hours, she and the other women, some of them grandmothers, were forced to strip. They were then raped repeatedly by the crew, who did not disguise their identities. By the following morning, her body was aching all over, her face bruised and her mouth swollen. The men's desires now sated, Nguyen Thi Thuy sat whimpering on the deck, leaning against a slightly older woman who was also sobbing uncontrollably.

Ahead, an island appeared, its presence obvious from the white spray around the rocks and the dark green of the trees and shrubs rising from the blue water. Another fishing boat was heading in the same direction, and the young girl now saw that aboard were other Vietnamese, some men, some women—prisoners of other fishermen. About three miles from the shore, she watched in horror as at least eight men were thrown into the water by their laughing captors. Both boats soon left the floundering men behind, but their cries for help still resonated over the calm waters.

Her helplessness gave way to shock as she realised that these men had been abandoned to drown. Now she knew that she would never see her uncle or cousin again. These fishermen had no respect for life or dignity. Trying to put her worst thoughts behind her, she watched the island drawing close. She did not see its idyllic beauty. She just hoped there might be a chance to escape from the horror.

The small bay already contained a number of other craft. As her boat slowed, ready to discharge the brutalised women, a body of a young naked girl floated past. Any lingering hopes that the ordeal was over were shattered. On the beach, she saw two young fishermen chasing and then catching a frail elderly figure. The next moment, he was on the ground, the two men kneeling on him as he shrieked in agony. From a tree above some reddish rocks a body was hanging by the neck. Whether the victim had killed himself to end his suffering or had been murdered was impossible to judge.

A group of about 30 women were being pushed toward another waiting boat, but Nguyen Thi Thuy did not understand why. Had they served their purpose? Were they going to be taken to the mainland and freed? No matter. She was on dry land. She ran, to where she did not know, but it was not far—just till she was out of sight of her torturers. Exhausted, she lay on some rocks beneath a giant canopy of thick foliage. But more men found her and raped her where she lay.

How often she was raped that day or on subsequent days she will never know. There were so many women of all ages, and even a few men who seemed to have the task of rounding them up if they strayed too far from the main beach. Their faces were forever changing as new ones arrived, just as she had done. Others left but how or why she did not know.

How long she spent on Koh Kra she was unsure but it was certainly months. As suddenly as her life had already changed, it all changed again. One morning, a boat arrived, and though she did not understand who it was at the time, it was evident that here there was warmth and kindness in contrast to the unspeakable way that she and the others had been treated. The boat was organised by UNHCR representative Ted Schweitzer, who had arrived from the refugee transit camp at Songkhla on the east coast of Thailand.

'Precisely how many Vietnamese drowned or died at sea is still uncertain, still less how many perished or were brutalised on this evil island.' Ellen recalls: 'When we ran our 1987 conference at Woods Hole Oceanographic Institution in the USA, we had some powerful speakers; one who made a vivid impression spoke from UNHCR papers. These described in detail the suffering on this little island. Schweitzer saved around 1,250 victims from what was reported to us as "certain death." Pascal Boulanger, the speaker, had evidence of bodies floating in the sea, of mutilated people found lying dead or dying on the island. Many injuries were to the head and face. Screwdrivers, pincers and hammers had been used to rip out gold teeth, leaving many with broken jaws.

'It is hard to capture the degree of suffering, but one particular example sticks in my memory. The fishermen, having moored at Rape-Island, would search out the women, who often tried to hide in vain. One woman, much wanted for sex, fled into the long grass to hide. Instead of wasting time looking for her, the grass was set on fire to smoke her out. But she did not come out. So great was her suffering in the hands of these animals that she preferred to let the fire sweep over her, burning her dreadfully. She chose the lesser evil.'

There were 22 successful prosecutions in the six years from 1982 to 1986 against the pirates, though piracy was not an offence with which they were charged. It was mainly gang robbery, gang rape and violence including murder. A few convictions early on with severe sentences might have prevented this entire episode taking on such vast dimensions. Only later were there some stiff sentences. By contrast, the death penalty was imposed on any Vietnamese who fought their captors, but no such sentence was passed against a pirate until December 1986, when the problem was over 10 years old.

'I know that not enough was done to get witness statements to secure convictions. It goes back to a lack of desire from the Thai authorities to take firm measures. In December 1980, six pirates from the fishing-smack *Suchinnawa* were charged with rape, indecent acts and false imprisonment of seven Vietnamese on Koh Kra. The Court found there was no case to answer because of inadequate proof of identity. In the same month, a Thai fisherman was charged with robbery and with causing several Vietnamese to drown near Koh Kra. Allegedly, he had rammed and sunk the boat used by the refugees. He was not charged with murder, but it was academic as he was acquitted due to lack of adequate identification.'

'We don't know if these men might have been convicted with stronger evidence. They were acquitted and are therefore innocent. The problem was getting these terrified young women to give convincing evidence about their captors. Today we have DNA and far better technology available, though often the offences were committed long before the arrests. The fishermen could have been charged with piracy as well, but if the evidence does not meet the burden of proof of identification, then it doesn't matter what the charge is.'

Koh Kra was used as a staging post. Besides pleasuring the fishermen and other guests, probably including the Thai police, those departing were almost certainly destined to become sex slaves in Bangkok or elsewhere. The extent to which organised crime was involved in the atrocities is less clear. Criminal gangs running brothels in Pattaya, Phuket and Bangkok were certainly beneficiaries of the abduction of these women. It must be assumed that money changed hands when the fishermen sold the women on, or alternatively, the gangs had muscled in on *a good thing*.

What had started out as a chance to rape and rob turned into something far more sinister. Decisive action at once might have prevented the spread of a cult of atrocity. Not all female boatpeople ended up at this hellish place. On many boats that were attacked, the women ended up ashore and were able to go to the transit camps. But thousands of others passed through *Rape-Island*. For the fortunate few, UNHCR came to their rescue. For the rest, it was a staging post—a one-way ticket to a life of prostitution and drug addiction.

Despite so much needless suffering, UNHCR believes that from the boatpeople years lessons were learned and much rehabilitation was achieved. At least 500,000 refugees from Laos, Cambodia and Vietnam were repatriated of the around two million who fled. Most, though, are now settled in other parts of the world. Many of the later refugees were escaping poverty rather than an intolerant regime and so international sympathy dwindled.

Though UNHCR can take some satisfaction on the humanitarian side, Ellen is not entirely happy with the refugee camps, and still less with the maritime community. 'I remain concerned that the transit camps were run in a way that *destroyed* families rather than bonding them together. Apparently on religious grounds to do with the Roman Catholic faith, survivors were segregated—male from female—and sent to different camps, children separated as well. Even years later, I wonder how this could ever have been dreamed up, let alone tolerated. These frightened and impoverished people may have survived theft, rape, terror and the perils of a dangerous crossing. Yet here they were as survivors being separated, husband from wife, mothers from children. I trust nothing so inhumane is ever done again, especially in the name of religion.'

Inadequate naval and other patrols, scant air cover, and ships too concerned with their own business left crime rampant right up until the last refugees sailed. The shipping world and governments have little cause to look back on the episode with much satisfaction. Ellen would like to think this could never happen again, but fears that would be over-optimistic. 'No doubt after Auschwitz, it was said then that such barbarism must never again be permitted.'

CHAPTER NINE

Bodies in the Fridge - The Phantom Journeys of *Erria Inge*

It was December 1992. The temperature was in the 60s and about average for the time of year. The ship breaker's yard was teeming with local Chinese workers. Everywhere people were shouting over the constant whine of metal against metal. Oxy-acetylene cutters sent showers of sparks in all directions as rusting ships, once the pride of the shipyards, were broken up, section by section. Here in Guangzhou, in the Province of Guangdong on the South Chinese mainland close to Hong Kong, poorly paid labourers in faded dungarees were dismantling the 17,000-ton freighter *Hai Sin*. She had entered port for the last time. Indeed, the IMB and other authorities had been looking for the vessel for over 12 months. But never under the name *Hai Sin*!

Guangzhou is a large city, with its population of nearly seven million crammed around the north end of the Pearl River. The team at the Guangdong Shunde Shipwrecking Company were well set in their tasks when work had to be halted. In one of the ship's holds, they came upon a refrigerated section. Electricity to keep the contents chilled had long ago been turned off for the last time. The stench in the area made the men reel back in disgust. When it was opened, the putrid smell of rotting human flesh filled the companion ways and cabin areas. The stench was unbearable.

Those in the area knew what they had seen and left well enough alone, an easy decision considering the advanced state of decay. The police were called and the gruesome contents removed, then wrapped and placed in giant pots. Almost alone in his determination, Eric Ellen worked hard to try to resolve the mystery. 'The corpses were unlikely to have been those of a previous crew of the vessel. The pathologist considered the victims had *probably* all been Caucasians. The dead crew of an attacked ship would scarcely be stored in a fridge by the invading pirates. Normally, if a ship in these Far East waters is pirated, the crew are abandoned on a liferaft or just murdered. Sharks destroy the evidence.'

Keeping the corpses on board made no sense. The crew hired to take the vessel to the breakers probably did not know the bodies were there. It would have been their predecessors who would have known how the corpses came to be aboard. Despite appeals, not one of them ever came forward to volunteer any information. If that crew had been innocent, someone would have come forward, volunteering that they had rescued burned corpses from the sea.

The 10 bodies had all been burned to a greater or lesser extent. Some were partially clothed, some naked. All but one had been stripped of any valuables. There was no clue of identity. Ten bodies, perhaps murder victims, were lying on a quayside in big pots, and yet before Ellen took up the challenge nobody had made any serious effort to unravel the mystery. Nobody even reported 10 persons missing. It says much for life at sea that an entire crew can disappear with no enquiry.

Ships' crews are usually multiracial. Masters often come from the Nordic countries, engineers from Greece, deck hands from the Asian subcontinent or West Indies. Many cooks and ratings come from poor countries. Maintaining contact with families is more difficult. Crews at the time could be hired from quaysides without proper paperwork—men who were not necessarily criminals or ready to become pirates but who might be happy to be anonymous for tax or family reasons. Many already had or were then provided with false passports, although since 9-11, controls on crew identification have been tightened. This alone cannot ensure that every crew member on every vessel is precisely who he claims to be.

Crew members may make a single voyage or stay at sea for years, travelling from port to port. Many lose track of families and friends as their travels take them far from home. But a crew of ten *Caucasians* not being missed is harder to explain. Were they murdered, or had they died of burns before being taken aboard? If the latter, why did the master of the *Hai Sin* not radio to shore to report the location where the bodies were picked up from the water? The questions remain under-investigated and unanswered. The Chinese police were certainly not going to waste money on investigations. The official view was that *if there had been a crime*, and this was unclear, then it had not happened in Chinese waters, so not their problem! Ellen found nobody really cared. The Chief Constable in him did not like an unsolved file.

Those nations which should have investigated included Panama, Honduras, Singapore and Thailand. For various reasons, none of them did. Interpol, the international police agency in Paris, was informed but made no progress. At the Bureau, Ellen maintained a file in the hope of a breakthrough.

In April 1990, *Hai Sin* was known as *Erria Inge*, registered in Panama, a large shipping register with a popular *flag of convenience*. Subsequently, she was registered in Honduras, a lax registry not particular about what quality of business came its way. Ellen was disappointed but not surprised when both registries failed to act. The Panamanian authorities were not going to squander resources on 10 bodies thousands of miles away in China. Neither was the much smaller Honduran Registry interested.

Cyprus, Belize and the Bahamas are other registries that have received criticism for being more interested in fees than in any obligations toward owners and crews. Every vessel must be registered in an official registry somewhere by law. Around 14,000 vessels of various sizes are registered in Panama. Ships registered there will probably have no connection with that country; it will have been chosen because its laws are less strict than those governing ship registration in London or New York. Registration may also be cheaper. Criminals have used these registries to their advantage, aware that they lack both the resources and the will to investigate possible crimes. These registries also attract legitimate business because of their less stringent laws on crew's rights, ship maintenance and perhaps tax advantages.

The police in Singapore, who knew much more than they have ever revealed about this strange incident, decided to take no action. Indeed, in November 1992, before the ship reached China, the Bureau believes they may even have been tipped off that there were dead bodies aboard. The vessel was close to Singapore in the Strait of Malacca, but they took no action as the vessel was not in their waters.

If 10 corpses were found in a New York apartment, the story would not die until who, how and why had been investigated. The entire history of the apartment and neighbourhood would be checked. Forensics teams would seek to create identities from the remains. But this was *not* New York. The corpses were an international problem, but whose problem? No country had the budgets or any pressing need to spend money investigating. As the nationality of the victims was unknown, there was no government or pressure group obsessed with discovering the truth. Nobody had been reported missing. It was easy for everybody to do nothing.

The *Erria Inge* saga started in April 1990, when shipowner Erik Boas, originally from Denmark but latterly living in Australia, set up a bareboat charter. *Erria Inge* was chartered to Erria Marine Inc. of Singapore as a vessel without crew. In a bareboat charter, the owner waves goodbye to control of his vessel, perhaps for years, but retains ownership. It is prudent, therefore, to know that the charterer possesses integrity and the ability to pay the ongoing fees and to manage the ship well. Boas thought he had been careful. Day-to-day management of his ship was to be provided by a Hong Kong company called Parakou.

In 1990, Boas, after a life of hard work, was looking to take things easier. A smooth charter arrangement would be ideal—no management worries, he could sit back and watch the charter payments arrive. Sadly, the charter did not work out. Boas was dragged into dangerous and enervating attempts to recover his ship. He was not a member of the Bureau. The IMB first became involved later when the new '*owner*' of the ship, who had bought the vessel for scrap, discovered the bodies.

The first hint of trouble came in February 1991, when Boas got news that his bulk carrier had been arrested and was in Mumbai. Apparently, the charterers had failed to pay substantial port charges, wages and other bills. At least, Boas rationalised, the vessel was safe and located. He packed hurriedly and flew several thousand miles to India in search of facts. *Why were bills not being paid? What was his ship being used for?* He quickly established that aboard was bulk chickenfeed worth $2.5 million. Before she was seized, his ship had been scheduled to sail for Manila.

After several meetings, discussions and frantic phone calls, Boas negotiated a deal. *Erria Inge* was to remain under arrest in Bombay while the case was resolved in Singapore, a regime known to have an excellent legal system based on English common law principles. The charterers were from Singapore, so this was a sound choice. In the fine colonial-style court buildings overlooking the Padang, not far from the Singapore River, legal proceedings demanding the return of *Erria Inge* were launched. Boas hoped for a quick result. He wanted to protect his ship and get her released. It was essential to stem the tide of mounting debts and to get the charter up and running again so that the charterers could earn money and thus pay him.

But Boas sustained a second body blow in April, whilst awaiting justice in Singapore, when he got news that his ship had broken arrest, the maritime equivalent of a jailbreak. Without permission, she had simply sailed away. Enquiries suggested her destination was probably Singapore. 'That was a red herring!' Ellen scoffs. 'The last place that the master would have sailed was Singapore, nor would he even enter its territorial waters! With litigation pending and Erria Marine Inc. registered there too, Singapore offered no attraction. The charterers obviously had other ideas when they stole the ship away from Bombay.' This gross misconduct was too much for the owner.

Justifiably, Boas terminated the charter, serving a formal demand on Erria Marine Inc. seeking return of his ship for a breach of contract and seeking indemnity for the debts incurred. The vessel now *had* to be returned. The law said so.

Erria Marine Inc. ignored the court order.

The commercial risks of a bareboat charter with a rogue charterer are stark. The ship was somewhere on the high seas. The charterers mocked court orders. Ellen summarised the problem. 'The gang, acting on orders, had stolen the ship and cargo and knew that nobody would use legal force to seize back the ship while at sea. Boas knew this too. No international police force retrieves stolen ships. Boas had to get the ship arrested in a port. But first he had to find her.' Nowadays, ShipLoc and similar modern technology would have enabled the vessel to be secretly traced and caught, but such tracking technology was not available then.

Boas was suffering the downside of bareboat chartering. Knowing the charterers is crucial: organised crime bosses flit from one Southeast Asian city to another to spread confusion. His charterers may have been Triads from China or Hong Kong using Erria Marine Inc. of Singapore as a front. 'This,' said a frustrated Boas, referring to the disappearance from Bombay, 'was when the ship was first pirated.' An understandable comment from a frustrated owner who realised his ship had been stolen; yet there had been no act of piracy in the accepted legal sense. The ship had simply sailed away from arrest.

There had been no attack on the high seas. Reports suggested the ship was close by yet outside Singapore's waters and the clutches of its navy. The Singapore police took the narrow view that there was no evidence of any crime committed in *their* waters and that there was no evidence of any Singapore national being involved. True, it was a Singaporean charter company, but that did not mean it was controlled by a Singapore resident. Boas explained their attitude. 'The police there are better than most, but from their perspective, jurisdiction to act had been a government matter.'

Boas involved the office of Singapore's Prime Minister, because theft of a ship by charterers based in his country was a serious matter. It was to no avail. Ellen explained that the Singapore Government had to abide by the international laws of the sea on jurisdiction, frustrating though it was for the owner. With no act of piracy, the Singaporeans felt unable to assist so long as the ship remained outside their waters. Had it entered port, it would, they said, have been different.

The crew had a cargo worth selling. They also had a large ship ready for further voyages carrying new cargoes. The opportunities around India and the Far East for selling stolen goods in small or corrupt ports are abundant. The chances of being caught are remote. There are no policemen about. A lick of paint to change the name, maybe a few bits of paperwork in a shipping registry, and ships were easily reinvented with a changed identity. Erria Marine had done just this: created a phantomship to operate in the apparently lawful business of carrying cargo for profit.

Phantomships were big business, especially among the astute Chinese who weighed up the odds and realised they had a winner *every* time, far better than the turn of a card or the spin of a wheel. Steal a ship and then use it for commercial gain over and over. The single theft gives profits of tens of millions—enough to fund drug-running or prostitution, with ultimate profits laundered into real estate or distant stock exchanges…or frittered away around the Macaogaming tables with a young and lovely mistress at your elbow.

To experts in the shipping community, *Erria Inge's* problems were just another example of theft and the risks of bareboat charters. A lesser man than Boas could have taken the easy way out and found someone like the notorious Captain Changco to steal his vessel back. A word in the right place around a Far Eastern dockside and he would have found a gang prepared to attack his vessel in a flurry of violence and bloodshed and steal back his ship. But this was not his style. Discouraged and angry though Boas was, recapturing his ship *lawfully* was his aim.

He needed to get his ship seized in port. That meant finding it under its false name. He put himself in the position of the crew and their paymasters. *What were their options? Firstly, they had valuable chickenfeed to sell. Who would want to buy stolen chickenfeed in a port with the necessary bunkering services? A port where no questions would be asked about ownership? Where would they re-register the ship? Somewhere with relaxed laws? Honduras? Belize, maybe?*

Boas had travelled widely and put his experience to good use. He reckoned there were two likely destinations for chickenfeed. One was the Philippines, some 1,500 miles away across the South China Sea to the east and north—where his ship should originally have gone. Manila was a hotbed of corruption, and there were many small ports dotted around the islands where the cargo could be discreetly offloaded. Otherwise, Thailand, with its huge poultry-breeding industry—sailing either north up the Strait of Malacca from Singapore or up the east coast of Malaysia through the Gulf of Thailand to Bangkok.

Boas put out enquiries in both countries and quickly received a tip-off that a vessel answering the description of *Erria Inge* but now called *Palu 111* was at Ko Se Si Chang at Bangkok, unloading chickenfeed. After a frantic dash, he saw the truth for himself. The name *Erria Inge* had previously been welded to the bow and stern. It was still there. The name *Palu 111* had been crudely daubed on, betraying the arrogance of the gang behind the theft.

Boas had found his ship. The quartered red, white and blue with two stars of Panama had been replaced by a new flag with three parallel stripes, two blue and one white. *Palu 111* was now registered in Honduras, Panama's neighbour. Honduras offered a bonanza to maritime criminals; nobody in the Honduras Registry enquired whether anyone applying to register actually *owned* the vessel.

Full of eager expectation, Boas laid evidence of his ownership before the Thai police, who were supportive. A squad of 13 heavily armed riot police stormed the vessel. The crew were arrested and held for questioning. They denied involvement in any fraud. Their explanations convinced senior police officers. If, they protested, the ship *had* been stolen from Bombay, it had not been by them. Boas reluctantly accepted their evidence and agreed to permit them to remain aboard. He had to accept it was *possible* that the crew now aboard were not those who had stolen the ship in Bombay. But what, then, had become of the original crew? If they had stolen the ship under orders from Triads, they might well have been switched between Bombay and Thailand for a crew innocent of that crime. Alternatively, the present crew were skilled liars, well trained by their big bosses, and, despite their protestations, they had stolen his ship.

Boas reasoned that his ship was secure in port and would have a crew available when the litigation was concluded. But then he was conned again. The crew asserted they were in terrible danger from the gang who had really stolen the ship—plausible, but untrue. Boas was a reasonable man. He believed the spiel and hired armed guards to protect his ship and crew.

He had done all he could. Now it was up to the law to help him reclaim his vessel, still under arrest in port. Fortified by advice from his local legal team, Boas flew back to Australia, reasonably satisfied that he could have done nothing more. The ship was now virtually his again.

Back in Australia, Boas's plans for a return to the quiet life were once again interrupted before he even had time to put his feet up and enjoy a glass of Chardonnay.

The bombshell came. *Palu 111* had disappeared. Yet again, his ship had escaped arrest. Boas flew back to Thailand to investigate how, despite the arrest and his hired armed guards, his ship, and the sympathetic crew whose safety he had paid for, had vanished. He now realised he had been cleverly duped by a crew acting under orders from some criminal mastermind.

The trail of enquiries led Boas to Danilo Siroy, whom he had left in charge as the master of the vessel. The ship had sailed without him. Siroy's explanation was that the gang behind the theft had used a mix of threats and bribes. He claimed, credibly, that he and his family had been threatened. He alleged that bribes had been paid to get the armed guards removed from the ship. The Thai authorities had then allegedly turned a blind eye to the ship's departure. The people behind the theft had muscle. Their threats were not empty. The murky waters around Bangkok have been the final resting place for many a dumped body down the years. The successful theft of a ship is worth big money. A determined gang will not let a few guards or bureaucrats impede their plan.

Boas obtained fresh evidence to put to the Singapore authorities. Once again, he met a polite rebuff. He had obtained passport details of two Singaporean nationals personally involved in the theft of his ship. But the passports may have been false; there are many bogus Singapore passports in circulation. The crew Boas found on board in Thailand had been hired in Singapore—or so they claimed. The Singapore Government were being asked to seize a ship flying another nation's flag while on the high seas. No nation wants to start an international incident like that.

Boas told them that the ship's master took orders from someone using a Singapore telephone number. But that did not mean that the person behind the number was Singaporean—probably the contrary. A gang boss from Singapore is unlikely to operate in his home country. The mysterious Mr Wong from Singapore masterminded his criminal activities from Indonesia. Chinese Triads visit Singapore or Hong Kong to plot crimes behind a front as legitimate businessmen. Gangs distance themselves from their home base to make the police's task harder. This *modus operandi* worked well for the gang against Boas.

Ellen continues: 'It is far more likely that this was a Hong Kong or Chinese-run operation, fronted up in Singapore. Precisely what the Singapore authorities themselves knew from their own enquiries is unclear, but Boas did get a clear warning from the generally excellent local police. He said the Singapore Commercial Crime Division confirmed there *was something* to his story, but they would not give him the details because it would be *unhealthy* for him to know. In effect, he was being told: don't risk your life digging deeper. Get the insurers to pay for the theft and forget the whole thing. Good but unpalatable advice.'

For the 14 or so months between October 1991 and Christmas Day 1992, there was no sighting of a vessel answering the description of *Erria Inge,* although there was another regional alert out for her. Ellen and other experts suggest, through educated guesswork, that she was probably operating in and around the Strait of Malacca. A vessel of 17,000 tons answering her description *was* spotted—probably *Erria Inge*, disguised yet again.

She was surely engaged in some form of illegal activity, otherwise there would have been no point in arranging her release from Bangkok. She may well have been used as a mother-ship; piracy was rampant in the Strait and mother-ships were often used to launch small speedboats for attacks. She may have been carrying legitimate cargoes but then stealing them by diversion. Or she might have been transporting illegal immigrants across the Pacific to the USA.

In their search for the truth, both Ellen and Boas worked backward from Christmas 1992, when the bodies were discovered. The aim was to fill the gap. The Guangdong Shunde Shipbreaking Company confirmed that they had purchased a vessel called *Hai Sin* from a Hong Kong company called Modern Richer. They in turn told the local police that they had bought the vessel as the *Hai Sin* from a Singaporean company, Hua Seng Ocean Engineering. But this company did not exist! Presumably, a forged set of papers had been produced to *prove* ownership. *Erria Inge* had become *Palu 111* but had then become something else again—perhaps *Hai Sin*, or that name may have come later.

'In this phantom game,' Ellen explains, 'at that time, ships changed names like people change socks. It could be hard to keep up. Names were not always registered as they should be, though in this case *Hai Sin* had been registered in Honduras. But there could have been an intermediate name used for carrying cargo that the gangsters never registered. Clearly what happened eventually was that a decision was made to dump the ship.' Maybe she was getting too hot to own or too expensive to maintain.

And then there were the corpses, which could be precisely why the vessel had to be sold for scrap. In order to distance the gang from the sale to the breakers, a dummy company was set up as a buffer, making it pretty much impossible to trace back to the gang behind Erria Marine and the crew who knew how the corpses came aboard. Modern Richer's crew would have sailed the vessel into Guangdong but need not have known of the corpses. It would have been their predecessors who knew the truth. Yet, for crew-members anxious to cover their tracks, the obvious solution would have been to weight and dump the bodies at sea. For guilty crew-members to keep the corpses aboard made no sense.

Use of a buffer company was a typical ploy. The gang had created a series of blind alleys veiled in impenetrable secrecy. The crew members could not be traced. Perhaps a determined effort by a body like Interpol might have achieved something, but with nobody reported as missing, there was no impetus. As for the Bureau, it could not throw the necessary resources at a complex operation, identifying members of a long-departed ship's crew, just to try to identify 10 corpses that nobody had even missed. Probably the crew would have remained silent even if traced.

Nor is Ellen critical of the Singapore authorities. Perhaps the police there knew much of the truth but recognised that proving it would be impossible. The criminals, the gang bosses, whether Triads or not, are so powerful. Terrified crews refuse to testify. They know what to expect for betrayal. Ellen has often encountered witnesses too frightened to speak or people changing their story from the obviously true to a pack of lies. Witnesses are reluctant to upset a gang boss who has already sent three thugs to their door to intimidate them and their family. Organised crime in the Far East will only end when some brave witnesses tell the truth—an unlikely event. The criminal grip is too strong, the threats of violence too often implemented.

As for the 10 corpses, there is no definite answer to the puzzle. The pathologist, faced with the difficult task of analysing the decomposed and burned evidence, had done a remarkable job. In his view, the victims were *probably* Caucasians and not Chinese. That ruled out the original crew who had sailed *Erria Inge* to Bombay. His examination confirmed that the men had been relatively young and fit, consistent with being mariners. On some corpses, remains showed hair colours to be red, brown and blonde. The men had been well-nourished, tall and of heavy build.

Ellen believes the ship was involved with or responsible for a collision in the Malacca Strait in September 1992, not long before she ended up in the breakers' yard. At 2320, long after dark, the containership *Ocean Blessing* collided with the tanker *Nagasaki Spirit*, with appalling loss of life. Everybody aboard the containership died and only two of the tanker's crew survived. The tanker was carrying over 40,000 tons of crude oil and 12,000 tons escaped. Even if *Erria Inge* were not responsible, Ellen is sure she was probably there.

With up to 2,000 vessels of all sizes operating at any one time in this narrow stretch of water, collisions are a statistical certainty, as any marine underwriter knows. At the southern end, the Strait is a bottleneck and only 11 miles wide. Further north, it broadens to perhaps 60 miles across, but sandbanks and shallow water make it a route that needs special care and good seamanship. This collision was one of several during the '90s. 'Forty-four seamen lost their lives in the explosive collision,' Ellen continues. 'Only 28 were accounted for. Some evidence points to a collision brought about by piracy—perhaps from *Erria Inge* acting as a mother-ship. *Something* odd was happening aboard *Ocean Blessing*. She was a well-run ship from a reputable background, yet in these difficult waters, she was zigzagging across shipping lanes and changing speed dramatically. That pattern is consistent with the master trying to shake off a perceived attack. None of the crew survived, so we have no explanation of what was happening on the bridge. It is possible there were even pirates actually aboard, taking control and causing confusion on the bridge.

'That is one scenario—*Erria Inge* operating as an attack vessel for pirates chasing or boarding the container ship. But there is at least one other possibility. The first distress signal came from *Nagasaki Spirit:* ***Have been fired upon and now have fire in nos 5 and 6 Central Tanks. Abandoning vessel immediately…***'

'The words *have been fired upon* are sinister, if accurate. Sometimes, though, messages get garbled or misunderstood. After all, there must have been pandemonium on the tanker, where fire or explosion are terrifying prospects. That raises the possibility that the tanker was being attacked, but if Erik's ship was being used as a mother-ship or had been attacking either vessel, then why pick up the corpses? That makes no sense.'

For this reason, Ellen's view is that during the missing months, *Erria Inge*, as *Hai Sin* or using another name, was crewed by a bunch of innocents, hired somewhere after she left Bangkok. As a phantom ship's crew they would know nothing of her history. Their task would be to carry cargoes for profit. Sometimes this is legitimate, in the sense that the cargo will reach the destination. Other times, the cargo, if valuable, will be stolen and sold in a remote port with the ship using yet another name to conceal the operation. If the crew aboard were innocent of stealing the ship, then when faced with a humanitarian crisis, simply by being close to the collision and innocent of blame, they could easily have picked up burned bodies from *Nagasaki Spirit*. One of its lifeboats had been caught up in the inferno, and bodies from that may be the answer.

'The corpses were saturated with petroleum as well as burned, consistent with the known facts of a fire or explosion. None showed any signs of having been murdered. Only an *innocent* crew would have placed the corpses in an unused refrigerated area. Pirates wouldn't have picked up bodies. If pirates aboard *Erria Inge* had attacked these ships, then surely they would never have kept the evidence.

'Once the dead were aboard and the master reported this to the shore, this would have placed the gang in considerable difficulty, because the corpses would need to be taken into Singapore, the last place the gang would want their ship to go. Any such conversation between ship and shore would have been terse when gang bosses learned of *a humanitarian gesture* that had blown a hole in the ship's anonymity. The master would have been told to say nothing to the authorities about the corpses.

'If the ship had entered Singapore, Boas could have got her arrested. So I believe the gang had to get rid of the ship, bodies and all. The phantom ship's days were over. The crew would have been dispersed in some small port other than Singapore to avoid questioning. Using false papers, the vessel was then sold to the non-existent company that in turn sold her to Modern Richer of Hong Kong.'

This theory is plausible but does not explain the zigzagging by *Ocean Blessing*, nor the distress call by *Nagasaki Spirit*. But it is possible that the collision occurred because one of the vessels was indeed under attack, just not from Boas's vessel. Unlike some flag-of-convenience countries, Liberia operated a first-class investigative team. From Reston, just outside Washington, D.C., Liberian Services investigated this incident because the tanker, *Nagasaki Spirit*, was flying their flag, but they did not attempt to identify the corpses in the fridge.

Their report was prepared by Captain William Chadwick, veteran of the *Salem*, *Silver Med* and *Acdir II* investigations. 'To lose 44 lives is a serious disaster. Besides the cost in human terms, the claims arising from hull and cargo interests and for pollution issues could be massive.' Rights and wrongs had to be established. They needed answers to questions including who was to blame for the collision and what the consequences would be in legal terms.

'I concluded,' confirms Chadwick, 'that *Ocean Blessing* was under attack. Her speed changes and zigzagging, as observed by others, were consistent with manoeuvres to shake off a boarding party.' However, even this does not explain why the containership, when under attack for some considerable time, had failed to send any distress message. 'As for the message that our ship *had been fired upon*, I could not interpret that as evidence that there had been gunfire. I am sure there was some confusion.' It certainly seems unlikely that both vessels were being attacked at the same time. The eyewitness evidence of evasive manoeuvres is convincing, but it does seem odd that no distress call was put out by the vessel—unless these were not evasive procedures but signs of a ship already in the process of being taken over by pirates. The eyewitness accounts do not say that there was any sign of speedboats positioned to attack.

Other vessels, including tankers, had been fired upon in the region. Pirates had also got aboard and threatened to start fires by dropping flares down the vents, but the words *have been fired upon* is inconsistent with that.

'In April 1992,' Ellen explained, 'just a few months earlier, *Valient Carrier*, laden with fuel oil, was sailing from Singapore to Indonesia. It was fired at and a flare landed on deck. The crew started to put it out, and while they were distracted a dozen armed pirates clambered aboard. This nasty bunch even injured the master's seven-month-old baby in their furious demands to rob the safe. The engine room was set ablaze and the ship lost power and went out of control. The gang left with a mere $3,800. Though the ship was only four miles from the Indonesian coast, neither we nor the master could raise anyone there to assist.'

Chadwick and Ellen agreed to differ on whether the 10 corpses were from the 16 mariners unaccounted for in this collision. They agreed that those aboard a liferaft might have died abandoning ship, but Bill Chadwick does not believe the missing 16 fit the profile of Caucasians observed by the pathologist. Ellen can think of no better explanation for 10 burned bodies of Caucasians who, unless they were from this collision, were never ever missed. Amongst the missing were two Indians and two other Caucasians from the former Yugoslavia. Northern Indians can have the characteristics of Caucasians.

'The pathologist was not *positive* that all were Caucasian anyway. It was a matter of probability only whilst working from imperfect evidence. To find 10 crew, all Caucasian, in these waters would be most unusual.' Ellen added, 'And if I'm wrong, just who were these 10 people? They can't have been refugees, and there are no reports of any missing crews, least of all ones with a profile to match the autopsy reports. This may yet be a case of mass murder. I still wish that Reston had done more to investigate the remains found in China.'

Today, the mystery remains. In the words used in the English Coroner's court, nobody knows just how and why these men came about their tragic deaths. But enough people know the truth. One day the story may break, though more probably fear of retribution may mean that silence will prevail. As Erik Boas was warned, it is sometimes better to forget.

CHAPTER TEN

Somalia
The Scourge of the Red Sea

Vessels sailing northward from the Red Sea pass through a narrow bottleneck into the Gulf of Aden and the Indian Ocean. This is a pivotal route for global trade. At any one time, around 100,000 crew are preparing to enter or are sailing in these most dangerous waters, bordered by Somalia. From the 1990s until about 2011/12, these waters provided ever richer spoils for the pirates and became increasingly used by organised crime and terrorists as lawless Somalia became a training ground for international terrorists. In 2009, Al-Qaeda called for its supporters in Somalia to attack merchant ships. The plunder was growing increasingly richer.

The Somali government, such as it is, cannot control the entire large country. With a civil war raging and rival warlords rampaging, the country has been a perfect breeding ground for piracy and terrorism. Currently, there is a worldwide relief effort aimed at resolving the famine in Somalia, but such efforts have been hampered by organised criminals and terrorists such as the Al-Qaeda–linked *Al-Shabaab*, who have masterminded piracy from Somalia.

In September 2013, terrorists operating from Somalia, believed to have been from the *Al-Shabaab* group, attacked an upmarket shopping mall in Nairobi, the capital of neighbouring Kenya. A further bloody massacre took place in Nairobi in May 2014. Apparently, these attacks were retribution for Kenya's stance against terrorism. Somali pirates arrested in the region had been tried in a Kenyan court. An attack on an *Al-Shabaab* terrorist stronghold by Kenyan forces inside Somalia had further incensed them. In October 2013, four pirates were jailed in this specially established court in Mombasa.

To get some perspective on why piracy here succeeded for so long, the expanse of sea *immediately* to the east of Somalia is around two million square miles in size—30 times larger than England, 10 times larger than Germany. In the early 1990s, when attacks were less frequent and more amateurish, the best advice to masters was to keep at least 50 miles off the Somali coast. However, attacks have increasingly occurred much farther from land. Even 500 miles off the coast and occasionally 900 miles further south, toward the Seychelles and Tanzania, cannot be regarded as pirate-free.

The use of mother-ships extended the pirates' fiefdom 500 miles into the Indian Ocean eastward to the Maldives. The entire area in question then became extended to around five million square miles. Hence, being 500 miles from Somalia is no passport to safety. In November 2013, Somali pirates mounted an attack 900 miles away, indicating that some pirates have moved their operational area to avoid the naval patrols further north.

This huge expanse of sea is heavily used by vessels heading to and from the Suez Canal on east-west routes. Vessels heading down Africa's eastern seaboard also pass the Somali coastline, the longest in East Africa. Nearly 50% of the world's food, raw materials and fuel has to pass through these waters.

Whereas the waters of Southeast Asia dominated the piracy statistics in the 1980s and 1990s, by 2011 Somalia easily topped the charts. More ominously, Somalia had developed into a spawning ground for terrorists. Piracy had morphed from an *opportunistic* local venture into a major war against shipping—a war that had to be met with a powerful united show of force. The figures are constantly changing, but the ICC-International Maritime Bureau's contrasting figures for the comparative years 2011 and 2013 for *actual and attempted attacks* showed that in 2011 there were 160, but in 2013 the figure had dropped to only 7. In 2011, the Somali pirates had taken 362 hostages, killed 7 and held 23 vessels for ransom, but in 2013, the dramatic change was that there were no deaths or injuries reported.

Activity peaked in January 2011, when there were estimated to be 736 hostages held and 32 vessels seized. Up to September 2013, the number of hostages seized by pirates off Somalia and in the Gulf of Aden had fallen to 34. 'Not a single vessel has been hijacked by these pirates since 10 May 2012,' confirms Captain Mukundan—but vessels have been fired upon.

Protection Group International is the largest private ship security operator, with over 100 in the company and some 600 contracted personnel who provide shipboard support. PGI gathers intelligence from government, non-governmental organisations and especially from its own sources, including the teams operating at sea. The IMB acknowledge that piracy is under-reported; this is confirmed by PGI. They believe there were 160 incidents to mid-November 2013 with two (very brief) hijackings. However, Eric Conway, the Managing Director, agrees that the rash of vessels being seized and crews and ships held for ransom has ceased. The question of how long this success will continue still needs to be reviewed.

The terrifying attack on the *Maersk Alabama* in 2009 was interesting but by no means unique. That containership, while successfully boarded with the crew held hostage, never reached coastal waters. Although aspects of the events as depicted in the 2013 movie *Captain Phillips*, starring Tom Hanks, proved controversial, the film accurately dramatized the horrific ordeal faced by *any* crew. Its importance is in educating people sitting safely in comfy chairs in Phoenix, Chicago or London that behind every statistic lies real suffering—trauma capable of blighting the lives of survivors forever. A less well-known 2012 movie, *A Hijacking*, presents an even more forceful re-enactment of a typical attack. That story is fiction but based on real events.

Eric Conway, of Protection Group International, agrees: 'The movie does reflect the reality. It is very representative of a pirate attack, with the varying attitudes of the pirates and differing levels of aggression.' The film effectively portrays the effects of khat, commonplace around the Horn of Africa. This amphetamine is illegal in many countries but not in Somalia and surrounding regions. When chewed, the plant acts as an appetite suppressant but at the same time provides an exhilarating high, which may explain some of the mood swings and ferocity that sometimes characterise piracy attacks.

Since 2008, over 4,000 crewmen have been taken hostage; the Far East, Somalia and Nigeria are particular hotspots. Even a strong international naval presence around the Somali region since the late 2000s did not stop the attacks, such was the scale of the problem and the vastness of the ocean to be protected. But their presence, along with other measures, underpins the success in curbing the power of these gangs. But it should never be forgotten that hostages, some of whom have been held captive for nearly three years either ashore or on a mother-ship at sea, may have nobody powerful or wealthy enough to negotiate or pay the excessive and unrealistic sums demanded for their release.

If their own vessel has not been sunk, then a captured crew may be released on payment of the ransom for the ship and crew. But, for example, experience with the MV *Albedo* demonstrates the difference if there is no ship to be retrieved. After capture in November 2010, some crew were released in 2011 on payment of a ransom but the rest were held as hostages until more money was paid. However, the vessel sank in a storm in 2013 and evidence suggests that when the vessel sank, the hostages were taken ashore to Somalia. Relatives of the crew from India, Bangladesh, and elsewhere have continued to plead for their release. Because they have no means of paying ransom demands and the owners, having no ship, now have less interest in paying a ransom, there is a sense of despair. The Maritime Piracy Humanitarian Response team are working on this and other hostage situations. This organisation is a pan-industry alliance of shipowners, managers, manning agents, insurers and welfare associations, and its sole aim is to help seafarers and their families in piracy and hostage situations.

Al-Shabaab is a Somali terrorist group that is regarded as part of the loose Al-Qaeda framework. The UN has confirmed that it is associated with piracy and a beneficiary of ransoms paid. Though there is no certainty of the precise sum paid to pirates to get crews and ships freed, it is likely to have exceeded $30 million according to the UN—much of this money going to fund this terrorist group.[5] The logic is impeccable: as pressure is applied to the Al-Qaeda network in one country, such as Afghanistan or Pakistan, so a new centre can be used to harbour and nurture terrorism for export. Lawless Somalia is ideal; early warnings that some of the ransom money would fuel international terrorism have proved prophetic.

The *lads-of-the-village* style of operation was serious enough to be a danger throughout the 1990s and into the 2000s. The IMB constantly sent stark warnings to seafarers to steer clear of Somalia, warning crews to keep a distance of 50 miles from shore. Back then, this distance was sufficient to avoid these unsophisticated attacks. Then came the use of mother-ships, meaning that this is no longer so. Warnings then emphasized the need for extra vigilance through the entire area that the pirates now claimed as their hunting ground.

In the earlier years, attacks were based on opportunism and the chance of easy pickings. Young men seized the chance to rob small pleasure craft and sometimes to steal the entire boat. Emboldened by the typically feeble response of nations which could have nipped the problem in the bud, the pirates grew more ambitious and started to target larger vessels

---

[4]In September 2014, US air-force drones killed Ahmed Abdi Godane, the leader of this terror group. He was one of America's "most wanted." It is reassuring to know that the group behind the Westgate Shopping Mall massacre in Nairobi in 2013 and piracy in the region is still being targeted.

with increasing violence. The pace accelerated rapidly after the turn of the century. With no adequate measures taken to stop piracy in its tracks, from around 2005 until peaking in 2011, the problem had become a serious threat to cargo vessels.

If UN figures are correct, over $31 million has been paid in ransom demands. Most demands have started out at absurd figures, higher than the amount finally paid. Ransom-paying is problematic: Firstly, the pirates are enriched and able to buy larger and faster small craft for their next attacks. Secondly, surrendering to blackmail encourages criminals to become more active and for others to join in the spree, precisely what happened in the years following 2005. Thirdly, the profits may finance terrorism. Fourthly, news of the easy spoils can spread to other areas, as has happened now with Nigeria, whose ports were already dangerous enough.

Hijacking is now a feature here, alongside a wide variety of attacks in port or in the Gulf of Guinea. In 2014, there have been mounting concerns that a terrorist organisation called Boko Haram that operates in Nigeria is being funded by piracy. Boko Haram is associated with Al-Qaeda. The sharply rising number of shipping attacks in this region has prompted fears that the failure to act quickly enough off Somalia has encouraged the previously generally more amateurish crime at sea around Nigeria to become slick, more lucrative and deadlier as part of a strategy to fund terrorism.

In April 2014, Bolo Haram kidnapped around 300 young schoolgirls from their village, and over four weeks later are still mockingly holding them. The power and wealth of Boko Haram has been growing, and thus governments and especially the US Government have been working on proving the link between piracy and this terror group. In Somalia, the small-time opportunist thugs of the early 1990s became well-organised criminal gangs. They bought better vessels and became bold enough to target bigger ships with valuable cargo. Some hijacked vessels then became mother-ships, enabling gangs to roam far out into the Indian Ocean. By 2011,at least eight hijacked mother-ships were reckoned to be operating in the region—one of them being a VLCC, the MV *Samho Dream*!

The advantage of the mother-ship goes way beyond its ability to roam the wider expanses of the Indian Ocean. In the days when pirates were just a few locals seeking opportunities, the monsoon season kept them ashore in the summer months. Now, the mother-ships ride out the weather, so piracy can continue all year round, whatever the season.

Ransom demands are now commonplace. The money is usually dropped by GPS-controlled parachute to land on the vessel. Occasionally, there is a hand-to-hand transfer, a fraught situation requiring a brave and cool character to meet up with the gang's representative. Typically, US dollars are paid over; sometimes, the notes may be electronically tagged so that the money trail can be followed.

Though cargo ships are the main victims, cruise ships have also been attacked in the region. Fortunately, around Somalia there have been no serious casualties on cruise ships, which is why the newsworthiness of incidents was transient. For example, the violent 2005 attack on *Seabourn Spirit* had been long forgotten by the wider public when in September 2008 pirates attacked and seized the *Faina*, a Ukrainian cargo vessel. This second attack prompted widespread media attention because the ship was carrying 33 Russian tanks, 42 anti-aircraft guns, 36 rocket-propelled grenades, six rocket launchers and 13,000 125mm rounds of ammunition bound for south Sudan.

Whether the pirates knew details of the cargo before the attack is unclear, but having hijacked the vessel, they were pursued by both the American and Russian navies. Recent Wikileaks data shows that the US Secretary of State was even considering attacking the vessel to prevent the weaponry falling into the hands of terrorists and criminals in Somalia. In the end, the vessel was released, but apparently a ransom of around $3 million was paid.

With this story fresh in people's minds, the scale of the next attack just a month or two later again became hot news globally. Pirates in small, fast craft hijacked the *Sirius Star*, a VLCC over 300 metres long carrying a cargo of crude oil worth over $250 million. Weighing in at 318,000 tons, this was the largest vessel ever attacked. The top speed of a VLCC is usually about 18 knots; others can make only 14 knots, well within the capability of pirates in their skiffs.

The nature of its cargo and its lack of speed make a VLCC vulnerable. Pirates, heavily armed with rocket-propelled grenades, pose a serious threat to the vessel's cargo and thus the crew and entire ship. As one pirate reportedly said, *We are prepared to die, crews are not*—a philosophy which makes threats to blow up the entire ship all too credible The trick, as ever, is to prevent pirates getting near enough to attack or board. Now at last systems are much improved for tackling problems even after pirates get aboard.

Eventually, a ransom of around $3 million was paid for the release of the *Sirius Star*, but as the pirates grew bolder, a spate of attacks followed involving a wide range of vessels, including more oil tankers. In February 2011, the *Irene SL* was seized for 58 days; reputedly, a ransom of $13.5 million was paid to secure the release of crew, cargo and vessel. It is noteworthy how the figure has risen with the value of the cargo, no doubt fuelled by the knowledge that ransoms have been paid. However, ransom figures are unofficial and should be approached with caution. Pirates even came to use negotiators, who may well peddle exaggerations and half-truths.

Depending on the vessel involved, the pirates may be taken prisoner or, more rarely, be killed in a fire fight. This has happened around Nigeria, where a private security company may provide an experienced leader with appropriate military know-how to lead four or five armed Nigerians with licence to shoot when needed. Under international law, when force may be appropriate is a thorny area. The blurred legal position has led to a varied response to piracy on the high seas.

Consent is needed for the security team to carry weapons aboard the vessel to be protected, and again to leave the ship with them. Regulations vary from one country to the next. The Nigerian approach differs from that of its neighbour, Cameroon. Somalia, lacking a strong government, was a lawless and undemocratic area ruled to large extent by warlords. The absence of maritime legislation enabled some security firms to adopt a gung-ho approach to killing pirates.

After arrest, some Somali pirates have been taken to Kenya; some have then been freed while others have been given deterrent or non-deterrent sentences. Pirates may now also be taken to Yemen to be prosecuted. Others, though caught, do not get arrested, as Captain Mukundan explains. 'If a naval vessel identifies a mother-ship, perhaps from aerial intelligence or by spotting suspicious use of a skiff, the mother-ship will be boarded. A dhow towing two or even three skiffs would be a suspicious pointer. Contrary to some impressions, the mother-ship will frequently only be a dhow or fishing boat, which makes it hard to identify among the mass of them in these waters. But once identified as a suspect, the vessel will be boarded and searched, and if piracy equipment like masks, weapons, ladders and boarding equipment are found, these will usually be dumped overboard and the crew then left to continue on a harmless basis. There is no great appetite for arrests and prosecution.'

The London-based private security company Protection Group International is one of perhaps 200 now operating around the world. The quality and size varies considerably, and PGI prides itself on operating lawfully at the top end of the market. They have provided security for some 5,000 transits. The company was only founded around 2006/7 and all the key figures are former Royal Marine Commandos. They believe it is essential to operate on a vessel with a team of four highly trained personnel, whereas some companies try to get away with two or three and using guards with possibly inadequate experience.

In one particular incident in 2013, Eric Conway is convinced by reports from his team on board that the pirates would not have been repelled had there been fewer than four armed guards, such was the ferocity and determination of the attackers.

'When private security companies started to be increasingly used,' continued Mukundan, 'there were no guidelines, rules of engagement or even regulations. Then an ISO emerged, and now, with IMO approval in 2013, there is what is known as the 100 Series of Rules of Force.' This lays down a graduated approach so that firstly the armed security team must identify themselves to give the pirates fair warning—attackers could assume that crews would not be armed and would not fight back. Then, if the pirates are not deterred by this, shots are fired in the air over the approaching skiff. Only if essential can reasonable force be used, which includes firing at the pirates when there is a threat to life. Even then, no more shots must be fired than reasonably needed. These Rules may not be followed by some less-reputable security personnel, and thus pirates have been killed around Somalia, whether justifiably in law or not.

PGI operates to its own Rules of Force, a version of the 100 Series mentioned above. One offering, as opposed to placing security specialists on board a vessel, was provision of an escort vessel for shipowners willing to pay for this. However, the concept presents problems in practice because of the Rules of Force. Intervening with force from a *separate vessel* does not fit comfortably unless the escort interposes itself between the pirates and the ship under attack.

Two examples in November 2013 show the effectiveness of the new procedures and the value of having an armed response unit. Both incidents are reports from the Bureau's Kuala Lumpur Piracy Centre. On 6 November, a product tanker sailing some 450 nautical miles east-southeast of Mombasa was approached by a skiff, presumably operating from a mother-ship somewhere in the area. Aboard were five heavily armed pirates. The skiff was spotted and emergency procedures were implemented at once. The authorities were informed and the crew alerted. Speed was increased, evasive manoeuvres undertaken, and the fire-pumps were started. When the pirates opened fire, they were met with an armed response and retreated.

Just a few short years ago, those pirates would have fancied their chances of getting aboard and seizing the ship and crew for ransom. So would the gang of five or six pirates—possibly the same bunch—who, just three days later, attacked from their skiff a chemical tanker about 277 nautical miles north-northwest of Madagascar. They got to within 200 metres of the tanker but the master had commenced evasive action and had activated the Ship

Security Alert System (SSAS), a beacon alerting supporting naval vessels and aircraft. The master also sent a distress message, while non-essential crew scurried to the citadel (as explained below, a location like a panic room provided in some high-value homes in the USA). However, once again, it was only when fire was met with fire from the specialist team on board that the pirates backed off. As Conway has commented, with an increased risk of arrest and prosecution plus stiff resistance from armed specialists on board, increasingly pirates are having to abort and seek out softer targets with no armed response.

Piracy has been less of a problem directly for Kenya than for its lawless neighbour to the north, but most African ports present some degree of risk for visiting ships. Many other nations have been far better equipped to prosecute and imprison pirates arrested on the high seas, but Ellen and the Bureau have had to campaign for too long to get the support of governments to make the arrests and then to take the pirates back to Germany, France, Italy, the UK, etc. However, because there was no chance of any prosecutions taking place in Somalia, Kenya was encouraged to handle piracy prosecutions until, in April 2010, it decided it no longer wished to be at the sharp end because of its straitened finances.

This led to international funding for a special maritime court to be created at the Kenyan port of Mombasa. In 2013, that court jailed nine pirates for five years and another four got seven years. A Spanish naval vessel had made one of these arrests when a Kenyan fishing boat was attacked. This commendable determination to play a part in stamping out piracy is very welcome. While appropriate prison sentences were imposed, they were nothing like the 33-year sentence handed down in the USA to the pirate tried for the hijacking of the *Maersk Alabama* involving Captain Phillips.

Though some countries that have captured pirates have brought them to trial in their own courts, it is not something that is viewed with enthusiasm. Prosecutions are costly, complex and time-consuming. Whereas India, for example, has a solid record, Europe generally has no great appetite to bring pirates back, and with its overcrowded prisons and stretched criminal courts, neither has the UK.

One gang made a huge error when they attacked an American *naval* vessel, the USS *Nicholas*. The gunship was on piracy patrol and naturally did not surrender but instead captured the five pirates. Their skiff was sunk and the pirates taken to the USA, when the judge sentenced them to life imprisonment…plus 80 years for firearm offences. It is not yet apparent whether such penal sentences have made any difference. The chances of being arrested and taken before an American court are slim.

MV *Maersk Alabama* was a container vessel belonging to international shipping giant Maersk, flying under the American flag, with a mixed nationality crew. She carried 17,000 tons of cargo, some of it foreign aid, and was heading for Mombasa. Allegedly, when attacked in April 2009, she was within 300 miles of the Somali coast, which, if true, would be closer than recommended. She was boarded by four pirates. The master was Captain Richard Phillips. After his encounter with the pirates, he became an American national hero and was invited to the White House to meet the president. Certainly, he and his crew underwent a challenging and at times terrifying ordeal, but probably little different from that suffered in scores of other pirate attacks, and certainly one far less brutal than the murderous attacks in the Far East described earlier.

Probably Hollywood and the PR folk handling his book both *bigged up* the master's role. That in no way disparages the master's resilience and steadfast courage. Whatever the rights and wrongs of decisions made in circumstances none of us would want to face, the crew are now blaming Captain Phillips and suing his employers, Maersk, in the US courts for compensation. They contend that Phillips ignored piracy warnings and sailed too close to shore—allegedly because he wanted to take a shorter route to cut costs. Damages of $50 million are sought, but frequently claims like this are settled for substantially less than the reported demand.

Captain Mukundan makes the valid point that today the vessel might have had a citadel and there would be no question of Captain Phillips and two of his colleagues remaining on the bridge after the pirates boarded and Phillips had rightly ordered the rest of the crew to hide. A citadel is like a panic room within the ship, where the entire crew remain in an unassailable position and can shut down all the power to the vessel. This obviously has dangers for the crew in some circumstances because the vessel is drifting; the crew have no control, but neither do the pirates.

In his book, *A Captain's Duty* (Hyperion), Richard Phillips admits he made a mistake in remaining too long on the bridge. Partly he did not wish to abandon it and partly he was taken by surprise by the speed with which a pirate armed with an AK47 reached the bridge and threatened him, having shot away locks on doors intended to keep the bridge impregnable. The preferred procedure at the time was for the *entire* crew to go to a safe hidden point away from the bridge, but the right course of action is easier to recognise when you sit in an armchair than when a pirate appears beside you brandishing an AK47. It is also easier to abandon the bridge if there is a citadel specially designed for this type of emergency. As it was, Phillips went outside to the bridge wing at huge personal risk to fire off flares at a pirate who in turn tried to kill him with his AK47.

Phillips was a hostage sitting in a lifeboat with the pirates when the long ordeal came to an end. Negotiations had started following a show of force from the US navy. A destroyer, the USS *Bainbridge*, and a frigate, the USS *Halyburton*, came on the scene after the emergency contacts had been made. When it came to the point that Commander Frank Castellano judged that Captain Phillips's life was in danger, three Navy Seals fired three fatal shots into the heads of the pirates in the lifeboat. The fourth pirate was arrested and sentenced to 33 years in jail, way more than sentences handed down elsewhere.

'The flag of the vessel is not a deterrent,' confirms Captain Mukundan. The highly effective intervention by the US navy made no difference in slowing down the rate of attacks, which peaked two years later. 'Pirates do not think of the flag. They seize an *opportunity*, and only after gaining control do they consider the nation behind the flag.' That is consistent with Captain Phillips's book, where he describes how the first pirate he spoke to was delighted to discover he had captured an American vessel. He had not known in advance.

Prior to the *Maersk Alabama* movie, the plight of a British couple in Somalia had probably attracted more global coverage than any other incident. The Chandlers were middle-aged retirees from Tunbridge Wells in Kent. They had been sailing the globe in their 38-foot yacht *Lynn Rival* for about three years. In October 2009, they were sailing from the Seychelles to Tanzania when their tiny craft was seized by pirates and they were taken into a Somali port. A British naval vessel had the opportunity to intervene en route but was ordered not to engage the pirates for fear of risk to the Chandlers.

In the subsequent 388 days while the Chandlers were held prisoner ashore in Somalia, there must have been moments when they wished there had been a successful fire fight at sea. In the end, after being forced to live apart in wretchedly inhumane conditions in the searing heat, a ransom was paid for their release. A ludicrous ransom demand of $7 million was initially put forward—way beyond the ability of friends of the Chandlers to raise. The British Government, while supportive and sympathetic to their plight, refused to assist with meeting any ransom demand.

Eventually, £282,000 was dropped to the gang, who double-crossed the rescue planners and did not release their prisoners. A Somali taxi driver living in London played a pivotal role in their eventual release when a further £219,000 was paid, and in nerve-racking circumstances the couple were taken in an armed convoy to the British High Commission in Mogadishu. It seems that even during that journey, there was a high risk of a further criminal attack to recapture the Chandlers for more ransom money.

A two-pronged approach was belatedly taken to combat piracy in these waters. Due to the increasing number of attacks, the size of vessels seized and the links to terrorism, a massive amount of resources are now concentrated in the region. The EU NAVFOR, supported by 26 countries, has operated under direction from an HQ in Northwood just west of London since December 2008. From here, an international naval operation is masterminded to protect shipping. One of the frequent casualties of piracy had been ships carrying food for starving people in Sudan—part of the World Food Programme. Since the creation of EU NAVFOR, not one such ship has been seized.

The seriousness of the problem is evidenced by the number of nations that also now maintain a physical presence: the USA, Russia, India, China, Japan and Taiwan. All have seen it as worthwhile to take part in the patrols. There are also NATO operations, and CTF 151, part of the Combined Maritime Forces (CMF) is also patrolling. This has not completely stopped attacks in this vast ocean, but not one ship has been successfully seized since May 2012.

The Combined Maritime Forces operation has been headed up by an American vice-admiral; 25 countries are involved. It has three main task forces devoted to maritime security and counter-terrorism, counter-piracy, and security and cooperation in the Gulf of Aden. CTF 151 is involved solely in anti-piracy operations. Its HQ is with the US Fifth Fleet in Bahrain. EU NAVFOR and the CMF share data in their common goal.

Vessels entering the high-risk zone are expected to give four to five days' notice so that the naval vessels and their HQs can monitor the position. Once in the danger area, ships are expected to keep in regular touch.

Useful if a vessel is hijacked is the ShipLoc system, a tracking device that can be secreted aboard vessels, enabling their position to be monitored. In any event, under IMO regulations, an Automatic Identification System must now be installed on vessels over 300 tons gross weight. This tracks location, speed, cargo, course and so on. However, some masters believed it was aiding the pirates and so mandatory use was diluted to *expected* use, with a discretion given to masters to switch off if in the better interests of crew safety.

The other main thrust of countering piracy has been better education of shipowners and crews—both about how to protect their vessels and how to prevent pirates boarding. Prevention remains a priority. Ships are advised to sail at full sea speed in the region. Evidence points to the value of travelling at over 18 knots and to having a freeboard of over 8 metres, though many vessels cannot meet these recommendations. The creed lies in Best Management Practices 4 (BMP4), which lays down procedures for all scenarios. This education has no doubt helped any number of crews evade attack or capture.

Preventing pirates from boarding is the priority. Advice dating back to when Eric Ellen was Director of the International Maritime Bureau still holds good: starting a fire fight aboard the ship is not the answer. Captain Mukundan endorses the widely held official view that with pirates aboard, avoiding a violent shootout is essential. The firepower of the pirates is likely to be such that the crew will much more likely be killed or seriously injured. Captain Phillips was fortunate not to have been shot when he attacked a pirate with a flare. The AK47 bullet hit the ship's frame, which probably saved his life.

That said, there is a wide body of support for the view that having armed security on board is effective in prevention. No pirates have successfully boarded and captured a vessel where they have been met with an armed response. Not surprisingly, with so much money at risk and with safety a vital consideration, increasingly shipowners have decided to employ armed guards. A private security company may provide skilled ex-Armed Forces personnel trained in weaponry or may offer a vessel to act as an escort. The cost of an escort for guarding a single vessel would make most shipowners think twice. Such protection is more likely to assist with a convoy of four or five vessels.

In contrast, private security guards on board have proved very effective, to the extent that, around Somalia, the pirates' easy pickings have gone. That of course raises the question of when the naval presence will back off to save expense or when shipowners decide once again to run the gauntlet of these waters without a hired security team aboard. When that happens, piracy might once again pick up speed, unless a political solution to the governance of Somalia is found.

The introduction of citadels has indubitably played a significant part in frustrating the pirates' ability to sail a vessel back to a Somali port or a safe haven. In 2011, the South Korean Government insisted that its vessels traversing this region should have a bulletproof citadel. This followed the 2010 successes of citadels aboard the *Taipan* and the *Magellan Star*, where pirates were held off until rescue came. In this panic room, the crew have emergency supplies and two-way communications and the ability to disable the engines to prevent pirates from powering the ship away. The drifting ship can be reached by the nearest naval patrol alerted by the emergency messages. But the pirates do not readily accept defeat. In one incident, a crew member was shot when the pirates fired on the citadel door.

Frustrated pirates are dangerous, and the risk from citadel use must be that unless crews open up the citadel on demand, sooner or later a vessel may be deliberately scuppered or set on fire, the pirates escaping by skiff. Pirates may also use explosives to breach the citadel. Or rescue may not even come; certainly the crew within the citadel must be prepared for an uncomfortably long stay. It could take a naval vessel three days to travel from the Somali coast to a distant point near the Maldives where attacks have occurred. But in general, citadels have often proved very effective in buying time for calls for help to be answered. The advantage is that the rescuers know that anybody encountered on the vessel is a pirate and can react accordingly.

The MV *Arrilay-1* is a good example of the citadel proving effective, although she was attacked not in the Somali trouble zone but nearby in the Arabian Sea. She was a 38,000-ton bulk carrier returning from Australia to Jebel Ali, near Dubai. When the pirates boarded, the security guards and crew took refuge in the citadel. The pirates unsuccessfully tried to shoot their way in and then tried to smoke them out. Cleverly, the citadel contained breathing apparatuses; the pirates were foiled yet again. Better still, from their refuge the crew were able not simply to disable the vessel's power but to operate her. By communication with aerial reconnaissance, they were able to steer toward the UAE, where a combined operation with the US Navy led to UAE forces boarding and seizing control of the ship.

But what of mother-ships? These are the key to the attacks now so far from shore. Although a hijacked vessel may become a mother-ship, most are only dhows and fishing boats. A problem arises when a hijacked vessel is identified as operating as a rogue mother-ship but the original crew are still aboard. They may have sealed themselves in a citadel, but if the engines are still operating, the vessel can be used as a mother-ship. Disabling the engines from the citadel is essential. With no citadel, a captured crew may be held as prisoners while their ship is used as a base from which to launch attacks. Intervention by naval vessels is then complicated by the need to save the crew.

The crucial factor is to prevent pirates from boarding by whatever means—using armed security guards, hoses jetting water from vulnerable parts of the ship to force the pirates back, razor wire or even lifelike dummies. Using crew members to aim hoses is no longer seen as ideal because of the risk of being shot, but automated hoses or discharging hot water or foam are effective measures. Finally, use of non-lethal 9,000-volt electric fencing, while not suitable for every type of cargo, is successful. Besides hurting the pirates, if touched, the fence triggers alarms and switches on floodlights, removing any element of a surprise attack.

Currently, three factors place the metaphoric foot on the throat of pirates around Somalia: the naval presence, the use of armed guards provided by private security companies, and the sound guidance of BMP4. The EU NAVFOR will remain until some date to be fixed in 2014. Its presence has been vital. In November 2013, Eric Conway of PGI commented that the state of the shipping industry makes owners very price-sensitive. The very success that has been achieved inevitably makes it tempting to consider cutting an expensive budget item like the cost of security.

As we have seen, in piracy the ratio between risk and reward is crucial. In the experience of PGI, pirates around Somalia back off when faced with armed security; there have been some 100 occasions when pirates have intended to attack and been deterred. Without the private security companies and with no naval presence, the attraction of attacking ships will increase. Better procedures on board merchant shipping, the use of citadels and the like, will certainly be effective, but these alone are unlikely to be sufficient to prevent pirates regaining their confidence and their hopes of boarding and then holding a vessel and crew to ransom.

CHAPTER ELEVEN

Terrorism at Sea– *When* and Not *If*

'We've seen…plans from intelligence of attacks on merchant shipping…there is a threat.'

- Sir Alan West (when First Sea Lord)

'I believe it's just a matter of time before the terrorists try to use a maritime attack against us.'

- General Ralph Eberhart, Head of US Northern Command

Many of today's problems stem from the generally pitiful response by most governments to the IMB's urgent calls for a united effort to fight crime at sea. Such calls have been made for the past *30 years*. In turn, the rich profits enjoyed by *organised crime* benefiting from sloppy maritime security subsequently encouraged terrorists to view the sea and ports as a way of attacking society. The failure to address the Somali problem swiftly and effectively enabled a thriving terrorist-supported industry to develop. In consequence, the problem exploded into enormous proportions until curbed by forceful international action from about 2008. It should surprise nobody that fears are growing that the Boko Haram terrorist group in Nigeria are using piracy to fund their operations.

In assessing the dangers of a terrorist attack involving a vessel, conflicting viewpoints make it harder to unravel the truth. Some experts, and some politicians when it suits them, ramp up the risks of a maritime version of 9-11. Others downplay the chances of a marine incident, arguing that too much credit has been given to scare stories and overblown warnings. They argue, fallaciously, that spotlighting vulnerable areas merely helps the terrorists.

Nearly 13 years after 9-11, the nightmare scenarios outlined in this chapter have happily not yet materialised. But there is no room for complacency.

Downplaying the maritime threat or that of border security *helps the terrorists* by diverting public concern and media focus to less pressing issues. As 9-11 proved, the new breed of terrorists have *imagination*, enabling them to push the envelope of opportunity. The West was poorly prepared for an event of this magnitude. Nobody in Florida even noticed anything odd about Arabs wanting to learn how to fly commercial jets without bothering to learn about landing. Terrorists and would-be terrorists now live secretly in our midst and are alert to what they see and what they hear. They need no media help to find the weaknesses in security, but gift horses like the disclosures by Edward Snowden involving highly confidential CIA documentation are gratefully accepted.

The experts who know best, including Dame Eliza Manningham-Buller, the Director-General of Britain's Security Service in the mid-2000s, have no doubts about what their intelligence resources are learning daily. Terrorists are *already* planning ways to use loopholes in maritime security to their advantage—indeed, they have already exploited them. Containers have featured in arms-running and in a probable but unproven attempt to smuggle a possible terrorist.

Between the first attack on the World Trade Center in 1993 and the second in 2001, eight years had passed with no apparent terrorist activity within the USA. Nobody in the security services believed they had given up or gone away. The public, however, grew complacent. Since 9-11, Al-Qaeda has again shown no urgent need to rush into more attacks on this scale, though intelligence services confirm that any number of possibilities have been checked out by terrorists and approved for development or discarded.

It must be assumed that since 9-11, terrorists have been planning scenarios quite beyond the range of routine foresee ability. Mention has already been made of the thwarted attack on the US Navy in Singapore in 2002. Another plot to blow-up *10* transatlantic flights using legal liquids to create explosives was thwarted in August 2006. This was a clear pointer that grandiose plans still appeal.

The sea offers just such opportunities.

To the public, the 2004 Madrid train bombings came out of nowhere, as did the London bombings in July 2005. Neither came as a shock to the intelligence services. Intense Al-Qaeda activity in Spain was being monitored. In Britain, MI5 had warned that an attack was *inevitable*. In November 2006, Dame Eliza Manningham-Buller warned that at least 30 *known* plots were under development in Britain. Today, the UK remains on constant substantial risk alert, with security officers infiltrating and monitoring terrorists living among British citizens. On several occasions, last-minute arrests have prevented a major atrocity in the UK. All Western governments are alert to the dangers but, as is often said, the terrorists only need to get lucky once to cause the mayhem and bloodshed that they crave. The intelligence services need to be lucky every time and that is not possible.

Bearing in mind the already well-publicised weaknesses in shipping procedures and in port security in many countries, the only sensible view is to assume that the use of ports or a ship for terrorist purposes is *inevitable.* That is not to say that society should surrender and lie back waiting for the bang. Rather, the challenge should be accepted and every effort made to outwit the terrorists by using the latest technology and applying greater resources to tighten security.

The overhaul of archaic maritime procedures has advanced by leaps and bounds since 9-11, so far successfully preventing an attack on mainland USA or in European ports. The real problem is that some loopholes cannot be eliminated without severe damage to the economic viability of maritime freight. Terrorists presumably understand the economic and practical difficulties presented by the sheer scale of reforms needed in shipping practice.

An increasing number of British Muslims, attracted into terrorism, may already be working in ports, involved in stuffing containers with cargo or hired as members of crews. In 2011, a Muslim British Airways employee was charged with terrorism offences relating to an alleged plot to blow up a US-bound flight. Before his arrest in 2010, he had been working as a computer expert since 2006.

He probably has his counterparts in the shipping world. Trying to identify this dangerous minority is a task that stretches the British security services. Ellen has no illusions. 'There is a long history of terrorism at sea, yet most people know nothing about it. Only after 9-11 did serious measures really start to be taken to combat this known danger.' Ellen had been trying for years to improve security both at sea and in port—measures designed to prevent crime and to combat terrorists. 'While the best remembered incident is the hijacking of the *Achille Lauro* in 1985, other atrocities have been going on with nobody really noticing, some of them unspeakably callous.

'Shipping presents problems because of the freewheeling nature of seamen. Crews are drawn from a wide variety of backgrounds, many from regions rife with pro-Muslim extremist sympathisers, like the Philippines and Indonesia. False identities and qualifications have been rampant.'

Until 9-11, people without any marine qualification, perhaps doctors or telephonists, had been able to buy a Master's Licence for a couple hundred dollars. They could sail away in a supertanker—a charter for terrorists! It takes only a few extremists among a crew to achieve a dramatic event, such as seizing command of an oil tanker at night close to Singapore and setting it full speed on a course to cause maximum pollution or other physical damage around the port. Just as the 9-11 hijackers trained as pilots, other terrorists may now have been secretly trained to command ships for terrorist purposes.

The US Government has attempted to make ports safer by adopting strict new laws, but only a fool would believe that any Western democracy can be a fortress against terror. 'In movement of cargo,' Ellen adds, 'security has been so lax that terrorists can scoff. It used to be gun-running, but now the greater risk is of nuclear material or chemical weapons being shipped secretly to the USA or Britain to be used in major cities.'

These are some of the biggest threats related to maritime security:

- Hijacking of a packed cruise liner to blackmail a government or governments—as happened in the *Achille Lauro* incident.
- Attacking a cruise liner, perhaps savagely with explosives, to cause death, fear of travel and financial instability.
- Exploding a ship in a major port, perhaps involving an oil terminal or Liquefied Natural Gas (LNG) storage facility.
- Causing global economic chaos by blowing up a ship at the Miraflores Lock in the Panama Canal, coinciding with blocking the Suez Canal by sinking other ships.
- Hijacking or even commanding a vessel carrying an inherently dangerous cargo such as Liquefied Natural Gas or petroleum and using it as a *weapon, a floating bomb or missile* in a port or as a political blackmail opportunity. The Singapore region is especially vulnerable.
- Carriage of concealed nuclear or biological or chemical material in containers or in cargo, for immediate or later use in Western cities.
- Movement of terrorists in containers or aboard cargo ships.
- Use of terrorist-controlled merchant ships as disguised warships.
- Training of terrorists to become crew members for a later mutiny or hijacking.
- An underwater attack using divers.
- The fleet of vessels allegedly secretly once owned by Osama bin Laden. The existence of the bin Laden fleet of over 20 vessels was

> widely reported after 9-11,but hard evidence that it existed is scarce or non-existent. Assuming that the original story was leaked to the media from intelligence agencies, it may be that the fleet is as illusory as the Iraqi weapons of mass destruction! Captain Mukundan is sceptical. 'I have no reason to believe this fleet exists. The overheads now of ship ownership are high, the essential bureaucracy quite demanding, so why own ships? If Al-Qaeda need to ship something, then they can bareboat charter the vessel they need without all the burdens of ownership.'

Of course, the Somali experience is that some eight pirated vessels became mother-ships. There is little doubt that the Somali operations in recent times have been driven by *Al-Shabaa*b, part of Al-Qaeda. To that extent, these dangerous mother-ships are already operating under terrorist control, and the stolen spoils and huge ransoms paid are helping to build a war chest to finance future terrorist operations. The IMB has always been well aware of how terrorists have exploited the sea. Here are some examples of past incidents that passed most of us by.

Though it was the plight of Paul and Rachel Chandler, seized from their small yacht, that triggered a media frenzy and raised popular awareness of the Somali piracy problem in 2009, the first major media story involving the Red Sea/Gulf of Aden was the 2005 attack on the cruise ship *Seabourn Spirit*.

As modern cruise ships go, the *Seabourn Spirit* was not large, measuring around 113 metres in length and only 10,000 gross tonnage. But the attack with grenade launchers and machineguns was dangerous. Only thanks to the cool head of the captain and crew was a worse incident avoided. As it was, the ship was hit and damaged, but by zigzagging away at speed the captain was able to outrun the pirates in their small craft.

Somali pirates also attacked MS *Nautica* in November 2008, but again the captain was able to use size and speed to escape. Not so fortunate was the cruise ship *Le Ponant*. In April 2008, the three-masted sailing ship was attacked and boarded at a time when only the crew of 30 was aboard. Having fired on the vessel, undaunted by firehoses, the pirates stormed aboard and took the ship into port with the crew held as prisoners until a ransom was paid—reputedly $2 million.

There is minimal risk of a successful pirate *invasion* of a cruise ship. A ship with a huge hull is virtually impossible to access.[6] Terrorism remains

---

[6]When I sailed through the Malacca Strait in the tiny cruise ship Sea Goddess, at a time of virulent pirate activity, Cunard took several Ghurkha soldiers aboard and they patrolled the deck constantly.

a greater threat, though again more stringent security checks on passengers and crew have helped to minimise the risk. Divers have been checking for explosives around the famous cruise-ship terminals like Miami and Fort Lauderdale. Since 9-11, the absence of any major and concerted attack on a cruise ship, whether by explosive device or by rogue elements of a crew seeking to hijack control, may have created an unjustified expectation that normality has returned. Increased security and undercover operations have successfully counteracted the threat, but only a fool would imagine that there is no group out there even now plotting to create terror through an act of atrocity.

The best hope for pirates when attacking a large vessel is to intimidate the master and crew into surrendering by using a show of weaponry and forcing the vessel into port so as to prevent further damage and possible bloodshed. However, the speed and size of most cruise ships are major defensive factors. Though in several parts of the world there remains a risk of piracy, it should not deter people from taking a cruise. The high-risk areas are well known and extra vigilance is taken. The officers of cruise ships are well trained in how to cope with a piracy attack. In the Red Sea zone, as described in the previous chapter, there is now a strong naval presence to protect shipping—although even this is no guarantee of total security.

The attacks on the cruise ships off Somalia were a pointer to the aspirations of the Somali pirates as they graduated to becoming organised criminals with terrorist backing. However, there had been a long history of incidents which should long before have galvanised governments into ensuring the safety of passengers at sea. Though not the most bloody, the highest profile attack was on the *Achille Lauro*—and its sensational aftermath.

This cruise liner was launched in 1947. She was around 200 metres long and weighed about 24,000 tons. Her twin blue funnels were each emblazoned with a white star; her hull was blue, her superstructure gleaming white. She had a dramatic career: after fairly uneventful early years, she suffered severe fires in 1965 and 1972. In 1975 she was in a major collision with a livestock carrier, which sank. In 1981, there was another fire in a bar and three passengers died during the evacuation. Not surprisingly, after these contretemps, by 1985 the vessel was showing her age. That was the year when her past troubles were eclipsed by a hijacking that left her name as more than a footnote in history. Even the hijacking was not the last sorry chapter: in 1994, the *Achille Lauro* was gutted by yet another fire and sank.

Among 19 Americans who decided to take a Mediterranean cruise in 1985 was a group from New York. There were some British passengers, too, but the majority of those who joined *Achille Lauro* in the Mediterranean port of Genoa were Italians. It was 3 October 1985, with blue skies and pleasingly warm temperatures. When the ship's horn blasted on departure, there were over 1,000 aboard, including a largely Italian crew of over 300.

The New Yorkers were friends. Among them were the Klinghoffers. The group had vacationed together before and were eager to sail through the sun-drenched beauty of the eastern Mediterranean, calling at Port Said and Alexandria in Egypt and at the Israeli port of Ashdod. The vessel was scheduled to sail alongside the notorious Gaza Strip, a flashpoint for so much trouble and bloodshed. Egypt itself was not directly involved in the Palestinian–Israeli conflict but, as an Arab country, it was sympathetic to the Palestine Liberation Organisation.

Terrorism was certainly not a concern to those aboard *Achille Lauro*, though the drama of this hijacking would recall a spate of attacks on commercial flights by Middle Eastern terrorists. In 1973, a Greek ship sailing in the same region had been sunk near Beirut by a bomb concealed on board, though none of the 250 Americans passengers were killed. Between 1979 and 1984, there had been over 500 assorted attacks, with hundreds slain in embassies, military garrisons, plane hijackings, airport lounges or hotels. One pointer to special risks for Americans had been the execution of Robert Stetham on a hijacked TWA flight. Just four months earlier, he was executed in cold blood by Hezbollah terrorists, his dead body thrown to the tarmac at Beirut airport.

Many of these crimes involved Middle East politics and hatred of Americans. In 1985, the warning signs had been written large, yet there were no worthwhile security arrangements on board *Achille Lauro*—entirely typical of the time. On arrival, passengers had been greeted by the ship's officers and their baggage delivered unchecked to their cabins or staterooms. Frisking a passenger for weapons was unthinkable. In the absence of *mandatory* security checks, cruise operators did not want to alarm the often elderly passengers.

Once aboard, the usual party atmosphere developed. The traditional Captain's Welcome Reception was followed by dinner. Captain Gerardo de Rosa, 51, was an experienced married mariner whose charm was appreciated by the passengers as they got acquainted and enjoyed their cocktails. The New Yorkers had journeyed nearly 4,000 miles to join their ship; after dinner, they, like most guests, retired early, though others stayed in the bars or danced to the ship's band.

Four of the passengers were travelling on false Norwegian passports, although they had no connection with that country. They were all members of the Palestine Liberation Front, a splinter group from Yasser Arafat's PLO. None of them even *appeared* Nordic, yet nobody thought to question this oddity. The terrorists were mocking security by using passports from a country of which they knew nothing and whose language they certainly could not speak.

Leon and Marilyn Klinghoffer were senior citizens but still loved life and fit in well on *Achille Lauro*. Marilyn was 58. Leon, 69, was confined to a wheelchair. He was in good form but poor health, having suffered a stroke that had left him with weakness and some paralysis down his left side. His speech was affected and talking was a struggle. As American Jews, this decent, respectable couple were high on any hate list for Middle Eastern terrorists.

On Monday 7 October, when the ship reached Alexandria, having sailed for four days south and east through the shimmering blue of the Mediterranean, many passengers went ashore to visit the pyramids while the vessel set sail mid-morning for the short cruise to Port Said at the mouth of the Suez Canal. There, the shore passengers would return to the ship. The Klinghoffers were among the 400 still aboard, including about 19 Americans and British.

The terrorists' true intentions remain unclear, though it is possible to distil the probable truth from the different versions expressed by credible witnesses. Abul Abbas, 50, was a key player in the events about to unfold on *Achille Lauro*. He had planned the assault but was not aboard. Abul Abbas was his *nom de guerre*—his real name was Mahmoud Abbas or Abu al-Abbas. He was the leader of the PLF faction and a close associate of Yasser Arafat.

After this incident he was put on America's *Most Wanted List* when he lived in the Gaza Strip and Iraq. However, years later in 1995, he became a leading proponent of peace and even gained the trust of the Israelis in peace discussions. Following 9-11, he was removed from America's Most Wanted List for the first time since 1985. In April 2003, during the fall of Saddam Hussein's regime, he was captured and in March 2004 he died in custody of a heart attack, though others claim he was murdered by being thrown from a roof.

Because of the way events turned out on *Achille Lauro*, it makes sense that Abul Abbas would want to distance himself from them. The four terrorists on board claimed they, too, never intended what happened. They later contended it was the result of a bungled plot. Allegedly, their original plan was to go ashore at Ashdod in Israel to seize hostages as revenge for an Israeli attack on the PLO headquarters in Tunisia.

They claim this plan was ruined when, through a partly open cabin door, a steward spotted them armed to the teeth with Kalashnikovs, grenades and detonators. If that is true, then it was startling that they had left the door open. If true, could they seriously have gone from such a modest plan to the grandiose scheme of hijacking a ship without orders from ashore? It seems more plausible that they *were* always aiming to hijack the ship or, when prematurely spotted, received orders to do so.

At Monday lunchtime, shortly after leaving Egyptian territorial waters, the terrorists seized the ship. For sceptics who dismiss the idea that a few dissident crew members could seize an oil tanker or luxury liner, these four terrorists showed how easy it was. Their timing was excellent. Most passengers were in the dining room at lunch, a daily highlight for many. The meal was well advanced, so that latecomers had arrived but nobody had yet finished. To the elderly passengers, the sudden appearance of two men brandishing automatic weapons must have been terrifying. The men burst in and shots were fired but with no apparent intent to kill. Everybody froze, too stunned to resist. There were shouted orders to get down and everybody but Klinghoffer lay on the thick carpet awaiting their fate. Some thought it was a robbery; others realised it was a terrorist attack and lay motionless, fearing for their lives.

Up on the bridge, Captain de Rosa heard the shots and started to head toward the noise but found himself confronted by two gunmen brandishing Kalashnikovs. Sensibly, he surrendered. The PLF were now in command of the vessel; he was under their orders. Al Molqi, the leader of the gang, directed him to sail for Tartus in Syria, where he assumed a warm welcome awaited.

The captain's message of a hijacking was picked up in Sweden and immediately crisis meetings were set up in Italy, London, Washington and all the Middle Eastern countries. Nobody knew how many hijackers were aboard but their message was stark: Israel must release 50 Palestinians, including Samir Al Qantari, in return for the release of the ship. If not, the Americans would be killed one by one. Israel has never yielded to threats, and the omens were bleak: in 1979, Al Qantari had killed a five-year-old Israeli girl by smashing her head against a harbour wall.

Some passengers wept but generally they were shocked and silent, putting up no resistance as they filed to the ship's main saloon. There they waited, surrounded by cans of kerosene. The warning was brutal: *one false move and we'll set you alight*. Passengers later described just how nervous the attackers seemed, despite their bravado. One of them was a youth of only 16, and the eldest only 23.

To add tension, three women were each made to hold a grenade with the pin removed. If their grip slackened, the grenade would explode. De Rosa helped identify most of the British, Americans and Jews. Their passports were sifted and sorted, and on top of the stack was Leon Klinghoffer's. That of an American woman, Mildred Hodes, 60, was next in the pile. In all, 29 'special cases' were identified and taken to the Arazzi Lounge. Leon and Marilyn, fearing the worst, were among them. At least they were together and alive. Hours passed. Nothing happened.

The Italian government of Bettino Craxi was at the centre of the crisis, constantly in touch with interested nations. In particular, though, Yasser Arafat was asked to state his position. Was he condoning or condemning the hijack? Back came his answer: *he condemned it. The hijacking hindered his peace efforts*. He denied involvement and sought to distance himself but Israeli intelligence, usually reliable, claimed Arafat had endorsed the attack.

Significantly, Arafat offered to mediate and appointed an emissary to travel to Egypt to help resolve the crisis. His emissary was none other than Abul Abbas, the organiser of the attack, using his other alias, Abu Khaled!

In Washington, President Reagan's crisis team had started plans for a military intervention, though a face-saving deal without negotiating with terrorists was the preferred option. Surrender to the PLF's terms was not on any agenda for Washington or Israel. The American aircraft carrier *Saratoga* and units from the Sixth Fleet had been in the Mediterranean on exercise and they steamed toward the crisis zone in readiness for military intervention. On the island of Cyprus, the British airbase at Akrotiri started receiving the spearhead of an Italian taskforce, ready to be helicoptered to the ship. Their plan assumed a shootout with the terrorists with predicted heavy passenger casualties, not an attractive prospect.

By now it was Tuesday 8 October. At Tartus, Al Molqi, the terrorist leader on board, suffered a setback. The vessel was refused entry. Syria, usually happy to support terrorist activity, was not keen to get involved. Worse still, all other ships anchored near the port left the area, leaving *Achille Lauro* alone. The implication of her vulnerability was clear.

Al Molqi issued a threat to start killing the hostages if negotiations did not commence. It was ignored. He then ordered the 19 special hostages to file onto an open upper deck. It was a potential helicopter pad, and so the prospect of a helicopter landing was now stymied. Leon Klinghoffer, in his wheelchair, could not get there and so was ordered to remain on the lower open deck, separated from his wife. Angered by the lack of Syrian support and with his threats ignored, Al Molqi ordered the ship to sail. He broadcast a warning that the first execution would take place at 1500 hours. Still the politicians ignored the warning. The terrorist leader had little choice now. He had to give in or start the killing. He decided to start killing.

Rather than have pity for an elderly invalid, Al Molqi chose Klinghoffer as his first victim. Without ceremony, Klinghoffer was executed in cold blood on deck, shot in the head and chest. A member of the crew and the ship's barber then jettisoned his dead body and wheelchair into the sea. The leader, innocent blood on his clothes, returned to the bridge clutching the dead man's passport and one other. A broadcast was made announcing 'two dead.' This may have added pressure on the Americans and Israelis, but it remains unclear who released this incorrect information.

None of the other hostages knew of the murder until much later. When Mrs Klinghoffer came down from the upper deck, her husband was missing, but she had no idea he was dead. Mildred Hodes was only told by de Rosa that she had been next in line *after* the terrorists had left the ship. More intriguing is what the rest of the diplomatic world knew. From now on, *double-speak* was on the political agenda. Abul Abbas later claimed that Leon Klinghoffer had brought it on himself by encouraging others to protest. It is even said that Abul Abbas joked that 'perhaps he wanted to swim for it.' This sick jest appears to have been in keeping with his callous character.

Al Molqi apparently then received a message from the PLO forbidding more killing. If that is true, just who outside the ship knew *for sure* of the execution? The killing *did* stop. It had achieved nothing anyway. There is no point in killing hostages unless the world knows. Stetham's body had been dumped from the TWA plane in front of the cameras, the effect both stark and immediate. Klinghoffer had been discreetly tipped overboard. It seems probable that the PLO or PLF did order the killing to stop *and* to keep quiet about the death in order to enable negotiations to be more effective.

De Rosa was now ordered to head for Libya, another nation then nurturing bitter anti-Western hatred. As Tuesday ended, Reagan was ready for military action but was dissuaded by Craxi, who contended that there had been no *evidence* of any murders aboard. So—was the broadcast of two deaths even made? It is probable that it was, but that it suited the Governments to ignore or dismiss it.

The breakthrough came when Arafat's emissary, Abul Abbas, arrived in Egypt and negotiations started with Egyptian representatives. The news reached the ship, causing elation among the hijackers. Al Molqi was ordered by the PLO to force de Rosa to head for Port Said to await developments. By Wednesday morning, *Achille Lauro* was anchored 15 miles from shore.

A safe exit for the four terrorists was agreed in return for the release of the ship and hostages. The deal was that the four men would be taken to the PLO headquarters in Tunis, under guarantee of safe passage from Egypt's President Mubarak. There they would be tried. Releasing Israeli-held prisoners was *not* on the agenda.

The Italians, Germans and Egyptians signed the agreement but the British and American Governments distrusted the deal and refused. However, by mid-afternoon on Wednesday, the agreement was signed. The four terrorists left the ship and de Rosa spoke to the Italian Prime Minister's Office at the Palazzo Chigi and confirmed that *all the passengers were well.* Prime Minister Craxi was about to announce that the crisis was over without bloodshed when the captain was quizzed about this again. De Rosa then confirmed the murder. Had the master previously really not known of Klinghoffer's execution? Had he been forced to lie? If Al Molqi went to the bridge with fresh blood on him, had de Rosa not been there? It seems most unlikely.

Just how much was known to the negotiators about the murder when the deal was made remains clouded in diplomatic evasions. It seems likely that it was convenient for *both* sides to work on the basis that there had been no bloodshed, but Abul Abbas must have known the full story. Other governments using bugging techniques to pick up messages from ship to shore may have known the truth. At the Klinghoffer home in Manhattan, the unsuspecting family celebrated the successful end of the crisis.

News of Klinghoffer's murder reached President Reagan and then the daughters of the dead man. Relief turned to despair. America was stunned. Outraged, Reagan demanded that Egypt prosecute the four terrorists but Mubarak denied knowledge of any murder and claimed that the four had already left the country. This was untrue. The terrorists were still in Egypt.

Reagan was furious at the double-cross. Confident in his intelligence that the terrorists were still in Egypt and would be sent to Tunisia on an Egyptian Boeing 737 with Abul Abbas, he decided to act. His anger reflected the mood of the American people. The murder of a helpless elderly American Jew from New York City attracted a storm of media attention.

Attempts by the Italians to get the murderers sent to Rome for trial were ignored. At 2300 on Thursday 10 October, the four Palestinians were shepherded onto an Egyptian jet to be flown to Tunis. The American Sixth Fleet received urgent orders to scramble fighters. It was a race against time, seeking an elusive quarry. Admiral David Jeremiah dispatched two F-14A Tomcats and two E-2C Hawkeyes from USS *Saratoga*. From Washington, the Tunisian Government was warned not to let the Boeing 737 land. It agreed. The 737 switched course for Greece, but when landing rights were again refused, it was forced to head south again for Egypt.

Using night intercept techniques, the planes criss-crossed the target area until at last, at 0030 on Friday 11 October, 30 miles southeast of Crete, the two Tomcats closed on Egyptian 737 number 2843 flying at 34,000 feet and 450 mph. The fighters identified themselves and ordered the pilot to fly to Italy.

President Reagan, from his hospital bed, persuaded Craxi to agree to let the plane land at Sigonella Airport on Sicily. On landing, in an episode worthy of Monty Python, Italian troops surrounded the plane only to find *themselves* surrounded by fifty Americans, who had just landed with orders to seize the terrorists and to whisk them off to the USA. There was a standoff as two friendly nations confronted each other with weapons primed.

The crime had been on an Italian ship; the perpetrators were now in Italy. The law was on Italy's side. Craxi refused to hand over the four, forcing Reagan to back off. Mubarak of Egypt was furious, protesting air piracy as the four terrorists walked into Italian captivity. But Abul Abbas remained aboard and claimed to be using an Iraqi diplomatic passport. It was decided to send the plane to Rome.

Dramatically, US General Carl Stiner, working on Washington's instructions, ordered that the Egyptian plane be escorted by American fighters. Over Italian airspace and without consent, the legality of this was nil but the gung-ho approach suited the mood of the American people. They wanted Abul Abbas brought to the USA for trial. An enraged Craxi would have none of it. In a major diplomatic showdown between friendly nations, the Italian Air Force then scrambled four of its own jet fighters and muscled in on the Boeing 737, forcing the American jets to withdraw.

Undeterred by this setback, when the Boeing landed at Rome, General Stiner's own plane landed and pulled up right alongside. A further demand for a handover was refused. Stalemate ruled on the tarmac throughout the day until three Italian judges ruled three–nil that American legal justification for extradition of Abul Abbas or the terrorists was non-existent. Instead, America's public enemy number one flew to Croatia and on to freedom before the US could serve any legal proceedings on him for piracy or other crimes. He was to remain free till 2003.

To American disgust, he never faced any trial but was convicted as a conspirator *in absentia* by the Italian Court and sentenced to life imprisonment. Al Molqi was convicted and went to jail for 30 years; his accomplices were all jailed too. In 1996, although Al Molqi was being held in a top-security prison near Rome, he was allowed under Italian law to take a vacation of 12 days. Not surprisingly, he failed to return but, amazingly, was later recaptured in Spain.

Was the hijacking an act of piracy or terrorism? The distinction had been critically important to the Americans. The PLO officially denied that the act was undertaken on its behalf. Whether or not it met the narrow legal definition of piracy affected what action could be taken in international waters. The definition of piracy has too often produced cogitation and confusion rather than swift and decisive action.

In 1985, lawyer Abraham Sofaer had just joined the US State Department under Secretary of State George Schultz. As he later testified to a Congressional Committee, when Schultz asked what laws were available on which they could rely to try to get the culprits arrested, extradited and prosecuted, Sofaer's advice was not well received. 'I told him then that it was uncertain that the seizure would be considered piracy because a Harvard study in the 1930s had suggested that politically motivated seizures of vessels should not be treated as piracy, a suggestion that some claimed had found its way into governing international conventions.'

He continued: 'Schultz was outraged, saying *what good is the law*, almost throwing me out of his office!' But Sofaer was correct. He was just the messenger bringing bad news. The impotence of American power following the murder led the Government to force some changes internationally. The United Nations asked its marine agency, the London-based International Maritime Organisation, to tackle the issue. A special subcommittee published guidelines that were widely accepted and raised safety standards for crew and passengers alike. That said, proper security for those boarding ferries and cruise ships right up to 9-11 remained far from adequate. The guidelines raised the level from a very low base indeed.

One hundred and thirty countries accepted the guidelines but few passed them into law. Different approaches were taken on ship security (widely honoured in spirit at least) and on port safety (largely ignored). A benchmark as to what was *a reasonable standard of safety* from attack was laid down. It thus opened the way for legal compensation claims, something pursued later by passengers on the *Achille Lauro* against the Italian port authorities and against the PLO.

It took the December 1988 bombing of Pan-Am Flight 103 over Lockerbie to expedite a safety law in the UK with the passing of the Aviation and Marine Security Act 1990. In the USA and Canada, legislation has also now been enacted.

'The *Achille Lauro* is not the most deadly example of a ship being hijacked,' remarks Ellen. 'That attack caught media attention because it was high drama involving a cruise ship with Americans aboard. Despite the dreadful circumstances of the murder of Leon Klinghoffer, another more bloody incident has been largely forgotten.'

The attack aboard *City of Poros*, a Greek island-hopping ferry, in July 1988 involved one of the most feared Palestine terrorist groups, the ANO—the Abu Nidal Organisation.

'These ferries are packed with locals and tourists, everybody enjoying warm sunshine and the splendours of the Greek islands in a relaxed atmosphere. Suddenly, on this ferry, all hell broke loose. The terrorists opened fire with machine guns and hurled grenades. Around 10 people were killed and 70 injured. The gang were making a political point, though as far as I know without any effect.

'There have been several other examples of terrorism, often involving ferries, around the Far East and the Indian subcontinent. In 1999, the Tamil Tigers in Sri Lanka attacked and sank a passenger ferry at Trincomalee. In the Far East, a ship and passengers were hijacked and held to ransom. So you see from these examples what happens if security is lax. Any passenger ship is vulnerable. It's urgent to introduce procedures at *every* port to prevent something far worse occurring.'

The laxity which continues to allow border crossing with fake documents is a major concern. A BBC-TV investigation in December 2006 showed how easy and cheap it was to get illegal passports in Europe. The researcher was advised to enter the UK by sea rather than air because security at ports was regarded as less tight! She did so successfully on both occasions. Ellen notes: 'Eighty-four percent of shipping crimes occur in or around ports, so a big plus is that the American post-9-11 reforms to counter terrorism, if implemented widely enough, could reduce opportunities for crime in ports.

'My fear is that it will take the marine equivalent of the WTC disaster to get some countries to wake up. What America has been trying to achieve since 9-11 is long overdue. Perhaps the richer nations are going to have to fund upgrades in port and loading procedures in poorer countries. Any weak link will be exploited by today's terrorists. It's no use having 100% security in ports like Liverpool, Le Havre or Hamburg so long as terrorists can stuff a container in Dar es Salaam, destination USA, with deadly content. It is then up to the Americans to spot the rogue using intelligent profiling among the millions of containers.' Under the Container Security Initiative (CSI), the US Coast Guard are confident such a container would now be spotted.

'People have short memories. Governments have private agendas,' says Ellen. 'There was an attempt to plant a car bomb on the ferry *Val de Loire* in June 2001. At that time, this ship operated between the Spanish port of

Santander in northern Spain and Plymouth, England, a highly popular route for British tourists travelling to Spain with their cars. In the summer, there could be 2,000 people aboard. This Basque separatist plot by the terrorist group ETA was foiled. It was a *near thing*, but you can only have so many *near things* before that one occasion when the terrorists win.

'A catastrophic disaster with huge loss of life was avoided by some excellent work by Spanish anti-terrorist police. They'd arrested two ETA members the previous week in the Spanish town of Mondragon. Their homes were raided and police found 35 kg of dynamite, maps of Santander and the sailing schedule for the vessel. The bombers had planned to take a car bomb aboard, this being one of their specialities. Was this big news? Not really. The Spanish Government, in contrast to the police, played down the threat. You mustn't scare off the tourists!

'In July 2001, ETA terrorists also threatened *Seabourn Legend*, a luxury cruise ship, when she was at anchor near the Franco-Spanish border. So soon after the *Val de Loire* incident, the threat was taken with due seriousness. Nothing was found. The ship was delayed, distressing the 324 people aboard. The terrorists had made their point. Later, in 2005, another vessel from the same fleet, *Seabourn Spirit*, was attacked by Somali pirates.

'Passengers on a ship to Ibiza got lucky too—through a more unlikely turn of events. In 2000, the Spanish police discovered a car bomb in the town of Benabarre in northern Spain, a Basque stronghold. This was pure chance—the bombers' car had broken down on the way to the ship! That vehicle was scheduled for the ferry sailing from Valencia to the holiday island of Ibiza. It would not have been picked up by dockside security. Once aboard, untold carnage could have occurred.'

Whatever their goals, many terrorist groups support each other. Libya under Colonel Gaddafi was a powerful benefactor of the IRA, providing sophisticated weaponry to support their campaign against the British. Without this support, many atrocities in Northern Ireland and mainland UK would have been impossible. It is unlikely that Colonel Gaddafi gave a toss for centuries-old Irish grievances. To him, the logic was simple: *I hate the USA. Britain is its poodle and supports them against me. So they are my enemy too. The IRA wants to attack the United Kingdom by a terrorist campaign. So, we have a mutual enemy...therefore the Irish Republican Army are my friends.*

Colonel Gaddafi and his cohorts in government were reputedly behind the Pan-Am 103 bombing, but arguments still continue about the ultimate truth about the atrocity. What other international terrorist activities his regime has supported will hopefully become clear following his overthrow and death in October 2011. However, even since the end of his regime, Libya has been a troubled country simmering with hostility and ongoing violence. The overthrow of Gaddafi has yet to bring stability. There is tension and fighting in Egypt and elsewhere along the North African Mediterranean coast, the so-called Arab Spring creating an uneasy instability.

On the same basis that Gaddafi once supported the IRA, there would be some logic for extremist nationalists in Ireland to make common cause with Al-Qaeda, which has the resources and a shared hatred of the United Kingdom. Though this is possible, Dr Rohan Gunaratna, PhD, a Research Fellow once based at the highly respected Centre for the Study of Terrorism and Political Violence and who now heads up the International Centre for Political Violence and Terrorism Research in Singapore, does not think it likely.

Following the 2001 attack on USS *Cole*, Dr Gunaratna was retained by the American Government to advise on terrorism issues and capabilities. His opinions and advice are widely sought after, not least because of his authorship of the controversial book *Inside Al-Qaeda*. 'I don't believe these two, the Irish terrorists and Al-Qaeda, will make a common cause. Al-Qaeda is still well organised in Europe. Its cells are in place. It has no need to seek assistance from non-Muslim groups. That might create weaknesses that do not exist in its close network.'

Though the IMB works closely with intelligence services and other international agencies, the war against terrorism is not a true part of their role. They see this as the task of the intelligence services. But they shared a mutuality of interest to the extent that arms shipments could only occur through false documents, disguised ship ownership and slack port security, all of which were very much the concerns of the IMB. The sea has been used by most terrorist groups to transport weapons under any number of guises. The IRA was no exception. The cargo manifest would hardly refer to several hundred Russian AK47 assault rifles or two tons of Semtex.

Even before 9-11, some experts had predicted that Al-Qaeda would turn its attention to merchant shipping. In October 2000, Islamic extremists had already demonstrated an ability to humiliate the American Navy by blowing a hole in USS *Cole* at a cost of 17 lives, 30 injured and around $250 million. USS *Cole* was a guided missile destroyer—505 feet long, displacing 9,000 tons. She was four years old when she entered the dangerous port of Aden in Yemen. Yemen has never been far from the centre of Middle Eastern troubles. It remains a hotbed for terrorism and should have been regarded as a port offering a high degree of risk for Americans, perhaps even an *unacceptable* degree of risk.

The vessel docked at 0930 local time on 12 October 2000. The *Threat Level* of an attack under the five levels of the *Threatcon* procedure had been assessed at the raised level of BRAVO. This level should have ensured a high state of readiness for trouble. It did not.

Level BRAVO meant that the ship should have appeared alert to the risk of terrorist attack. On deck, the vessel should have had armed personnel. In reality, the crew were armed but without bullets! Fire hoses should have been ready to prevent small craft getting too close or anyone boarding. They were not. No audio system was available in Arabic to warn off those coming too close, by sea or otherwise. No orders were given to the crew to demand identification from small craft approaching. In short, the safeguards of Level BRAVO were not being used when, at 1030, refuelling commenced.

At 1118, a small motor boat crossed the harbour, sailing toward the warship. Aboard were two men and what is now known to have been a mass of explosives. Small craft criss-crossing the harbour were common enough, and aboard the *Cole* there was no apparent alarm as the sailors waved cheerfully to the locals, acting with typical open-heartedness. To the terrorists, they were just suckers. This was a suicide mission, and when the vessel pulled up alongside as if on official business, it erupted in a massive explosion, blowing a hole 40 feet by 20 feet in the warship's hull.

Some might say this was predictable, though other vessels had refuelled there without incident. Yet complacency appears to have ruled even though the dangers of Yemen and Aden were known. In 2000, the first report into the tragedy came from two retired military figures, who concluded that naval forces were not adequately prepared for an attack during refuelling. A formal naval investigation also decided that about half the *preventative measures* were not used.

Among the various measures to be taken under *Threatcon* was the following:

'*Measure 16. Water taxis, ferries, bum boats, and other harbor craft require special concern because they can serve as an ideal platform for terrorists. Unauthorized craft should be kept away from the ship; authorized craft should be carefully controlled, surveilled, and covered.*'

That seems clear enough. Following Measure 16 plus the procedures in Level BRAVO should have kept the USS *Cole* safe. The list of failures looks extraordinary and allegations of neglect seem appropriate, but that was not the final official view. The last report on USS *Cole* was the Judge Advocate General Manual (JAGMAN) published in January 2001. This manual determined that ignoring 12 procedural rules was within reasonable performance standards—surely an encouragement to Al-Qaeda as well as a shock to many Americans.

The real concern is that, despite the JAGMAN conclusions, this incident appears to have been both predictable and preventable. The boat was in sight across the harbour. True, the suicide bombers would have ignored an oral warning in Arabic to stay clear, but their defiance would have provoked an alarm signal to fend off the craft with hoses or by opening fire. Instead of being repelled under Measure 16, the terrorists were welcomed alongside—to the extent that first reports stated that the craft was part of the refuelling operation.

The efforts to arrest the team behind the suicide bombers have had some success—small consolation to families who lost loved ones. The permanent lingering image is of friendly American servicemen waving to the terrorists who were about to kill them.

Though the USS *Cole* incident had the higher profile, the attack against the French-registered *Limburg* 12 months later in October 2002 might have been more serious. MV *Limburg* was attacked at sea in the Gulf of Aden by a small craft which exploded alongside the 330-metre oil tanker. There was one fatality and a dozen wounded—far fewer than the score intended by the murderous terrorists, who no doubt hoped the tanker would erupt in flames, killing everyone. The repair bill came to $45 million. The ship still operates today, now renamed as *Maritime Jewel.*

In February 2014, a Saudi held by the Americans at Guantanamo Bay, Cuba, pleaded guilty to his role in this attack. Al-Darbi had joined Al-Qaeda after training in Bosnia and with the approval of Osama bin Laden. He had planned and orchestrated the attack but was actually in US custody already when the incident took place. He is not going to be sentenced until he has given evidence against another prisoner who was allegedly involved both in the attack on *Limburg* and also against USS *Cole*.

The *Cole* and *Limburg* attacks involved the same hierarchy of Al-Qaeda terrorists. Though arrests and convictions followed in Yemen, in a mass prison breakout in 2006 13 other terrorists convicted of these crimes escaped.

Perhaps deliberately, to de-sensationalise the headlines, official reports played down any terrorist element in the *Limburg* attack for nearly two weeks, thus diluting the story. Most people will barely remember the incident. This is one reason why a terrorism expert like Brian Jenkins, who advised the Clinton administration, has spoken publicly about the need for caution when making sweeping assertions that a terrorist attack by ship is *inevitable*. While the *vulnerabilities* exist, experts like Jenkins argue that harping on about them only leads to the media turning what is a plausible *possibility* into a real threat—something very different.

Captain Mukundan adds his own note of caution, recalling reports that a ship in the Malacca Strait had been kidnapped by Al-Qaeda and then piloted by terrorists for hours as a practice run for a major incident. Before long, the ship was being described in the media as a VLCC, a true giant of the oceans. 'When we investigated and spoke to the master, the truth was very different. The vessel was small and certainly no VLCC! It had *not* been in the Malacca Strait and the attack had been by pirates, who had not kidnapped the ship but had merely boarded for a short time and stolen just over a thousand dollars.'

In September 2001, too many ports, not least in the USA, were unsafe. The WTC attack thrust American port security onto the agenda. Warnings were at last taken seriously. Ports like Boston and Houston were seen to be especially vulnerable. Harbours close to city centres and used by schooners 200 years ago now present potential opportunities for use of a tanker or LNG carrier *as a weapon* to destroy an entire city. Fuel storage tanks, power stations and container depots all rub shoulders by the quays, simply a waiting a detonator such as an exploding ship or a rogue container stuffed with explosives and a timer. Urgent measures have been taken to prevent what was an invitation to attack a soft target.

One of the gravest dangers might be if terrorists somehow commandeered or controlled a Liquefied Natural Gas carrier, which could have 125,000 cubic metres of high explosive—30 million gallons of LNG aboard. A *successful* blast would cause devastation. An LNG explosion has been compared by some experts to the force of a small nuclear bomb, though in a study arranged by Lloyd's Register, such devastation was played down, with the claim that terrorists would be 'very unlikely' to achieve even a fireball. Their view was that unconfined gas cannot explode and cannot even burn in its liquid state. But other safety experts believe that because the gas is transported at 1/600th of its original volume, if it were exploded or ignited *aboard* the vessel, there *would* be a massive fireball.

The dangers these carriers represent are self-evident, yet that did not stop a bunch of amateur armed robbers from being able to invade an LNG carrier in Santos, a notoriously violent port in Brazil. If a bunch of small-time thugs could get aboard, then so can Al-Qaeda—and *they* would not be content just to steal $10,000 from the safe like the Brazilians. Happily, a new regime providing heightened security when these vessels are near port is now in place.

Despite acceptance of the increased dangers of an attack on an American port, approval has been given post 9-11 by the US Federal Energy Regulation Commission for an enlarged LNG storage depot at Cove Point, Maryland. The size has since increased by 80%. LNG deliveries come from countries like Algeria, Nigeria, Trinidad and Norway via the Chesapeake Bay, even though the vessels must pass close to a nuclear power station at Calvert Cliffs, Maryland, three miles away. One central aspect of the decision is that the facility will not receive such carriers without clearance from the US Coast Guard and only once *that* agency is satisfied that it will be able to ensure safe passage. A no-boating zone has been created and a *cordon sanitaire* will operate around the LNGs. However, remembering the training of the 9-11 pilots and the ingenuity and patience of Al-Qaeda, is it really wise to increase such an obvious flashpoint?

Dr Rohan Gunaratna, for one, is worried about the decision at Cove Point. 'An LNG represents a threat. I do not know of any precise range of the fireball if an LNG carrier were attacked or exploded, but the effect would be devastating for a considerable distance. To route LNGs close to a nuclear power station seems to me to be an unacceptable risk. When I was first retained after USS *Cole*, I felt that the American intelligence agencies were significantly under-informed on the threats. However, they learned fast and well. I am less sure whether their new learning has sufficiently infiltrated other government agencies. That may explain why a decision like Cove Point has been taken.

'The Tamils have tried to use mini-submarine technology (for an intended attack). One attempt was in March or April 2000. The sub was being built in Phuket in Thailand. Then the Thai police confiscated it. However, the Tamils got the sub back because it was legal for them to build one under Sri Lankan law. Terrorists operate on a copycat basis, and there is every reason to believe that other terrorists might now use this capability. Korea has made many, many mini-subs. In Colombia, even two *full-size* submarines are in use by criminals.

'An attack on an LNG using a mini-sub might be a suicide mission, but that would not be normal. In my view, they are ideal for delivering frogmen to a target so that limpet-style mines can be fixed to a hull. They are only about 20 feet long and so are suited for an attack in an unprotected stretch of coastal water or port.'

A congressional report into 9-11 stated that the attacks succeeded because of a failure of *imagination*—the failure to think like a wealthy, cunning foe ready to use imagination to create unprecedented havoc. General Ralph Eberhart has warned that he believes the attack could come in terms of bringing a ship into port, either carrying high explosives...or weapons of mass destruction. That is why the Cove Point decision is so controversial.

Use of an LNG carrier (or indeed a supertanker) as a weapon of mass destruction could come from a rebellious crew or by hijack from air or sea. These cumbersome vessels have an autopilot facility. If commandeered in Chesapeake Bay, say by parachute drop or from a helicopter and the vessel set to full engines, it could speed to its target, such as the nuclear power station or the storage terminal. Employing sea marshals aboard the ship would not necessarily be sufficient to foil a violent attempt to take control.

The LNG facility on the Charles River at Boston is a similar problem. It can store at least 13 billion cubic feet of gas. If a single tank were pierced, the entire storage plant would be expected to follow, with an estimated force of 2,000 megatons. According to a distinguished scientist, that is equivalent to 200 nuclear weapons. Nothing was done about this risk even after a TV documentary in 1978 warning about it. Now, since 9-11, confronting much greater danger from terrorists, Bostonians must hope that new measures now adopted under the ISPS Code will reduce the dangers from the air or sea.

Germ warfare is another problem. There are at least 48 different organisms now available, including toxins and viruses. The former Soviet Union had an advanced programme developing germ warfare. Additionally, they had a means of delivery via missiles. Some suspect that this type of know-how was being smuggled aboard the *Estonia* when she sank. The breakup of the Soviet Union has added to worries about chemical warfare among those who should know—like William Cohen, former Defence Secretary in the Clinton Administration.

Cohen has publicly voiced concern about the *inevitability* of a germ or chemical attack. With the near impossibility of preventing transit of these weapons by sea, the danger is far closer than people realise. The sad fact is that tomorrow's headlines could be filled with the story of a devastating germ attack on any city of the terrorists' choosing. The fact that efforts are being made to reduce the risk is of small comfort. Even establishing a foolproof detection system (if that is possible) could now be too late.

On 20 March 1995, a rather amateurish terrorist gang planted sarin nerve gas on trains running on three different Tokyo subway lines. Eleven people died and over 5,500 were harmed—and all by the tiny contents of a few lunch boxes and soft drinks containers. If the attack had succeeded as the criminals intended, thousands would have died. The gang had pierced the containers with umbrellas to release the gas before fleeing to safety.

Secret Services everywhere are concerned by the proliferation of germ and nerve gases. The potency of agencies such as sarin or germs used in biological warfare make large quantities unnecessary. Material for a dirty bomb could be imported in a ship's container with no certainty of detection. In police raids in 2003, Scotland Yard recovered only some of large quantities of the deadly nerve gas ricin being made in premises in north London. The ringleader was jailed in 2005 amid evidence of a campaign to spread panic in Britain by placing ricin on vehicle door handles and on toothbrushes in stores. As to the remainder, never found, it could easily have been slipped into the USA concealed in a container with a good chance of successful delivery. Ricin is alarmingly easy to make; the skill is taught by Al-Qaeda at its training camps.

An alternative target is hijacking a vessel carrying toxic waste. Judging by what happened in April 2000, this is not hard to achieve. Fourteen containers of toxic waste from American military bases in Japan had been shipped on the MV *Wanhe* to the USA and Canada. Carriage of these Polychlorinated Biphenyls (PCBs) attracted a storm of protest; they were not permitted to be unloaded. The vessel returned to Yokohama in Japan. Here, a group of Greenpeace protesters were able to board the vessel illegally to make their protest. If a few demonstrators can get aboard so easily, what chance is there of stopping a team from Al-Qaeda?

Before the 2004 tsunami in the Indonesian region, Captain Mukundan was concerned about the prevalence of hostage-taking as a new form of terrorism involving Indonesia and the rebellious Aceh Province in particular. That crime wave was partly politically motivated, whereas the current Somali problem stems from poverty and links with gangsters and terrorists associated with Al-Qaeda. The IMB's annual figures at the time pointed to this mounting threat to merchant seamen. In viewing the figures in the years up to the tsunami, the director commented: 'The overall trend of piracy attacks remained on the increase, but the two most disturbing aspects were the degree of violence and the number of hijackings by terrorists. Many crews were taken hostage for political ends.'

A welcome development was that the Indonesian Navy increased patrols to combat these attacks. There are vessels permanently in the Aceh waters and in the rest of the Malacca Strait. 'There has been very active patrolling by Malaysia on the other side. We know that the people involved in piracy are also making money from people-smuggling. I'm hopeful that this proactive role from Indonesia will curb this rash of hijackings by terrorists.'

No question, the Malacca Strait and the waters of the region were the vortex of piracy and potential terrorism until the 21st century. The 2004 initiative was boosted by the involvement of the Indian Navy in 2006, which worked wonders in stemming the tide of hijackings and kidnappings. However, the forces of nature also had a significant if transient effect.

As it turned out, something far more devastating than increased patrolling hit the region in December 2004. Following a severe earthquake off Indonesia, Aceh Province bore the brunt of the ensuing tsunami that swamped coastal communities, causing over 120,000 deaths. 'By mid-February, there had not been one reported attack in the Malacca Strait,' confirmed Captain Mukundan. 'We believe that, like the rest of the population of Northern Sumatra, many pirates may have died. The pirate gangs would certainly have lost their equipment and boats. This may account for the lack of attacks.' Realistically, he did not expect an end to shipping crime but hoped that the lull might have given the Indonesian Navy a chance to get on top of the problems.

Alas, a spate of attacks since mid-February 2005 proved that kidnapping and piracy in general was still a problem despite the presence of warships. In March 2005, 35 well-drilled pirates armed with rocket-launchers and machineguns seized a methane carrier in the Strait, but fortunately their intent was armed robbery rather than use of the ship as a weapon for an attack on a port. In July 2006, a Japanese crew fought off an attack, but two UN vessels providing relief aid to tsunami victims were both boarded and pillaged. Lloyd's Insurance of London reclassified the Malacca Strait as a warzone because of the dangers—a decision that triggers entitlement to higher premiums. However, with the drastic action taken to safeguard shipping, the 'war risks' decision was reversed the following year.

Whereas Mukundan accepted that many attacks pre-tsunami involving hostage-taking had political motives, the subsequent spate of attacks from Indonesia had a different motive: extorting money from shipping companies to get a crew (and perhaps the vessel) released. Again, these past seven years or so, the combined naval and aerial presence in the Malacca Strait has largely curbed the worst excesses. However, payment of cash encourages repetition; yet the psychological pressure on owners to free a crew or ship is self-evident.

Until reinforcement by the Indian Navy, the prospects for travelling safely through these dangerous waters were not good, despite improved international cooperation. Singapore's Prime Minister publicly acknowledged that he was aware of terrorist threats to shipping. The Al-Qaeda-linked group known as Jemaah Islamiyah was responsible for the massacre of 225 clubbers in Bali in 2002. Jailed supporters of these Muslim extremists have admitted that the group is seeking the right opportunity to strike terror by using a ship.

Attacks in Southeast Asia have not disappeared, but the days of easy pickings have gone. Whereas stealing ships to use for phantom trading was commonplace, today's crime may be the theft of tugboats and barges—small beer in comparison to much larger vessels laden with oil or high-value minerals. Tracking devices secreted on board now make the phantom ship industry harder for criminals. Whereas ships used to be spirited away, now the pirates can usually be followed and found. Given cooperation between Malaysia, Thailand, Singapore and Indonesia (with Indian support), success here was much easier to achieve (albeit very belatedly) because the Malacca Strait is a much smaller area than the vast expanse of the Indian Ocean infested by Somali pirates.

Besides the danger of attack by mini-submarine, evidence has surfaced of terrorists being trained as divers to plant mines or other explosives. Captured terrorists have admitted that some Al-Qaeda groups have been planning underwater attacks, especially in the Far East. The Philippines Military uncovered evidence that Jemaah Islamiyah militants were being trained in diving and explosives. A senior figure from the British Ministry of Defence expressed concern that terrorists had been training in Western diving schools.

In the Netherlands, Dutch security are sure that militant extremists have been trained there in diving techniques. In the USA, the FBI has been investigating reports of possible terrorists seeking training. The prospects remain ominous, even though so much time has passed without the type of spectacular outrage that has been dreaded. An underwater attack using trained divers is hard to counter except by costly measures that are impractical on a routine basis for civilian shipping. That said, divers inspect the hulls of cruise liners before departure to ensure no limpet-mines have been affixed.

During research for this book and shortly after 9-11, a most reliable contact told me that two incidents *worse* than the WTC had also been prevented. Since then that number has risen to at least five. Congratulations are due to the intelligence services, but the implications remain chilling. Dangers to shipping remain grave because, as hijacking planes gets more difficult and security specialists get smarter at infiltration and surveillance of terrorists, *they will want to make their point* by staging some other dramatic atrocity. Foiling the 10 jetliner explosions was a serious setback for them. That is why the maritime risk had to be tackled, and much has been achieved over the past 13 years. Before 9-11, regulation of the sea, of ships and of crew identities was so slipshod that there could have been a welcome mat at the door for terrorists. In relative terms, rapid progress has been made, but it is like blocking every hole in a large sieve. However, below are the main measures now taken to block the largest holes.

In February 2005, the US Coast Guard announced new underwater precautions designed to protect vulnerable structures like Cove Point LNG terminal and strategically important vessels such as naval ships, LNGs and large tankers. There will still remain the vast majority of other vessels that might be blown up around important ports to disrupt trade and cause terror.

In September 2005, the White House published the *National Strategy for Maritime Security*—the culmination of different agencies working toward joined-up thinking for the future. It highlighted in stark terms the entire array of dangers from the sea. The Strategic Plan had many components, one of which was the *Container Security Initiative* (CSI). Top priority is preventing weapons of mass destruction (WMD) from entering the USA by sea (the most likely method). A concerted drive to tighten security, whether in preventing movement of terrorists or WMD, came from the CSI. This is a multi-layered approach combining the intelligence services, software, experience and technology.

The plan introduced screening every container for WMD or their components. The Domestic Nuclear Defense Office developed techniques to improve detection. However, with 30,000 containers arriving each day, the Strategy accepts the impossibility of any physical inspection of the contents of all containers. Rather, the concept is to profile which containers present the greatest risks based on data compulsorily supplied from the private sector. These containers are then vetted *before* shipment to the USA.

Before 9-11, the major weakness in defence against terrorism came from container transportation. Two hundred million containers enter the USA each year through main ports like New York, Los Angeles, Long Beach, Charleston, Houston and Miami. The stark truth was that a container had a 2% chance of being checked on arrival. For Customs personnel to empty a container might take an entire day. The cost and delays quash the viability. Even using technology, a computer scan was taking 15 minutes, far too long in a busy commercial port.

The big CSI breakthrough was international acceptance in 2004 of an American initiative for checking containers *before* shipment. Customs and Border Protection personnel now use the latest high-tech equipment while based in major foreign ports where loading occurs. This procedure has now been recommended for use in many other non-US ports; the concept will hopefully spread. Vessels loading in other small ports will be scrutinised with extra care by profiling criteria now adopted to target suspect containers.

As this approach draws heavily on *intelligence* to select high-risk containers, it is far from infallible. Computer software incorporates an *Automated Targeting System* that assesses the total facts and selects containers with the highest risk factors. Sixty-two percent of containers come from long-established and trusted companies, and so, while these may still be checked at random, this profiling reduces the seriously high-risk field to the remainder. Customs experts add their own experience to spot oddities so that, even if the final in-depth examinations are statistically few, the most dangerous have the greatest chance of being caught.

The next security initiative is that vessels loading cargo for the USA (or carrying cargo to stay aboard for another destination) must give notice 24 hours pre-departure of what is being carried (loose generic terms such as *Household Goods* are unacceptable and can lead to a *Do Not Load* order). Ninety-six hours' notice then has to be given of intended arrival in the USA. The master must describe the cargo, name all ports visited on the voyage, and list the crew so that their identities can be checked. If need be, the ship can be denied entry if places visited, cargo or crew present unacceptable risks.

Once unloaded, containers may then be subjected to a third check by technology or (very rarely) by a thorough physical inspection. US Customs reacts sharply today to suggestions that only 2% or possibly 5% of containers are being checked. They claim that 100% of containers are checked. This sounds impressive, but the reality is less reassuring. While it is true that 100% are checked, this process combines examination of the paperwork describing the contents and their history rather than an internal physical check. Then, taking into account the container's risk profile, Customs decide whether to select the container for more detailed scrutiny by scanning or stripping it. Initially, technology designed to identify nuclear, chemical and explosive materials was a disappointment, but by March 2006 it was announced that handheld detectors were now working efficiently, with over 80 million containers screened.

Getting much-needed reforms through at international levels is usually a painfully slow exercise, but there have been noteworthy successes since 9-11. Under the IMO's rules, reform is achievable only as fast as the slowest vessel in the convoy; 9-11 acted as a sharp reminder that urgent action was needed to bring about the type of changes to counter piracy and maritime crime for which Eric Ellen and Captain Mukundan had been lobbying for years. The result was a raft of new measures to counter terrorism (certainly helpful against piracy). These were brought into force in July 2004 as the *International Ship and Port Facility Security Code* (ISPS).

Central to the philosophy is a uniform international approach to carrying out a risk assessment for ports and ships. The burden of checking ports is vested in national governments, but there was no blacklist of governments who declined to adopt ISPS. Ports are now *less insecure*. The likelihood is that improved systems have reduced dangers, but prevention of all attack scenarios is impossible.

By 1 July 2004, vessels of over a modest 500 tons used on international voyages had to be certified by their flag states as meeting basic criteria. A major change was the introduction of compulsory *Automatic Identification Systems* (AIS), which enable a ship's master to identify what vessels are in the vicinity. Radar identifies a *presence*, but AIS provides details, warning a master of suspicious vessels in the region. Exempt from this new law on AIS are oil tankers and passenger vessels. The advantage of being able to track vessels containing a device means that pirated vessels have been recovered. But unfortunately this powerful initiative does have a risky downside that pirates or terrorists can exploit: terrorists might access valuable data and turn it to *their* advantage. Masters can therefore turn off the device in sensitive situations so that their identity is concealed.

New vessels must now have a black box installed, in line with those used on aircraft. Every vessel covered by the regulations must now have an identification number for life, making creation of phantom ships more difficult. It has always been absurd that ships could disappear so readily, only to reappear with a new name and identity. Those below 500 tons and those not undertaking international voyages are exempt. The gangsters have scrutinised the rules: since 2005 there has been a flurry of hijackings of tugs towing barges in the Malacca Strait. Tug and barge are then separated and the barge is towed into a friendly port and its cargo stolen. Barges need no identity numbers; this flaw needs urgent rectification.

Other significant changes involve the need to carry a permanent record of the vessel's history—useful in countering phantom ships—compulsory fitment of alarm systems to alert authorities on land such as the IMB's Piracy Reporting Centre in Kuala Lumpur, and permission to use electric fencing.

Under the Seafarers' Identity Document Convention 2003, the problem of false crew identities was tackled. The use of biometric data such as retina scans and fingerprints gathered from the individual helps to plug this gaping loophole. Tom Whalen, a specialist with New York attorneys Carter Ledyard & Millburn, regarded counterfeit and forged licenses as the area most in need of tighter controls. 'This [false identities] left a gap for terrorists to masquerade as legitimate seamen and take over control of vessels.' Making the data now internationally accessible is a giant leap in knowing who is aboard a vessel, so that if need be a ship can be denied access to port. What cannot be catered for is the closet terrorist with no criminal record, who, with others, infiltrates a ship as a legitimate crew member with the intention of carrying out an act of terrorism at some future time.

A further post 9-11 American initiative, Boarding Officers, has spread to other countries. Previously, US Customs carried out inspections as vessels approached the USA, especially in the war against narcotics and illegal immigration. It was always a dangerous job, with a potential for violent confrontation. The role of Boarding Officers goes further. Up to six officers board any vessels carrying dangerous cargoes or perceived as high risk. They secure the bridge area, the engine room and emergency steering gear to prevent terrorists from taking control or using the vessel as a weapon to strike a target. They are not pilots, simply armed guards alert to the risks and ready to act if needed. Again, this approach provides some comfort regarding Cove Point and other high-risk destinations.

After such prolonged inertia, these are remarkable strides, and no doubt they have inhibited much terrorism and piracy. But as the number of incidents shows, the problems at sea have not gone away. Nigeria and the Far East represent an ongoing festering sore; other areas are far from immune. Bearing in mind the IMB's opinion that the bosses behind piracy view any criminal activity as a profit centre involving risk against reward, it is likely that some in the Far East have turned away from the sea toward software piracy, prostitution, narcotics, people-smuggling or other profitable trades.

The risks of being caught in Southeast Asia have increased and measures like ship identification and tracking have proved effective against the lucrative phantom ship crimes. One may cautiously conclude that the Somali situation is coming under control, but shipping crime flourishes around Nigeria. Only once the paymasters realise that the rewards do not justify the risks will piracy be curbed. In poor or war-ravaged countries, finding men to be trained and used as pirates will continue to be easy. Other opportunistic local thugs will continue to engage in low-level piracy. Efforts are being made to find ways to arrest and prosecute the financial masterminds who crouch like spiders at the centre of their webs. Seizing the fruits of their crimes would help, but still today no way ahead has yet been internationally agreed, despite the continued threat to crews, commerce and the global economy.

Without those planes exploding into New York's twin towers that September morning, progress *would* have continued to be made against piracy and maritime crime. It would have been slow and piecemeal. Since that horrific crime, there have been important strides to make up for many wasted years of apathy. But the chain of protection against crime is only as strong as the weakest link.

'There remains no room for pussyfooting,' agrees Ellen, reviewing progress since 9-11. 'Rightly, there has been much talk of a war against terrorists, but *we* have been trying to fight a war against organised crime involving murder, violence and theft for too long with nobody caring enough to support us. We must continue to combine our assault against terrorism and maritime crime.'

ACKNOWLEDGEMENTS

I could never have completed this book without so much generous assistance from old friends and new ones made along the way. A key figure throughout the book is Eric Ellen, former founder-director of the ICC International Maritime Bureau, who has worked tirelessly with suggestions, comments, and quotes. Through his many friendships, door have opened that I never knew existed, let alone could have entered.

Captain Pottengal Mukundan, although stretched with the pressures of his demanding role since succeeding Eric as director at the Bureau, was never too busy to keep me abreast of fast-moving events around the globe.

One of Eric's vital introductions proved to be S. Lin Kuo (Shiao Lin), who had worked as an investigator for the Bureau. She gave me considerable background about the dangers of her work. Another was Captain William Chadwick. Bill and Genny made me feel really at home when I quizzed Bill. My wife Bridget and I left with fond memories and a suitcase full of Bill's archived material. Once home, updates from Bill just kept on coming, totally consistent with his devotion to maritime safety. Dr Frank Wiswall, an introduction from Bill and a legend in marine legal circles, was a willing resource with valuable judgments on topical trends and past history alike.

Members of Legalink, an international network of independent law firms of which I am honorary president, have excelled. Of particular help were Tom Davis of Carter, Ledyard and Millburn and his maritime law partners. Joseph Brand of Patton Boggs of Washington, D.C., Tony Olsen of Olsens in Jersey, Lawrence Miller, sadly now deceased, and his anonymous colleague in Cape Town, Jorgen Hammarstrom of Attorney's House ANPR in Helsinki, Peter Polak of Fiebinger Polak, and Leon of Vienna also helped with comments and material. Peter arranged for me to talk on the *Lucona* scandal at Café *Demel*, where the outrageous plot was hatched.

I was also given significant insight into the latest measures against piracy from Protection Group International, a major private security company operating at the sharp end with armed personnel on vessels. Thanks to Richard Deely of the Liberian Shipowners Council in delightful Tarrytown and to (former) Det. Supt. Suzanne Williams at New Scotland Yard, who assisted on more than one aspect of shipping crime. Many others helped on details, including Mark Dickinson of Nautilus International, and Ivor Stoneham, a relative of the notorious pirate Mary Read. Richard Sayer, formerly a solicitor at Ince & Co of London and a marine consultant rated in the top five shipping lawyers in the UK.

Andreas Harsano, a Far Eastern journalist, Captain Alister Crombie, a veteran of the *Salem* investigation (also sadly now deceased), and Nicholas Dawe, who understood the mysteries of deep-sea searches for wrecks, were most helpful, and Joseph Discenza of Daniel H Wagner provided great insight into how wrecks from the deep can be found, something very pertinent today as, six weeks after its disappearance, efforts are still being made to find Malaysian Airlines flight 370 somewhere deep under the ocean.

My great friends Ray and Anne Foot assisted with background on the Bahamas, a notorious area for sea crime. My son Fraser carried out valuable research, and Bob Bashforth, brother of Captain John Bashforth, assisted with background on *Baltimar Zephyr*—as did Andrew Linington of NUMAST, who was helpful with data about attacks on crews.

Dr Rohan Gunaratna, a leading figure in the study of terrorism, was most generous with his time and experience. In London, Captain Hartmut Hesse, Gurpreet Singhota, and Alexander Petrovat the International Maritime Organisation in London were most helpful. On the MV *Estonia*, the comprehensive published work by Dr Peter Holtappels was essential reading, and he was kind enough to answer my queries about this extraordinary and mystifying tragedy. Retired solicitor and friend Graham Fisher, who sadly died in 2012, also helped with comments and an appraisal of this controversial chapter.

Finally, though my wife Bridget knows little of shipping, she has been a constant source of encouragement, suffering with a smile my strange hours. Without the help of all of you, this book would have been an impossibility. I hope I have accurately absorbed and reflected your views. To you all and to anyone unwittingly missed, my warm thanks.

ABOUT THE AUTHOR

Born in Glasgow but brought up in southern England, Douglas was educated at Cranbrook School, Kent, and Durham University. After qualifying as a solicitor and working in the west of England, he moved to London, ending up as senior partner of the firm he founded, which still flourishes following his move abroad. Alongside this career, Douglas had his first novel published in 1980 and has been writing mystery thrillers and works of non-fiction ever since.

In 2001, Douglas moved to the USA, where he developed both his legal and writing interests but has now returned and settled in Europe. He is married with three children.

CPSIA information can be obtained at www.ICGtesting.com
Printed in the USA
LVOW07s0526030715

444852LV00002B/9/P

9 781849 823319